A MIND FOR WHAT MATTERS

A MIND FOR
WHAT MATTERS

Collected Essays of

F. F. BRUCE

William B. Eerdmans Publishing Company
Grand Rapids, Michigan

TO THE
FACULTY OF DIVINITY
UNIVERSITY OF ABERDEEN

A belated thank-offering
from an adopted son

Copyright © 1990 by Wm. B. Eerdmans Publishing Co.
255 Jefferson Ave. S.E., Grand Rapids, Mich. 49503

Printed in the United States of America

Library of Congress Cataloging-in-Publication Data

Bruce, F. F. (Frederick Fyvie), 1910-1990
    A mind for what matters : collected essays of F. F. Bruce
    p.   cm.
    Includes bibliographical references.
    ISBN 0-8028-0446-2
    1. Bible. N.T.—Criticism, interpretation, etc. 2. Theology.
3. Dead Sea scrolls—Criticism, interpretation, etc. 4. Qumran
community. I. Title.
BS2361.2.B78 1990
22506—dc20   90-41599
                                                    CIP

Contents

Contents

Preface

The papers reproduced in this volume cover a period of half a century. They have been delivered as lectures or composed as essays for varying bodies of listeners or readers, and are collected and presented here because I have been encouraged to believe that they may have some interest for a wider public. They relate to fields of study which have particularly attracted me over the years.

Some of them, were they reproduced without alteration, would have been unacceptably out of date in certain respects, especially in bibliographical references. They have therefore been brought up-to-date in such matters, while retaining their essential identity.

The original location of each paper is indicated in a note appended to its title. I am greatly indebted to librarians, publishers and editors for their ready permission to reissue this material: my thanks are due especially to Dr. Michael Pegg, director of the John Rylands University Library of Manchester, and also to the Paternoster Press, Exeter; Marshall Pickering, publishers, Basingstoke; the editors of *New Testament Studies, Faith and Thought* and *Interpretation;* and the Rev. David Staple, General Secretary of the Free Church Federal Council, London. Nor must I omit a word of sincere gratitude to my friends of the William B. Eerdmans Publishing Company for their willingness to publish this volume.

June 1990   F. F. B.

Abbreviations

ANF	The Ante-Nicene Fathers (Eerdmans, Grand Rapids)
Ann.	*Annals* (Tacitus)
ANRW	*Aufstieg und Niedergang der römischen Welt*
Ant.	*Antiquities* (Josephus)
ASV	American Standard Version (1901)
AV	Authorized Version (1611) = KJV
BASOR	*Bulletin of the American Schools of Oriental Research*
BGBE	Beiträge zur Geschichte der biblischen Exegese (Mohr, Tübingen)
BJ	*Jewish War* (Josephus)
BJRL	*Bulletin of the John Rylands (University) Library, Manchester*
CBRF	Christian Brethren Research Fellowship
CD	Book of the Covenant of Damascus (= Zadokite Work)
CIJ	*Corpus Inscriptionum Judaicarum*
CIL	*Corpus Inscriptionum Latinarum*
Conf.	*Confessions* (Augustine)
CSEL	Corpus Scriptorum Ecclesiasticorum Latinorum (Vienna)
Cyrop.	*Cyropaedia* (Xenophon)
De ciu. dei	*On the City of God* (Augustine)
DJD	*Discoveries in the Judaean Desert* (Clarendon Press, Oxford)
EKK	Evangelisch-katholischer Kommentar zum Neuen Testament
Ep.	*Epistle*
E.T.	English translation

FEUNTK	Forschungen zur Entstehung des Urchristentums des Neuen Testaments und der Kirche (Kiel)
GL	*Grammatici Latini*, ed. H. Keil (Leipzig)
GNB	Good News Bible (= Today's English Version)
HDB	J. Hastings (ed.), *Dictionary of the Bible* (T. & T. Clark, Edinburgh, 1898-1904)
Hist.	*History* (Thucydides, Herodotus)
Hist. Eccl.	*Ecclesiastical History* (Eusebius)
HKAT	Handkommentar zum Alten Testament (Göttingen)
HTK	Herders Theologischer Kommentar zum Neuen Testament (Freiburg i/B)
HTR	*Harvard Theological Review*
Ibid.	In the same place *(ibidem)*
ICC	International Critical Commentary (T. & T. Clark, Edinburgh)
IGRR	*Inscriptiones Graecae ad Res Romanas Pertinentes*
JBL	*Journal of Biblical Literature*
JQR	*Jewish Quarterly Review*
JRS	*Journal of Roman Studies*
JSOT	*Journal for the Study of the Old Testament*
JSS	*Journal of Semitic Studies*
JTC	*Journal for Theology and the Church*
JTS	*Journal of Theological Studies*
KJV	King James Version (= AV).
Leg.	*Legation to Gaius* (Philo)
LXX	Septuagint (Greek version of OT)
MNTC	Moffatt New Testament Commentary (Hodder & Stoughton, London)
MT	Masoretic Text (of Hebrew Bible)
NEB	New English Bible
N.F.	Neue Folge
NICNT	New International Commentary on the New Testament (Eerdmans, Grand Rapids)
NIGTC	New International Greek Testament Commentary (Eerdmans, Grand Rapids/Paternoster Press, Exeter)
NIV	New International Version
NovT	*Novum Testamentum*
n.s.	new series
NT	New Testament
NTL	New Testament Library (SCM Press, London)
NTS	*New Testament Studies*

Od. Sol.	*Odes of Solomon*
Op. cit.	The work cited above *(opus citatum)*
Or. Sib.	*Sibylline Oracles*
OT	Old Testament
OTS	*Oudtestamentische Studiën* (Brill, Leiden)
PL	*Patrologia Latina*, ed. J.-P. Migne
P.Mich.	University of Michigan Papyri
RB	*Revue Biblique*
Ref. Omn. Haer.	*Refutation of All Heresies* (Hippolytus)
RSV	Revised Standard Version
RV	Revised Version (1881-85)
Sat.	*Satire* (Juvenal)
SBL	Society of Biblical Literature
SBLDS	Society of Biblical Literature Dissertation Series
SBT	Studies in Biblical Theology
SD	Studies and Documents
SIG	*Sylloge Inscriptionum Graecarum*, ed. W. Dittenberger
SJT	*Scottish Journal of Theology*
SNTS	Society for New Testament Studies
SNTSM	Society for New Testament Studies Monograph
SUNT	Studien zur Umwelt des Neuen Testaments (Göttingen)
Suppl	Supplement
s.v.	under the word in question *(sub voce)*
TB	Babylonian Talmud
Tert.	Tertullian
Thuc.	Thucydides
TLZ	*Theologische Literaturzeitung*
TNTC	Tyndale New Testament Commentary
TU	*Texte und Untersuchungen*
VT	*Vetus Testamentum*
WBC	Word Biblical Commentary
WC	Westminster Commentaries
WUNT	Wissenschaftliche Untersuchungen zum Neuen Testament (Mohr, Tübingen)
WVSS	Westminster Version of the Sacred Scriptures
ZAW	*Zeitschrift für die alttestamentliche Wissenschaft*
ZNW	*Zeitschrift für die neutestamentliche Wissenschaft*
ZTK	*Zeitschrift für Theologie und Kirche*

For abbreviations of Qumran manuscripts see pp. 33f.
For abbreviations of works of Marius Victorinus see pp. 216f.

I. PROLOGUE

1. The New Testament and Classical Studies

I. ABERDEEN AND ITS UNIVERSITY

My first word must be one of grateful appreciation of the honor which the Society has conferred on me—the highest honor in its gift—in inviting me to preside over this year's meeting and to follow such a distinguished succession of predecessors, including not least my immediate predecessor, Professor Béda Rigaux. As in private duty bound, I cannot but recall that among other predecessors were two eminent scholars whom I am proud to remember also as predecessors in my Manchester chair—Professors T. W. Manson and C. H. Dodd, who presided over the Society in 1949 and 1951 respectively. For any student of the New Testament there could be no more warmly cherished honor than to be called to follow such men in this presidential office.

Let me next express to you all my personal welcome to the northeast of Scotland and the University of Aberdeen, as a native of the former and a graduate of the latter.

Pope Alexander VI has had a less favorable press over the centuries than most occupants of the Holy See; yet in this place he should be remembered with special gratitude because it was he who, on 10 February 1494, issued the Bull (still preserved, I believe, in King's College

---

Presidential address delivered to the Society for New Testament Studies on August 26, 1975. (The Society met that year in King's College, University of Aberdeen.) The address was published in *New Testament Studies* 22 (1975-76), pp. 229-242 (Cambridge University Press).

Library) which authorized the foundation of the University of Aberdeen. The initiative in the matter was taken by William Elphinstone, Bishop of Aberdeen and Chancellor of Scotland, who enlisted the interest of King James IV. The king wrote to the Pope, describing the insatiable thirst for learning manifested by the inhabitants of these parts, cut off as they were from ready access to higher education by mountains and firths, and representing the climate of Old Aberdeen as particularly salubrious. The inhabitants of these parts were not so completely cut off from higher education as the king suggested: before this University was founded financial aid was available to enable a few promising lads from my own old school, some 70 miles W.N.W. of Aberdeen, to attend the University of Paris. But the Bull was forthcoming; King's College was founded in 1505, and a young Scots lecturer in the University of Paris, a native of Dundee, by name Hector Boys or Boece—duly latinized as Boethius— was inducted as first Principal, with Bishop Elphinstone as first Chancellor.[1] Here, then, we are today.

II. ABERDEEN AND NEW TESTAMENT STUDIES

So far as biblical scholarship is concerned, I think it would be agreed that Aberdeen and its hinterland have in the past made more lasting contributions to Old Testament than to New Testament study. Certainly we have produced no one in the New Testament field comparable to Andrew Bruce Davidson, William Robertson Smith or George Adam Smith in the Old Testament and Semitic field. But the New Testament field has not been left uncultivated. Sparing the blushes of our esteemed colleagues in the Department of New Testament Exegesis, I may remind you of work done in our field by members of other departments and faculties here. Readers of *New Testament Studies* are acquainted with Professor Francis Lyall's interest in Roman law in its bearing on the New Testament,[2] and it should not be forgotten that our colleague Professor David Daube held the Chair of Jurisprudence here for some years in the early 1950s. But for half a century some of the most notable New Testament work associated with Aberdeen was done by two Professors of Humanity—as Latin is traditionally called in the Universities of Scotland. My own former teacher Alexander Souter did his greatest work in the study of the Latin Fathers (outstandingly Ambrosiaster and Pelagius), but his handbooks for students of the Greek New Testament, especially his *Pocket Lexicon to the Greek New Testament* (Oxford, 1917) and his *Text and Canon of the New Testament* (London, 1913; revised by C. S. C. Williams in 1954), along with his introduction and apparatus to the

Novum Testamentum Graece (Oxford, 1910; revised 1947), are still known
and used. To him Augustine was "the greatest man that ever wrote
Latin,"[3] while he regarded the epistles of Paul, to whom he professed
himself "passionately devoted,"[4] as "the most valuable writings in the
world."[5]

His teacher and predecessor Sir William Ramsay established for
himself in the 1880s a scholarly reputation which was unfortunately
overlaid from the later 1890s onward by a reputation as a popular
apologist. Ramsay tells us how in 1876 he offered the Epistle to the
Galatians as a subject for the theological examination which he had then
to take as part of the requirement for Greats at Oxford, and studied it
with the aid of Lightfoot's commentary. Being at the time "full of
Aristotle's most advanced treatises," he "came to Paul with a new mind,
finding him the true successor of the Stagirite."[6] This led him on to what
he recognized as his "proper work, the study of Roman institutions in
Asiatic Greece, and the influence of Asia on the Graeco-Roman administration."[7]

The Ramsay of the *Historical Geography of Asia Minor* (London,
1890) and the two parts of *Cities and Bishoprics of Phrygia* (Oxford, 1895,
1897), outstanding samples of his "proper work," was a very great man,
and while the exploration of Roman Anatolia has forged ahead since his
day, those studies and others in which he touches on the geography,
epigraphy and sociology of that area can still be consulted with profit by
the student of Acts and the "Anatolian" documents of the New Testament. He built up a fine team of workers in the same field, among whom
J. G. C. Anderson and W. M. Calder bear specially distinguished names.
Something of the early promise of this team was published in a symposium, *Studies in the History and Art of the Eastern Provinces of the Roman
Empire* (Aberdeen, 1906), edited by Ramsay for the quatercentenary of
the University of Aberdeen.

It was in his earlier and more severely scholarly studies that
Ramsay laid the foundation for many positions which later received
wide circulation through his popular writings. For example, in the
preface to his fourth (1896) edition of *The Church in the Roman Empire* (first
published in 1893) he says that all the evidence for the South Galatian
hypothesis, which he so vigorously championed after he was converted
to it, is to be found in the first part of *Cities and Bishoprics of Phrygia*
(1895)[8]—and so it is, although the hypothesis as such receives no mention in that volume.

Again, Ramsay's keen appreciation of the importance of the sociological implications of his chosen field of study continued to find expression in his later writings—as, for example, in his remarks on early

Christian baptism. The theological aspects of baptism lay beyond his special interest, but his knowledge of the place of the family in the social structure of the Eastern Roman Empire in the mid-first century A.D. left him in no doubt about the significance of the household baptisms of Acts and 1 Corinthians.[9] That his interest in this area was maintained to the end is shown by the fact that his last contribution to scholarly literature was his posthumously published *The Social Basis of Roman Power in Asia Minor* (Aberdeen, 1941).[10]

Let this tribute to scholars of an earlier day serve as a prolegomenon to the following remarks on the New Testament and classical studies.

III. THE NEW TESTAMENT AS HELLENISTIC LITERATURE

The New Testament is a collection of Greek documents chronicling the rise and early progress of a new religious movement in Palestine and the Eastern Mediterranean in the first century A.D. Linguistically it has its place in the study of Greek literature: if Plutarch, Epictetus and Lucian are not too late to attract the attention of classical Greek students, neither is the New Testament. Culturally it belongs to the Graeco-Roman world—to the area which was Hellenized as a result of Alexander's conquests and which in due course came under the imperial domination of Rome. A classical student finds himself at home in this world, and he does not feel that he is visiting a foreign land when he reads the New Testament. True, he recognizes that the New Testament has features which it does not share with most Greek literature—features which are to be explained in terms of its Semitic, Old Testament and Judaic back-ground and environment. But there is much in the New Testament on which his Graeco-Roman studies cast direct light, and he believes that he has, as a classical student, a vital contribution to make to New Testament study which complements contributions made by theologians, Semitists or specialists in apocalyptic or rabbinical literature.

It will be plain from what has just been said that Jewish Palestine is not, in my opinion, to be excluded from the Hellenistic or Graeco-Roman world, and no sharp dichotomy is to be made between the Palestinian and Hellenistic spheres of Judaism or Christianity in the New Testament period. Of course there are elements in the New Testament which are essentially Jewish-Palestinian, and others which are equally recognizable as Hellenistic; but there is no hard-and-fast line of demar-cation between the two: in the broad central band of the spectrum they merge into each other.[11] The Hellenizing process in Palestine which began with Alexander's conquest was not reversed by the Hasmonaean victory, and it received fresh impetus under Roman and Herodian rule. This is as true in matters linguistic as in other areas of culture.[12] The presence of an Aramaic substratum here and there in the New Testament may indeed be evidence for a Jewish-Palestinian basis, but the absence of an Aramaic substratum is no argument against such a basis: what is basically Jewish-Palestinian can easily be expressed in Hellenistic Greek.

We can easily exaggerate the difference between Greek and Jew if we construct stereotypes of the one and the other which emphasize their distinctive features and ignore those which were common to both. In a book entitled *The Greeks and the Gospel,* published eleven years ago by a classical scholar who is a member of our Society, Professor J. B. Skemp, the stereotype Greek in the minds of some biblical theologians is described as a philosophical thinker, who holds a cyclic view of time and the universe, makes a strict division in his mind between soul and body, usually regarding soul as good and body as evil, and conceives of God as an abstraction devoid of true personality. I think most of us have met this stereotype Greek, especially in studies contrasting the Greek and Jewish thought-world. But it is a composite picture, bringing together a number of beliefs held by some Greeks at one time or another; many Greeks at all the relevant times held different beliefs, and most Greeks did not think in any such systematic way. The student of classics finds it difficult to recognize in this composite picture the flesh-and-blood inhabitants of the Graeco-Roman world whom he knows from his own studies.[13]

IV. HISTORICAL SOURCES

The classical historian is quite familiar with the task of using as source-material for his study literary and other documents which are not primarily historical, and were not written to preserve historical facts. If he wishes to reconstruct, for example, the career of Themistocles and the circumstances of the battle of Salamis, Themistocles's finest hour (480 B.C.), he will not confine himself to the historians Herodotus and Thucydides, the former of whom covers a great part of Themistocles's career,[14] while the latter provides information about his last phase.[15] He will study the geography of the Saronic Gulf and its approaches,[16] so as to master the probabilities of the movements of Persian and Athenian ships. He will examine contemporary epigraphic material and archaeological research dealing with fifth-century Athens. He will pay careful attention to the speech of the messenger in Aeschylus's *Persae* who describes the naval disaster at Salamis to the Persian court.[17] Aeschylus's purpose was not historical, but the battle had taken place within the memory of his audience, and some of them—perhaps even Aeschylus himself—had taken part in it. On the other hand, the historian will also consult a writer who was far from being a contemporary—Plutarch, whose *Life of Themistocles* (paralleled by that of Camillus) was written not so much to impart factual information as to illustrate a particular virtue. In making a selection from variant accounts given by his literary authorities (whom he mentions by name) Plutarch is guided more by suitability for his moral purpose than by the canons of historical probability; yet the material he preserves is so valuable that the historian will not ignore it but examine and evaluate it critically.

So, when we are told that the Gospels (say) were not written to provide us with source-material for writing a life of Jesus in his historical and local setting, we may agree. But documents which were not written with this purpose may nevertheless provide the historian with the raw material of his craft. Dr. Dennis Nineham once described the task of today's historian of Christian origins as being "to wring truth relevant to the history of Jesus from the increasing stock of remains of the Judaism of his time."[18] That is indeed a necessary task, although the non-Jewish evidence should not be neglected; for example, every advance made in the study of contemporary Roman administration and jurisprudence provides grist for our mill.[19] But "the increasing stock of remains of the Judaism of his time," apart from the works of Josephus, does not include much historical writing, and the extraction of historical data from documents which did not primarily set out to provide such data is a delicate undertaking—an undertaking, however, in which the classical historian is not inexperienced.

Even documents which did primarily set out to provide historical information call nevertheless for critical assessment. Take Thucydides, for example, by common consent the most "scientific" of all the Greek historians.[20] He aimed at satisfying those who wished to have before their eyes "a true picture of the events which have happened" during the Peloponnesian War, "and of the like events which may be expected to happen hereafter in the course of human affairs," and succeeded in his ambition of producing a "possession for all time."[21] Yet even Thucydides had his built-in presuppositions, without which he would not have been what he was, an exceptionally intelligent and public-spirited Athenian of the fifth century B.C. One Cambridge scholar, F. M. Cornford, went so far as to call him (in the title of a once well-known study) *Thucydides Mythistoricus*, explaining that by *mythistoria* he meant "history cast in a mould of perception, whether artistic or philosophic, which, long before the work was even contemplated, was already inwrought into the structure of the author's mind."[22] This mold could not be broken by any amount of "hard, rational thinking—an exercise which Thucydides never intermitted."[23] It was the result of "an early education consisting almost exclusively in the study of the poets," thanks to which his *History* is informed by "the tragic theory of human nature" imbibed, apparently, from Aeschylus.[24]

Even if Cornford overdid his thesis, it has only to be stated for the reader of Thucydides to recognize its validity. The juxtaposition of the Athenians' *hybris* over Melos and their disastrous Sicilian expedition is the most obvious instance.[25]

V. LUKE'S HISTORY

Of all the New Testament books, the twofold Lukan history is especially attractive to the classical student. It belongs to a literary genre with which he is well acquainted. The prologue to the history, promising the reader something better researched and more coherent than earlier narrators of the same events have provided, follows a well-established tradition, going back to Thucydides. Luke writes statedly in order to give his reader an orderly and trustworthy account of what has happened. If the classicist finds himself in a strange world in Luke 1:5–2:52—apart from the historical and administrative conundrum posed by the reference to the census in 2:1-3—he feels at home again when he comes to the synchronism of 3:1f. That the synchronism comes here and not at the beginning of the work does not surprise him: he recalls that the elaborate synchronism by which Thucydides dates the outbreak of the Peloponnesian War does not appear until the beginning of his second book.[26]

It is a commonplace of New Testament criticism that Luke, for all his care to follow stylistic precedents set by classical historians, is a theologian as well as a historian. So he is (and not necessarily the worse historian for being a theologian). But the recognition of this fact about Luke does not mean that he must be put in a different category from his classical predecessors: if Luke sets the course of events in a pattern of salvation-history, while Thucydides sees the course of events in terms of Aeschylean tragedy, that makes them the more, not the less, comparable.

Luke's twofold history places the course of Christian origins in the setting of contemporary world-history in a manner unparalleled elsewhere in the New Testament, and thus presents the student of Graeco-Roman antiquity with territory in which he finds a welcome avenue of approach to New Testament study. *Experto credas.*

For it would be vain to try to conceal the autobiographical character of this paper. It was not through the door of a theological curriculum that I entered the New Testament fold; I climbed up some other way—the way of classical study. More particularly, when I was a teacher of classical Greek I undertook to produce a commentary on the Acts of the Apostles, which was published nearly a quarter of a century ago.[27] Since then, I have devoted a constantly increasing proportion of my time and study to the letters of Paul, so that when I turn to Acts today I view its contents from a vantage-point which I did not then command. This new approach does not invalidate the conclusions which I reached when I studied Acts as a work of Greek literature, but it helps to set those conclusions in a better perspective. Yet I think that the study of Acts in a classical context is marked by a degree of objectivity which is not always found in more theological assessments of the book. Let me simply say here that, while Paul's own writings are primary sources of incomparable value for our knowledge of his life and thought, the value of Acts as our principal secondary source is much greater than some theologians of more recent times have allowed. To approach the Pauline letters through Acts is to put the cart before the horse, no matter how time-honored a procedure it may be; yet the student of Paul's letters who ignores the record of Acts cuts himself off from what can supply, time and again, an illuminating commentary on them.

In fact, whether we view Acts in broad outline or in some particular detail, it mirrors the world in which Paul and his fellows lived. As for broad outline, we may recall the opinion of Lord Hewart, a former English Lord Chief Justice, "that the best short general picture of the *Pax Romana* and all that it meant—good roads and posting, good police, freedom from brigandage and piracy, freedom of movement, toleration and justice—is to be found in the experience, written in Greek, of a Jew who happened to be a Roman citizen—that is, in the Acts of the Apostles."[28] As for one particular detail, we may recall the judgment of H. J. Holtzmann that Luke's account of Paul's voyage and shipwreck is "one of the most instructive documents for the knowledge of ancient seamanship."[29]

VI. THE SPEECHES IN ACTS

One feature of Acts which the classical student finds quite familiar is the presence of speeches at salient points in the narrative. He will be quite prepared to recognize them as Thucydidean—as saying the kind of thing that the speakers would have said on the various occasions, not as being *verbatim* reports. Not all Greek or Hellenistic historians, of course, shared Thucydides' concern "to give the general purport of what was actually said";[30] for some of them the speeches interspersed throughout their works were little more than rhetorical exercises—which called forth the censure of a sober historian like Polybius.[31] But the classical student may find it difficult to identify the speeches in Acts as rhetorical exercises by the author and nothing more. He will see clearly enough, for example, that the attitude to the temple expressed in Stephen's defense is not the attitude of Luke-Acts as a whole—and why, he will ask, should the author have introduced it in Stephen's speech if he did not believe that it was the attitude of Stephen personally or of the segment of Hellenistic opinion of which Stephen is made the spokesman?[32]

It is especially, perhaps, in the account of Paul's visit to Athens and his speech before the Court of the Areopagus that the classical reader of Acts feels himself to be on home ground. The local color is right; the delicately adapted allusions in the speech are appropriate to a Christian apologist trying to establish a point of contact with such an audience, and the incredulous reaction to his mention of resurrection from the dead is just what might be expected from cultured hearers who had it, on what to them was the highest authority, that "when the earth has drunk up a man's blood, once he has died, there is no resurrection."[33]

As Henry J. Cadbury put it, "the classicists are among the most inclined to plead for the historicity of the scene of Paul at Athens."[34] Among those "classicists" none was more positive than Eduard Meyer. "How any one has been able to explain this scene as an invention," said he, "is one of those things which I have never been able to understand";[35] and we recall his claim that he succeeded in persuading even the learned author of *Antike Kunstprosa* and *Agnostos Theos* to concede at least the possibility that Luke reproduces the genuine content of Paul's speech.[36] Had he lived in a later generation, he might have found greater difficulty in exercising such persuasion on Martin Dibelius than he found with Eduard Norden—not to mention scholars who have written on this subject more recently.[37]

Once I myself approached Luke's Athenian narrative with the naïveté of a classicist. But, after immersing myself for several years in the study of Paul's capital epistles, I now find myself approaching it as follows. Take the author of Romans 1–3 and bring him to Athens. Bear in mind that he has experienced remarkable success for a number of years as a Christian missionary to the gentile world—which suggests an ability to get on to his hearers' wavelength and exploit an initial area of common ground so as to gain their attention. Bear in mind also his unusual versatility and his avowed policy of making himself "all things to all men, in order by all means to save some" (1 Cor. 9:22). Invite him to expound his message before the Court of the Areopagus: what will he say? If I express my suspicion that he will say something not utterly unlike the *Areopagitica* of Acts 17:22-31, you may conclude that I am still more of a classicist than a Paulinist. So be it.

VII. PAUL'S EPISTLES

Not only Luke-Acts, however, but the Pauline letters have their place in the history of Greek literature. This was recognized by no less than the great Wilamowitz—ἀνὴϱ Ἑλληνικώτατος (as he was described on the occasion of his receiving an honorary degree from the University of Athens)—who in *Die griechische Literatur des Altertums*, written over sixty years ago, devotes two important pages to Paul, to whom he refers as *einem Klassiker des Hellenismus*. Paul, according to Wilamowitz, did not directly take over any of the elements of Greek education—the Pastoral Epistles and the Areopagus speech must not come into the picture here[38]—yet he not only writes Greek but thinks Greek; without realizing it, he acts as the executor of Alexander's testament by carrying the gospel to the Greeks.

> At last, at last, once again someone speaks in Greek out of a fresh inward experience of life. That experience is his faith, which makes him sure of his hope. His glowing love embraces all mankind: to bring them salvation he joyfully sacrifices his own life, yet the fresh life of the soul springs up wherever he goes. He writes his letters as a substitute for his personal activity. This epistolary style is Paul, Paul himself and no other.[39]

That Paul is a Hellenist in the ordinary sense of the term—one whose habitat was the Hellenistic world and who made a unique contribution to Hellenistic literature—cannot be doubted. Yet he might not have appreciated being called a Hellenist. When he does claim such a cultural (rather than ethnic) designation, he calls himself not a Hellenist but a Hebrew—"a Hebrew born of Hebrews" (Phil. 3:6).[40] We are not compelled, of course, to interpret this language on Paul's lips in the sharply antithetical sense in which "Hebrew" is set over against "Hellenist" in Acts 6:1, yet some suggestion of that antithesis is present when he speaks of himself as a Hebrew. For all his Hellenism, he felt and knew that the roots of his life and thought were Hebrew. In this regard he can be contrasted with Philo[41] who, while remaining a pious and practicing Jew, reinterpreted the Hebrew scriptures (in their Greek rendering) in terms of that Platonic and post-Platonic philosophy which he intuitively embraced as ultimate truth. This being so, then the most intensive study of the life and culture of Tarsus at the beginning of the Christian era, and of the influence which that life and culture must have exerted on an intelligent and sensitive youth like Paul, will make only a marginal contribution to our understanding of the apostle—quite apart from the possibility that he was taken to Jerusalem at too early an age for Tarsus to have influenced him at all in his boyhood.[42] The classical student can come to terms with Paul the Hellenist, but a classical education alone will not equip him to assess the essential Paul, Paul the Hebrew, any more than it will equip him to assess him whom Paul proclaimed as Lord.

If, however, the classical student realizes these limitations, he will nevertheless find much in the area of his special interest which will throw light on the milieu in which Paul accomplished his lifework. There are indeed institutes specially devoted to the exploration of the common ground between classical culture and Christian origins. One may think in particular of the F. J. Dölger-Institut in Bonn and the Institute for Antiquity and Christianity in Claremont, California.

In an article in the annual associated with the Dölger-Institut, the *Jahrbuch für Antike und Christentum,* Professor Edwin A. Judge refers to P. R. L. Brown's *Augustine of Hippo* (London, 1967) as "an outstanding study . . . distinguished by its sense of the subtleties of relating a complex figure to changing times," and adds, "It is precisely this kind of study we lack for Paul."[43] In the article mentioned, which bears the title "St. Paul and Classical Society," Professor Judge indicates some of the lines along which such a study might be conducted.[44]

VIII. PAUL'S ENVIRONMENT

Whether Tarsus influenced Paul in his boyhood years or not, he spent his life after his departure from Jerusalem in the third year following his conversion (Gal. 1:21) in one Graeco-Roman city after another. Graeco-Roman city life forms the milieu of his letters—especially of the people to whom his letters were addressed. A study of city life in the eastern provinces is bound to illuminate many aspects of his writing.[45] Such a study is rendered the more difficult because of the variety of legal and social institutions between one city and another, and the scantiness of our knowledge of these institutions in the first century A.D. as compared with the abundant information available on the civic and imperial institutions of Rome. What we can learn from classical authors finds welcome augmentation in inscriptions; it is from them that we are most likely to gather data bearing on local conditions.[46]

It helps to know what the commonly accepted presuppositions of thought and behavior were in the cities to which Paul sent his letters. Sometimes he goes along with these presuppositions, as when he appeals to the common disapproval, even in permissive Corinth, of cohabiting with one's father's wife (1 Cor. 5:1), or to the general agreement that it was natural for a woman, in contrast to a man, to have long hair (1 Cor. 11:14f.). At other times he insists that these presuppositions must be revised or reversed in the light of the gospel, which turns accepted secular wisdom upside down (1 Cor. 1:18ff.) and excludes certain moral patterns which were tolerated in pagan life (1 Cor. 6:9-11). These are instances which lie on the surface, but there must be many more which can be unearthed only by epigraphic and other research. Could someone do for the Pauline world the kind of service lately performed by Professor K. J. Dover for another period in his *Greek Popular Morality in the Time of Plato and Aristotle* (Oxford, 1974)?[47]

If the man in the street whom we know today still embraces as an article of faith that progress (no matter whither) is a good thing and reaction (no matter against what) is a bad thing, that one must never put the clock back (even when it is going fast), what did his Macedonian or Galatian counterpart accept as a matter of course nineteen centuries ago? Did he think *gnosis* was a good thing? Did he venerate the ideal of the θεῖος ἀνήρ, or would he have recognized that expression?[48] How did he contemplate death, and the possibility of existence after death? Had he been initiated into a mystery religion or did he use mystery terminology in an extended sense? What kind of rhetoric, if any, did he find impressive? What were his ideas of public and private decency? (If we ask the same questions not about the man in the street but about the woman in the home we shall have even greater difficulty in getting an answer, because her thoughts had minimal opportunity of finding open or permanent expression—Paul's affirmation that in Christ there was neither male nor female must have made a difference here.) The answers to these and similar questions may differ from city to city, or from province to province, but it could be that sociological inquiries along these lines will substantially fill out the context of Paul's letters and enable us to see better how their first readers would have understood them. The classicist, more particularly the classical epigraphist, may consider that he still has contributions to make to New Testament studies in such ways as these.

IX. NEW TESTAMENT VOCABULARY

When he comes to examine the vocabulary of New Testament anthropology, particularly in the writings of Paul, the classical student quickly recognizes that it cannot be understood entirely in terms of Platonic thought and language. The Old Testament portrayal of the "vitality of the individual"[49] has made its contribution, but in Paul especially full allowance must be made for an original line of thought in which Hebrew and Greek concepts or terms have been given a new significance in the light of the Christ-event and the reality of life in the Spirit.

But we should not too readily set the New Testament doctrine of resurrection over against the Platonic teaching about the immortality of the soul. In view of his personal experience of the risen Christ, Paul propounds a doctrine of resurrection which advances beyond that which he had been taught by his Pharisaic instructors—although we should not be overassured about the nature of that; the Jewish, and even the Pharisaic, doctrine of resurrection and immortality in those days was not so uniform as we are prone to imagine.

In the work by Professor Skemp to which reference has been made already we are reminded of Plato's insight in the *Timaeus*, that if there is a morally good creator of the world, then all souls apart from himself exist by his will, even if his will decrees their immortality. In this sense they have no independent immortality; such immortality belongs to the creator alone.[50]

X. CONCLUSION

The conclusion of the whole matter is that the Graeco-Roman contribution to early Christianity should not be depreciated as though it were an alien accretion upon the pure gospel. Part of the genius of the gospel lies in its adaptability, in its capacity for becoming naturalized among people of widely varying cultures. If the existence today of a distinctively Indian or African Christianity is an enrichment of the church's faith and life, the appropriation of Christianity by Greeks, Romans and others in the first century did not impoverish it. John the seer in his last vision saw "the glory and the honour of the nations" being brought into the new Jerusalem (Rev. 21:26), and this may best be understood not in the material sense of its Old Testament *Vorlage* (Isa. 60:5b) but as a parable of the contributions made by converts of all nations to the many-hued splendor of the city of God. If at this point someone interjects *timeo Danaos et dona ferentes*,[51] I reply that I do not acknowledge Virgil's Laocoon as a prophet for all seasons. When, according to the Fourth Evangelist, certain Greeks at the last Passover asked that they might see Jesus, he replied that, when once he had been lifted up from the earth, he would draw all sorts of people to himself[52]—including, as the event proved, very many from the Greek world, who came not only to receive his saving grace but to present their gifts of gratitude.

There was indeed the danger that the gospel might be so completely adapted to this or that cultural environment that its *novum*, the very thing that made it the gospel, might be obscured or lost; but this danger was as great in a Jewish as in a gentile environment. To guard against this danger Paul waged a constant warfare on two fronts— against the judaizers and the gnosticizers alike. But this does not detract from the value of the Gentiles' gifts. The Greeks brought welcome gifts—first and foremost their language, apart from which the gospel would have made no headway in the Graeco-Roman world. The Romans, too, brought their gifts—first and foremost the imperial organization, thanks to which the headway of the gospel in the Graeco-Roman world was greatly expedited from the first Christian generation onward. Today, the student of the resources from which the Greeks and Romans derived those gifts may likewise venture to offer his tribute to the exposition of the earliest Christian writings.[53]

II. EARLY JUDAISM

2. Josephus and Daniel

I. THE STORY OF DANIEL IN JOSEPHUS

The story of Daniel as told by Josephus in the tenth book of his *Jewish Antiquities* is based almost entirely on the contents of the canonical Hebrew-Aramaic text of Daniel; he shows no knowledge of the deutero-canonical additions found in the Septuagint. Such additions as Josephus makes to the biblical narrative are based on other sources. The statement, for example, that some of the young Jews to whose company Daniel belonged were made eunuchs by Nebuchadnezzar (*Ant.* 10.186) is plainly derived from Isaiah's words to Hezekiah in 2 Kings 20:18 = Isa. 39:7. It is one of Josephus's characteristic literary amplifications or modifications of the narrative, like his adding dates to the "pulse" that Daniel and his three companions ate (§ 190), or his synchronizing Daniel's deportation with the exile at the end of Zedekiah's reign (§ 186) instead of following the biblical dating in the problematical "third year of Jehoiakim" (Dan. 1:1).

The chronological difficulty in Dan. 2:1, where Nebuchadnezzar's second year is mentioned, although Daniel and his companions have already had three years' education at his court, is resolved by Josephus with the statement that it was the second year "after the devastation of Egypt" (§ 195).

This was the year in which Nebuchadnezzar had his dream of the great image. Josephus's account of this dream and its interpretation by

Presidential address to the Society for Old Testament Study, London, January 1965, published in *Annual of the Swedish Theological Institute* 4 (1965), pp. 148-162.

Daniel follows the pattern customary from the first century A.D. onwards; he does not specify the identity of the three kingdoms which are
to follow the Babylonian empire, but he clearly takes them to be respectively the Medo-Persian, the Graeco-Macedonian and the Roman. The
head of gold represents not only Nebuchadnezzar but also "the Babylonian kings who were before you" (§ 208); the fact that the silver part
of the image includes the two arms signifies that the Babylonian empire
"will be brought to an end by two kings" *(ibid.)*—in other words, by
"Cyrus king of the Persians and Darius king of the Medes," as he calls
them later (§ 232). The third kingdom comes "from the west" (§ 209)—a
detail borrowed from Daniel's vision of the he-goat (Dan. 8:5), marking
this kingdom as Alexander's. Nothing is said by Josephus about the
weak latter state of the fourth kingdom, since this kingdom was interpreted of Rome, and any such detail would be impolitic. As to Josephus's
remarks about the great stone, we shall revert to these.

The story of Daniel's three companions and the burning fiery
furnace (Dan. 3) is abridged by Josephus (§§ 213-215), and there is
nothing in his account of the incident to excite comment. The narrative
of Nebuchadnezzar's second dream and its sequel (Dan. 4) is also
abridged (§§ 216-218). Josephus evidently reflects that the story of Nebuchadnezzar's madness may be thought farfetched, especially his statement (an embellishment of the biblical account) that no one ventured to
usurp the throne during its seven years' enforced vacancy, and he
defends himself by reminding his readers of his stated policy of reproducing only what he has found written in the Hebrew scriptures,
without addition or omission—a policy to which he does not always
adhere so rigidly. Indeed, when he comes to record Nebuchadnezzar's
death immediately afterwards, he amplifies his account with a long—
and, to us, very valuable—excerpt from Berossus's history of this king's
reign,[1] to which he adds testimonies from three other historians of the
Hellenistic age[2] (§§ 219-228).

The reigns of Nebuchadnezzar's successors are summarized on the
basis of other sources than the book of Daniel—partly biblical, as when
the release of Jehoiachin by Evil-merodach (Abilmathadachos) is recorded (§§ 229f.; cf. 2 Kings 25:27-30 = Jer. 52:31-34) and partly extrabiblical (§ 231). Then the narrative of Daniel is resumed with the story
of the feast of Belshazzar, "Baltasares, who was called Naboandelos by
the Babylonians" *(ibid.)*—a wrong identification of the crown prince
with the king his father. The odd alternation of two Greek words for
"wall" in the statement that "a hand came out of the τεῖχος and wrote certain syllables on the τοῖχος" (§ 233) may conceivably be due, as Thackeray
suggests, to the influence of a version like the later one of Theodotion

which says that the hand wrote "on the plaster of the wall (τοῖχος) *and* of the king's palace" (Dan. 5:5);[3] but it is much more likely due to a not very happy variation of vocabulary on the part of Josephus or his amanuensis. The queen of the story is called the king's grandmother (μάμμη, § 237)—perhaps from a desire to identify her with Nebuchadnezzar's widow or with the Nitocris of Herodotus.[4]

The interpretation of the writing on the wall follows the biblical text except that where that text says "God has numbered your kingdom and finished it" (Dan. 5:26) Josephus makes Daniel say, "God has numbered the time of your life and reign, and there still remains for you a brief time" (§ 243)—perhaps meaning "only a brief time." Accordingly, whereas the Bible says that "*in that night* was Belshazzar the Chaldaean king slain" (Dan. 5:30), Josephus says that "*not long afterwards* he and his city were taken" (§ 247).

"Darius the Mede"—unknown apart from the book of Daniel—was, according to Josephus, "the son of Astyages and bore another name among the Greeks" (§ 248). Perhaps he had in mind the doubtfully historical Cyaxares II of Xenophon's *Cyropaedia*.[5] The 120 satrapies into which Darius the Mede divided his kingdom, according to Dan. 6:1, become 360 in Josephus (§ 249), as though each of the three "presidents" (Aram. *sāreḵîn*) of Dan. 6:2 had 120 satrapies under him. Josephus (or at least his textual tradition) is confused about the relations between these three presidents (whom he calls satraps) and the satrapies. The following narrative of Daniel and the den of lions is embellished with moralizing features, especially at the end, where the lions are fed to satiety before Daniel's enemies are thrown to them, that it might be seen that their rending and devouring these enemies was due "not, I think, to the beasts' hunger, . . . but to the men's wickedness, which would be obvious even to irrational animals, so that they were punished by God's design" (§ 262). In Hellenistic style, Daniel is then proclaimed First of the King's Friends (§ 263).

An apocryphal addendum to this narrative is the account of Daniel's building a fortress (βάρις) for himself at Ecbatana (§ 264)—possibly based on a midrash of Dan. 8:2, where Daniel is at *Susa* in the *bîrāh* (βάρις in Theodotion). In this well-preserved fortress, says Josephus, "the kings of Media, Persia and Parthia are buried to this day, and the person to whose care it is entrusted is a Jewish priest" (§ 265). An odd tale; but to this day the alleged tomb of Daniel is venerated by Shi'ite Muslims in the village of Shush (Susa). In speaking of Ecbatana, Josephus may have confused this city, where according to Ezra 6:2 there was also a *bîrā* (LXX βάρις), with Susa, or he may have followed an independent tradition.[6]

Of the four visions of Dan. 7–12 the only one which Josephus reproduces at any length is the vision of the ram and the he-goat of chapter 8; he sees clearly enough in the climax of this vision the profanation of the Jerusalem temple under Antiochus Epiphanes (§§ 269-276). But the 2300 evenings and mornings of Dan. 8:14 are replaced (on the basis of other time-indications in Daniel) by 1296 days[7] during which Antiochus would "disrupt the temple service and prevent the sacrifices from being offered" (§ 271).

"In the same manner," Josephus adds (summarizing the remaining visions), "Daniel also wrote about the empire of the Romans, how Jerusalem would be captured by them and the sanctuary laid waste" (§ 276).[8] The fulfillment of Daniel's visions is seen as a proof that, contrary to the Epicurean belief, God is indeed concerned about human affairs (§ 280). It is noted especially that while Daniel, in common with other prophets, foretold future events, unlike them he also foretold the fixed time at which they would take place (§ 267). As for the details of interpretation, Josephus will not be dogmatic: "I have written of these things," he says, "as I have found them in my reading; if any one chooses to form a different opinion, he is at liberty to do so" (§ 281).

II. ALEXANDER THE GREAT AND THE BOOK OF DANIEL

The briefest reference will suffice to the story in *Ant.* 11.337 of how, when Alexander the Great visited the temple in Jerusalem and offered sacrifice there, "he was shown the book of Daniel, in which it was declared that one of the Greeks would overthrow the empire of the Persians, and believing himself to be the one indicated" he showed the Jews great favor. The historicity of Alexander's visit need not concern us here; with Tcherikover, we may recognize the narrative as "a Palestinian folk-story" devoid of factual content.[9] The incident of Alexander's being shown the book of Daniel has a parallel in *Ant.* 11.5f., where Cyrus is said to have been moved to authorize the Jews' return from exile and rebuilding of their temple through reading Isa. 44:28. A more recent parallel is presented in the experience of an Italian Protestant in the 1930s who had an interview with the late Benito Mussolini and interested him greatly by telling him how the Bible (presumably the books of Daniel and the Revelation) foretold just such a revival of the Roman Empire as Mussolini himself was believed to have in mind, and procured for the Duce's perusal a little book published in England with the title *The Roman Empire in History and Prophecy*.[10] But at least the book of Daniel does have something to say about the Greek overthrow of Persia, whereas it is silent on the subject of a revived Roman Empire.

III. THE SEVENTY HEPTADS

In Josephus's account of Daniel's visions he has nothing explicit to say about the oracle of the Seventy Heptads (Dan. 9:24-27), although he probably had it in mind when he pointed out that Daniel was enabled to define the time at which his prophecies would be fulfilled (*Ant.* 10.267). Yet, even if Josephus himself did not always realize it, this oracle has influenced his narrative at a number of points, especially in his chronology. It is well known that in Josephus the period of the Second Temple is consistently made too long by about half a century. For example, he says, "from the rebuilding of the temple in the second year of Cyrus [he means Darius I[11]], for which Haggai was responsible, to its capture under Vespasian, was 639 years, 45 days" (*BJ* 6.270); it was in fact 589 years. What is the reason for this discrepancy? Josephus himself probably did not know; but the chronology which he took over from one of his sources was based on a reinterpretation of Dan. 9:24-27 which made the seventieth heptad begin with the reign of Alexander Jannaeus in 103 B.C.—an interpretation which evidently regarded Jannaeus as the perpetrator, if not the embodiment, of the "abomination of desolation." The principal evidence for this interpretation appears in *Ant.* 13.301, where Aristobulus I becomes king 481 years and 3 months after the people's deliverance from the Babylonian captivity.[12] The "word to restore and build Jerusalem" of Dan. 9:25, with which the seventy heptads began, was equated with the edict of Cyrus. Since Aristobulus I reigned for one year, Jannaeus's accession fell towards the end of the sixty-ninth heptad. The actual interval between the edict of Cyrus and the accession of Aristobulus was about 434 years;[13] its extension to 481 years was due to its being stretched on the Procrustean bed of a reinterpretation of Daniel's oracle. It was not the first or the last time that the corpus of true chronology was either stretched or curtailed on that bed.[14] The traditional Jewish chronology of *Seder ʿOlam*, for example, reckons the seventy heptads as running from the destruction of Solomon's temple by the Babylonians to the destruction of Herod's temple by the Romans, thus reducing the true chronology by over 160 years.[15] An earlier reinterpretation of the seventieth heptad is probably reflected in *Ant.* 20.237 (following 1 Macc. 9:54–10:21), where it seems to be equated with the seven years' interregnum in the high-priesthood between Alcimus's death in 159 B.C. and Jonathan's investiture in 152 B.C. This time-note contradicts and corrects that of *Ant*. 13.46, where Jonathan puts on the high-priestly robe four years after the death of Judas Maccabaeus; here another of Josephus's sources apparently "neglected the seven years of the interregnum between Alcimus (Jacimus) and Jonathan (wishing for patriotic reasons to endow Judas Maccabaeus with the High Priesthood),"[16] and "could do no better than cut Jonathan's time in two and credit Judas with his first three years."[17]

Josephus's sources might reflect earlier interpretations of Daniel's seventy heptads; a closer examination will show that Josephus had his own interpretation of the oracle and that, while he does not make explicit mention of the oracle, his interpretation of it comes to the surface repeatedly in his *History of the Jewish War*.

IV. THE ABOMINATION OF DESOLATION

In Josephus's eyes the abomination of desolation—the profanation of the sanctuary and of the priestly office—was manifested increasingly as the war went on; he records, in fact, a succession of "abominations."

The insurgent Zealots, concerning whom he can find no words condemnatory enough, reached the point where, "sated with crimes against humanity, they turned their outrageous conduct against God, and entered the sanctuary with polluted feet" (*BJ* 4.150). Ananus the ex–high priest upbraided the citizens of Jerusalem for allowing this state of affairs to develop (*BJ* 4.163-192). He pointed to the filling of God's house with countless abominations and the intrusion into its inviolable precincts of men whose hands were red with blood; he bade them ironically take it easy when they saw the sanctuary thus trampled underfoot—the sanctuary which even the Roman army of occupation had treated with respect. The populace, stirred to action by his appeal, tried to dislodge the Zealots, and in the ensuing fighting, while those of the citizens who fell were carried home by their friends and relatives, wounded Zealots were carried up into the temple, "leaving bloodstains on the holy floor," says Josephus, "so that it might truthfully be said that it was only by *their* blood that the sanctuary was polluted" (*BJ* 4.201).

The election by lot of the last high priest, Phanni ben Samuel, cannot dispassionately be thought a more unworthy appointment than some of those which had been made in the preceding decades by the Roman governors or members of the Herod family. But Josephus describes it as though it were a profanation at least as shocking as the appointment of Menelaus by Antiochus Epiphanes. Phanni was at least a priest, though of humble peasant stock; this last point in Josephus's aristocratic eyes was a positive disqualification for the office, "a monstrous sacrilege," he calls it, which moved its perpetrators to ungodly mirth but the other priests to tears of indignation and grief as they witnessed this "mockery of their law" and "travesty of the sacred rites" (*BJ* 4.157). The latter, adds the Slavonic text, "thought that the desolation of the city would follow and prophecy would cease, if abominations were found in the holy place" (cf. Dan. 9:24, 27).

Phanni's appointment was, for Josephus, a sacrilege all the worse because there was still alive and available a patriot worthy of the sacred office—the ex–high priest Ananus the younger. There is a curious discrepancy between the picture of Ananus's character during his brief highpriesthood in A.D. 62, given by Josephus in *Ant*. 20.197-203, and the picture of Ananus's patriotic activity during the war. However that may be, when Josephus comes to record Ananus's death, at the beginning of A.D. 68, at the hands of the Idumaeans whom the Zealots had brought into the city to strengthen their side, he does so in terms which suggest that he recognized in this event the "cutting off" of the anointed one of Dan. 9:26.[18] "I should not be far wrong," he says, "if I were to say that the fall of the city began with Ananus's death, and that the overthrow of the wall and destruction of the Jewish polity dated from the day when they saw the high priest and champion of their cause butchered in the midst of the city" (*BJ* 4.318).

Incidentally—although this has nothing to do with Daniel's prophecy—there is a striking parallel between the exposure of the naked corpses of Ananus and his colleague Jeshua ben Gamala (high priest *c*. 63-68), who was killed at the same time, and the exposure "in the street of the great city" of the corpses of the two witnesses in Rev. 11:7-11, after their murder by the "beast from the abyss." Neither the seer of Revelation himself, nor the source which he appears to have remolded in Rev. 11:1-13, can have identified the two witnesses with Ananus and Jeshua, but it is possible that Josephus knew the short Jewish apocalypse which lies behind this section of Revelation, and saw it fulfilled, or partially fulfilled, in the fate of these two former high priests.

Further profanation of the holy place came when the Roman siege of Jerusalem began in earnest. "The heavy missiles came over with such velocity that they reached the altar and sanctuary, falling on priests and sacrificers; and many visitors from the ends of the earth who came eagerly to visit this renowned and sacred place, were themselves struck down in front of their offerings, and sprinkled the altar with their own blood . . ." (*BJ* 5.16f.).

From time to time in his account of the last days of Jerusalem,

Josephus makes reference to ancient oracles which we cannot now readily identify. For example, "the Jews, after the destruction of Antonia, reduced the temple to a square (τετράγωνος), although they had it recorded in their oracles that the city and the sanctuary would be captured when the temple became foursquare (τετράγωνος)" (*BJ* 6.311).

"Authority unknown," says Thackeray in a footnote to this passage in the Loeb edition.[19] But the mention of the capture of the city and sanctuary is reminiscent of Dan. 9:26, "the people of the prince who is to come shall destroy the city and the sanctuary." That being so, can the reference to the temple being made foursquare have been a misinterpretation or an imperfect reminiscence of Dan. 9:25, "it [the city] shall be built with square and water-channel"?[20] It is admittedly easy to be over-influenced by the English word "square," which in this place represents Heb. *rᵉḥōḇ* ("broad place") and not *rᵉḇûʿāh*;[21] but I am assured by colleagues whose knowledge of biblical and postbiblical Hebrew far exceeds mine that the meaning "square," even in the sense of τετράγωνος, is not out of the question for *rᵉḥōḇ*.[22]

Another "age-old saying of divinely inspired men," twice referred to by Josephus (*BJ* 4.388; 6.109), foretold that the city would be taken and the temple burnt down if ever the citizens fought with each other and Jewish hands took the initiative in defiling the house of God. The Jewish hands, Josephus reckons, were the hands of the Zealot defenders of the temple area; but what was the ancient oracle which was thus fulfilled?[23] It might conceivably be Jeremiah's oracle of Jer. 7:14 and 26:6, or the vision of judgment described in Ezekiel 9, judgment which was to begin at the sanctuary (v. 6) and pollute its precincts with piles of corpses (v. 7; cf. *BJ* 6.110)—except that the sanctuary thus defiled and doomed was the First Temple. It might, on the other hand, be based on the prophecy of Daniel 11, where there is evident opposition between those Jews who "forsake the holy covenant" and those who "know their God" (vv. 30, 32), and where the internal strife is accompanied by the profanation and desolation of the temple (v. 31) and the shattering of the power of the holy people (Dan. 12:7).

The particularity with which Josephus records the cessation of the daily sacrifice, on 17 Panemos (Tammuz) of A.D. 70 (= 5 August)—three and a half years, coincidentally, after Vespasian's arrival as commander-in-chief in Judaea—suggests strongly that in this event he recognized the fulfillment of the repeated prophecy in Daniel about the taking away of the daily sacrifice (Dan. 8:11-14; 9:27; 11:31; 12:11). Historically, of course, Daniel's references are to the cessation of the daily sacrifice through the edict of Antiochus IV at the end of 167 B.C.; this is the interpretation found in 1 Macc. 1:45, 54, 59, and probably followed by some of Josephus's other authorities for the distress under Antiochus. But for Josephus the cessation which took place almost under his own eyes was much more important. On that day, he says (*BJ* 6.94), Titus was informed that the continual sacrifice had been discontinued through lack of lambs[24] to offer, and Josephus was put up to address one further appeal to the defenders, pointing out that now at last they might give up hope of having God on their side, since they had left off paying him his ordained tribute of sacrificial worship.

Josephus, as usual, is preeminently distasteful when from his position of security he taunts his fellow-citizens moralizingly for their impiety; but it is plain that he himself thought the cessation of the daily sacrifice to be the final act which sealed the doom of the holy place—the final act which sealed its doom, but not the crowning profanation.

The crowning profanation was surely the incident which followed the firing of the sanctuary: "while the flames were consuming the sanctuary itself and all its surroundings, the Romans brought their standards into the temple area and, erecting them opposite the East Gate, offered sacrifice to them there,[25] and with loud acclamations hailed Titus as *imperator*" (*BJ* 6.316). Since the military standards bore aloft the imperial images, they might not even be introduced into the city without an infringement of the Second Commandment, and Pilate, over forty years before, had been compelled to remove them when he brought them into Jerusalem;[26] but now the legionary eagles are brought into the temple court and sacrificial worship is rendered to them—an appalling abomination the like of which had not been witnessed since the cult of Olympian Zeus was installed in the holy place under Antiochus Epiphanes. Josephus simply records the incident; he says nothing of his own feelings on the matter, although earlier he speaks very freely of his horror and despair at the defilement of the sacred precincts by the activities of the Zealots, and represents even Titus as shocked by it (*BJ* 6.126).

That Josephus expected any improvement in the situation at the end of 1260 or 1290 or even 1335 days[27] after the cessation of the daily sacrifice and the setting up of this abomination of desolation is most improbable; a longer period than the longest of these had elapsed when he published the Greek edition of his *History of the Jewish War*.

V. THE COMING PRINCE

As for Josephus's assurance that Vespasian was the predicted ruler who was to emerge from Judaea, he is not the only writer of this period to mention this prediction and see it fulfilled in Vespasian. Tacitus (*History* 5.13) tells how the Jews' ancient priestly writings foretold that at that very time (*eo ipso tempore*) the Orient would recover strength and men from Judaea would gain supreme power—an ambiguous oracle which really pointed to Vespasian and Titus but was popularly misconstrued. Suetonius (*Vespasian* 4), in almost identical words, says that the Jews rebelled because they applied to themselves this oracle, widespread and persistent throughout the whole Orient, that at that time (*eo tempore*) men from Judaea would gain supreme power—although the oracle really referred to the Roman Emperor.

What Josephus says on this subject is: "The Jews' chief inducement to go to war was an equivocal oracle also found in their sacred writings, announcing that at that time (κατὰ τὸν καιρὸν ἐκεῖνον) a man from their country would become ruler of the world. They took this to portend the triumph of their own race, and many of their scholars were widely out in their interpretation; the oracle in fact pointed to the accession of Vespasian, who was in Judaea when he was acclaimed emperor" (*BJ* 6.312f.).[28]

All those references to the oracle represent it as Delphic in its ambiguity, like the oracles which led Croesus to his doom because he interpreted them in the obvious, but wrong, sense.

What does Josephus mean by saying that the oracle in question announced the emergence of a world-ruler *at that time?* The only oracle in the Hebrew scriptures which makes such an announcement in chronological terms is the oracle of the seventy heptads in Dan. 9:24-27. Josephus must have identified Vespasian with the "prince who is to come" of Dan. 9:26, and perhaps also with the "anointed prince" of the preceding verse. (This "anointed prince" of Dan. 9:25 is actually the high priest Jeshua ben Jehozadak, who entered on office at the end of the first seven heptads, *c.* 539 B.C., but the passage has sometimes been punctuated, as in KJV/AV,[29] to point to the emergence of the "anointed prince" at the end of the sixty-ninth heptad. For the rest, we may recall that the interpretation of the events of A.D. 66-70 as the *terminus ad quem* of the seventy heptads is that perpetuated in *Seder 'Olam* and the traditional Jewish calendar.)

The Jews who, according to Josephus, thought that the oracle portended the triumph of their own nation may well have identified the "coming prince" with the ruler of the house of David whose unending and worldwide sovereignty is foretold elsewhere in Hebrew scripture, whose "dominion will be from sea to sea and from the River to the ends of the earth" (Ps. 72:8; cf. Isa. 9:6f.).

The earliest explicit prophecy of a ruler from Judah comes in the Blessing of Jacob (Gen. 49:10):

The scepter shall not depart from Judah,
   nor the ruler's staff from between his feet,
until he comes to whom it belongs;
   and to him shall be the obedience of the peoples.

This was most probably the oracle referred to by Tacitus and Suetonius, which foretold how men from Judaea would attain world dominion. There is no note of time in this oracle, however, and if its fulfilment was expected "at that very time," it must have come to be interpreted with the help of Daniel's oracle of the seventy heptads. Josephus (*Ant.* 2.194f.) passes swiftly over the Blessing of Jacob, pausing only to make a brief mention of the promise of special prosperity for Joseph. But with the sudden insight he had gained at Jotapata, Josephus was quite capable of identifying "the one to whom it belongs," the one who would receive "the obedience of the peoples," not with any Davidic prince but with Vespasian, whom he hailed as sovereign of "land and sea and all the human race" (*BJ* 3.402).

When, as he claims, he was inspired to understand certain equivocal utterances of the Deity in this sense, he perhaps had in mind not only the Blessing of Jacob and the visions of Daniel but also Balaam's prophecy of a star that would arise from Jacob and win the victory over all the sons of tumult (Num. 24:17)—a prophecy which we know influenced the eschatological thought of the Qumran community[30] and was revived later in the Bar Kokhba revolt. In the same context of Num. 24 there is Balaam's further prophecy about ships coming from the coast of Kittim to afflict Aššur and Eber (v. 24). If, like Dan. 11:30 and the Qumran commentators, Josephus interpreted these Kittim of the Romans, then he no doubt found further ground for his belief that God was on the side of the Romans—a belief which he reiterates to the point of tedium.

We cannot pass from this subject without a reference to Yoḥanan ben Zakkai's hailing Vespasian as emperor (*malkā*) when he came before him after being smuggled out of Jerusalem, and predicting his conquest of Jerusalem. Yoḥanan based his prediction on Isa. 10:34, "Lebanon shall fall by a mighty one." "A mighty one," he said, "is an epithet applied only to a king" (cf. Jer. 30:21), and "Lebanon" is made to refer to the sanctuary, on the strength of Deut. 3:25 (TB *Giṭṭin* 56b).[31]

VI. THE STONE

In the Qumran commentary on Habakkuk it is made plain that the particular form of inspiration with which the Teacher of Righteousness was endowed was the ability to interpret accurately the prophetic

oracles, with special reference to the *time* of their fulfillment.[32] This was
the form of prophetic inspiration which Josephus claimed for himself,
and which impelled him to salute Vespasian as emperor-to-be. When in
Ant. 10.267, 277-280, he appeals to Daniel's visions as evidence that God
does have a concern for human affairs and does reveal to his servants
not only *what* must come to pass but *when* it must come to pass, we may
surmise that he has in mind his own prophetic gift and what he describes
as "the dreams by night in which God had foretold to him the impending
fate of the Jews and the destinies of the Roman rulers." He himself, he
goes on, "was an interpreter of dreams and skilled in divining the
meaning of ambiguous utterances of the Divinity. Being a priest himself
and the descendant of priests, he was not ignorant of the prophecies in
the sacred books. At that hour [in the cave after the fall of Jotapata] he
was enabled by divine inspiration to master these prophecies, and
recalling the awesome appearances of his recent dreams he offered up
to God a silent prayer:

> "Since thou, Creator of the Jewish nation, art now pleased to bring it low,
> and fortune has passed entirely to the Romans; since thou hast chosen me
> to declare the things that are to come, I willingly surrender to the Romans
> and consent to live, and I call thee to witness that I go over to them not as
> a traitor, but as thy minister" (*BJ* 3.351ff.).

This was the rationalization of his inglorious action, and no doubt
as the years went on he looked back more and more on his whole career
in the light of his prophetic calling. He was not the first Jew to incur the
suspicion and hostility of his people for prophesying the triumph of the
enemy—Jeremiah springs to mind as an earlier example, but Jeremiah
refused to live in luxury as the Babylonians' pensioner when his city fell,
nor can he be charged, as Josephus can, with unfeeling complacency in
reviling braver men than himself.

Did Josephus, then, remain content with the new order as the
consummation of God's will—Jerusalem captured, the temple destroyed, priesthood and sacrifice brought to an end, and the Flavian
dynasty supreme throughout the Mediterranean world?

In his account of Daniel's explanation of Nebuchadnezzar's
dream-image, where Josephus clearly takes the fourth empire to be the
Roman, he passes over with an eloquently delicate touch the significance
of the stone cut out without hands. "Daniel also showed the king the
meaning of the stone, but I have not thought fit to inquire into this, for
it is my duty to write about things of the remote and more recent past,
not of things which are yet to be. However, if anyone in his desire for
precise information will not abstain from inquiring more closely, so as

to gratify his curiosity about things which are still hidden in the future, let him give diligence to read the book of Daniel: he will find it among the sacred writings" (*Ant.* 10.210).

Josephus knew well enough what the current interpretation of the stone was among his people. It was interpreted of the reign of the saints which would follow the overthrow of the fourth empire (Dan. 7:18, 22, 27): one form of this interpretation, indeed, doubtless encouraged the Zealots to resist to the bitter end of A.D. 73. These Zealots, as Josephus saw the situation, were wrong; but were they altogether wrong? Josephus had ample time to reflect on such questions between the end of the war and the writing of the *Antiquities*. Whatever he may have thought at one time, in A.D. 93 Josephus did not think of Daniel's fourth empire as the Julio-Claudian dynasty doomed to fall before the Flavians; had that still been his opinion there would have been no reason for reticence. No: Daniel's fourth empire, he saw, was Rome absolutely, not this or that imperial dynasty; then Rome itself would one day disintegrate beneath the great stone.[33] Josephus kept his counsel about the meaning of the stone, but at the end, it may be suggested, his patriotism triumphed and he foresaw his people's vindication. His nation had had a glorious past, as he did his best to emphasize; but its future would be even more glorious. Long delayed it might be; nevertheless the day would come.

3. Qumran and the Old Testament

[Qumran is an area on the northwest shore of the Dead Sea (where the Wadi Qumran debouches into the coastal plain), in which a Jewish religious community—probably an Essene group[1]—had its headquarters for the greater part of 220 years, c. 150 B.C.–A.D. 70. Our knowledge of the community is derived partly from the excavation of their buildings but mainly from the study of ancient manuscripts (largely fragmentary) found in eleven caves in the vicinity between 1947 and 1956; they have come to be known popularly as the Dead Sea Scrolls. The community was organized by an exceptionally gifted man, known to his followers by a Hebrew title which is conventionally rendered the Teacher of Righteousness, but which perhaps means rather "the right guide."[2] He taught his followers to recognize themselves as the true Israel, the righteous remnant which God would use as his agent for putting down wickedness and establishing righteousness in a new order which would soon replace the current "epoch of Belial."[3]]

I. THE QUMRAN DOCUMENTS

The Qumran documents include an abundance of material bearing on the Old Testament—Hebrew texts, Greek texts, Targums and commentaries.

(1) Some 175 copies of Old Testament books in the Hebrew (or

Presidential address to the Victoria Institute, delivered in London, 2 June 1959, and published in *Faith and Thought* 91 (1959-60), pp. 9-27.

Aramaic) original have been identified among the nearly 600 books represented by the Qumran finds. Most of these have survived only as fragments, but there are a few reasonably complete copies, notably one of the book of Isaiah from Cave 1 (1QIsa^a),[4] and substantial portions of others have been preserved, such as copies of Leviticus and the Psalms[5] from Cave 11. All twenty-four books of the Hebrew Bible are represented with the exception of Esther; there are also fragments or larger portions of some books of the Apocrypha and Pseudepigrapha.[6]

(2) Some Septuagint fragments of two manuscripts of Leviticus and one of Numbers have been identified from Cave 4; Cave 7 has yielded fragments of the Septuagint text of Exodus and also of the Epistle of Jeremiah, which appears in most editions of the Apocrypha as the last chapter of Baruch, although it is an independent composition.[7]

(3) Of all the Targumic material found, greatest interest attaches to the Targum of Job found in Cave 11 because we have independent evidence for the existence of a written Targum of this book in the period of the Second Temple, which Gamaliel I ordered to be built into the temple walls[8] (presumably not later than A.D. 63, when Herod's temple was finally completed). We remember, too, the note appended to the Septuagint text of Job which is said to have been "translated from the Syriac book" (probably from an Aramaic Targum). Fragments of a Leviticus Targum (16:12-15, 18-21) have been found in Cave 4. The *Genesis Apocryphon* from Cave 1 certainly contains Targumic sections, although J. T. Milik says that it is "no true Targum."[9] Other scholars, however, disagree with him; M. Black, working out a hint dropped by P. Kahle, says that it "is almost certainly our oldest written Palestinian Pentateuch Targum."[10]

(4) One of the most important groups of writings found at Qumran consists of commentaries *(pesharim)* on various Old Testament books or parts of books. These not only tell us much about the biblical interpretation and religious outlook of the Qumran sectaries, but also have a contribution of their own to make to the history of the biblical text.

[(5) In addition to these there are a number of community documents (as they might be called) which, while not in themselves biblical texts, versions or commentaries, are more or less Bible-related and throw light from time to time on the community's understanding of the sacred text.[11] Among these are:

(a) the Rule of the Community (1QS), a manual of discipline for the community's life and practice, doubtless laid down originally by the Teacher of Righteousness;

(b) the Rule of the Congregation (1QS^a), setting out procedures to be followed by the elect congregation in the new age that is to come;

(c) a collection of benedictions (1QS^b);

(d) the Book of the Covenant of Damascus (CD), often called the Zadokite work, comprising a historical retrospect and ethical admonition, with a body of rules for national life, originally known from two early mediaeval manuscripts found in the ancient synagogue of Old Cairo at the beginning of the twentieth century but now identified as a product of the Qumran community;[12]

(e) a collection of hymns of thanksgiving or *hôḏāyôṯ* (1QH);

(f) the Rule of War (1QM), a manual prescribing how the end-time conflict between the sons of light and the sons of darkness is to be waged;[13]

(g) the Temple Scroll (11QT), the longest of the Qumran manuscripts, a second-century-B.C. updating of the material in Exodus, Leviticus and Deuteronomy dealing with the temple, its ministry and its sacrificial worship.][14]

In the light of these different species of Qumran literature we now propose to consider what can be learned about (a) the literary criticism of Old Testament books; (b) the text of the Old Testament; (c) the canon of the Old Testament; (d) the interpretation of the Old Testament current at Qumran.

II. LITERARY CRITICISM

The evidence which the Qumran discoveries provide for the literary criticism of Old Testament books is exiguous. The reason for this is simply stated: the Qumran literature for the most part belongs to an age when all, or nearly all, the Old Testament books had acquired their final form (questions of textual variation excluded).

When at first the report of the complete Isaiah scroll from Cave 1 was released, there were excited surmises in various quarters about the light which might be shed upon the question of the composition and authorship of Isaiah. All that it does tell us about this, however, is that the book of Isaiah existed in its present form at the beginning of the first century B.C. (when this manuscript appears to have been copied); but that was already known. It is clear, for example, that Ben Sira (*c.* 180 B.C.) knew the book of Isaiah in substantially its present form, for in his eulogy of the prophet Isaiah (Sir. 48:22-25) he assigns to him indiscriminately passages from all three of the main divisions of the book. The Septuagint text of the book is a further witness to the same effect. The fact that there is no space between the thirty-ninth and fortieth chapters of the book in 1Q Isaᵃ (chap. 40 beginning actually on the last line of a column) tells us as little about the earlier history of the book as does the fact that there *is* a space between the thirty-third and thirty-fourth chapters (chap. 34 beginning at the top of a column, although there is room for three lines of writing at the foot of the preceding column).[15]

To be sure, the Qumran evidence does appear to refute conclusively arguments to the effect that the book of Isaiah did not receive its present form until after the Maccabaean revolt. We may think, for instance, of R. H. Kennett's suggestion[16] that the portrayal of the Suffering Servant in Isaiah 52:13–53:12 was inspired by the martyrdom of faithful Jews under Antiochus Epiphanes (between 168 and 164 B.C.), or of B. Duhm's dating[17] of the "Isaiah Apocalypse" (Isa. 24–27) in the reign of John Hyrcanus (135–104 B.C.). If we now have a copy of the book of Isaiah, complete with Servant Songs and "Isaiah Apocalypse," assignable on palaeographical grounds to the early period of the Hasmonaean regime, there is no further need of argument. So, at least, one might have thought; but in a book actually dealing with the Qumran discoveries one French scholar hazarded the suggestion that the portrayal of the Suffering Servant could have been based on the historical experience of the Teacher of Righteousness, the revered leader of the Qumran community, whose death he placed between 66 and 63 B.C.![18]

III. TEXT

If little light is thrown by the Qumran documents on questions of date, composition and authorship, it is far otherwise with questions of textual criticism.[19]

The text of the Old Testament has come down to us along three principal lines of transmission.[20]

There is, first of all, the proto-Masoretic Hebrew text.[21] This is the consonantal text of the Hebrew Bible which is commonly supposed to have been fixed by Jewish scholars in the days of Rabbi Aqiba (*c.* A.D. 100), the text to which the Masoretes of the sixth to ninth centuries A.D. affixed an elaborate apparatus of signs which standardized the pronunciation, punctuation and (up to a point) interpretation of the text. Although the earliest surviving manuscripts of this text belong, with fragmentary exceptions,[22] to the ninth century A.D., we have witnesses to its earlier stages in quotations in the Mishnah and Talmud, in the

Midrashim and Targumim, and in the Syriac (Peshiṭta) and Latin (Vulgate) versions of the Old Testament.

There is, secondly, the Greek version of the Old Testament commonly called the Septuagint, produced in Alexandria in Egypt in the last two or three centuries B.C., and reflecting a Hebrew text which sometimes deviates from that of the Masoretes, and which may reasonably be labeled as an Egyptian text-type.

Thirdly, so far as the Pentateuch is concerned, there is the Samaritan Bible, an edition of the Hebrew text which has for at least 2,000 years been preserved along a line of transmission quite independent of the Masoretic text of the Jews. Before the discovery of the Qumran texts, P. Kahle expressed the view that the Samaritan Bible, apart from certain adaptations in the interest of Samaritan claims, "is in the main a popular revision of an older text, in which antiquated forms and constructions, not familiar to people of later times, were replaced by forms and constructions easier to be understood, difficulties were removed, parallel passages were inserted."[23]

The discovery at Qumran of biblical texts a thousand years older than the earliest Hebrew biblical manuscripts previously known naturally gave rise to considerable excitement and speculation, especially as the possibility of our ever finding Hebrew biblical manuscripts substantially earlier than the Masoretic period had been dismissed for all practical purposes by the highest authorities.[24] The general reader of the Bible asked if the new discoveries involved much alteration in the traditional text of the Old Testament; the specialist asked to which, if to any, of the known text-types the newly discovered texts could be assigned.[25]

It was possible immediately to reassure the general Bible reader that he could go on using the familiar text with increased confidence in its substantial accuracy. The new evidence confirmed what there was already good reason to believe—that the Jewish copyists of the early Christian centuries carried out their work with the utmost fidelity. To be sure, it was inevitable that a number of scribal errors should find their way into the text in the course of a thousand years of copying and recopying the Scriptures, in spite of all the care taken to prevent this; and it seemed probable that here and there the new discoveries would help to correct some of these.

For example, when the text of 1Q Isa[a] was made available, the Revised Standard Version of the Old Testament had reached an advanced stage of production, but the revisers saw fit to adopt thirteen readings in which that manuscript deviates from the traditional Hebrew text.[26] Thus, whereas Isaiah 14:4 appears in RV as "How hath the oppressor ceased! the golden city [margin, "exactress"] ceased!," RSV renders it "How the oppressor has ceased, the insolent fury ceased!," and adds a footnote to the word "fury" as follows": "One ancient Ms Compare Gk Syr Vg: The meaning of the Hebrew word is uncertain." The Masoretic text reads *madhēbāh*, which was interpreted as related to the Aramaic *dhb* ("gold"); but this was almost certainly a scribal error caused by the close resemblance between the letters *d* and *r*, and 1Q Isaᵃ (which, of course, has no vowel-points) reads *mrhbh*, which the RSV relates to the root *rhb* ("be proud"). The renderings of the Greek, Syriac and Latin versions could represent *mrhbh*, but not *madhēbāh*.

Again, in Isaiah 21:8 RSV says: "Then he who saw cried: 'Upon a watchtower I stand, O Lord . . .'" and in a footnote invokes the authority of "one ancient Ms" for this reading against the unsuitable Masoretic reading "a lion." The "one ancient Ms" is 1Q Isaᵃ, which reads *hr'h* as against MT *'aryeh* (whence AV "And he cried, A lion . . . ," and RV "And he cried as a lion . . ."). The reference is to a watchman looking for the approach of a messenger across the Syrian desert from Babylon.

In Isaiah 60:19 1Q Isaᵃ adds the phrase "by night" to the second clause, thus completing the parallelism. Here too RSV follows it, reading: "The sun shall be no more your light by day; nor for brightness shall the moon give light to you by night" (with a footnote which appeals to the evidence of the Greek and Old Latin versions and the Targum, as well as of "one ancient Ms"). RV, on the other hand, following MT, renders: "The sun shall be no more thy light by day, neither for brightness shall the moon give light unto thee."

There is, however, one place where RSV does not follow a significant reading of 1Q Isaᵃ, although it might have been expected to do so, the more so since this reading appears also in 1Q Isaᵇ (which in general is much closer to the Masoretic text than 1Q Isaᵃ is). That is in Isaiah 53:11, where these two manuscripts add the word "light," so as to read: "After his soul's travail he will see light." It had frequently been suggested that "light" originally stood in the Hebrew text here, but had fallen out accidentally, since it was present in the Septuagint version; but now this suggestion was confirmed by the appearance of the word in these two ancient texts of Isaiah. Yet RSV does not adopt this reading, but paraphrases MT: "he shall see the fruit of the travail of his soul."[26a]

Another attractive reading of 1Q Isaᵃ which is not mentioned in RSV is in Isaiah 40:12, where we find "Who has measured *the waters of the sea (my ym)* in the hollow of his hand?" as against MT "Who has measured *the waters (mayim)* in the hollow of his hand?"

Although some of the readings in which 1Q Isaᵃ differs from MT are attested by the Septuagint,[27] 1Q Isaᵃ does not in general exhibit the

type which we may presume to have lain before the Septuagint translators. It is rather a popular and unofficial copy produced by amateur
scribes for the use of readers who were not very familiar with Hebrew,
but its text-type is in general that from which the Masoretic text-type is
descended.

The widespread destruction of copies of Hebrew Scripture in the
persecution of Palestinian Jews in 168 B.C. and the following years
created a great demand for fresh copies when the persecution died
down. While this demand may have been met in part by the production
of such popular copies as 1Q Isa^a, something more accurate and reliable
must have been required for synagogue services and for study in the
schools. Not only would fresh copies be made on the basis of those which
had escaped the destruction, but trustworthy copies would be imported
from Jewish communities outside Palestine.

As examination of the biblical manuscripts from Qumran pro-
gresses, it becomes ever clearer that they do not represent one text-type
only, but all three of those we have already mentioned, if not indeed
others as well. In addition to those manuscripts which exhibit the
proto-Masoretic text-type, there are several which exhibit the sort of
Hebrew text which must have lain before the Septuagint translators, and
yet others which have close affinities with the Samaritan Pentateuch. If
the Septuagint *Vorlage* is an Egyptian text-type, and the Samaritan Bible
in essence a popular Palestinian text-type, then it may be that the
proto-Masoretic text is of Babylonian provenience.

During the study of the biblical fragments which were found when
Cave 1 was explored by an archaeological party in 1949, it was
announced that a Hebrew fragment of Deuteronomy (1Q Dt^b) exhibited
a reading in 31:1 which agreed with the Septuagint ("And Moses finished
speaking all these words") and not with MT ("And Moses went and
spoke these words"). But with the discovery of Cave 4 in 1952 much more
evidence of the same kind came to light.

For example, a Hebrew fragment of Exodus (4Q Exod^a) agrees with
the Septuagint against MT by giving the number of Jacob's descendants
in 1:5 as seventy-five instead of seventy (cf. Acts 7:14, where Stephen, as
throughout his speech, relies upon the Septuagint text).

A tiny fragment of Deuteronomy from Cave 4 presents us for the
first time with documentary evidence for a Hebrew reading which had
long been inferred on the basis of the Septuagint. According to MT, "the
Most High . . . set the bounds of the peoples according to the number of
the children of Israel," but the Septuagint says ". . . according to the
number of the angels of God," whence it had often been deduced that
the underlying Hebrew read (in place of MT *b^{e}nê Yiśrā'ēl*) *b^{e}nê 'ēl* or *b^{e}nê*

ĕlōhîm, "sons of God."[28] It is the latter phrase that is shown by this fragment from Cave 4 (4Q Dt^q).

Another interesting reading in the same chapter is exhibited by the same roll from Cave 4, which contains this chapter only (the Song of Moses). The end of the Song in the Septuagint diverges markedly from MT, especially in verse 43, which is twice as long in the Septuagint as in MT. (It is from this longer text that Hebrews 1:6 derives the quotation, "Let all the angels of God worship him.") The Hebrew original of these Septuagint readings is preserved in this roll from Cave 4 (4Q Dt^q).

In the summer of 1958 J. T. Milik identified a passage from the middle of Deuteronomy 32 on another fragment from Cave 4, presenting further Hebrew readings previously known only from the Septuagint—notably the expansion at the beginning of verse 15, "But Jacob ate and grew fat, and Jeshurun kicked," and the reading "was moved to jealousy" (Heb. *wyqn'*) instead of MT "abhorred" (Heb. *wayyin'aṣ*) in verse 19.[29]

The best-preserved biblical manuscript from Cave 4 is a copy of Samuel in Hebrew (4Q Sam^a). This scroll originally contained fifty-seven columns, of which parts of forty-seven survive. It is of particular interest, because not only does it exhibit very much the type of text which the Septuagint translator of Samuel must have used, but a type of text closer to that which the author of Chronicles appears to have used in the compilation of his work than to the MT of Samuel. P. W. Skehan[30] suggests that the MT of Samuel is a "scissored" text, in which certain material has been removed from an earlier "vulgar" text of which 4Q Sam^a and the Septuagint together give us information.

Among the prophetical books, Jeremiah shows the greatest divergence between the Septuagint and MT, the Septuagint attesting a shorter text. This shorter text is exhibited in a Hebrew copy from Cave 4 (4Q Jer^b), but the longer recension is also represented at Qumran.

A fragmentary scroll of Exodus from Cave 4, written in palaeo-Hebrew script, shows a type of text hitherto regarded as distinctively Samaritan. The Samaritan text is characterized by expansions, only a few of which reflect a sectarian tendency. This scroll exhibits all the Samaritan expansions for the area which it covers, except the supplement to the Tenth Commandment at the end of Exodus 20:17, which is one of the expansions where a sectarian tendency is evident. There is thus nothing sectarian about this scroll, and its evidence confirms Dr. Kahle's suggestion, quoted above, that the Samaritan Pentateuch in essence is a popular recension of the traditional text.

The well-known document 4Q *Testimonia*,[31] which brings together a number of "messianic" proof-texts from the Old Testament, quotes as its first proof-text part of the expanded Samaritan text of Exodus 20:21, where the words "Moses drew near to the thick darkness where God was" are followed by a conflation of Deuteronomy 5:28f. and Deuteronomy 18:18f.

In addition to manuscripts which can be classified quite confidently as belonging to one or another of these three main text-types, there are others which exhibit a mixed text, while others may belong to text-types not yet identified. Thus, from Cave 4 we have a manuscript of Numbers (4Q Num[b]) whose text is midway between the Samaritan and Septuagint types, and one of Samuel (4Q Sam[b]) which J. T. Milik considers to exhibit a text superior to the Septuagint and MT alike.[32]

The biblical manuscripts proper are not the only Qumran documents which provide us with the information about the biblical text; indeed, reference has already been made in this respect to 4Q *Testimonia*, which is not a biblical manuscript in the strict sense. The biblical commentaries are also useful in this respect,[33] the more so because the commentators make skillful use of textual variants. Where one variant suits a commentator's purpose better than another, he will use it, although his exposition may show plainly that he is well aware of an alternative reading. Out of several instances that might be given, let one suffice.

The MT of Habakkuk 2:16, as rendered in RV, runs: "Thou art filled with shame for glory: drink thou also, and be as one uncircumcised. . . ." For "be (as one) uncircumcised," however (Heb. *hēʿārēl*), the Septuagint and Peshiṭta read "stagger," which presupposes Heb. *hērāʿēl;* and this is the basis of the RSV rendering, "Drink, yourself, and stagger!" It appears that the Qumran commentator on Habakkuk (1Q p Hab) read *hērāʿēl* ("stagger") in his biblical text, for he quotes the first part of verse 16 in this form. But when he comes to give his exposition of the words, he indicates that he was acquainted with the alternative reading *hēʿārēl* ("be uncircumcised"), for he combines both ideas in his application of the prophet's denunciation to the Wicked Priest: "Its interpretation concerns the priest whose shame was mightier than his glory, for he did not circumcise the foreskin of his heart but walked in the ways of drunkenness to quench his thirst."

As between the three main text-types, that which formed the basis of the Masoretic is superior to the other two. In a considerable number of places the new discoveries have helped us to emend it, or have confirmed emendations previously conjectured; but in general neither the Septuagint *Vorlage* nor the Samaritan text can approach the proto-Masoretic for accuracy. It is evident that down to the end of the Second Commonwealth no one text-type was fixed as authoritative among

Palestinian Jews, even in so strict a community as that of Qumran. But when, about the end of the first century A.D., a uniform consonantal text was fixed by Aqiba and his fellow-rabbis, they proceeded with sound judgment. It is significant, by the way, that the biblical Hebrew manuscripts found in the Murabba'at caves, whose presence there evidently dates from the years of the second Jewish revolt against Rome (A.D. 132-135), uniformly exhibit one text-type—the text-type recently standardized by Aqiba and others, the text-type which some centuries later formed the basis on which the Masoretes worked.

IV. CANON

It is difficult to make a definite pronouncement on the limits of the biblical canon recognized by the Qumran community. It is clear that they recognized the Law and the Prophets as divinely inspired. The commentaries which are written on those books, or on excerpts from them, presuppose that they are to be treated as divine oracles, whose interpretation was a closely-guarded mystery until it was made known in the latter days to the Teacher of Righteousness. The Psalter was evidently accorded the same recognition as the Law and the Prophets. But what about the other books in the third division of the Hebrew Bible—the "Writings"? We cannot simply infer that they were regarded as canonical from the fact that all of them (except Esther) are represented in the Qumran literature, for many other books are represented in the Qumran literature. The Qumran library evidently included many apocalyptic and pseudepigraphic works which enjoyed considerable prestige in certain sections of the population of Judaea in those days, such as Jubilees (in Hebrew) and 1 Enoch (in Aramaic),[34] which appear to be closely related to the distinctive theology of Qumran, with the *Testament of Levi* (in Aramaic) and the *Testament of Naphtali* (in Hebrew) both representing an earlier recension than that found in the Greek *Testaments of the Twelve Patriarchs*. It also included fragments of Tobit (in Aramaic and Hebrew), of Ecclesiasticus/Ben Sira (in Hebrew) and, as has been already mentioned, of the Epistle of Jeremiah (in Greek). Were these works, which large tracts of the Christian church were to venerate as deuterocanonical, if not canonical, venerated in any such way at Qumran? We cannot say with certainty, for the mere fact of their presence among the Qumran fragments provides no evidence one way or the other.[35]

   A book may be authoritative in a religious community without being given the status of a divine oracle. The *Book of Common Prayer* is an authoritative document in the Church of England, but it is not part of Holy Writ. The *Rule of the Community* was an authoritative document at Qumran, but no one suggests that it was regarded as canonical scripture. Jubilees was also an authoritative document at Qumran; the community apparently accepted the solar calendar of Jubilees as that instituted by God in the beginning (Gen. 1:14), and it is very probably the work referred to in the Zadokite document (16.3f.) as "the book of the divisions of times into their jubilees and weeks." But was it regarded as canonical in the sense of being divinely inspired? We cannot as yet give a confident answer to this question.

What can be said about the fact that thus far no fragment of Esther has turned up at Qumran? Obviously no sound inference can be built upon the argument from silence. Its nonappearance among the Qumran texts may be accidental. On the other hand, we know that its right to a place in the sacred canon was questioned in some Jewish quarters,[36] as also later in some Christian quarters,[37] and it would not be surprising if it were not accepted at Qumran.

Daniel was clearly a favorite book with the Qumran sectaries, and apparently enjoyed canonical status among them.[38] Two copies of this book have been identified from Cave 1, five from Cave 4 and one from Cave 6. These follow MT, apart from a few variant readings related to the Septuagint *Vorlage*. Fragments from Caves 1 and 4 have preserved the two places in Daniel where the language changes—from Hebrew to Aramaic in 2:4 and back from Aramaic to Hebrew in 8:1. No light is thrown by the Qumran finds to date on the problem of the two languages in Daniel.

The deuterocanonical additions to Daniel (*Susanna, Bel and the Dragon,* the *Prayer of Azariah* and the *Benedicite*) have not been identified at Qumran. It appears from these additions that the cycle of stories about Daniel continued to grow after the publication of the canonical book,[39] and indeed we can recognize among these additional stories a variant account of one of the canonical incidents (Daniel's six days' imprisonment in the lions' den in the story of *Bel and the Dragon* is patently a variant of the incident narrated in chap. 6). And even the canonical book has been thought to have "the appearance rather of a series of excerpts than of a continuous narrative, and the hypothesis that the present book is an abridgment of a larger work (partly preserved in its original language and partly translated) has much in its favour."[40]

Now, alongside the fragments of the canonical Daniel found at Qumran fragments have also been found of one or more Daniel cycles not represented in either the canonical or deuterocanonical documents. One of these fragments, the *Prayer of Nabonidus*, written in Aramaic, represents that king as telling how he was afflicted with a sore inflammation for seven years "in the city of Teman," and how, when he confessed his sins, he received help from one of the Jewish exiles in Babylon. This may well be a variant of the story of Nebuchadnezzar's madness in Daniel 4, but it is attached to another Babylonian king, Nabonidus (556-539 B.C.), and preserves a reminiscence of his historical residence at Teima in North Arabia.[41] Further fragments of a Daniel cycle, also in Aramaic, represent Daniel as rehearsing events of biblical history from the Deluge and the Tower of Babel down to Hasmonaean times, and going on from there to predict what is to happen in the end-time.[42]

These discoveries may not add to our knowledge of the history of the Old Testament canon, but further study of them may illumine a number of the literary problems of the book of Daniel.

V. INTERPRETATION

The interpretation of Old Testament scripture exhibited by the *pesharim* and related Qumran documents is based upon the following principles.[43]

(a) God revealed his purpose to his servants the prophets, but this revelation (especially with regard to the time of the fulfillment of his purpose) could not be properly understood until its meaning was made known by God to the Teacher of Righteousness, and through him to the Qumran community.[44]
(b) All that the prophets spoke refers to the time of the end.
(c) The time of the end is at hand.

These principles are put into operation by the use of the following devices:

(a) Biblical prophecies of varying date and reference are so interpreted as to apply uniformly to the commentator's own day and to the days immediately preceding and following—that is, to the period introduced by the ministry of the Teacher of Righteousness and the emergence of the eschatological community of the elect.
(b) The biblical text is atomized so as to bring out its relevance to the situation of the commentator's day; it is in this situation, and not in the natural sequence of the text, that logical coherence is to be looked for.
(c) Variant readings are selected in such a way as best to serve the commentator's purpose.

(d) Where a relation cannot otherwise be established between the
text and the situation to which *(ex hypothesi)* it must refer, allegorization is resorted to.

The most important of the Qumran *pesharim* is the commentary on
the first two chapters of Habakkuk found in Cave 1. As I have devoted
some attention to this document elsewhere,[45] it is appropriate to consider
here rather some of the shorter or more fragmentary samples of the same
genre.

In a commentary on Isaiah from Cave 4 (4Q p Isa[a]) the Assyrian
advance and downfall of Isaiah 10:22ff. are interpreted of the eschatological "war of the Kittim."[46] The leader of the Kittim (or so it appears,
for the document is sadly mutilated) goes up from the plain of Acco to
the boundary of Jerusalem. Then follows a quotation of Isaiah 11:1-4,
which is (very properly) interpreted of the "shoot of David," the Davidic
Messiah, who is to arise in the latter days to rule over all the Gentiles,
including "Magog," but takes his directions from the priests. This is in
line with the general messianic expectation cherished at Qumran, in
which the priesthood (and particularly the "Messiah of Aaron") is
envisaged as taking precedence over the Davidic Messiah, whose main
function is to lead his people to victory in battle.

A fragmentary commentary on Micah from Cave 1 provides a good
example of allegorical interpretation. Here the words, "What is the
transgression of Jacob? is it not Samaria?" (Mic. 1:5), are interpreted of
"the Prophet of Falsehood, who leads astray the simple," while the
following words, "and what are the high places of Judah? are they not
Jerusalem?," are interpreted of "the Teacher of Righteousness, who
teaches the law to his people and to all those who offer themselves to be
gathered in among God's elect, practicing the law in the council of the
community, who will be saved from the day of judgment." The Teacher
of Righteousness we know; the Prophet of Falsehood is evidently the
leader of a rival sect—the Pharisees, in my opinion. But the only way of
reading these two rival leaders out of Micah's reference to the transgression of Jacob and the high places of Judah is first of all to read them
in—by arbitrary allegorization.

Considerable portions have survived of a commentary on Psalm
37 from Cave 4. Here "those who wait upon the LORD," those who "shall
inherit the land" (v. 9), are "the congregation of his elect who do his
will"—i.e., the Qumran community. The "little while" after which "the
wicked shall not be" (v. 10) is the probationary period of forty years at
the end of the age, comparable to the probationary period of forty years
in the desert in Moses' day.[47] At the end of the eschatological period of

forty years "there will not be found in the earth any wicked man" (how the wicked are to be got rid of in just that period is explained in greater detail in the *Rule of War*). "The wicked," who "have drawn out the sword and have bent their bow, to cast down the poor and needy" (v. 14), are "the wicked ones of Ephraim and Manasseh who will seek to put forth a hand against the priest and the men of his counsel in the time of trial which is coming upon them."[48] The "priest" is certainly the Teacher of Righteousness.[49] But he and his followers will not be left to the mercy of their enemies; "God will redeem them from their hand, and afterwards they [the wicked] shall be given into the hand of the terrible ones of the Gentiles for judgment." The "terrible ones of the Gentiles" are no doubt the Kittim, who in 1Q p Hab are the executors of divine wrath against the persecutors of the Teacher of Righteousness. There is a further possible reference to the Teacher of Righteousness in the comment on verses 32f. ("The wicked watches the righteous, and seeks to slay him. The LORD will not leave him in his hand, nor condemn him when he is judged"); but the comment unfortunately is very defective: "Its interpretation concerns the Wicked [Pries]t who s[ent to the Teacher of Righteousness . . .] to slay him . . . and the law which he sent to him. But God will not le[ave him in his hand] nor [condemn him when] he is judged." But if the commentator did see a reference to the Teacher of Righteousness in this passage (which, on the analogy of Qumran interpretation of similar passages, is highly probable), the Wicked Priest's attempt to slay the Teacher seems to have been unsuccessful, for his deliverance is mentioned here as in the comment on verse 14.

It has, of course, become a major preoccupation of students of the Qumran literature to interpret the Qumran commentaries so as to elucidate their historical and personal references. The difficulty of doing so may be gauged by the greater variety of solutions proffered. One source of difficulty is that leading personalities are denoted by descriptive titles rather than by personal names. Many a religious minority will venerate a Teacher of Righteousness, complain of persecution at the hands of a Wicked Priest, and despise the easy-going majority of Seekers after Smooth Things, followers of a Prophet of Falsehood. Even the Gentile power which looms so largely in the literature is mentioned allusively as the Kittim, a term which in itself might denote either Greeks[50] or Romans.[51]

Occasionally we may think we have found a more definite clue. Thus the document 4Q *Testimonia* ends with these words:

> When Joshua had finished praising and giving thanks in his praises, he said: "Cursed be the man that buildeth this city: with his firstborn shall he

lay the foundation thereof, and with his youngest son shall he set up the gates of it." And behold, an accursed man, one of the sons of Belial, shall stand up, to be a very sna[re of the f]owler to his people, and destruction to all his neighbours. And he shall stand up[52] . . . [so that] they two may be instruments of violence. And they shall build again the . . . [and s]et up a wall and towers for it, to make a stronghold of wickedness . . . in Israel, and a horrible thing in Ephraim and Judah, . . . [and they shall w]ork pollution in the land, and great contempt among the sons of . . . [and shall shed b]lood like water on the rampart of the daughter of Zion, and in the boundary of Jerusalem.

This passage is said to be an extract from a work called the *Psalms of Joshua*, which is independently attested among the Cave 4 material. It does not belong strictly to the *pesher* category, but the passage quoted above certainly follows *pesher* principles in its interpretation of Joshua's curse on the rebuilder of Jericho (Joshua 6:26).

According to MT, Joshua said, "Cursed be the man before the LORD, that rises up and builds this city Jericho." It may be that the word Jericho was absent from the Qumran author's copy of Joshua (as it is from the Septuagint), but the context makes it clear that Joshua was referring to Jericho. It is not certain, however, that the Qumran author applied the curse to a rebuilding of Jericho; he may have had another incident in mind, such as one of the successive fortifications of Jerusalem; conceivably, but improbably, he may have intended the "city" in a metaphorical sense.[53]

If, however, we look for a man with two sons, all in positions of authority, who take a leading part in the rebuilding of a Judaean city, and cause great bloodshed in the precincts of Jerusalem, we have an embarrassing wealth of choices. F. M. Cross says that "the application of the passage to Simon and his older and younger sons Judas and Mattathias, and their deaths in Jericho seems to the writer almost inevitable. The slaughter in Jerusalem and its environs described in the last lines reflects the attack of Antiochus Sidetes upon Judaea in 134-132 B.C. immediately following Simon's death."[54] But the application is not so obvious to many other scholars. J. T. Milik[55] prefers to think of Mattathias (father of the Maccabees) and his two sons Jonathan and Simon, both of whom took part in the rebuilding of Jerusalem's fortifications (1 Macc. 10:10f.; 13:10; 14:37). (The reference to Jerusalem at the end of the passage does at least suggest that it, and not Jericho, is the city whose rebuilding the commentator has in mind.) If the idea that the pious Mattathias should be described as "one of the sons of Belial" makes one lift an eyebrow, let it be remembered that the Hasmonaean family as a whole enjoyed no good reputation at Qumran.

If we pass other members of the Hasmonaean family in review, we may think of Jonathan, whose two sons were unsuccessfully sent to Trypho as hostages for their father's release (1 Macc. 13:16ff.); of John Hyrcanus and his two sons Aristobulus I and Alexander Jannaeus; of Jannaeus and his two sons Hyrcanus II and Aristobulus II; or even of Aristobulus II and his two sons Alexander and Antigonus. If we cast our net wider, we may think of Antipater and his two sons Phasael and Herod; or of Herod and his two sons by Mariamne, Aristobulus and Alexander; or even of Vespasian and his two sons Titus and Domitian.[56] The later identifications in this list can probably be excluded on palaeographical grounds. For 4Q *Testimonia* is said to be the work of the same scribe as wrote out 1QS (the copy of the *Rule of the Community* found in Cave 1), which the palaeographers date in the earlier part of the first century B.C. If this date is upheld, it might be felt to rule out even the otherwise attractive identification of the parties concerned with Jannaeus and his two sons; but the palaeographical evidence must be carefully scrutinized before we dismiss an interpretation which would recognize the civil strife between Hyrcanus II and Aristobulus II, with the consequent intervention of the Romans, as the occasion of the bloodshed around Jerusalem. But at least this may serve as an example of the difficulty of correlating the biblical exegesis of Qumran with events in the relevant period of Jewish history.[57]

There is, however, one fragmentary *pesher* which actually refers to historical characters by name. This is the commentary on Nahum from Cave 4, which explains the prophet's description of Nineveh as a den "where the lion and the lioness walked, the lion's whelp, and none made them afraid" (2:11) as a reference to "[Deme]trius, king of Javan, who sought to enter Jerusalem by the counsel of the Seekers after Smooth Things." The personal name is unfortunately mutilated, but it can scarcely be anything but Demetrius. We have a choice between three Seleucid kings of that name—Demetrius I (162-150 B.C.), who sent Nicanor to seize Jerusalem at the instigation of the high priest Alcimus and his supporters; Demetrius II (145-139/8 B.C.), who sent a force against Jonathan; Demetrius III (95-88 B.C.), who invaded Judaea at the invitation of Jannaeus's hostile Jewish subjects. The Seekers after Smooth Things, who are mentioned in other places in Qumran literature, are best identified with the Pharisees, who led the opposition to Jannaeus throughout most of his reign.

The comment on Nahum 2:11 continues: "[Never has that city been given] into the hand of the kings of Javan from Antiochus to the rise of the rulers of the Kittim, but ultimately it will be trodden down [by the Kittim]." This Antiochus may well be Sidetes, whose demolition of the walls of Jerusalem early in the reign of John Hyrcanus (135-104 B.C.) was the last effective action by a Gentile ruler against the city until Pompey entered it in 63 B.C. In that case the Demetrius mentioned in the previous sentence of the commentary will surely be Demetrius III. It may also be pointed out that the reference in this context to "the rulers of the Kittim" makes the identification of the Kittim with the Romans practically certain.

Nahum 2:12 goes on: "The lion tore in pieces enough for his whelps, and strangled for his lionesses, and filled his caves with prey, and his dens with the kill"; in these words the commentator sees a reference to "the young lion of wrath, who smote with his mighty ones and the men of his counsel" and "took vengeance on the Seekers after Smooth Things, in that he proceeded to hang them up alive, [which was never done] in Israel before, for concerning one hung up alive on a tree the Scripture says. . . ." What the Scripture says is that such a person is "accursed of God" (Deut. 21:23); but our scribe evidently could not bring himself to pen such ill-omened words.[58]

In any case, the Scripture envisages the hanging of a dead body on a tree; the Qumran commentator on Nahum has something more dreadful in mind—hanging men up alive, in other words, crucifying them. That "such a thing was never done in Israel before" means that it had never been done by an Israelite.[59] We know that Jewish confessors were crucified by Antiochus Epiphanes, but the first Jewish ruler to punish his enemies in this way, so far as we know, was Jannaeus. The Seekers after Smooth Things were not approved of by the Qumran community, but to crucify them was a blasphemous atrocity. (It may be remarked in passing that there is no implication that the Teacher of Righteousness or his followers were among those crucified by the "young lion of wrath.")

The Nahum commentary, then, provides us with more certain criteria for relating Qumran exegesis to history than we find in the other commentaries published to date.[60] And these criteria may, with due caution, be used to throw light on ambiguous references in other Qumran texts. The Qumran commentaries plainly do not give us much help in understanding the Old Testament. But the serious student of Scripture can never fail to be interested in what was thought of its meaning by serious students of earlier days; and in this regard the Qumran commentaries on the Old Testament have opened a new world for our exploration.

4. *The Dead Sea Scrolls and Early Christianity*

I. INTRODUCTION

When the discovery of the Dead Sea Scrolls—more precisely, those from Qumran—was first announced, it appeared that their relevance for biblical studies lay chiefly in the Old Testament field. And naturally so: here were manuscripts of books of the Hebrew Bible a thousand years older than any previously known to be extant. Their value for the textual study of the Old Testament indeed remains very great; thanks to them we can now see, as we could not before 1947, at least three main types of Hebrew biblical text current at the turn of the pre-Christian and Christian eras.[1]

But, as time went on and more manuscripts were discovered and deciphered, it became clear that their relevance for *New* Testament studies and for the history of Christian origins held even more surprising implications, though in a less direct form. And in the course of the years New Testament students throughout the world have evinced as great interest in the Scrolls as have Old Testament students—even greater interest, if my impression is correct.

When, however, we ask students of the Qumran texts what affinities exist between these texts and the New Testament we are given the most varied answers. We are told that there are no affinities whatsoever;

A lecture delivered in the John Rylands Library, Manchester, on Thursday, 10 March 1966, during the Exhibition of Dead Sea Scrolls, and published in *BJRL* 49 (1966-67), pp. 69-90.

we are told on the other hand that the story of Jesus represents an "astonishing reincarnation"[2] of the activity, death and vindication of the Teacher of Righteousness. We are told that Jesus was the Teacher of Righteousness in person;[3] we are told on the other hand that the Qumran discoveries prove conclusively that Jesus never existed at all.

All these answers cannot be true. But people who are interested in the subject need not stand in bewilderment before them, wondering which (if any) they are to believe. Much of the material on which these divergent accounts are based is accessible to them in translation—pre-eminently, in the Pelican Book by Geza Vermes, entitled *The Dead Sea Scrolls in English* (1962)[4]—and if they compare this material with the New Testament, they can form their own conclusions, tentative though these may be. While by no means all the Qumran literature has been published as yet, either in text or in translation,[5] we may be sure that what is yet to be published will not essentially change the picture given by what has been published already, though it will amplify it and fill in details.

In comparing the Qumran texts with the New Testament, we shall bear in mind that these two bodies of literature are in some respects not on the same footing. In dealing with the New Testament, and especially with the Gospels, we are in the fortunate position of dealing with documents which during the past two centuries, to go no farther back, have been subjected to closer scrutiny and analysis than any other ancient texts. With the Qumran texts, on the other hand, we are dealing with documents which were discovered only the other day (compara-tively speaking); and for all the volume of literature which their study has already brought forth, it will require many further years of study before anything like an agreed account of their origin and significance can be expected.

Here is one important example of this disparity between the two bodies of literature. The period of Jesus' life can be dated fairly precisely, for we know—from extrabiblical as well as from biblical sources—that he was executed while Pontius Pilate was Roman governor of Judaea: that is to say, between A.D. 26 and the end of 36 or beginning of 37. Within that interval of ten or eleven years there is evidence enabling us to fix the date more precisely still, but we need not look at that; if it were possible to date the death of the Teacher of Righteousness, the effective founder[6] of the Qumran community, within a dozen years, we should count ourselves fortunate indeed. As it is, the Teacher has been identified with the high priest Onias III, who was assassinated in 171 B.C.,[7] and with the Zealot leader Menahem, son of Judas the Galilaean, who was killed in September, A.D. 66,[8] as well as with a number of other individuals who flourished at various times between these two terminal points. These widely divergent identifications have been propounded by scholars of the highest eminence—that with Onias III, for example, by H. H. Rowley,[9] and that with Menahem by G. R. Driver.[10]

Although only a minority of scholars who have worked on the Scrolls accept Professor Driver's dating, any view which has commended itself to his mind is worthy of respectful attention. If he is right, then the main events in the history of the Qumran community are later than the events of the ministry of Jesus and the greater part of the apostolic age; even so, in Professor Driver's opinion, "the Scrolls . . . are . . . more or less contemporary with the New Testament. Consequently they are documents of prime importance for the understanding of the New Testament and present a challenge which Christian scholars will neglect at their peril."[11]

It is clear that, to some extent at least, these chronological problems of Qumran history and literature must affect the relevance of the Scrolls to New Testament studies. My own preference, if I may state it briefly, would be not to attempt to identify the Teacher of Righteousness with any known figure in Jewish history, but to date his rise to a position of supreme influence over the Qumran community during the high-priesthood of Jonathan, brother of Judas Maccabaeus (152-143 B.C.). Jonathan might in that case qualify for identification with the Wicked Priest, the Teacher's bitter enemy and persecutor;[12] in any case, it is probably more than a coincidence that it is during Jonathan's period of power that the Essenes first make their appearance in history.[13] Professor Driver thinks of the men of Qumran as Zealots rather than Essenes. The line of demarcation between Essenes and Zealots was probably not so sharply drawn as is frequently thought;[14] but to me the men of Qumran seem to have more in common with the Essenes described to us by Philo, Pliny, Josephus and Hippolytus than they have with the Zealots.

II. THE TWO COMMUNITIES

The men of Qumran went out to their wilderness retreat, northwest of the Dead Sea, in order to organize themselves there as a new Israel, rather after the fashion of the tribes under the leadership of Moses in another wilderness. The nation as a whole had broken the covenant with the God of the fathers, but these men regarded themselves as the heirs of the new covenant, the righteous remnant, the hope of the future, a miniature Israel, whose faithfulness would be accepted by God as an atonement for the unfaithfulness of the nation at large. Their movement was pre-

dominantly under priestly control in its earliest days at least; they
maintained the sole right of the house of Zadok to exercise the high-
priesthood at Jerusalem, and one of their designations was "the sons of
Zadok." They abstained from participation in the sacrificial services of
the Jerusalem temple while it was controlled by an illegitimate priesthood, but they preserved in their community the priestly and levitical
orders so that, when the new age dawned, a pure sacrificial worship
might be restored without delay in a reconsecrated temple, administered
by men who had not gone astray as the majority of the priests had done.
The Teacher of Righteousness was himself a priest[15]—whether of the
house of Zadok or not is uncertain—and the nucleus of the community
consisted of twelve laymen and three priests.[16] Later, each of the groups
of ten men into which the community was divided for various purposes
must include one priest.[17]

The believing community of New Testament times similarly regarded itself as a new Israel, "a remnant chosen by grace" (Rom. 11:5),
"a chosen race, a royal priesthood, a holy nation, God's own people"
(1 Pet. 2:9). The kingdom of God had been taken away from those who
had shown themselves unworthy of their trust, and given to "a nation
producing the fruits of it" (Matt. 11:44). They were the "little flock" to
whom their Father had been well pleased to give the kingdom (Luke
12:32). In the early days of their fellowship they tried to practice community of goods[18] (which the men of Qumran did as a matter of course),
but in a much less systematic fashion than obtained at Qumran. They,
too, held themselves to be the people of the new covenant, although they
understood the new covenant differently from the men of Qumran; for
the New Testament community the new covenant was a new relationship with God which had been sealed in messianic blood. Instead of
maintaining distinct priestly and levitical classes, as the men of Qumran
did, the Christian community was taught to consider itself corporately
as "a holy priesthood, to offer spiritual sacrifices acceptable to God
through Jesus Christ" (1 Pet. 2:5).

The Qumran community, moreover, lived in the conviction that the
end of the current age, the "epoch of wickedness," was at hand. Its
thought and life were dominated by this eschatological conviction. Its
members believed that in the very near future all that the Old Testament
prophets had foretold would come to pass; indeed, they believed that
those predictions had already begun to be fulfilled in the emergence of
their community and the activity of the Teacher of Righteousness. Similarly, the early Christians looked on themselves as those on whom "the
ends of the ages" had come (1 Cor. 10:11); for them, in fact, the new age
had already dawned, although the old age had not completely passed

away; they were living in the overlapping period of the two ages, the "last hour" (1 John 2:18), between the passion of Jesus and his manifestation in glory.

III. FULFILLMENT OF PROPHECY

In both communities this eschatological emphasis appears very clearly in their interpretation of the Old Testament. The commentaries discovered among the Qumran manuscripts show us well enough how the Old Testament was interpreted by the followers of the Teacher of Righteousness; the New Testament writings indicate plainly how it was interpreted in the primitive Church.

The Qumran community, like the early Christians, but unlike the traditional rabbinical schools, interpreted the prophetic oracles of the Old Testament in their own right and not simply as supplements to the Law. According to the Qumran commentaries, God revealed his secret purpose to his servants the prophets, but that revelation (especially with regard to the *time* when his purpose would be fulfilled) could not be understood until the key to its understanding was placed in the hands of the Teacher of Righteousness. To him the mysteries were made plain by divine illumination, and he made known to the last generations what God was going to do in the last generation of all.[19] He taught his followers that all that the prophets had spoken referred to the time of the end, the time which had now set in; and he so interpreted all that the prophets had spoken as to teach his followers their duty in this critical situation.[20]

The parallel with the New Testament is striking. Mark sums up Jesus' early Galilaean preaching in the words: "The appointed time is fully come and the kingdom of God has drawn near; repent and believe in the good news" (Mark 1:15). The age of fulfilment has dawned. The prophets who foresaw the gospel blessing, we are told, "searched and inquired about this salvation; they inquired what person or time was indicated by the Spirit of Christ [i.e., the Spirit of messianic prophecy] within them when predicting the sufferings of Christ and the subsequent glories" (1 Pet. 1:10f.). Much had been revealed to those prophets, but not everything. But first-century Christians had no need to search and inquire in order to ascertain what person or time was indicated by the prophecies; they knew. The person was Jesus; the time was now. Their whole attitude to the Old Testament and its fulfillment is summed up in Peter's words in Jerusalem on the first Christian Pentecost: "This is that which was spoken by the prophet" (Acts 2:16).

If it was the Teacher of Righteousness who taught the Qumran

commentators and other members of the community their biblical exegesis, we need not search and inquire long to discover who taught the
apostles theirs. This note of fulfillment runs throughout Jesus' public
proclamation: "Today this scripture has been fulfilled in your hearing"
(Luke 4:21). "Blessed are the eyes which see what you see! For I tell you
that many prophets and kings desired to see what you see, and did not
see it, and to hear what you hear, and did not hear it" (Luke 10:23f.). The
Old Testament exegesis which pervades the apostles' preaching is based
on that which they learned from Jesus on every occasion when he
"opened their minds to understand the scriptures" (Luke 24:45).[21]

Here is one of the most important points of resemblance between
the Teacher of Righteousness and Jesus, in that each imparted to the
community which he founded its distinctive features of biblical interpretation. The resemblance does not amount to identity: there is an
important contrast. To the early Christians Jesus was the central theme
of the Old Testament revelation, which indeed reached its fulfilment in
him as the Messiah. With his triumph over death and exaltation by God,
the days of the Messiah had dawned; he was now exercising his kingly
power, not on earth but at God's right hand. To the men of Qumran the
Teacher of Righteousness, while he was certainly a subject of Old Testament prophecy, was not its central subject; Old Testament prophecy
reached out beyond him for its fulfilment. After his death, his followers
continued to look forward to the advent of the messianic age. In what
circumstances the Teacher died—was "gathered in," to use his followers' language of him[22]—we are not clearly informed. It is conceivable, but not probable, that some of his followers expected him to rise
from the dead in advance of the general resurrection of the just,[23] and
believed that in resurrection he would function as the priestly Messiah
of the new age.[24] Even if they did, it is nowhere suggested in the Qumran
literature that he did so rise, or that anyone thought he had done so.

IV. MESSIANIC EXPECTATION

The form which messianic expectation took in the Qumran community
is known to us from a number of documents,[25] and it is reasonable to
suppose that the community learned its messianic doctrine, as it learned
so much else, from the Teacher of Righteousness. Messianic expectation
at Qumran was directed towards two distinct personages who would
appear at the end-time and inaugurate the new age: a great priest and a
great military leader.[26] The great priest, the "Messiah of Aaron" (or
"priestly Messiah"), would be head of state in the new age. The military

leader, the "Messiah of Israel" (or "lay Messiah"), was the promised prince of the house of David, probably identical with the mighty man who would lead the people of God, the "sons of light," to victory over the hostile "sons of darkness" in the eschatological warfare which the prophets had foretold. In the new age he would rank beneath the Messiah of Aaron,[27] just as the Davidic prince in Ezekiel's blueprint of the new commonwealth of Israel would be subordinate to the priest-hood. (Where the title "the Messiah" appears without qualification in the Qumran texts, it is the Messiah of David's line that is meant.) With these two Messiahs is associated a third eschatological personage, who does not, however, receive the messianic title; this is the prophet like Moses, promised in Deuteronomy 18:15ff.[28]

While the Qumran community, to judge by the literature thus far published, never seems to have reached the point at which it believed the Messiah (or Messiahs) to have appeared, the New Testament is dominated by the announcement that the Messiah has come. And while the Qumran community distinguished the prophet, the prince and the priest of the end-time as three separate individuals, the New Testament presents Jesus as combining the three roles: he was "anointed"[29] in his baptism as the prophet of whom Moses spoke,[30] as the heir to David's throne,[31] and as the perpetual priest of Melchizedek's order acclaimed in Psalm 110:4.[32] The traditional doctrine of the threefold office *(triplex munus)* of Christ goes back to primitive times. His prophetic office speaks for itself, but his kingship was manifested in quite another way than that of military conquest,[33] while his priesthood could have nothing to do with the line of Aaron, since he belonged to the tribe of Judah, not Levi: the one New Testament document which enlarges on the priestly aspect of his messianic ministry finds in Psalm 110:4 authority for ascribing to him a greater priesthood than Aaron's.[34]

But the prophetic portrayals of the prophet, the priest, and the Davidic prince do not exhaust the New Testament presentation of Jesus' Messiahship. He himself did not often voice a messianic claim; had he done so, it would certainly have been misunderstood. On one notable occasion, however, when he did make such a claim he identified himself not only with the Messiah who is called in Psalm 110:1 to take his seat at God's right hand but with the "one like a son of man" who in Daniel 7:13f. is brought to God on the clouds of heaven to receive everlasting dominion (Mark 14:62).[35] Jesus' commonest self-designation, indeed, was "the Son of man"; but in his mind the figure of the Son of man is fused with that of the obedient Servant of Yahweh in Isaiah 42–53, and it is this conception of the Servant-Messiah that controls Jesus' accep-tance and fulfillment of his mission.[36]

The Qumran community, for its part, appears to have attached importance to the Old Testament figures of the Servant of Yahweh and the Son of man, without using these explicit terms, but it does not seem to have interpreted them messianically. Instead, the community itself felt called upon corporately to fulfill what was written concerning the Servant of Yahweh and the Son of man. As the Teacher and his followers devoted themselves to the study and practice of the holy law, as they endured persecution at the hands of the Wicked Priest and other ungodly oppressors, they believed that they were accumulating a store of merit which would avail not only to procure their own justification before God but also to make propitiation for the polluted land of Israel,[37] just as the Servant by his suffering was to bear the sin of many and cause them to be accepted as righteous (Isa. 53:11f.). But the men of Qumran also believed that when the epoch of wickedness came to an end, it would be their duty and privilege to be God's instruments in the execution of judgment on the ungodly,[38] in fulfillment of what was said in Daniel 7:22 about the "saints of the Most High" who are the counterpart of the visionary figure "like a son of man."

This corporate interpretation of the Servant and the Son of man is not absent from the New Testament. The apostles share in the mission of the Servant, carrying God's salvation "to the ends of the earth" (Acts 13:47), and the Corinthian Christians have to be reminded that "the saints will judge the world" (1 Cor. 6:2); but this twofold activity is viewed as a participation in work which belongs primarily to Jesus, and only then to his people as associated with him. (Where, on the other hand, the language of the Servant is used in the Qumran *Hymns of Thanksgiving* in the first person singular, we may recognize the community expressing itself through an individual spokesman, most probably the Teacher of Righteousness himself.)

The Qumran community, in addition to its prophetic exegesis, had its own interpretation of the Law, and a rigorous interpretation it was, one which "exceeded the righteousness of the scribes and Pharisees." Readers of the New Testament are prone to think of the Pharisees as being inordinately strict in their application of the Law, but in Qumran eyes the Pharisees were looked upon as compromisers, "seekers after smooth things" or (as the phrase should perhaps be rendered) "givers of smooth interpretations."[39] The Qumran marriage law was stricter than that of the Pharisees;[40] so was the Qumran sabbath law. When Jesus said that anyone whose ox or ass had fallen into a pit on the sabbath would certainly rescue it, for all the sacredness of the day, he plainly knew that the Pharisees would agree with him.[41] But precisely such a humane action to an animal in distress is forbidden in the sabbath regulations of Qumran.[42]

Again, the men of Qumran out-Phariseed the Pharisees in their separatism, even if the Pharisees received their name as being "separatists" *par excellence*. The men of Qumran were volunteers for holiness, but they understood holiness in a different way from Jesus. They tried to preserve their holiness by keeping themselves to themselves as far as possible, whereas Jesus deliberately sought the company of people who were no better than they should be, because, as he pointed out, it was sick people, not healthy people, who needed the doctor's care.[43] For this Jesus was criticized by the Pharisees of his day, but the Pharisees themselves were criticized by the Qumran community for not being half thoroughgoing enough in their separation from defiling associations.[44]

VI. QUMRAN AND THE NEW TESTAMENT

Let me now go through the New Testament quickly, mentioning certain documents or groups of documents in which affinities with Qumran literature have been noted, but not staying to assess the cogency of all these suggested affinities.[45]

1. The Synoptic Gospels

Resemblances between the Qumran community and the milieu in which the Gospel of Matthew took shape have been traced by Krister Stendahl in *The School of St. Matthew* (Uppsala, 1954). W. D. Davies, in *The Setting of the Sermon on the Mount*, has suggested that some of the polemic in the Sermon may have been directed originally against Essene sectarians, although its final formulation was determined by the encounter, later in the first century, between Palestinian Christians and Pharisees.[46] It may well be that some of the special material in Luke's Gospel, especially his nativity narratives, came from circles which shared in certain respects the outlook of Qumran. The humble and pious society into which both John the Baptist and Jesus were born, according to these narratives, could have included "associate members" of Qumran or a similar community, "men who are the objects of God's good pleasure," to use a Lukan term (Luke 2:14) not unfamiliar at Qumran.[47]

2. John and 1 John

It is with the Gospel of John, however, that the most striking and abundant affinities of thought and language have been detected, to the point where a common reservoir of terminology has been spoken of.[48] It would be wise to remember that practically every new discovery in the field of Near Eastern religion of the closing years B.C. and early years A.D. has been hailed in its time as the solution to "the problem of the Fourth Gospel." Even so, the affinities with Qumran certainly provide additional evidence for the Hebraic foundation of the Fourth Gospel. Some of the affinities are adequately accounted for by the fact that the Old Testament is the fundamental sourcebook both of the Fourth Gospel and of the Qumran texts—in the former case, the Old Testament as interpreted and fulfilled by Jesus; in the latter, the Old Testament as it had passed through the mind of the Teacher of Righteousness and his disciples. The antithesis between light and darkness, to take one example of the dualistic phraseology common to Qumran literature and the Fourth Gospel, goes back ultimately to the opening verses of Genesis, where God at creation separates the light from the darkness; yet the way in which light and darkness, truth and falsehood, good and evil are set in opposition in the *Rule of the Community* is especially reminiscent of the language of the Johannine Gospels and Epistles.[49]

How can this be explained? The early chapters of the Gospel of John deal with a phase of Jesus' ministry in Judaea, Samaria and the Jordan valley which was concurrent with the closing months of John the Baptist's ministry. The dispute about purification mentioned in John 3:25, which led John's disciples to question Jesus' activity, is the kind of dispute which must have been very common at a time when so many competing "baptist" groups were active in those parts. The disciples of John and the disciples of Jesus were not the only people engaged in baptizing there at that time. The men of Qumran had their distinctive ceremonial washings, and so had other communities.[50]

The unnamed disciple of the Baptist who, according to John 1:35-40, began to follow Jesus along with his companion Andrew, may well be identical with the beloved disciple on whose testimony the Fourth Gospel is based (John 21:24). If the beloved disciple was indeed at one time a follower of John the Baptist, then some fascinating possibilities are presented. For, among all the theories which have been propounded to establish a connection between Qumran and primitive Christianity, the least improbable are those which find such a connection in John the Baptist.[51] That John was brought up by the men of Qumran or a similar community is not a necessary inference from the statement in Luke 1:80 that "he was in the wilderness till the day of his manifestation to Israel"; but it is a guess which does not conflict with that statement. But if there is any substance in the guess, then we must conclude that, when the word of God came to John in the wilderness and sent him forth to preach his baptism of repentance in view of the approach of the Coming One, he must have realized that the way of Qumran, noble as its ideals were, was not the way in which preparation should be made for the divine visitation.[52]

With regard to the First Epistle of John, which bears such a close relation to the Gospel, mention should be made of Wolfgang Nauck's study, *Die Tradition und der Charakter des ersten Johannesbriefes* (Tübingen, 1957). Here a primitive order of Christian initiation is discerned which presents similarities to the procedure for admission to the covenant-community at Qumran.

3. Acts

The community of goods in the Qumran community and the early Church (Acts 2:44f.; 4:32-35) has been mentioned already; we may note in passing the difference between the penalty imposed on the member of the community who "lied deliberately in matters of property"[53] (one year's excommunication and deprivation of one-fourth of his food-ration) and the sad fate of Ananias and Sapphira in Acts 5:1-11 when they committed the same offense. More important, probably, in the narrative of Acts is the statement that, at an early stage in the life of the church, "a great many of the priests were obedient to the faith" (Acts 6:7). Nothing more is said expressly about these priests, but it may be significant that they are mentioned immediately before the account of the activity of Stephen and the inauguration of the Gentile mission. It has been suggested that they had Essene affinities, that they would have been among the first targets of attack in the persecution which followed the death of Stephen, and so migrated to the regions north of Judaea, to Samaria and then Damascus and other parts of Syria.[54] That they or their successors were the people to whom the Epistle to the Hebrews was addressed has been held by more than one scholar, although this is pure speculation.[55]

4. Paul

However, we have just referred to Damascus. Damascus, as we know, plays a part in the Qumran literature. If the "Damascus" of the Zadokite document is the literal Damascus,[56] then at an early stage of the Qumran community's existence the community, or part of it, migrated to Damascus. As we also know, Damascus plays a part in the New Testament; it was in its vicinity that Paul became a Christian, and the first Christians with whom he was associated in community fellowship were those of Damascus.[57] Is there any link between the part that Damascus plays in Qumran literature and the part that it plays in the New Testament? Here is one possible link: the designation "the way," which Luke uses six times in Acts for the Christian religion, is used twice in his accounts of Paul's conversion (Acts 9:2; 22:4), in contexts which make it likely that it belongs to the source on which he draws. Outside Acts, some of the most striking instances of "the way" used as a term for true religion come in the Zadokite document and other Qumran literature.[58]

More impressive than this possible link between Qumran and Paul is the twofold sense given in his writings and in Qumran literature to the term "righteousness"—in the sense both of God's personal righteousness and of that righteous status which he imparts to believers.[59]

In the Pauline corpus it is the Epistles to the Colossians and Ephesians that display closest resemblances to the terminology of Qumran.[60] A possible explanation of this is that in these two epistles Paul employs for purposes of Christian teaching terminology which was current in the "Colossian heresy"—employing it, it has been said, in a "disinfected" sense.[61] Over a hundred years ago Bishop Lightfoot of Durham, in his great commentary on Colossians, traced the distinctive features of the "Colossian heresy" back to Essene influence.[62] Perhaps he used the term "Essene" in rather a wide sense, but if we take "Essene influence" to mean the influence of Jewish nonconformity he was assuredly right; and his argument chimes in remarkably well with the affinities which K. G. Kuhn and others have recognized between the phraseology of Qumran and that of Colossians and its sister-epistle to the Ephesians.[63]

One feature of these two epistles which is not paralleled at Qumran is their presentation of the church as the body of which Christ is the head. At Qumran we have no lack of parallels to the picture of the church as the household of God or the temple of God—the whole Qumran community is a temple for God, and its inner nucleus is the holy of holies— but the conception of the church as the body of Christ, a particular application of the Hebrew idea of corporate personality, is probably original to Paul.

5. The Letter to the Hebrews

A variety of attempts has been made to establish some affinity between the Qumran sect and the Epistle to the Hebrews.[64] According to F. M. Braun, "of all the New Testament writings, the Epistle to the Hebrews is the one which gives the fullest answer to the basic tendencies of the sect."[65] Yigael Yadin has argued that it was addressed to Jews originally belonging to the Qumran community, who were converted to Christianity but carried with them some of their former beliefs and practices, with which the unknown author takes issue.[66] Hans Kosmala prefers to regard the people addressed as Jews holding views very similar to those of the Qumran sect and other Essenes, who had come a considerable part of the way towards Christianity, but not yet far enough.[67] C. Spicq regards them as the converted priests of Acts 6:7, who in his eyes were "Esseno-Christians" and included former members of the Qumran community.[68] J. W. Bowman thinks of the recipients as a community of Hellenistic-Jewish Christians at Sychar who had come under the influence of Qumran.[69] My own view is that all the evidence adduced in support of these views can be satisfied if we suppose that Hebrews was intended for a house-church of Jewish Christians at Rome. In the Roman Church there survived into the third century (as we know from the *Apostolic Tradition* ascribed to Hippolytus) elements derived from Jewish nonconformity.[70] If the new evidence suggests that this nonconformity was akin to the way of Qumran, then we have confirmation of an impression formed independently by comparing certain allusions in the epistle (e.g., the "instruction about ablutions" of Hebrews 6:2, which probably is not a reference to the once-for-all Christian baptism) with indications that the Jewish substratum of Roman Christianity had affinities with some of the "baptist" movements of Palestine.[71]

6. The General Epistles

In the Epistle of James[72] there is an enigmatic passage which some have attempted to relate to Qumran doctrine: "Do you suppose it is in vain that the scripture says, 'He yearns earnestly over the spirit which he has made to dwell in us'?" (James 4:5; the quotation from "scripture" might also be rendered: "the spirit which he has made to dwell in us yearns earnestly").

These words come from no known scripture. It is pointed out that the concept of "spirit" which they express—the concept of a good spirit, given to man by God at creation—corresponds to the Qumran concept of the "predestined 'spirit of truth' which takes the pious man to itself at the time of creation, of '*his,* the pious man's, spirit' which stands in battle with the 'spirit of perversion' ";[73] but we are still left without an answer to the question about the scripture from which James quotes, for he is not quoting from the *Rule of the Community.*

The quotation from 1 Enoch and the allusion to the *Assumption of Moses* in the Epistle of Jude[74] remind us that the former pseudepigraph was included in the Qumran library, while the latter displays features of outlook in common with that of Qumran.

7. The Apocalypse

Among a number of affinities between the book of the Revelation and the Qumran literature may be mentioned the vision of the New Jerusalem (Rev. 21:2, 10ff.), which is paralleled in a New Jerusalem apocalypse represented by fragments from several Qumran caves[75] (both the Johannine and Qumran visions of the New Jerusalem draw on Ezekiel 40–48), and the battle of Armageddon (Rev. 16:16), comparable to the eschatological conflict of the Qumran *Rule of War*. In general, however, where the New Testament Apocalypse uses traditional military phraseology to denote the Messiah's triumph, it does so with sovereign liberty: it is not by taking the lives of others, but by giving his own life, that the Messiah wins his victory; the conquering Lion of the tribe of Judah comes on to the stage as the slaughtered Lamb (Rev. 5:5f.). But one point of contact I find of special interest. The picture in Revelation 12:1ff. of the woman who gives birth to a man-child—in other words, Israel (or at least the true Israel) giving birth to the Messiah—has a remarkable parallel in one of the Qumran *Hymns of Thanksgiving,* where a spokesman of the community adopts the language of a woman in the pains of childbirth who bears a man-child as a "wonder of a counsellor," one of the four designations given in Isaiah 9:6 to the expected prince of the house of David.[76]

VII. AFTER A.D. 70

There is some reason to believe that, when the Qumran community was scattered towards A.D. 70 (as archaeological evidence indicates), some of its members, together perhaps with members of other Essene groups, made common cause with another body of refugees—members of the fugitive church of Jerusalem who left the doomed metropolis and settled east of the Jordan. A number of the distinctive features of the Ebionites, as they are described by Christian writers of later generations, could be accounted for in terms of influence exercised by such a body as the Qumran community on such a body as the second generation church of Jerusalem.[77] The presence of Essene elements in Ebionitism has long been recognized—by J. B. Lightfoot and F. J. A. Hort,[78] for example. If, indeed, some of these elements came from the Qumran community, we may conclude that those Qumran refugees who joined the Jewish Christians came to acknowledge that their messianic hopes were fulfilled, not along the lines laid down by their former instructors but in Jesus of Nazareth, envisaged more particularly in terms of the prophet foretold in Deuteronomy 18:15ff. Other survivors of the community have been linked, very speculatively, with the gnostic community of the Mandaeans, who survive in Lower Iraq to the present day.[79]

VIII. CONCLUSION

The Teacher of Righteousness and the Prophet of Nazareth taught their respective followers a way of life. The two ways of life did not completely coincide, and one might consider what were the factors which enabled the one to survive the catastrophe of A.D. 70 while the other disappeared then, to be rediscovered as a historical antiquity in our own day. We shall understand both better if we give due weight to the resemblances and differences between them.

The resemblances are due not only to the general fact that both movements drew upon the spiritual heritage of Israel's faith, enshrined in the Old Testament writings; they are due more particularly to the fact that both originated in a nonconformist environment within the Jewish nation. In *The Scrolls and Christian Origins* (1961)—one of the best books on this subject—Matthew Black traces the Essene and Qumran movements back to an ancient ascetic strain or wilderness tradition in Israel, represented in earlier days by the Kenites, Nazirites and Rechabites. This strain, he believes, continued to flourish in the postexilic period as a nonconformist tradition in two main groups—a northern and a southern. From the southern group came the men of Qumran; it was against the background of the northern group that, a century and more later, Jesus began to proclaim in Galilee the gospel of the kingdom of God (although the evidence of the Fourth Gospel[80] is that he had earlier and later associations with the southern group as well).

At one point after another throughout the New Testament some interaction between Qumran and early Christianity is indicated. It is of the essence of the gospel story that it is not something insulated from the contemporary world but part and parcel of the on-going course of first-century thought and action. The Christian account of this matter would, I think, be that when God does a new thing in the earth, as he did preeminently in the Incarnation, the event cannot be exhaustively accounted for in terms of what went before (although what went before constitutes a providential preparation for the event); but when once the event has taken place, it is fed into the stream of history as a real dateable occurrence, playing its part in the historical pattern of cause and effect, or challenge and response.

Even in their most sober and restrained presentation, the discoveries at Qumran, with the light they shed on biblical studies, are exciting enough. They do not constitute, as the publisher's blurb on one American book puts it, "the greatest challenge to Christian dogma since Darwin's theory of evolution"[81]—that is as rare a gem of wishful thinking as I have come across in this connection! But they do provide us with new and most welcome background and context for the more intelligent study of the New Testament and Christian origins. When any object is viewed against a new background, the object itself takes on a fresh appearance, and against the background supplied by the Qumran discoveries many parts of the New Testament take on a new and vivid significance. Above all, those passages which express the remnant consciousness and eschatological outlook of early Christianity take on a new significance, by comparison and contrast alike, when they are viewed in the light of this contemporary movement which was also characterized by a remnant consciousness and an eschatological outlook.

We should be restrained from premature dogmatism when we consider how incomplete our knowledge of the Qumran community still is. Even when all the documents that have been discovered are published the reflection that they may represent but a fragment of what the library originally contained will continue to impose counsels of caution.

Truth is one and indivisible; and the more truth we receive, the more light is shed on the truth we already know, and the better able we are to appreciate the old and the new together. It was a Christian apostle who said, "We cannot do anything against the truth, but only for the truth."[82] The men of Qumran would gladly have endorsed his words; we, too, may take their lesson to heart.

5. *Preparation in the Wilderness: Personal Religion at Qumran*

I. VOLUNTEERS FOR HOLINESS

It is easier to say something about the religious attitudes of the Qumran community as such than about the personal religion of its individual members. Most of the documents which throw light upon the subject are community documents, and what we learn from them has naturally to do mainly with the beliefs, aspirations, and practices of the community. Yet it is impossible to think that the beliefs and aspirations of the members were simply submerged in those of the community. No one became a member accidentally or automatically; each member had entered the fellowship in the first instance by his own decision, and that decision had to be reinforced by a prolonged novitiate and a rigorous examination. We should expect that only men of unusual strength of character would survive these tests and attain full membership.

The men of Qumran were "volunteers for holiness." (The more precise rendering of the passage in which these words occur [1QS 5.6] may describe them as "volunteering to be a sanctuary in Aaron and a house of truth in Israel," but this in any case implies their dedication to a life of holiness.) The holiness to which they devoted themselves involved the meticulous keeping of the law of God according to a *halakhah* which exceeded in strictness the "tradition of the elders" which we meet in the New Testament. It involved a degree of separation greater

Published in *Interpretation* 16 (1962), pp. 280-291.

than anything practiced elsewhere in Israel. It involved the endurance of privation and, at times, of active persecution. It involved submission to an austere discipline, such as cannot have come naturally to men of the necessary strength of personality to join the community.

II. THE ELECT OF GOD

But all these things, which by secular standards would be counted as disadvantages, were far outweighed by the privileges which the members of the community enjoyed. The assiduous study of the sacred Scriptures, which was enjoined upon them, could have been no hardship to men of their caliber, but a most congenial duty—all the more so since they were taught to interpret those Scriptures in a way which made their own calling and election plain to them. For *they* constituted the righteous remnant, the elect of God, the saints of the Most High, the people of the new covenant. Only they could understand the Scriptures aright, only they possessed insight into the wonderful mysteries of God, only they knew the way in which he was about to accomplish his eternal purpose—and in the accomplishment of that purpose they were to be his chosen instruments. Was it not abundantly worthwhile enduring their present toil and tribulation if such a glorious prospect lay immediately before them?

Within the Christian church (or on its fringes) we sometimes come upon small pious communities of people who have very similar ideas about their own place in the divine scheme of things. They alone can interpret the Bible (particularly biblical prophecy and apocalyptic) properly, and they look with mingled pity and disapproval on theological professors and church leaders who, for all their learning and fame, have obviously had concealed from them those revelations which God in his wisdom has communicated to babes like themselves. Such an attitude commonly leads to a profound sense of humility before God, a deep appreciation of his grace in so dealing with them, all unworthy as they are, an unshakable conviction that they are right and all others wrong, and a sublime disregard for the criticisms of scholars who point out that their cherished interpretations of Holy Writ violate the canons of history, philology, and exegesis. If they do, so much the worse for those canons! If we have any acquaintance with members of such groups, we shall have some insight into the personal religion of the men of Qumran. And at the same time we may have some insight into the picture that the church of apostolic days must have presented to the religious leaders of Judaism or to the heads of philosophical schools in the Graeco-Roman world. For those early Christians believed that to them, God's holy and elect people, had been revealed the secret of the divine kingdom which was hidden from the wise and prudent.

The hymn of praise which concludes the Rule of the Community (1QS 10.1–11.22) sets before us clearly many of the features of personal religion at Qumran. It is cast in the first person singular, and whereas in the first place the "I" of this hymn will be identifiable with the composer (whoever he may have been), there is nothing in it which could not have been sung by any member of the community as an expression of his own attitude to God. Theodore Gaster may well be right in describing it as the Hymn of the Initiants. The fact that the opening section of the hymn regulates the praise of God by the sacred calendar does not detract from the sincerity and spontaneity of the religious aspirations expressed in his praise. Christians who remember our Lord's nativity with special thanksgiving at Christmas and his passion and triumph on Good Friday and Easter Day do not find that this observance of the Christian Year imposes any artificiality upon their worship. Paul indeed deprecated the Galatian Christians' observance of "days and months and seasons and years" (Gal. 4:10), but not because it diminished the genuineness of their piety.

Along with the initiants' hymn we may take the whole collection of Hymns of Thanksgiving at Qumran (1QH). Here we find personal religion in unstinted measure. Here, too, the language is that of the first personal singular. Whoever is speaking in these hymns is expressing his own attitude to God, but at the same time he is the spokesman of his brethren. From the canonical Psalms down to the hymns of our own day there are many compositions in the first person singular in which the composer himself is the primary speaker, but in which the experiences and attitudes described are so representative that many others find them a most helpful vehicle of their own praise and prayer. If (as seems most probable) the "I" of the Hymns of Thanksgiving is the Teacher of Righteousness himself, his followers could most naturally make his words their own. We may compare the way in which many of the hymns of John and Charles Wesley, expressing the realities of religion in their own lives, are sung by Methodists (and others) today because they express the realities of religion in their lives too. Charles Wesley may sing as the true account of what happened to him:

> Long my imprisoned spirit lay
>   Fast bound in sin and nature's night;
> Thine eye diffused a quickening ray—
>   I woke, the dungeon flamed with light;
> My chains fell off, my heart was free,
> I rose, went forth, and followed Thee.

But probably since the publication of that hymn there has never been a Methodist who did not sing it as the account of what had happened to him or her as well as to Charles Wesley.

So, even when the Teacher of Righteousness (if it be he) thanks God for initiating him into his "wonderful mysteries" (an initiation which was granted to him as a special privilege), the humblest of his followers could take upon his own lips the same words of thanksgiving, for he too, because of his membership in the Teacher's community, had the entrée to those mysteries which remained veiled from the wisest of those outside the community. And in any case, a leader of the stamp of the Teacher of Righteousness tends to transmit to his followers not only his own pattern of religious language but his own pattern of religious experience.

III. HUMILITY BEFORE GOD

Basic to the personal religion of the men of Qumran, then, is an overwhelming appreciation of the greatness and holiness of God. Such is his majesty and power that they feel themselves to be as nothing before him. This induces a sense of deep humility which comes to repeated expression, and usually in very much the same form of words.

> What indeed is the son of man among Thy wondrous works?
> One of woman born, how can he dwell before Thee?
> From dust was he formed, and the food of worms is his dwelling;
> From clay was he fashioned and he is bound for dust again (1QS
> 11.20-22).

Time and again these words recur throughout the hymns, emphasizing the creaturely insignificance of man in himself. There are Old Testament adumbrations of this attitude, as when Abraham says, "I have taken upon myself to speak to the Lord, I who am but dust and ashes" (Gen. 18:27); but it is hardly to be paralleled in the New Testament. In the New Testament the gulf between God and man is the gulf between man's sin and God's holiness rather than between man's creatureliness and God's creative power; man is created indeed, but created in God's image, as Genesis 1:26ff. reminds us, and it is sin that has made him fall short of the glory of God. For a parallel to the Qumran insistence on the lowliness of man's origin we turn rather to the words of Aqabya in *Pirqê Abôth* 3.1: "Know whence thou camest, . . . from a putrefying drop; whither thou art going, to a place of dust, worms and maggots."

But this very consciousness of his lowly origin moves the man of

Qumran to wonder and praise that God should have made him one of his elect. For the person whom God elects is elected indeed; the predestinating decree of God is absolute.

> I know that in Thy hand is the inclination of all spirit; . . .
> Thou didst establish his work [?] before he was created.
> And how can any one change Thy words?
> Only Thou hast created the righteous, and from the womb Thou hast established him for the season of favor,
> To pay heed to Thy covenant and walk in it altogether,
> That Thou shouldest pardon him in the abundance of Thy mercy . . .
> And the wicked Thou hast created for the Epoch of Thy wrath,
> And from the womb Thou hast set them apart [literally, hast sanctified them] for the day of slaughter (1QH 15.13-17).

Elsewhere in the Qumran texts there may be passages which modify this picture of absolute double predestination, prescribing the character and destiny of the righteous and the wicked before their birth; but no such modification is suggested in the Hymns. Paul may remind the Romans that the destinies of Esau and Jacob were foreordained "though they were not yet born and had done nothing either good or bad, in order that God's purpose of election might continue, not because of works but because of his call" (Rom. 9:11); but his last word about the purpose of God in this part of his argument is that "God has consigned all men to disobedience, that he may have mercy upon all" (Rom. 11:32). The men of Qumran were deeply conscious of the mercy of God shown to them, but they did not think of his mercy as having such a wide embrace as this.

IV. JUSTIFIED SINNERS

It would be wrong, however, to think that the humility of the men of Qumran arose only from a sense of their creatureliness and not also from a sense of sin. Those who entered the covenant made humble confession of their sins and of the sins of their ancestors, they acknowledged the righteousness of God's judgment upon these sins together with "the compassions of His loving-kindness which He has shown us from age to age" (1QS 1.24–2.1). This sense of the defilement of sin and consequent need for cleansing persisted. It is only by the spirit of holiness that a man can be purified from his iniquities so as to see the light of life, the "outward and visible sign" of this inward purification being the "cleansing of his flesh by sprinkling with the water that removes impurity and by sanctification in purifying water" (1QS 3.6-9). This reminds us forcibly of 1 Peter 1:2, where the elect of God are spoken of as "sanctified by the Spirit for obedience to Jesus Christ and for sprinkling with his blood." The one difference—and it is the one that makes *all* the difference—is the personal reference to Jesus Christ in the Christian document. But it is certain that for the men of Qumran this cleansing and sanctification by the "spirit of holiness" was no mere matter of doctrine but an intensely real experience which gave character to their corporate and personal piety.

The sinner's need of cleansing may also be viewed as his need for justification in the sight of God. "I know," says one of the Hymns of Thanksgiving, "that righteousness does not belong to mortal man, nor perfection of way to a son of man. To God Most High belong all the works of righteousness, and the way of mortal man cannot be established except by the spirit which God has fashioned for him" (1QH 4.30f.). "I will call God 'my righteousness,'" says the Hymn of the Initiants, "and the Most High 'the establisher of my good'" (1QS 10.12f.). Now a man who can say that God is his righteousness has the root of the matter in him, according to the best biblical standards. The difference between the Qumran initiant and Paul is that Paul knew that God's righteousness had come near to him in Christ (1 Cor. 1:30; 2 Cor. 5:21). But the Qumran hymn writer lived before the coming of Christ; nevertheless he knew something of the meaning of the name which Jeremiah gives to the coming Prince of the house of David: "The LORD is our righteousness" (Jer. 23:6; 33:16).

This note recurs repeatedly in the Hymn of the Initiants:

> By His righteousness my sin is blotted out. . . . When I stumble in the iniquity of [my] flesh, my judgment [lies] with the righteousness of God, which will stand for ever. . . . In His compassion He draws me near and in His loving-kindnesses He brings my judgment. In the righteousness of His truth He judges me and in the abundance of His goodness He makes atonement for all my iniquities; in His righteousness He cleanses me from the impurity of mortal man and from the sin of the sons of men, that I may praise God for His righteousness and the Most High for His glory (1QS 11.3-15).

In these words it is not difficult to recognize the same twofold sense of "the righteousness of God" that we are familiar with in Paul's epistles—not only God's personal righteousness but also (in Luther's words) "that righteousness whereby, through grace and sheer mercy, He justifies us by faith." Man, according to the Qumran hymns, has no righteousness of his own—at least "not before God," as Paul says of Abraham (Rom. 4:2).

For none is righteous in judgment with Thee, and none is innocent when he contends with Thee. One mortal man may be more righteous than another; one man may have more understanding than another . . . but none can vie in strength with Thy mighty works and Thy glory is [unsearchable] (1QH 9.14-16).

As for me, I said in my rebellion, "I have been rejected from Thy covenant." But when I remembered the strength of Thy hand with the multitude of Thy compassions I was fortified; I arose and my spirit was strengthened, standing firmly in the face of affliction, for I have leaned upon Thy loving-kindnesses and the multitude of Thy compassions. For Thou makest atonement for iniquity and dost cleanse mankind from guilt by Thy righteousness—not for the sake of man [but for Thy glory] Thou hast done it (1QH 4.35-38).

The man who could speak like that could well have sung with Horatius Bonar:

I have no help but Thine; nor do I need
    Another arm save Thine to lean upon;
It is enough, my Lord, enough indeed;
    My strength is in Thy might, Thy might alone.

He could go on and sing:

Mine is the sin, but Thine the righteousness.

And perhaps, if he had lived on to see the day of Christ, he might have found just here the ultimate confirmation of his trust:

Mine is the guilt, but Thine the cleansing blood:
Here is my robe, my refuge, and my peace—
    Thy blood, Thy righteousness, O Lord my God.

Even if the hymns do not explicitly qualify this righteousness as being "by faith," it is plain that faith on the speaker's part and nothing else enabled him to lay hold on the righteousness with which God dealt with him in grace. In this connection, however, we are reminded of the interpretation of the words, "The righteous shall live by his faith," in the Qumran commentary on Habakkuk (1QpHab on 2:4):

Its interpretation concerns all the doers of the law in the house of Judah, whom God will save from the place of judgment because of their labor and their fidelity to the Teacher of Righteousness.

What is the nature of this fidelity to the Teacher of Righteousness, or faith in the Teacher, which procures for his followers deliverance and justification at God's hands? Probably faith in his teaching and loyal acceptance of his directions. But if (as seems highly probable) the Teacher is himself the author of many (if not all) of the Hymns of Thanksgiving, his own justification could not be based on "fidelity to the Teacher of Righteousness" but on his personal trust in the mercy of God. In that case, his followers' fidelity to his teaching would logically have meant that they too learned to look in trust to God for the justification which could come from no other source. True, they are described as "doers of the law," and their labor (or possibly endurance of hardship) is mentioned along with their "fidelity to the Teacher of Righteousness" as procuring their deliverance from the place of judgment; here we see a different viewpoint from Paul's.

In an earlier publication I stated that:

> The Qumran commentator, who ascribes saving efficacy to the "toil" [*'āmāl*] of the doers of the law in the house of Judah, would not have known what to make of Paul's statement that "to one who does not work but trusts him who justifies the ungodly, his faith is reckoned as righteousness" (Rom. 4:5). Justification by faith is not an unknown idea in Qumran literature, but justification of the ungodly would have been unthinkable.[1]

On this a colleague in the Republic of Ireland made the following comment in a letter:

> I think that both Paul and the Qumran writers would admit that the elect were ungodly before God forgave them and they turned away from evil; cf. Manual of Discipline, plate xi, lines 9-15 . . . Paul himself can say that the anger of God is revealed against all ungodliness and wickedness (Rom. 1:18), but that God can justify the ungodly (Rom. 4:5). I think the Qumran writers made a similar distinction between transgressors who continued in their perversity and "repentant transgressors" (plate x, line 20). The difference between Paul and Qumran is, I think, that for Paul, God's justice is revealed to all who believe, without reference to the Mosaic legislation, whereas the Torah is still essential in the Qumran view.

With this I am not really in disagreement, but I should still say that Paul in Romans 4:5 goes beyond what a member of the Qumran community would have thought proper. It seems clear that Paul is deliberately stating a paradox in Romans 4:5; when he describes God as justifying the ungodly, he is saying that God does the very thing which God, in Exodus 23:7, says he will not do (or, in the LXX text, forbids his people to do).[2] Of course, Paul would have agreed that the faith by which the ungodly turn to God and receive his justifying sentence is inseparable from repentance; there is no justification for the impenitent. But while the men of Qumran acknowledged their sin, I am not sure that they would have classed themselves along with the "ungodly"; they were too conscious of the predestined gulf which separated the ungodly on the one side from repentant and justified sinners on the other.

It is conceivable, moreover, that many of the Teacher's followers, especially after his death, did not maintain in its original purity his own high doctrine of justification by the grace of God alone, and came to attribute some share in their justification to their own works. We may compare the infrequency with which Christians of the postapostolic age, no matter how greatly they revered the memory of Paul, evince any real appreciation of what he meant by *his* doctrine of justification by faith. But we must not be unfair to the men of Qumran; the responsibility which they took upon themselves was a very heavy one. The righteousness at which they aimed exceeded the righteousness of the scribes and Pharisees ("seekers after smooth things," as they called them); their chosen privilege was, by the unremitting study and practice of the law of God, and by enduring affliction for his sake, to make atonement for their land (polluted as it was through the dominance of Belial), and it would be scarcely surprising if they thought that the labor and suffering which procured atonement for the land would incidentally procure atonement for themselves. Even so, this is not the view of personal atonement taken in the Hymns of Thanksgiving; there it is ascribed to God's grace, and all glory is given to him: *sola gratia, sola fide, soli Deo gloria!* All the more reason for attributing these hymns, and the Hymn of the Initiants too, for that matter, to an author of really independent mind such as the Teacher of Righteousness must have been.

V. ATTITUDE TO OTHERS

It is not easy for those who know themselves to be chosen and justified by God to resist the temptation to look down on others who have not been so blessed. The line of demarcation between "There, but for the grace of God, goes John Berridge," and "God, I thank thee that I am not like other men," is a very finely drawn line, but a very real one. On which side of the line should we place these words with which one of the Hymns of Thanksgiving begins?

> I give Thee thanks, O Lord, because Thou hast not caused my lot to fall in the congregation of vanity, and hast not set my portion in the council of dissemblers (1QH 7.34).

From the words themselves it is not easy to reach a conclusion; but from the fact that the writer, in the words which follow, appears to base all his hope in God's forgiving mercies and to "put no confidence in the flesh" (as Paul would have said), it is probable that his attitude is one of humble gratitude to God, but for whose grace he too might have been one of the "dissemblers." But religious people know (or should know) how easy it is to pass from this sense of sincere thankfulness to an attitude of censorious superiority.

One of the least attractive traits of the Qumran texts is their frequent inculcation of hatred. On initiation into the community, new members swore not only to "hate all that God has rejected" but also "to hate all the sons of darkness, each of them according to his guilt in [the time of?] God's vengeance" (1QS 1.4, 10f.). And the fidelity of a member is tested by the wholeheartedness of his hatred as well as of his love (1QS 9.15). There is little of the distinction which we like to make between hating the sin but loving the sinner. But the hatred inculcated at Qumran is not the hatred of personal enemies; anything of that sort is forbidden as unworthy. It is the hatred of the wicked because they are wicked, because they are the enemies of God; it is the hatred which will nerve the saints as the agents of God to execute righteous judgment against the ungodly when the day of his vengeance comes. It is, in fact, thoroughly in line with the sentiment of such Old Testament passages as Psalm 139:21f.:

> Do I not hate them that hate thee, O LORD?
>   And do I not loathe them that rise up against thee?
> I hate them with perfect hatred;
>   I count them my enemies.

Here the teaching of Christ certainly shows us a more excellent way. We may indeed be reminded of his words about the necessity of hating father, mother, wife, children, brothers, sisters, and life itself if one is to become his disciple indeed (Luke 14:26). If Christians are right in understanding this hatred to mean a lesser love, may the word not have the same sense in the Qumran writings? The reason for taking the word in the sense of a lesser love in Luke 14:26 is that this is the plain meaning of the language both in its immediate context and in the wider context of the general teaching of Christ. He who laid down, by contrast with what was said to the men of old, that his followers should love their enemies, certainly did not inculcate unnatural hatred towards their next of kin. But he did mean that, in his disciple's case as in his own, family ties should yield to the superior claims of the kingdom of God. The members of the Qumran community would have agreed that the divine kingdom and righteousness must take precedence over all such things as family ties, but it is not in reference to this situation that the inculcation of hatred recurs in their literature. Here we must simply say that Jesus went farther than the Teacher of Righteousness did, while bearing in mind (lest we condemn the Teacher and his followers) that the followers of Jesus have in this regard all too often manifested an attitude more in line with the Qumran oath of initiation than with the Sermon on the Mount. On this whole subject a paper by Father E. F. Sutcliffe in the *Revue de Qumran* for June 1960 demands careful study; it will preserve us from condemning the men of Qumran out of hand on this score.[3]

On the other hand, love to one's neighbor was warmly fostered (naturally with special reference to fellow members of the community, but not necessarily with exclusive reference to them): all were to live together "in true unity and kindly humility and loyal love and righteous thoughts one to another" (1QS 2.24f.), and angry language and a resentful spirit were alike forbidden (1QS 5.25; 7.8).

VI. CONCLUSION

The picture of personal piety that we can reconstruct from the Qumran writings, then, is one in the best traditions of Israel. We must remember, of course, that we are dealing with an ascetic group, whose way of life must inevitably differ from that of people living "in the world." We must remember, too, that we are dealing with men who believed that their days were the last days of the present age, and whose evaluation of life and its concerns was conditioned by this belief. When all that has been said, we can still learn something from their overwhelming sense of indebtedness to the grace of God, to which they owed their election, their cleansing, their justification, their enlightenment, their strength and protection, their refreshment and enabling, their guidance and hope. And we can learn something from their unreserved dedication to God, their resolution to know his will and do it, their readiness to be the instruments of his righteous purpose.

If we, as Christians, think that we are more enlightened than they were, let us remember to acknowledge that for this we are even more indebted to the grace of God than they were, and that we ought to be more utterly dedicated to the accomplishment of his will than they were. The difference between the followers of the Teacher of Righteousness and the followers of Jesus is that the latter have come to know the perfect revelation of God in the Word made flesh, as the former could not. We may well count them among those righteous men who desired to see and hear the things which came into the world with Jesus, but neither saw nor heard them because they lived too soon. But according to their light and strength, they prepared in the wilderness the way of the Lord and set up in the desert a highway for their God—and ours.

III. NEW TESTAMENT

6. The Romans Debate—Continued

I. INTRODUCTION

The title of this lecture was suggested by the title of a symposium edited by Karl Paul Donfried and published in 1977 as *The Romans Debate*.[1] This symposium brings together ten essays composed and published over the previous thirty years. The first of these essays originated as a lecture delivered by Professor T. W. Manson in the John Rylands Library in February 1948 and published in the Library's *Bulletin*, later in the same year, under the title "St. Paul's Letter to the Romans—and Others."[2] It seems, therefore, especially appropriate to devote this twenty-first Manson Memorial Lecture to the continuation of the debate.

The "Romans debate" is the debate about the character of the letter (including questions about its literary integrity, the possibility of its having circulated in longer and shorter recensions, the destination of chapter 16) and, above all, Paul's purpose in sending it. This lecture confines itself mainly to the last of these issues. With regard to other questions, suffice it to say that the lecture presupposes the literary integrity of the document (from Romans 1:1 to at least 16:23) as a letter addressed to the Christians of Rome, and the probability that a later editor (Marcion, it appears) issued a shorter recension of it which has influenced the textual tradition but has no relevance for our understanding of the original work or for the destination of chapter 16.

Since that symposium was published, further contributions have

The Manson Memorial Lecture delivered in the University of Manchester on 19 November 1981, and published in *BJRL* 64 (1981-82), pp. 334-359.

been made to the debate. A few distinguished new commentaries on Romans have appeared;[3] among them, in relation to our present subject, special mention should be made of Ulrich Wilckens' work in the Evangelisch-Katholischer Kommentar zum Neuen Testament. Apart from commentaries, there is an important monograph by Dr. Harry Gamble on *The Textual History of the Letter to the Romans*.[4] Here the various textual phenomena which Professor Manson discussed in his lecture of 1948 are reviewed afresh; the problem of chapter 16 is dealt with among others and answered—conclusively, in my judgment—in favor of a Roman destination. In fact I think that C. H. Dodd said as much as needed to be said on this subject in his Moffatt Commentary on Romans in 1932,[5] but Dr. Gamble has dotted the i's and crossed the t's of the case for Rome.

On several aspects of the Romans debate there is widespread agreement. When Paul dictated the letter he had completed ten years of apostolic activity both east and west of the Aegean Sea. In the great cities of South Galatia, Macedonia, Achaia and proconsular Asia the gospel had been preached and churches had been founded. Most recently Illyricum also had been visited. Paul now reckoned that his work in the eastern Mediterranean area was at an end: "I no longer have any room for work in these regions," he said (Romans 15:23). He was essentially a pioneer, making it his ambition to preach the gospel where the name of Christ had never been heard before. But where around the Mediterranean shores could he find such a place in the later fifties of the first century? Paul was not the only Christian missionary in the Gentile world, though he was the greatest, and several Mediterranean lands which he had not visited had probably been evangelized by others. But Spain, the oldest Roman province after Sicily, Sardinia and Corsica,[6] remained unevangelized; Paul resolved that he would be the first to take the gospel there. To Spain, then, he turned his eyes.

A journey to Spain would give him the opportunity of gratifying a long-cherished desire to visit Rome. He had no thought of settling down in Rome: it was no part of his policy to build, as he said, on someone else's foundation[7] (we know what he thought about certain people who invaded his mission-field and tried to build on *his* foundation).[8] But a stay in Rome would enable him to enjoy the company of Christians in the capital and to renew acquaintance with a number of friends whom he had met elsewhere and who were now resident there. After his missionary exertions in the east, and before he embarked on a fresh campaign in the west, it would be a refreshing experience to spend some time in Rome. No doubt there would be an opportunity, during such a visit, to exercise his ministry as apostle to the Gentiles.[9] But any converts that he made by preaching the gospel in Rome would be added to the

Christian community already existing in the city: there was no question of his forming them into a separate Pauline church.

One thing only remained on his program before he could fulfill this plan. He had to go to Jerusalem with the delegates of churches in his Gentile mission-field who were to hand over to the leaders of the mother-church their churches' contributions to a relief fund which Paul had been organizing among them for some years. When this business had been attended to, then, said Paul to the Roman Christians, "I shall go on by way of you to Spain" (Romans 15:28).

This, then, as may be gathered from information given in the letter, was the occasion of Paul's writing to the Christians of Rome. The letter was sent from Corinth, early in (probably) A.D. 57.

But if the primary purpose of the letter was to prepare the Roman Christians for Paul's visit to them, how is that purpose related to its main content? This question, indeed, is the crux of the Romans debate, and an attempt will be made to answer it. In trying to answer it, we shall bear in mind that Paul, while dictating the letter, had three places especially in mind—Rome, the home of the people to whom the letter was addressed; Spain, where he planned shortly to inaugurate the next phase of his apostolic ministry; and Jerusalem, which he was to visit in the immediate future to complete a project very close to his heart. A consideration of these three places, one by one, should help us to come to terms with some important aspects of the Romans debate.

II. THREE PROSPECTIVE VISITS

1. Rome

This document is, in no merely nominal sense, Paul's letter to the Romans—a letter addressed, in all its parts, to a particular Christian community in a particular historical situation. Communications between Rome and the main centers of Paul's mission-field were good, and Paul was able to keep himself informed, through friends who visited Rome or were now resident there, of what was happening among the Christians of the capital.

It is plain from Paul's language that the Christian community in Rome was large and active, enjoying a good reputation among churches elsewhere in the Mediterranean world.[10]

The origins of Christianity in Rome are obscure. The words of the fourth-century commentator called Ambrosiaster are frequently quoted in this regard: "The Romans had embraced the faith of Christ, albeit according to the Jewish rite, although they saw no sign of mighty works nor any of the apostles."[11] We know too little about Ambrosiaster's sources of information to accept this as an authoritative statement, but it certainly agrees with such other evidence as we have, not least in relation to the Jewish base of early Roman Christianity.[12]

It is probable that Christianity reached Rome within a few years of its inception, given the degree of social mobility in the Roman Empire in those days. The people most likely to take it to Rome were Hellenistic Jewish Christians, members of the group in which Stephen and Philip played a leading part. The name of the Synagogue of the Freedmen in Jerusalem, with which Stephen was associated,[13] suggests a link with Rome (if the *libertini* in question were the descendants of Jews who were taken as captives to Rome by Pompey to grace his triumph in 61 B.C. and subsequently emancipated). The introduction of Christianity into the Jewish community of Rome was bound to lead to the same kind of disputes as its introduction into other Jewish communities; and if such disputes played their part in the constant tumults in which, according to Suetonius, the Jews of Rome were indulging (*adsidue tumultuantes*) in the principate of Claudius, we can understand his further remark that these tumults were stirred up by "Chrestus" (*impulsore Chresto*).[14]

We have ample evidence for the use of *Chrestus*/Χρηστός and *Chrestiani*/Χρηστιανοί, in Latin and Greek alike, as mis-spellings for *Christus*/Χριστός and *Christiani*/Χριστιανοί.[15] It is about as certain as can be with such an allusion that the person referred to is Jesus Christ. Had he been another, otherwise unknown, bearer of the name Chrestus, Suetonius would probably have said *impulsore Chresto quodam*. It is not at all likely that the reference is to another messianic claimant, a rival Christ— e.g., Simon Magus (whose presence in Rome under Claudius is attested elsewhere).[16] There is no evidence that Simon Magus claimed to be the Messiah, and in any case a pagan writer would not have said *impulsore Chresto* if he had meant "at the instigation of a Messiah"—Chrestus for Suetonius was a personal name, as it was for pagans in general.

True, Jesus Christ was not in Rome during the principate of Claudius.[17] But Suetonius may well have understood his sources (wrongly) to mean that he was. Tacitus knew that Christ was executed under Tiberius,[18] but Suetonius had not the same concern for historical precision. If his sources told him that the rioting among the Jews of Rome was caused by disagreement about the claims of Christ, it was a natural, if mistaken, inference that Christ himself was in Rome at the time.

It was because of these riots, says Suetonius, that Claudius expelled the Jews from Rome. He does not date the expulsion edict: Orosius, early in the fifth century, says that it was issued in A.D. 49.[19] Orosius's inaccuracy in the very act of supplying this information does not inspire confidence, but the record of Acts makes A.D. 49 a probable date.[20] Luke says that, when Paul first visited Corinth, he met a Jew named Aquila, "lately come from Italy with his wife Priscilla, because Claudius had commanded all the Jews to leave Rome" (Acts 18:2). The reference in Acts 18:12 to Gallio as proconsul of Achaia during Paul's stay in Corinth enables us to date Paul's arrival in that city in the late summer of A.D. 50; it is therefore quite probable that Priscilla and Aquila left Rome the previous year.[21]

Since Paul, in his references to Priscilla and Aquila, never implies that they were converts of his own, the likelihood is that they were Christians before they left Rome—perhaps, as Harnack suggested, foundation-members of the Roman church.[22]

In Claudius's expulsion of Jews, no distinction would be made between those among them who were Christians and the majority who were not. The expulsion could have gone far to wipe out the Roman church. But perhaps it did not wipe it out altogether. If in A.D. 49 there were some Gentile Christians in Rome, they would not be affected by the edict of expulsion. By A.D. 49 Gentile Christianity was firmly rooted in several cities of the eastern Mediterranean, and if in the eastern Mediterranean, why not also in Rome, to which all roads led from the imperial frontiers? We do not know this for certain: what we can say is that by the beginning of A.D. 57, when Paul sent his letter to the Roman Christians, the majority of them were apparently Gentiles.[23]

After the expulsion of Jews from Rome, if the course of events may be so reconstructed, the small group or groups of Gentile Christians in the city had to fend for themselves. But they continued to receive accessions of strength in the years that followed. They were probably not organized as a single city church, but existed as a number of separate house-churches, conscious nevertheless of the bond which united them in faith and love. Some of these house-churches, indeed, may have been associated with the imperial establishment. It is at a later date that Paul refers to "saints . . . of Caesar's household" (Philippians 4:22).[24] But the evidence of Romans 16:10f. suggests that there were Christians in some of the groups that made up "Caesar's household" of slaves and freedmen—among the *Aristobuliani*, for instance, and the *Narcissiani*.[25]

When, around the time that Nero succeeded Claudius in the principate (A.D. 54), the expulsion edict became a dead letter (like earlier expulsion edicts of the same kind),[26] Jews began to return to Rome, and Jewish Christians among them. Priscilla and Aquila seem to have returned soon after the end of Paul's Ephesian ministry (A.D. 55); their residence in Rome served as the headquarters of a house-church (Romans 16:5), as their residence in Ephesus had done (1 Corinthians 16:19). There were no doubt other Jewish house-churches added to the Gentile house-churches already existing. What kind of reception did these returning Jewish Christians meet with from their Gentile brethren? It is implied in Romans 11:13-24 that the Gentile Christians tended to look down on their Jewish brethren as poor relations. Paul, discussing the place of Jews and Gentiles in the divine purpose, warns his Gentile readers not to give themselves airs: even if they are now in the majority, they should bear in mind that the base of the church—of the Roman church as well as of the church universal—is Jewish.

Caution must be exercised when evidence is sought in this letter for the state of the Roman church at the time of writing, lest we find ourselves arguing in a circle. It is all too easy to draw inferences from the letter about the state of the church, and then use those inferences to help us in understanding the letter.

Here, however, we have a letter from Paul explicitly addressed to the Christians of Rome: "to all God's beloved in Rome" (Romans 1:7). True, there is one textual tradition which omits the phrase "in Rome" both here and in verse 15, but this omission cannot be original. The sense requires a place-name, and no other place-name than Rome will fit the context (this is no circular letter in which a variety of place-names might be inserted in a blank space left for the address). The omission of the reference to Rome can best be explained, as T. W. Manson explained it, by the supposition that Marcion struck it out, after his rejection by the Christian leaders in Rome, to show that in his judgment such a church did not deserve the honor of being addressed in a letter from the only true apostle of Christ.[27]

Paul writes to the Roman Christians, he says, because he hopes to pay them a visit soon. He had planned to visit their city on earlier occasions but had not been able to put those plans into action. One of the occasions he has in mind may have been the time when he first set foot in Europe. Having crossed the Aegean to Macedonia in A.D. 49, he found himself traveling from east to west along the Egnatian Way, evangelizing first Philippi and then Thessalonica. Had nothing interfered with his program he might have continued his westward journey until he reached one of the Adriatic termini of the Egnatian Way, after which the natural course would have been to cross the Straits of Otranto to Brindisi and proceed along the Appian Way to Rome.[28] He was prevented from doing this by the riots which broke out in Thessalonica while he was there—*impulsore Chresto*, it might have been said there also, for he and his colleagues were charged with proclaiming "another emperor, namely, Jesus" (Acts 17:7). Paul was not only forced to leave

Thessalonica and proceed no farther along the Egnatian Way; as he turned south he found that there was no place for him anywhere in Macedonia, and he was unable to settle until he reached Corinth, where he stayed for eighteen months.

But even if he had been left in peace to continue along the Egnatian Way, it would have been an inopportune time for him to visit Rome: it was just then that Claudius issued his expulsion edict. A visit to Rome must await a more convenient season, and early in A.D. 57 the way seemed more propitious for such a visit than ever it had been before.[29] The situation had changed: Nero was now on the imperial throne, halfway through his first quinquennium, which was greeted, especially in the eastern provinces, as a kind of golden age.

This, then, is the background to the letter, and there is general agreement that Paul sent it to prepare the Roman Christians for his prospective visit. But why, it may be asked, did he send a letter with these particular contents? He mentions his visit only at the beginning and at the end; what is the relevance to the Roman Christians of the main body of the letter?

After his preliminary remarks about his occasion for writing, Paul launches into a sustained and coherent statement of the gospel as he understood it, with special emphasis on the justifying grace of God, available on equal terms to Jews and Gentiles (1:16–8:40). Then comes a careful inquiry into God's purpose in history, with special reference to the place of Jews and Gentiles in that purpose (9:1–11:36). Various ethical admonitions (12:1–13:14), including a problematic paragraph on the Christian's relation to the state (13:1-7),[30] are then followed by a particular paraenesis on the mutual responsibilities of the "strong" and the "weak in faith" within the Christian community (14:1–15:13). Next, Paul makes a short statement about his activity as apostle to the Gentiles thus far (15:14-21), together with an account of his plans for the immediate and subsequent future (15:22-33). The letter comes to an end with the commendation of Phoebe, who is taking it to its destination (16:1f.), and a series of greetings to twenty-six individuals, who belong to at least five groups or house-churches (16:3-15). Greetings are sent from "all the churches of Christ," presumably those of the Pauline mission-field (16:16). A final admonition (16:17-20) is followed by greetings from named individuals among Paul's present companions (16:21-23), and by a benediction (16:24) and doxology (16:25-27) of disputed authenticity.[31]

If we knew more about the current situation in the church of Rome, it might be seen that the detailed contents of the letter are more relevant to that situation than can now be established. But it will be rewarding to look at the contents section by section.

As regards his lengthy statement of the gospel (1:16–8:40), it was in any case expedient that Paul should communicate to the Roman Christians an outline of the message which he proclaimed. Misrepresentations of his preaching and his apostolic procedure were current, and must have found their way to Rome. It was plainly undesirable that these should be accepted in default of anything more reliable. Paul does not, for the most part, refute those misrepresentations directly (there are a few incidental allusions to them, as in Romans 3:8),[32] but gives a systematic exposition showing how, if the contemporary plight of mankind, Gentile and Jewish, is to be cured, God's justifying grace, without discrimination among its beneficiaries, is alone competent to cure it.

This exposition is carried on largely in terms of a debate or dialogue with the synagogue. Paul must have engaged in this kind of exchange repeatedly in the course of his preaching—what, for example, were the terms in which some members of the synagogue in Pisidian Antioch "contradicted what was spoken by Paul" (Acts 13:45)?—but it was probably relevant to the state of affairs in Rome. The rioting which attended the introduction of Christianity into the Jewish community of the capital some years previously was sparked off by arguments not dissimilar, perhaps, to those voiced in the Jerusalem synagogue where Stephen's teaching was first heard.[33] Paul's exposition of the new faith had different emphases from Stephen's, but was sufficiently like it to provoke the same kind of violent reaction, as indeed it did from one city to another.

Paul's gospel, we know, was charged with promoting moral indifferentism, if not with actively encouraging sin, and the form of his argument in this letter implies his awareness that this charge was not unknown in Rome: "Are we to continue in sin that grace may abound?" (Romans 6:1). He makes it plain, therefore, that the gospel which he preaches is not only the way of righteousness, in the sense of the righteous status which God by his grace bestows on believers in Christ, but also the way of holiness, in which "the righteous requirements of the law are fulfilled in us who walk not according to the flesh but according to the Spirit" (Romans 8:4).

The relation of chapters 9–11 to the plan of the letter as a whole has been much debated. It has been said that, if Paul had moved from the end of chapter 8, with its celebration of the glory which consummates God's saving work in his people, to the beginning of chapter 12, with its practical application of that saving work to the daily life of Christians, we should have been conscious of no hiatus. Yet Paul judged it fitting to grapple at this point with a problem which, as he confesses, caused him great personal pain.

Israel, the nation which God had chosen to be the vehicle of his purpose of grace in the world, had as a whole failed to respond to the fulfillment of that purpose in Jesus Christ. Paul was conscious of this as a problem for himself both on the personal and on the apostolic level. If in Israel's failure to respond he saw writ large his own earlier unbelief, that very fact brought hope with it: as his eyes had been opened, so his people's eyes would surely be opened. For this he prayed incessantly.[34] Indeed, if Israel's salvation could be won at the price of his own damnation, he would readily pay that price.[35] He would gladly have devoted his life and strength to the evangelizing of his people,[36] but he was specifically called to be Christ's apostle to the Gentile world. Yet he trusted that even by the evangelization of Gentiles he would indirectly do something for the advantage of his own people: they would be stimulated to jealousy as they saw increasing numbers of Gentiles enjoying the gospel blessings which were the fruit of God's promises to the patriarchs, and would waken up to the realization that these blessings were for them too—that in fact they should properly have been for them first, since they were the descendants of the patriarchs and the inheritors of those promises. This prospect enhanced the prestige of his apostleship as he contemplated it: "inasmuch as I am the Gentiles' apostle, I glorify my ministry in order to make my kinsfolk jealous and thus save some of them" (Romans 11:13f.).

But it is not simply to share with the Roman Christians his concern for Israel and his appreciation of the significance of his apostleship that he writes like this. His theme is relevant to the situation in Rome. It is in this context that he warns the Gentiles among his readers not to despise the Jews, whether the Jews in general or Jewish Christians in particular, because God has not written them off. They continue to have a place in his purpose, and his purpose will not be completed until, with the ingathering of the full tale of Gentile converts, "all Israel will be saved" (Romans 11:25f.). Gentile Christians must not pride themselves on the superiority of their faith, but remember that they are what they are only by the kindness of God. This will induce in them a proper sense of humility, and respect and understanding for their fellow-believers of Jewish stock.

The paragraph about the Christian's relation to the secular authorities (Romans 13:1-7) is best understood in the light of the Roman destination of the letter. This is not a universal statement of political principle. The injunction to "render to all their dues" (13:7) may indeed be viewed as a generalization of Jesus' precept: "render to Caesar what belongs to Caesar" (Mark 12:17).[37] That precept was addressed to a particular situation in Judaea, in face of a firmly held and violently defended doctrine that for Jews of Judaea to pay tribute to a pagan overlord was to take from God the things that were his and hand them over to another. That situation, of course, did not exist in Rome. But in generalizing the dominical precept Paul has in mind the situation which did exist in Rome and in other cities throughout the empire.[38]

Eight years previously, it appears, the introduction of Christianity into Rome had led to riots. About the same time, according to Luke, the arrival of Paul and his fellow-preachers in Thessalonica provoked the charge that they were the men who had subverted the whole world and kept on "acting against the decrees of Caesar" (Acts 17:6f.). The name of "Christian" had subversive associations in Rome and elsewhere: some at least remembered that the founder of the movement had been executed by sentence of a Roman judge on a charge of sedition.[39] It was most important that Christians in the imperial capital should recognize their responsibility not to give any support by their way of life to this widespread imputation of disloyalty, but rather refute it by punctilious obedience to the authorities and payment of all lawful dues. Thus far the representatives of imperial law had, in Paul's experience, shown at least a benevolent neutrality to the prosecution of his mission.[40] The time was to come, and that in Rome itself, when this would no longer be so. When Caesar demanded the allegiance which belonged to God, his demand had to be refused. But Caesar had not yet done so, and Paul does not mention this eventuality. His approach to the matter is relevant to the situation of Roman Christians at the time and in the circumstances of their receiving the letter.[41]

Equally relevant to the Roman situation is the practical section in Romans 14:1–15:7 in which Paul deals with the relation between the "strong" and the "weak" in the Christian fellowship—the "weak" being those who scrupulously abstained from certain kinds of food and paid religious respect to certain holy days, while the "strong" (like Paul himself) had a more robust conscience with regard to such externalities.

There is a degree of resemblance between what Paul says here and what he says to the Corinthian church on the issue of eating or avoiding the flesh of animals offered in sacrifice to a pagan deity (1 Corinthians 8:1-13; 10:14-30). But in this section of the letter to the Romans there is no direct word about eating *eidōlothyta* (an issue bound to be acute in a mainly Gentile church like that of Corinth). The distinction here is rather between the believer who can, with a good conscience, eat food of any kind and treat all days alike, and the believer whose conscience forbids the eating of any but vegetable food and the doing of ordinary work (however normally legitimate) on a holy day. The principle of mutual considerateness which Paul inculcates in this section would, of course, cover the issue of *eidōlothyta*, but if Paul has one particular situation in

mind here, it is a situation in which Jewish and Gentile Christians have
to live together in fellowship. It was to such a situation, indeed, that the
Jerusalem decree was addressed a few years before, but Paul takes a
different line from the decree. The decree urged abstention from *eidōlothyta* and flesh from which the blood had not been completely
drained;[42] Paul urges his readers to consider one another.

It was not simply that Jewish Christians continued to confine
themselves to kosher food and to observe the sabbath and other holy
days, while Gentile Christians practiced complete liberty in both respects. The situation was probably more complex. Many Jewish Christians had become more or less emancipated from legal obligations in
religion, even if few were so totally emancipated as Paul was. On the
other hand, some Gentiles were more than willing to judaize, to take over
the Jewish food restrictions and Jewish regard for holy days, even if they
stopped short at circumcision.[43] We have examples of this tendency to
judaize in our own day, even if it is not expressly called judaizing; and
in the apostolic age we have only to think of Paul's Gentile converts in
Galatia, who were not only beginning to keep the Jewish sacred calendar
but even to accept circumcision.

Among the house-churches of Rome, then, we should probably
envisage a broad and continuous spectrum of varieties in thought and
practice between the firm Jewish retention of the ancestral customs and
Gentile remoteness from these customs, with some Jewish Christians,
indeed, found on the liberal side of the halfway mark between the two
extremes and some Gentile Christians on the "legalist" side.[44] Variety of
this kind can very easily promote a spirit of division, and Paul wished
to safeguard the Roman Christians against this, encouraging them rather
to regard the variety as an occasion for charity, forbearance and understanding.

Instead of laying down rules which would restrict Christian freedom, Paul makes it plain that, religiously speaking, one kind of food is
no worse than another, one day no better than another. It is human beings
that matter, not food or the calendar. Christian charity, on the one hand,
will impose no limitations on another's freedom; Christian charity, on
the other hand, will not force liberty on the conscience of someone who
is not yet ready for it. The scrupulous Christian must not criticize his
more emancipated brother or sister; the emancipated must not look
down on the over-scrupulous. The only limitation that can properly be
imposed on Christian liberty is that imposed by Christian charity, and it
can only be self-imposed. No Christian was more thoroughly emancipated than Paul, but none was readier to limit his own liberty in the
interests of his fellow-Christians.[45] In such matters as abstention from

food or observance of days he conformed to the company in which he found himself: in themselves they were matters of utter indifference.[46] This example he recommends to others. For the rest, they should do what they believe to be right without forcing their convictions on others or thinking the worse of others if they do not see eye to eye with them.

2. Spain

If Spain plays a less crucial role in the letter than either Rome or Jerusalem does, it is no merely peripheral one. Not only did Paul's plan to visit Spain provide him with an opportunity to gratify his long-cherished desire to see Rome, but it enabled him to invite the Roman Christians' collaboration in the next phase of his apostolic enterprise. It meant, moreover, that he could tell the Roman Christians of his plan to visit them without giving them cause to suspect that he was coming to put down his roots among them or assert apostolic authority over them. At the same time, by assuring them of his ardent longing to make their acquaintance he makes it plain that he does not simply see in their city a convenient stopping-off place on his way to Spain. Rome probably lay no less close to his heart at this time than Spain did.[47]

But why should he think of evangelizing Spain? If he judged his task in the Aegean world to be complete and wished to adhere to his policy of confining his ministry to virgin soil, his range of choice in the Mediterranean world, as has been said, was limited. By A.D. 57 the gospel had certainly been carried to Alexandria and Cyrene, if not farther west along the African coast. The close association between proconsular Asia and Gallia Narbonensis would suggest that the evangelization of the former territory in A.D. 52-55 led quickly to the evangelization of the latter. But Spain, for long the chief bastion of Roman power in the west, beckoned Paul as his next mission-field.

We have no idea what contact, if any, Paul may have had with people from Spain who could have told him something of conditions in that land. Of this we may be sure: Paul could not hope to use the synagogue here as a base of operations as he had done in the eastern Mediterranean, or to find his first converts in "God-fearing" Gentiles as he had done elsewhere.[48] Moreover, the language which had served him so well in his ministry hitherto, and served him equally well in his present communication with Rome, would not be adequate for the evangelizing of Spain. Spain was a Latin-speaking area. Paul was probably not entirely ignorant of Latin, but he would require to speak it fluently if he was to do effective work in Spain. It was perhaps in order to spend some time in a Latin-speaking environment that he had recently paid a visit to Illyricum. We should not, in fact, have known about his visit to Illyricum but for his mentioning it in Romans 15:19 as the westernmost limit of his apostolic activity thus far.

If Illyricum provided him with some linguistic preparation, there were other kinds of preparation required for such an enterprise as he contemplated in Spain. In earlier days the church of Syrian Antioch had provided Paul and Barnabas with a base for the evangelization of Cyprus and South Galatia. Later, when Christianity had been established in Corinth and Ephesus, these two cities provided Paul with bases for the evangelization respectively of the provinces of Achaia and Asia. But where would he find a base for the evangelization of Spain if not in Rome? He does not in so many words ask the Roman Christians to provide him with such a base, but he sets the situation before them in such a way that they would see his need of one and could, if they were so minded, spontaneously offer to supply what was needed. "I hope to see you in passing as I go to Spain," he says, "and to be sped on my journey there by you, when first I have enjoyed your company for a little" (Romans 15:24). Here certainly is one facet of his purpose in writing—not, of course, the only one. What the sequel was—whether or not he did go to Spain, and whether or not the Roman church did provide him with a base—is quite unclear, and is in any case irrelevant to our investigation of the purpose of the letter.

3. Jerusalem

Towards the end of his personal remarks in Romans 15, Paul tells the Roman Christians that, before he can come to their city and spend some time with them on his way to Spain, he must for the present go to Jerusalem "with aid for the saints" (Romans 15:25). This is a reference to his involvement in the Jerusalem relief fund, which we know from his Corinthian correspondence to have been very much on his mind for some time back.[49]

One obvious reason for mentioning the relief fund to the Roman Christians was to explain why he could not set out for Rome immediately: this business of delivering the collected money to Jerusalem must be completed first. Therefore he could not give them even an approximate date for his arrival in Rome—as things turned out, it was just as well that he did not try to give them one! Even if nothing untoward happened, there was no way of knowing how long the business would take. According to Luke's record, he hoped to be in Jerusalem in time for Pentecost (which in A.D. 57 fell on 28/29 May).[50]

But evidently Paul is not merely advising his friends in Rome that there may be some delay in his setting out to see them: he tries, tactfully, to involve them in his Jerusalem enterprise. He does not, either expressly or by implication, invite them to contribute to the fund. It had been raised among the churches of Paul's own planting, in which the Roman church had no place. Indeed, just because the Roman Christians were not involved in the fund in this sense, Paul could tell them about it in a more relaxed manner than was possible in writing to people whom he wished to make a generous contribution. The Gentile churches, he says, are debtors to Jerusalem in respect of spiritual blessings; it is but fitting that they should acknowledge that debt by imparting to Jerusalem such blessings as they could impart—material blessings, monetary gifts.

It is plain from his Galatian and Corinthian letters that Paul was greatly concerned to preserve his churches' independence of Jerusalem. Yet here he himself acknowledges their dependence on Jerusalem for the gospel itself. Indeed, we learn more here than anywhere else of Paul's real attitude to Jerusalem. Throughout his letters there is an ambivalence in his relation to the Jerusalem church and its leaders: on the one hand, they must not be allowed to dictate to his churches or himself; on the other, he must at all costs prevent his apostolic ministry and the Gentile mission from having the ties of fellowship with Jerusalem severed. This appears clearly enough in Galatians: in the very context in which he asserts his independence of Jerusalem he tells how he went up to Jerusalem on one occasion and laid his gospel before the leaders of the church there.[51] Happily, they appear to have recognized the validity of Paul's gospel and his authority to communicate it to the Gentiles. What if they had withheld such recognition? Paul was under orders higher than theirs, but his work would be largely frustrated if he had to carry it on in isolation from Jerusalem. Luke does not always tell his readers why Paul's apostolic ministry was punctuated by the successive visits to Jerusalem which he records (Acts 9:26; 11:30; 15:2; 18:22; 19:21), but in the light of Paul's letters we can see why he was so careful to maintain contact with Jerusalem and we can accept Luke's account in this regard as being true to the facts.[52]

The place which Jerusalem occupied in Paul's thinking[53] is emphasized by his statement in Romans 15:19 about the range of his apostolic activity to the time of writing: "from Jerusalem and as far round as Illyricum I have fully preached the gospel of Christ." It is evident from Acts and from Paul's own testimony that it was not in Jerusalem that he first preached the gospel. Why then does he give Jerusalem pride of place in this statement? Perhaps because Jerusalem is the place where, by divine decree, the preaching of the gospel is initiated:

out of Zion shall go forth the law, and the word of the LORD from Jerusalem (Isaiah 2:3).

This primacy of Jerusalem is recognized in the Lukan tradition—for example, in the direction "beginning from Jerusalem" in the risen Lord's charge to his disciples (Luke 24:47; cf. Acts 1:8). Paul appears to acknowledge this primacy not only in Romans 15:19 but elsewhere in his letters. He had, in fact, a greater regard for the Jerusalem church and its leaders than they evidently had for him, and was indeed, as the late Arnold Ehrhardt put it, "one of the greatest assets for the Jerusalem church" because, either by his personal action or under his influence, versions of the gospel which were defective by the standards of Jerusalem were brought into conformity with the line maintained in common by Paul and the leaders of the mother-church.[54] And it is a matter of plain history as well as a "theological presupposition" that, from the inception of the church until at least A.D. 60, "Christendom" (in the words of Henry Chadwick) "has a geographical center and this is Jerusalem. Gentile Christians might be free from Judaism; they remained debtors to Zion."[55]

The agreement on the demarcation of missionary zones, according to which Peter and his Jerusalem colleagues would concentrate on the evangelization of Jews and Paul and Barnabas on the evangelization of Gentiles (Gal. 2:7-9), was not free from ambiguities, and could have been interpreted diversely in good faith on both sides. And even a cursory reading of Paul's letters reveals the tension between his resolve to maintain the fullest fellowship between the churches of his Gentile mission-field and the church of Jerusalem, and his resolve to maintain their independence of control by that church and its leaders. There appears to have been a sustained campaign waged by "trouble-makers" (as Paul calls them) who made it their business to infiltrate his churches and bring them into subjection to the Jerusalem leadership and the "super-apostles" (Gal. 1:7; 2:4; 2 Cor. 11:4-21; Phil. 3:2f.).

Jerusalem also played a central part in Paul's understanding of the consummation of God's purpose in the world. He himself, as apostle to the Gentiles, had a key place in that purpose as he understood it—not only directly, as the progress of the gospel prospered under his hand among the Gentiles, but also indirectly, when (as he hoped) the large-scale participation of Gentiles in the blessings of the gospel would stimulate the Jewish people to jealousy and move them to claim their own proper share in those blessings. This development would mark the climax of gospel witness in the world and precipitate the parousia. This seems to be the point of Paul's quotation of Isaiah 59:20f. in this context (Rom. 11:26f.). He quotes it in the form: "The Deliverer will come from

Zion, he will banish ungodliness from Jacob." The Hebrew text says "to Zion"; the Septuagint version says "for Zion's sake." Paul has apparently derived "from Zion" from Psalm 14:7 / /53:6, "O that salvation for Israel would come out of Zion!" The implication is that the climax of salvation is closely associated with Jerusalem. Not only did the gospel first go out into all the world from Jerusalem; Jerusalem (if we interpret Paul aright) would be the scene of its consummation. And Paul's own ministry, as he saw it, had a crucial role in speeding this consummation.[56]

No wonder, then, that Paul related his ministry closely to Jerusalem. This adds a further dimension of meaning to Paul's organizing of the Jerusalem relief fund and to his resolve to be personally present in Jerusalem with the messengers of the Gentile churches who were to hand it over. It was not only his response to the request of the Jerusalem leaders at an earlier date that he should "remember the poor" (Galatians 2:10); it was not only an acknowledgment on the part of the Gentile churches of their indebtedness to Jerusalem and a means of promoting a more binding fellowship of love between them and the church of Jerusalem. It was all that, but it was at the same time the outward and visible sign of Paul's achievement thus far, the occasion of his rendering to the Lord who commissioned him an account of his discharge of that commission. It was also, in his eyes, a fulfillment of prophecy.

One of the prophets of Israel had foreseen the day when "the wealth of nations" would come to Jerusalem, when foreigners would "bring gold and frankincense and proclaim the praise of the LORD." "They shall come up with acceptance on my altar," said the God of Israel, "and I will glorify my glorious name" (Isaiah 60:5-7). A careful study of Romans 15 leads to the conclusion that Paul sees this promise being fulfilled in the impending visit of Gentile believers to Jerusalem, carrying their churches' gifts and prepared to join their fellow-believers of Jerusalem in thanksgiving to God. It was this vision that prompted his earnest prayer that "the offering of the Gentiles might be acceptable, being sanctified by the Holy Spirit" (Romans 15:16). This language echoes that of Isaiah 66:20, where the brethren of the Jerusalemites will be brought "from all the nations as an offering to the LORD." In the Old Testament context the "brethren" in question are Jews of the dispersion; for Paul they are fellow-members of that extended family which embraces believing Gentiles and believing Jews—together children of Abraham.

The Gentile Christians brought their monetary offering, but they themselves constituted Paul's living offering, the fruit of his own "priestly service." Paul would not have thought of presenting this offering anywhere other than in Jerusalem. Hence his decision to accompany the Gentile delegates as they traveled there to hand over their churches' gifts to the mother-church. He may have had it in mind to render an account of his stewardship thus far and to rededicate himself for the next phase of his ministry in those very temple precincts where, more than twenty years before, the Lord had appeared to him and confirmed his commission to preach to the Gentiles (Acts 22:17-21).[57] His Gentile companions could not accompany him into the temple, but there in spirit he could discharge his *hierourgia* and present as a "pure offering" the faith of his converts through which the name of the God of Israel was now "great among the Gentiles" (Malachi 1:11).

He may indeed have hoped that on a later occasion, when his contemplated evangelization of Spain was completed, he might pay a further visit to Jerusalem with a fresh offering of Gentiles from "the limit of the west"[58] and render a further, perhaps the final, account of his stewardship.[59]

But at the moment his visit to Jerusalem with the fruit of his Aegean ministry had to be paid, and he could not foresee how it would turn out. He lets his Roman readers fully into his motives for paying the visit, and shares with them his misgivings about the outcome. That the "unbelievers in Judaea" would stir up trouble for him as on previous occasions was only to be expected; but would the gift-bearing Greeks *(Danaos et dona ferentes)*[60] be "acceptable to the saints" (Romans 15:31)? Paul could not feel sure on this score, and he invites the Roman Christians to join him in earnest prayer that his hopes and plans would be fulfilled. If things turned out otherwise, then all the care which had gone into the organization of the fund, all the high hopes which Paul cherished for the forging of a firmer bond of affection between the mother-church and the Gentile mission, would be frustrated. Whether or not the leaders of the Jerusalem church did in fact accept the gifts in the spirit in which they were brought is disputed, but it does not affect our understanding of Romans.[61] One thing is clear: Paul was anxious that they should so accept them, and he seeks the prayers of the Roman Christians to this end.

Did he seek more than their prayers? Their prayers were all that he explicitly asked for, but did he hope that they would read between the lines and do even more than he asked?

We may certainly dismiss the view that the letter is addressed only ostensibly to Rome but is essentially directed to the Jerusalem church— that Paul throughout the letter really develops the argument which he hoped would be effective in Jerusalem.[62] There is nothing in the letter to suggest that its contents are not primarily intended for Roman consumption; we have argued indeed that its contents are as a whole suited to the

Roman situation, as they are for the most part unsuited to the Jerusalem situation.

But might Paul be hinting that the Roman Christians could do something to pave the way for a favorable reception in Jerusalem?[63] We have no direct information on such contact as may have existed at this date between the Christians of Rome and the church of Jerusalem, but it would be surprising if there were no communication between them. There would, however, be no time for the Roman Christians to get in touch with Jerusalem between their receiving this letter and Paul's arrival in Jerusalem. Paul was evidently on the point of setting out for Jerusalem when he sent the letter ("I am on my way,"[64] he says in Romans 15:25). If the year was A.D. 57, he left Philippi about 15 April—"after the days of Unleavened Bread" (Acts 20:6)—and reached Caesarea with his companions about 14 May. Even if Phoebe left Cenchreae a month before Paul set out for Jerusalem (mid-March was the earliest date for the resumption of sailing after winter),[65] she would not have reached Rome much earlier than mid-April, and there was no way that messengers from Rome could reach Judaea before Paul did, even if they had set out as soon as the letter was received.[66]

But Paul certainly did wish to involve the Roman Christians as closely as possible with his Jerusalem enterprise, and if the Jerusalem leaders could be given to understand (tactfully) that Rome was being kept in the picture, this might have influenced their reception of Paul and his Gentile friends.

III. CONCLUSION

In short, not only in his impending visit to Jerusalem to discharge the relief fund and not only in his subsequent Spanish project, but in all the aspects of his apostleship Paul was eager to involve the Roman Christians as his partners, and to involve them as a united body. He did not know how much longer time he had to devote to the evangelization of the Gentile world. He may have believed himself to be immortal till his work was done (he never explicitly says so), but for one so constantly exposed to the risk of death it would have been irresponsible to make no provision against the time when death or some other hazard would prevent him from continuing his work. He had his younger associates, we know—men like Timothy and Titus—who could bear the torch after his departure. But if he could associate with his world vision a whole community like the Roman church, the unfinished task might be accomplished the sooner. The influence of that church sprang not only from the centrality of the imperial capital and its unrivaled means of communication with distant regions, but even more (he had reason to believe) from the outstanding faith and spiritual maturity of which the Roman Christians gave evidence. An individual might suffer death or imprisonment, but a church would go on living. Therefore in all the parts of his letter to the Romans he instructs them, he exhorts them, he shares with them his own concerns and ambitions in the hope that they may make these their own. These hopes and ambitions embraced not only the advance of the Gentile mission but also the ingathering of Israel which, he was persuaded, would follow the completion of the Gentile mission. Because of its history and composition, the church of Rome was uniquely fitted for this ministry. That its members might see the vision and respond to it Paul sent them this letter.

Did the Roman Christians rise to the occasion? The witness of history is that they did. From now on, and especially after A.D. 70, Christendom, which could hitherto be represented by a circle with its center at Jerusalem, became rather (in Henry Chadwick's figure) an ellipse with two foci—Jerusalem and Rome.[67] The influential part played henceforth by the Christians of Rome in the life of the ecumenical church is due not so much to their city's imperial status as to the encouragement given them by Paul in this letter.[68]

7. Paul and "the Powers That Be"

I. "THE POWERS THAT BE"

The expression "the powers that be" is found at the end of Romans 13:1 in older English versions of the Bible: "the powers that be," says Paul, "are ordained of God." It comes near the beginning of a self-contained paragraph, which may be translated freely as follows:

> Let every person submit to the superior authorities. There is no authority that is not derived from God; the established authorities have been appointed by God. Therefore, whoever opposes constituted authority resists the ordinance of God, and those who resist will bring judgment on themselves. It is not when people are engaged in a good activity but in a bad one that they have any need to fear the magistrates. Do you wish to live free from the fear of whoever is in authority? Do what is good, and you will earn his commendation. He is God's servant for your good. But if you do what is bad, you may well be afraid; it is not for nothing that he bears the sword. He is God's servant, the agent of divine retribution in punishing the evildoer. Therefore you must submit, not only because he is the agent of retribution but also as a matter of conscience. This, too, is why you should pay taxes; your taxes go to the maintenance of the authorities who are God's ministers as they attend to this very business. Therefore, pay everyone his due: pay taxes to the tax-collector and duty to the customs officer; pay reverence and honor to those who are entitled to receive your reverence and honor (Romans 13:1-7).

A lecture delivered in the John Rylands University Library, Manchester, on Wednesday, 7 December 1983, and published in *BJRL* 66.2 (1984), pp. 78-96.

II. A QUESTION OF AUTHENTICITY

So far as textual evidence is concerned, the authenticity of this paragraph is unquestionable. It has been argued indeed that it may have been absent from Marcion's edition of the New Testament.[1] This is not proved, and even if it were true, the absence of a passage from Marcion's edition is no argument against its genuineness. Yet several scholars have presented a case for regarding the paragraph as a non-Pauline interpolation.[2]

One of the most thorough statements of this case was put forward in 1965 by Professor James Kallas.[3] Pointing out that there is some textual doubt about other passages towards the end of Romans, he says that nowhere else does Paul discuss the state or the Christians' relation to it. More specifically, the paragraph, he says, is not only self-contained but interrupts the context, which runs on more smoothly without it. But above all, he argues, it contradicts basic Pauline ideas and forms of expression. It assumes the indefinite continuance of the present order which, according to Romans 13:11f., is on the point of disappearing. The "authorities" envisaged here are Roman rulers, whereas everywhere else in Paul the word relates to cosmic powers—"the world-rulers of this darkness," as they are called in Ephesians 6:12. Far from being appointed by God, these authorities are controlled by "the god of this age" (2 Corinthians 4:4). It is because it is subject to this demonic control that this age is called "the present evil age" (Galatians 1:4). In such an age the people of God are naturally under attack by the authorities instead of enjoying their protection.

In Romans 13:1-7, on the other hand, what Professor Kallas calls the "Pharisaic" view of retribution is expressed:[4] it is evildoers who are punished by the state, in discharge of its commission from God, while the good have nothing to fear. He compares 1 Peter 3:13 ("who is there to harm you if you are zealous for what is right?") and asks if the section of 1 Peter where these words appear forms the earliest commentary on Romans 13:1-7.

Nowhere else, it is further argued, does Paul in his letters suggest that the state (or its representatives) is worthy of respect from Christians. Indeed, we are assured, there is one passage where the opposite attitude is expressed. In 1 Corinthians 6:4, where Paul deprecates the spectacle of Christians washing their dirty linen in public by prosecuting one another before pagan judges, he asks his readers why they lay their trivial disputes "before those who are least esteemed by the church."[5] But this, I think, implies no disparagement of the custodians of civil law and order as such; what is meant is that pagan judges have no status whatsoever in the church, whereas a Christian who suffers an injury, real or imagined, at the hands of a fellow-Christian should (if he has not enough of the spirit of Christ to accept the injury uncomplainingly) have the matter adjudicated within the Christian fellowship.

Professor Kallas's arguments are of varying weight. He is right, of course, in pointing out that there is textual doubt about some other passages in the closing chapters of Romans. There is, for example, manuscript evidence for placing the concluding doxology at the end of chapter 14, chapter 15 and chapter 16; and a closing benediction appears at Romans 15:33; 16:20 and 16:24.[6] But the textual doubt is raised in these places by the manuscript evidence itself: no such doubt is raised by the evidence for Romans 13:1-7.

If Paul nowhere else discusses the state or the Christian's relation to it, that may simply be because in his other surviving letters he had no occasion to do so. He discusses the Eucharist in 1 Corinthians 10:16-21 and 11:20-34 only because reports from Corinth gave him occasion to discuss it: no one would base an argument on the textual genuineness of these two passages on the fact that "nowhere else in any of his epistles" does Paul discuss this subject. The subject of the Christian's relation to the civil authorities must have been one of practical concern in Paul's churches: if there is any cause for surprise, it is not that Paul discusses it once only but that he does not discuss it elsewhere.

That the paragraph is self-contained is obvious: it is not so obvious that it interrupts the flow of the argument. There is not the same kind of sustained argument in Romans 12–15 that we have in the first eight chapters of the letter. In these later chapters we find rather a sequence of ethical injunctions relating to Christian life within and without the believing community. Smooth transitions are not so characteristic of Paul's style that there is any need for surprise at an abrupt change of subject here. Earlier in the same letter there is another self-contained section—the discussion of Israel's place in the divine purpose in Romans 9–11. Without these three chapters, the beginning of chapter 12 would follow on quite naturally from the end of chapter 8; but this has not served as a basis for questioning the authenticity of Romans 9–11.

In fact, a discussion of the Christian's relation to the state is introduced quite appropriately at this point in the letter. The preceding paragraph deals with the Christian's attitude to non-Christians, not least to those who try to injure them, and contains the injunction: "If possible, so far as it depends upon you, live peaceably with all" (Romans 12:18). As a general injunction this would be unexceptionable; but the question might readily arise of living peaceably with the representatives of the state. Their demands on the Christian, as on any other subject, were undoubtedly backed by power; were they also backed by authority—authority of a kind which a Christian ought to recognize?

"Never avenge yourselves," Paul goes on in the preceding paragraph, "but leave it to the wrath of God; for it is written, 'Vengeance is mine, I will repay, says the Lord'" (Romans 12:19).[7] If evil is done, there is a principle of divine retribution at work in the universe, but Christians are ministers of God's grace, not agents of retribution. There are others whom God has entrusted with this responsibility: it is the civil magistrate who is his duly appointed agent of retribution in punishing the evildoer. The language in which the magistrate's province is described in Romans 13:4 echoes the language of Romans 12:19. The word for "wrath" or "retribution" (Gk. ὀργή) is common to both texts, and the term "vengeance" (Gk. ἐκδίκησις) in the former is caught up by "avenger" (Gk. ἔκδικος) in the latter.

Again, the aorist imperative of the verb "pay" (Gk. ἀπόδοτε) in Romans 13:7—"pay everyone his due"—echoes the present participle of the same verb (ἀποδιδόντες) in Romans 12:17, "pay no one back evil for evil." And the idea of dues or debts is caught up in the clause immediately following the controverted paragraph: "Let the only debt you owe be the debt of love" (Romans 13:8). When rates and taxes have been paid, those particular debts are discharged in full; but the debt of love is continuous: no amount of loving one another can relieve the Christian of the obligation to go on paying this debt. It can be argued, then, that the controverted paragraph has links in thought both with what goes before it and with what comes after; it is, in fact, integral to its paraenetic context.

Professor Kallas's most serious argument against the authenticity of the paragraph, however, is its alleged contradiction of basic Pauline ideas and forms of expression. The word rendered "authorities" (Gk. ἐξουσίαι), it is said, relates everywhere else in Paul to cosmic powers, evil powers at that.

The noun itself is perfectly common and nontechnical, used in the ordinary sense of authority. But in the plural it is used, both in Pauline Greek and in current English, of the bearers of authority—"the authorities," as we say. And it is probably true that, wherever else in Paul's writings the plural is used, it is cosmic powers that are meant. But if Paul ever had occasion to mention earthly authorities, the same plural form (ἐξουσίαι) was the most natural term for him to use. It is with reference to earthly authorities that the plural is used in Romans 13:1-7, but that is no argument against the Pauline authorship of the paragraph.

Does the paragraph envisage the indefinite continuance of the present world order? If it does, then indeed it contradicts the sense of a later passage in the same chapter: "Recognize what hour it is: it is high time now for you to wake up from sleep. Our salvation is nearer to us now than when we first believed; the night is far spent, the day is at hand" (Romans 13:11f.). The point of this eschatological urgency is that Christians must live as Christians should: this is no time to idle or engage in unworthy practices. Elsewhere Paul sounds the same note of urgency by way of warning his converts in Corinth not to become excessively involved in earthly attachments, whether domestic or mercantile, but to maintain the measure of detachment proper to those who are heirs of the new and impending age (1 Corinthians 7:29-31).

But I can find nothing in Romans 13:1-7 inconsistent with this outlook. Paul expected the new age, the kingdom of Christ, to break in quite soon, but he made no attempt to say how soon. Until the day dawned, the civil authorities occupied their divinely appointed sphere of power, and should therefore receive the respect and obedience due to them.

III. A NON-PAULINE STRATUM?

To what extent the powers that be, who are ordained by God, could also be regarded as controlled by cosmic powers is a question to which we shall return. First, however, mention must be made of a further argument against the authenticity of Romans 13:1-7 that has been presented recently. In a monograph entitled *Authority in Paul and Peter*, Professor Winsome Munro identifies a "pastoral stratum" in the Pauline letters (excluding the Pastorals) and 1 Peter. This stratum she calls "pastoral" because it has the same origin as the Pastoral Letters; it is characterized by the note of subjection to authority. "The subjection material of the New Testament," she says, "does not belong with the more primitive, eschatological strata of tradition, but . . . was introduced later, it is suggested in the first half of the second century."[8]

This "subjection material" contains, first and foremost, the sections commonly called the household codes, in which the mutual responsibilities of husbands and wives, parents and children, masters and slaves are laid down. These codes prescribe the duty of subjection for wives to their husbands, children to their parents, slaves to their masters. The New Testament household code appears to be the christianization of a Stoic literary form. When Paul speaks spontaneously the subjection he enjoins is reciprocal; thus the household code in Ephesians 5:22–6:9 is introduced by his own direction: "Be subject to one another out of reverence for Christ." This is in line with his words elsewhere: "outdo one another in showing honor" (Romans 12:10); "in humility count others better than yourselves" (Philippians 2:3). But this does not imply that the household codes were later additions to the Pauline letters in which they occur: they seem to have circulated among the Gentile churches as elements in a primitive Christian catechesis, and like other such elements were incorporated from the first in the letters in which they appear.

To the allegedly later "pastoral stratum" Professor Munro assigns Romans 13:1-7, in which certainly the note of subjection is struck—subjection to the "higher authorities." She is not impressed by Kallas's argument that the paragraph is isolated from the context in which it is now placed: she recognizes its links both with what precedes and with what follows. But these links lead her to assign part of what precedes and what follows to the "pastoral stratum"—specifically, Romans 12:9-11a, 12c-21, and 13:8-10. This really weakens her case against the genuineness of Romans 13:1-7. But, leaving her treatment of the adjacent passages aside, we note her argument that the subjection to the ruling powers inculcated in the paragraph under discussion is in line with the attitude to the Roman state found in Acts, but inconsistent with Paul's own teaching, as expressed in 1 Corinthians 2:8, where the "rulers of this age" are hostile to the cause of God rather than ordained by him.[9]

While scholars like Professor Kallas and Professor Munro are led to their conclusions by literary-critical reasoning, it must be acknowledged that some people welcome such conclusions on other grounds. The call for submission to the powers that be has often been made the basis for an insistence that Christians are bound to render uncritical obedience to the existing government in all situations. Those who find this insistence unacceptable are sometimes relieved to be told that Romans 13:1-7 is probably not the work of Paul. If it is not, then (they feel) they need pay no further attention to the passage or to the corollaries drawn from it. They may be told that, whether it is by Paul or not, it is still canonical scripture; but that has not the same weight with them as Pauline authorship has.

The exegete's task is to ascertain the meaning which the text had in its historical setting, whoever the author might be. The task of discovering what guidance, if any, can be derived from the text for the practical life of readers today is not to be overlooked, but it is not the task of exegesis and should not be allowed to influence exegesis.

Professor Munro speaks of some friends of hers who found themselves in prison in her native South Africa with nothing to read but the Bible, "one of whom wanted to know how Paul the prisoner could have written Rom 13:1-7."[10] She does not say if her friend was relieved to learn that, in Professor Munro's judgment, it was not Paul who wrote those verses. Paul was not a prisoner when he sent this letter to the Christians in Rome, but when, a few years later, he found himself a prisoner in Rome, it was because he had sufficient respect for the superior authorities to appeal to Caesar—to submit to the judgment of the supreme tribunal of the Roman Empire. This, at least, is the account given in Acts; how far it should be given a hearing in the discussion of Romans 13:1-7 will be considered anon.

IV. OTHER PAULINE REFERENCES

But first it is proper to consider other passages in the Pauline writings which may have a bearing on our subject. According to Professor Munro and others, the teaching of Romans 13:1-7 is inconsistent with 1 Corinthians 2:6-8, where "the rulers of this age" are said to be on their way out because, through ignorance of God's eternal wisdom, they "crucified the Lord of glory." But Paul is not referring there to such minor characters as Caiaphas the high priest and Pontius Pilate the Roman prefect, who share the responsibility for Jesus' death in the passion narratives of the Gospels; he is referring to cosmic powers, to whom Caiaphas and Pilate were merely instruments for the execution of their plan to thwart the divine purpose. In fact, they overreached themselves; it was their own plan that was thwarted. In vivid words in Colossians 2:15 Paul describes how Jesus on the cross disarmed them, turning the cross (so to speak) into his triumphal car before which they were driven as his vanquished foes. They maintain their malignant opposition to the cause of God, those "world-rulers of this darkness," but they have no more power over the followers of Christ, who are sharers in his victory; to them they are now "weak and beggarly elemental forces" (Galatians 4:9).

Granted, however, that "the rulers of this age" in 1 Corinthians 2:6-8 are cosmic powers, it is implied that they use human authorities as their instruments. Is not this as true of the highest human authorities, such as the Roman emperor, as it is of minor functionaries like Caiaphas and Pilate?

The idea that the nations of the world have angelic rulers, who operate above and behind their earthly rulers, goes far back in Hebrew thought. Its earliest attestation probably comes in the "Song of Moses" (Deuteronomy 32:8):

> When the Most High gave the nations their inheritance,
>   when he separated the children of men,

he fixed the bounds of the peoples
according to the number of the sons of God.[11]

That the "sons of God" are angels is the interpretation of the Septuagint. In early Hebrew thought they are members of the "council of Yahweh," the "gods" among whom, according to Psalm 82, the Most High executes judgment when he "stands in the heavenly court." If he finds injustice on earth, that is ultimately their responsibility; unless they mend their ways, they will "die like men, and fall like any prince."[12]

This idea was further developed in apocalyptic literature. In the book of Daniel, the first and chief of the Jewish apocalypses, the angel Gabriel comes from heaven to acquaint Daniel with what is destined to happen to his nation (it is already written in the heavenly book), but he is held up for three weeks by the "prince of Persia" and has to thank the archangel Michael for help in getting away from him. On his way back from delivering his message to Daniel he expects to have an encounter with the "prince of Greece" also (Daniel 10:13, 20). These "princes," who are powerful enough to impede an angel of the divine presence in the execution of his commission, are plainly not the human rulers of the empires mentioned; they are superior angel-princes. Israel is in the fortunate position of having Michael as her angel-prince; he ensures her final victory (Daniel 12:1).

When, however, the present age gives way to the coming age, world sovereignty will pass to "the saints of the Most High" (Daniel 7:18, 22, 28). Exegetes today are divided on the identity of those "saints": it is debated whether they are holy angels or human beings.[13] But it is clear how Paul understood them: when he reminds the Corinthian Christians that "the saints will judge the world," it is before his readers that he holds out this prospect. "Do you not know," he goes on, "that we are to judge *angels*?" (1 Corinthians 6:2f.). If such judicial authority is to be exercised by them in the age to come, surely they are able here and now to adjudicate on their own internal disputes.

From this it appears that Paul did accept the apocalyptic outlook. Does it not follow, then, that in his eyes the Roman emperor and other rulers were but the instruments of discredited angel-princes, and therefore not entitled to the obedience of Christians, who were heirs of the age to come? Not necessarily. In the visions of the book of Daniel angel-princes have their part to play, but elsewhere in the book it is God who bestows imperial authority directly on human rulers, and they are directly responsible to God for the way they govern. It is "the God of heaven" who has given Nebuchadnezzar the kingdom, the power and the glory, and calls him to account for his actions, teaching him through painful experiences that "the Most High God rules the kingdom of men and gives it to whom he will" (Daniel 4:17, 25, 32). The affirmation of Romans 13:1, that "the established authorities have been appointed by God," is completely in agreement with this, and can well be the language of Paul, who in that case follows this apocalyptic line here rather than that which envisages the Gentile powers as controlled by angel-princes.

V. HUMAN RULERS OR ANGELIC POWERS?

It has been assumed thus far that the authorities of Romans 13:1-7 are human authorities. But attempts have been made to interpret them as angelic powers. Of all the arguments put forward for understanding them in this way the most influential have been those of Oscar Cullmann.[14] Starting from 1 Corinthians 2:8, where it is invisible world rulers who are ultimately responsible for the crucifixion of "the Lord of glory," Professor Cullmann concludes that in Romans 13:1 "it is by far the most natural thing to give to the plural ἐξουσίαι no other sense than that which it always has for Paul, that is, the meaning of 'angelic powers'."[15] True, the context makes it plain that Paul is referring to the state, but the "authorities" are the *"invisible angelic powers that stand behind the State government."*[16] Cullmann knows that in the second century this interpretation was maintained by some gnostic teachers and opposed by Irenaeus,[17] but he thinks that Irenaeus was mistaken in holding, with the gnostics, "a false dualistic conception of the angelic powers"[18] which would imply that the state, if controlled by them, was essentially evil instead of being, in the words of Romans 13:4, God's servant for the good of its subjects.

But Professor Cullmann's view is unacceptable. The authorities in Romans 13:1-7 are authorities to whom taxes are paid, and it is unnecessary to import angelic powers into the picture. If angelic powers did figure here, that would indeed be inconsistent with Paul's general emphasis. He nowhere suggests that Christians should be submissive to angelic powers, but rather that they should resist them (Ephesians 6:12-17), confident of victory over them through Christ, who defeated and disarmed them when they assailed him on the cross (Colossians 2:15).

True, the picture of Christ's victory over these principalities and powers has been seen by some interpreters as having a bearing on our present subject. Human beings, and especially Christians, it is said, are called upon to be subject to the cosmic powers because those powers, having been overcome by Christ, are now subject to him. But this christological perspective on the "superior authorities" of our text, although it can claim the distinguished sponsorship of Karl Barth,[19] consorts ill with the pragmatic and even pedestrian note which is struck in these seven verses. Moreover, the powers defeated by Christ have lost whatever potency they once had; even if they are supposed to have changed their character for the better, there is no point in submitting to them.

VI. EARLIEST COMMENTARIES ON ROMANS 13:1-7

The earliest commentaries on Romans 13:1-7 are found in some of the later New Testament letters—notably the Pastoral Epistles and 1 Peter[20]—and in them the "authorities" are clearly understood to be human rulers. In 1 Timothy 2:1f. it is directed that prayers and thanksgivings should be offered by Christians "for all human beings" and specifically "for kings and all who are in high positions, that we may lead a quiet and peaceful life." Rulers, wisely guided, are able to ensure tranquil lives for their Christian subjects; this indeed contributes, under God, to the working out of his saving purpose for the human race. In Titus 3:1 Titus is told to remind the naturally insubordinate Christians of Crete "to be submissive to principalities and powers, to be obedient, to be ready for any honest work." Here again the principalities and powers are human, not angelic. In 1 Peter 2:13f. the Roman imperial hierarchy is in view when the readers are urged to "be subject for the Lord's sake to every human institution, whether it be to the emperor as supreme, or to governors as sent by him to punish those who do wrong and to commend those who do right."[21] This exhortation, which closely follows the thought of Romans 13:1-7, is summed up in the fourfold admonition: "Honour all; love the brotherhood; fear God; honour the emperor" (1 Peter 2:17).

If we move into the postapostolic period, we find the same very positive attitude to the state expressed in the letter of Clement of Rome and, later, in the *Martyrdom of Polycarp*. Clement reproduces a prayer for the rulers who have received "glory and honour and power" over earthly things from God, the eternal king, "that they may administer with piety, in peace and gentleness, the authority given to them."[22] Polycarp is said to have told the proconsul of Asia that "we [Christians] have been taught to render honour, as is meet, to rulers and authorities appointed by God, if it does not harm us."[23] The saving clause, "if it does not harm us," implies that the only honor withheld by Christians from the secular authorities is that which would compromise their faith.

The New Testament does indeed present another attitude to the state. In Revelation 13:1-10 the Roman empire, instead of subserving the divine purpose, is energized by the devil and sets itself with deadly hostility against Christ and his people. This, to be sure, is the persecuting empire, with Caesar demanding not only the things which are rightfully his but those which belong to God also. The empire had not yet manifested itself as a persecuting power when the letter to the Romans was composed. But even after it had so manifested itself, the same positive attitude to it as appears in Romans 13:1-7 is maintained (as we have seen) in 1 Peter, Clement of Rome and the *Martyrdom of Polycarp*. The reaction seen in Revelation is by no means the only Christian response to the persecuting empire; there were Christians who persisted in regarding its persecuting activity as an aberration from its true nature and role.

VII. THE THESSALONIAN APOCALYPSE

There is an apocalyptic passage in the Pauline corpus where the Roman Empire probably figures: 2 Thessalonians 2:1-12.[24] Here, as in the Revelation, the rise of Antichrist is foreseen. But, whereas in Revelation Antichrist is embodied in the last Roman emperor, in 2 Thessalonians the Roman emperor imposes a temporary check on the emergence of Antichrist. In my opinion the attitude to the empire in 2 Thessalonians agrees rather well with that expressed in Romans 13:1-7; but this cannot be used as an argument for the genuineness of the latter passage because there are too many uncertainties about the interpretation of 2 Thessalonians. The Pauline authenticity of 2 Thessalonians is disputed, and it is by no means agreed that the restraining power which prevents the immediate revelation of the "mystery of lawlessness" is to be identified with the Roman Empire. Let me say briefly that I take 2 Thessalonians to be what it claims to be—the joint composition of Paul, Silvanus and Timothy (2 Thessalonians 1:1)—and that at one point in the apocalyptic passage Paul takes personal responsibility for what is said about the coming rise of Antichrist (2 Thessalonians 2:5). As for the identification of the restraining power with the forces of law and order, represented by the empire (or embodied in the emperor), holding the spirit of anarchy in check, this is at least as early as Tertullian. "What is this," Tertullian asks of the restraining power, "but the Roman state, whose removal, when it has been dispersed among ten kings, will bring on Antichrist?"[25] Chrysostom, two centuries later, reviews various interpretations but expresses his preference for that which identifies the restrainer with the

Roman empire: if Paul had meant something else, he says, "he would have said so plainly and not obscurely, . . . but because he meant the Roman empire, he naturally glanced at it, speaking covertly and darkly."[26] Tertullian wrote under the persecuting empire and Chrysostom under the Christian empire, but this distinction was irrelevant to their exegesis.

If this exegesis of 2 Thessalonians 2:6, 8 is correct (as I believe it to be), then the empire plays the same part there as it does in our text, acting for the encouragement of good and the coercion of evil.

It was, of course, conceivable that the imperial power itself might abandon its proper function in the divine economy and take on the role of Antichrist: something like this had happened in the principate of Gaius, with his insane insistence on being worshipped as a god. It was to happen again, in the view of many Christians, when later emperors claimed divine honors for political purposes, not (like Gaius) on personal grounds. Did Paul foresee this possibility? No doubt he did: he was no starry-eyed optimist. He would have agreed with Peter and his companions when they were called to account before the Sanhedrin for preaching the gospel in defiance of a court order to desist: "We must obey God rather than men" (Acts 5:32). When it came to a stark choice between the two, no Christian of the first three centuries would have answered differently—not even the alleged interpolator of Romans 13:1-7. But, so long as the secular authorities continued to discharge their divinely-appointed functions, they were to receive the obedience of Christians, not only because of the painful consequences of disobedience but (much more) because proper obedience to rulers was part of their obedience to God. They should render obedience to them and pay the taxes due to them "for conscience' sake." A moment's reflection will show that disobedience for conscience' sake on the part of people who are normally obedient and law-abiding should make a greater impression than disobedience on the part of people who are habitually unruly and against the government.

VIII. THE IMPERIAL CONTEXT

The direction to "pay everyone his due" probably echoes Jesus' concise reply when he was confronted with a question about the pious Judaean's obligation to the Roman state: "Is it lawful to pay tribute to Caesar?" When, at his request, a sample of the coinage acceptable for the paying of Caesar's tribute was produced, he pointed out that what bore Caesar's name and likeness was self-evidently Caesar's property. Therefore, he said, "give Caesar back[27] what belongs to him; give God what belongs to *him*" (Mark 12:17). The political context in which that question was put to Jesus was an exceedingly delicate one:[28] his questioners, it is suggested, hoped to impale him on one horn or the other of a dilemma. By his answer he not only avoided being trapped; he reminded his questioners of their higher duty. God was not impoverished if Caesar was paid back, literally, in his own coin; but it was all too easy to withhold from God the tribute which was of real importance—justice, mercy and faith.

For Paul, addressing Christians in Rome, no such dilemma presented itself. In Rome above all, in Caesar's own city, the propriety of paying him his dues could scarcely be questioned. Indeed, throughout Caesar's empire, it might be argued, those who benefited from the *pax Romana* could reasonably be called upon to share the cost of maintaining it.

Was it necessary, then, for Paul to direct the Christians of Rome to be subject to Caesar and his officers of state? For one thing, "one might say," with C. E. B. Cranfield, "that it would have been surprising, if in such a relatively full section of exhortation as [Romans] 12.1–15.13 he had nothing to say on a subject which must have been of great importance to Christians of the first century just as it is to Christians today."[29] In addition, there were probably some idealists in the Christian movement who argued that citizens of the kingdom of heaven had no responsibility to any earthly authority. And the spirit of insubordination was widespread. At Thessalonica in A.D. 50 Paul was accused of being one of those who went about subverting ordered society and urging defiance of imperial decrees.[30] The terms of the accusation suggest that such characters were known to be active in Jewish communities throughout the empire at that time. There was insurgency in Judaea itself in those years; there had recently been unrest in the Jewish communities of Alexandria and even of Rome.[31] Moreover, at this very time, in Rome itself, there were public and well-founded complaints against the system of taxation, which gave tax collectors too many opportunities for abuse. In A.D. 58 Nero proposed the abolition of all indirect taxation. His advisers, however, persuaded him that such a move would be against the interests of the state, but it was agreed that some of the heaviest taxes should be reduced, and that various forms of exaction practiced by tax collectors should be forbidden by law (Tacitus, *Annals* 13.50-51; cf. Suetonius, *Nero* 10.1).[32]

Paul may well have been informed of the unrest in Rome which led up to the easing of the burden. His readers should respond to such situations conscientiously. It was necessary that Christians everywhere, and not least in Rome, should live in such a way as to dissociate themselves from any spirit of unruliness. The gospel which they proclaimed was subversive enough; indulgence in other forms of subversiveness would not advance its cause.

The secular ruler is God's servant, responsible to carry out the service entrusted to him. If the servant is not content to remain within his sphere of service and begins to usurp his master's authority, he cannot rightly command obedience. If rightful disobedience to him, when his orders clash with God's, lands the Christian in trouble, the Christian will accept such trouble as God's will for him. When Paul was deprived of liberty because of his apostolic activity, he was Caesar's prisoner in the eyes of Roman law, but in his own eyes he was the "prisoner of Christ" (Ephesians 3:1). His place of custody was the place where he was currently "posted for the defence of the gospel" (Philippians 1:16). "Sometimes," as Ernst Käsemann has put it, "the Lord of the world speaks more audibly out of prison cells and graves than out of the life of churches which congratulate themselves on their concordat with the State."[33] He speaks against the background of German church-state relations in the period 1933-45. But the idea of a concordat with the Roman state was not even on the church's horizon in A.D. 57. When, a few years later, Paul looked forward to making his defense before Caesar, the most he could have hoped for from the state might be a readiness to recognize Christian congregations as *collegia licita*—a recognition already extended to Jewish synagogues. If he did cherish such a hope, it was not to be realized.

If 1 Peter provides a commentary on Romans 13:1-7, it is relevant to note that Christians are there encouraged not to take it amiss if they are penalized for the profession and practice of their faith; but they are warned not to put themselves in a position to be charged with any other offense against the law. The situation in 1 Peter is later than that of Romans. When Romans was written, the question of state persecution of Christians for Christ's sake had not yet risen, and so it was not dealt with. In 1 Peter the situation is changing before the reader's eyes. In the third chapter it is unlikely that harm will befall those who pursue what is good; the possibility of suffering for righteousness' sake is mentioned, but as a remote contingency—although, even in this remote contingency, Christians are recommended to take courage from the example of Christ.[34] But in the fourth chapter the suffering of disrepute, and worse, specifically "as a Christian" is no remote contingency, but an imminent certainty; "the time has come" (1 Peter 4:17). The Christian apologists, following the instructions of Romans and 1 Peter, argued from a position of strength when they insisted on their innocence in relation to imperial law: the one charge against them was that they were Christians (and this did not become a statutory crime until the beginning of the third century).

IX. THE EVIDENCE OF ACTS

One final question: is the evidence of Acts relevant to the interpretation of Romans 13:1-7? Some of those who see a post-Pauline interpolation in Romans 13:1-7 would acknowledge that the evidence of Acts is relevant to its interpretation in the sense that both documents reflect the shift in perspective resulting from the failure of the end to come when Paul and his first-generation fellow-Christians had expected it.[35] This view of a shift in perspective calls for critical scrutiny:[36] for the present, however, as one persuaded of the high historical value of the evidence of Acts for the course of Paul's ministry in the fifties of the first century I consider its evidence for Paul's relation to the Roman state.

According to Acts, Paul was a Roman citizen by birth. On more than one occasion he claimed the privileges to which his citizenship legally entitled him, and outstandingly so when he appealed to have his case transferred from the jurisdiction of the Roman governor of Judaea to the imperial tribunal in Rome. I can find no reason in the data of Paul's own writings to doubt this representation of his status.

When he sent his letter to the Roman Christians, he planned to visit Rome, but he did not foresee that his plan would be carried out by his being taken there under armed guard for his appeal to be heard by Caesar. He was encouraged to make his appeal (in my reading of the situation) by the favorable impression he had received of Roman judicial impartiality during his apostolic activity. In the very city of Corinth where the letter to the Romans was written he had experienced this impartiality when he was charged before Gallio, proconsul of Achaia, with propagating an illegal religion. Gallio refused to take up the charge, and his refusal meant that Paul was free to continue his preaching of the Christian message.[37] If the emperor's representative had given a ruling which effectively promoted the advance of the gospel, the emperor himself might reasonably be expected to do no less.

However, when this letter was written, the occasion for appealing to Caesar had not yet arisen. But Gallio's precedent was still valid, and Paul had good cause to appreciate it. This situation depicted in Acts provides a background against which the positive attitude to the state expressed in Romans 13:1-7 can be accepted as Paul's attitude. At the same time, there is nothing elsewhere in Paul's letters which conflicts with this attitude.

The emotional response which some readers make to this paragraph arises very often from attempts made by themselves or others to apply its teaching without qualification to Christians living under a wide variety of political regimes today. How far its teaching is applicable to postapostolic times is an important question of Christian ethics,[38] but it is not our present concern. Paul was not writing with future generations in mind; he was writing for the Christians in Rome (and no doubt for Christians in other cities of the empire) in the earlier part of Nero's principate. He knew that the empire would not last forever: the state is to wither away; "the city of God remaineth." He knew, too, that when the state encroaches on the sphere which belongs to God, disobedience to its commands may be not only a Christian right but a Christian duty. But while the empire lasted, and while it discharged the ministry divinely committed to it, it should receive submission, not rebellion, from its Christian subjects. This is not only the teaching of Romans 13:1-7; it is, I believe, the teaching of Paul himself.

8. *Christ and Spirit in Paul*

Some time ago I gave a lecture here on "Paul and the Historical Jesus"—a lecture which was designed in part as a protest against the tendency to represent Paul as having no interest himself in the character and teaching of the historical Jesus, and as deprecating any such interest on the part of others. "The empty tomb and the resurrection appearances," I said, "mark the transition from the historical Jesus to the exalted Christ."[1] Paul maintained the continuity and identity of the historical Jesus with the exalted Christ. But the historical Jesus was known to him only by hearsay, whereas he claimed a profound personal acquaintance with the exalted Christ.

I. THE GLORY OF THAT LIGHT

The present lecture is designed to examine Paul's conception of the exalted Christ. The exalted Christ appeared to him on the Damascus road, but he makes little attempt to describe that appearance—perhaps because words were inadequate for the purpose. Radiant light is the chief feature of the appearance which emerges from Paul's references to it, for when he speaks of the ministry of the new covenant with which he was then entrusted, he contrasts it with the inferior ministry granted to Moses by setting over against the fading glory reflected on Moses' face the unfading glory associated with the gospel. He describes the dawn of

---

A lecture delivered in the John Rylands University Library, Manchester, on Wednesday, 13 October 1976, and published in *BJRL* 59 (1976-77), pp. 259-285.

faith as "seeing the light of the gospel of the glory of Christ, who is the image (εἰκών) of God"—"for," he goes on, "it is the God who said, 'Let light shine out of darkness,' who has shone in our hearts to give the light of the knowledge of the glory of God in the face of Christ" (2 Cor. 4:4, 6). As the old creation was inaugurated by the shining of light to dispel the darkness which lay "upon the face of the deep" (Gen. 1:2f.), so the new creation was inaugurated by the shining of light to dispel the blindness of unbelief; and Paul's choice of this figure was probably dictated by his own experience. We recall the reference in Acts 9:3 to the "light from heaven" which "flashed about him" on the Damascus road; in the parallel account of the experience in Acts 22:11 Paul himself says that he could not see "because of the glory (δόξα) of that light," and in all three records of the incident in Acts it is made fairly clear that in that light the risen Christ appeared to him (9:17; 22:14; 26:16).

While Paul had no doubt about the personal identity of the earthly Jesus and the heavenly Christ, he equally had no doubt that the heavenly Christ's mode of existence was different from that of the earthly Jesus. When he affirms that "flesh and blood cannot inherit the kingdom of God" (1 Cor. 15:50)—i.e., the resurrection order—he makes it plain that this is as true of the Lord as of his people. The earthly Jesus was a man of woman born who endured a real death; but the risen Christ, while still man, was now vested with heavenly humanity, a different order of humanity from that of this present life. "The first man was from the earth, a man of dust; the second man is from heaven" (1 Cor. 15:47). While the creation narrative of Genesis 2:7 tells how "the first man, Adam, became a living soul," the character of the new creation is disclosed in the affirmation that "the last Adam became a life-giving spirit" (1 Cor. 15:45). The risen Christ, for Paul, exists no longer in a body of flesh and blood but in a "spiritual body" (1 Cor. 15:44).

Those who, even while living on earth in mortal bodies, are by faith united to the risen Christ have something of this new order of existence communicated to them. This is a different kind of personal union from those which bind human beings together in their present life. The closest personal union in this life is that between man and woman, described in the words of the creation narrative as their becoming "one flesh" (Gen. 2:24)—"but," says Paul, "one who is united to the Lord becomes one spirit with him" (1 Cor. 6:17). It is difficult to dissociate "one spirit" in this sense from the "one Spirit" in whom all the people of Christ are united into one body with him, just as it is difficult to dissociate the "life-giving spirit" which Jesus became in resurrection from the Spirit of life which indwells his people. To this we shall return.

If even while in mortal body a believer in Christ becomes "one spirit" with him, this unity is to become more fully experienced in resurrection. For the "spiritual body" worn by the risen Lord is the prototype for his people, who are to share his resurrection and have their present bodies of humiliation transmuted into the likeness of his body of glory (Phil. 3:21). "As we have borne the image of the man of dust," says Paul, "we shall also bear the image of the man of heaven" (1 Cor. 15:49). It was as the "man of heaven" that Jesus appeared to Paul on the Damascus road, we gather, vested with his body of glory; but when Paul attempts to describe what he saw, the only vocabulary he can use is that of light.

Paul looked forward to the parousia of Christ, his manifestation in glory; but the appearance of Christ at his parousia would be of the same character as his appearance on the Damascus road, except that it would not be a momentary flash but a more enduring experience, and that it would be accompanied by the instantaneous glorification of his people—whether by the resurrection of those who had died or the transformation of those still alive. The revelation of the Son of God would be attended by the simultaneous "revelation of the sons of God" (Rom. 8:19), a prospect also described as their liberation from bondage to decay and futility, their adoption as sons, the redemption of their bodies (Rom. 8:20-23). This is the climax of their salvation, the consummation of God's eternal purpose of grace towards them.

"In this hope," says Paul, "we were saved. . . . But if we hope for what we do not see, we wait for it with patience" (Rom. 8:24f.). The subject-matter of this paper relates to the present period of hope—the interval between the past event of Christ's death and resurrection and the future event of his parousia.

II. THE EXALTED LORD

Paul may well have been brought up to think of the days of the Messiah as an interval separating this age from the age to come, the resurrection age.[2] But whether he had entertained the belief in such an interval before his conversion or not, the logic of the Christ-event imposed it on him now. Only, the days of the Messiah were not characterized by Messiah's reigning from an earthly throne, like the throne of his father David, but by his reigning from the right hand of God. The oracle of Psalm 110:1 (109:1 in the Greek Bible), "Sit at my right hand till I make your enemies your footstool," is one of the most primitive Christian *testimonia*. If, as was widely held, this oracle was addressed to the Messiah,[3] then, since in the eyes of his followers Jesus was the Messiah, the oracle was fulfilled in him.

Paul does not often use the expression about the right hand of God; when he does so, it is probably because it had already become familiar to Christians when they confessed their faith in the Christ "who died, ... who was raised from the dead, who is at the right hand of God, ..."— as Paul puts it in Romans 8:34, apparently quoting such a confession of faith. (That is the only place where the expression occurs in his "capital" epistles; it appears also in Col. 3:1 and Eph. 1:20.) Like his fellow-Jews, he knew "the right hand of God" to be a metaphor denoting supreme authority, but he may have preferred to use it sparingly lest some of his Gentile hearers or readers should imagine that it had physical or local significance. It is, of course, difficult to think or speak of exaltation or supremacy without the use of spatial imagery. Christian astrophysicists who recite the historic creeds are not charged with inconsistency for employing the terminology of the three-decker universe; this terminology provides serviceable metaphors for the expression of transcendence, or of communication in both directions between God and man. Even in the first century such terminology was recognized by many thinking people as metaphorical, and among those thinking people Paul is entitled to be included.

Instead of referring to Christ as being seated at God's right hand, Paul speaks of him as "highly exalted,"[4] endowed with "the name which is above every name" (Phil. 2:9).[5] The "name which is above every name" is the designation "Lord." It is the divine purpose, says Paul (or the source which he quotes), that "every tongue should confess that Jesus Christ is Lord" (Phil. 2:11). The Greek noun he uses is χύριος, which because of the Septuagint usage lent itself happily to this exalted connotation. In the Septuagint it is used not only to render such a Hebrew word as *'āḏôn* ("lord") but also to render the ineffable name of the God of Israel—the name which we commonly reproduce as Yahweh. Thus the Septuagint of Psalm 110:1 uses χύριος twice—"The χύριος said to my χύριος"—just as most of our English versions use "Lord": "The LORD said to my lord." But the Hebrew text means "Yahweh's oracle to my lord *('āḏôn).*" The person addressed by the psalmist as "my lord" was probably the Davidic king, so that the later messianic interpretation was not inappropriate.[6] But in the Septuagint the person addressed in the oracle is designated by the same word as Yahweh himself: in that sense he shares "the name which is above every name."

The wording of Philippians 2:10f. is based on Isaiah 45:23, where Yahweh swears by himself: "To me every knee shall bow, every tongue shall swear."[7] Here, however, it is in Jesus' name that every knee shall bow, and it is Jesus' lordship that every tongue shall confess. Nor is this by any means the only instance in the New Testament where an Old

Testament passage containing κύριος as the equivalent of Yahweh is applied to Jesus.[8] In any case, the title "Lord" in the highest sense which it can bear belongs distinctively to the risen and exalted Jesus, and not for Paul only. Luke's testimony is to the same effect: his account of Peter's address in Jerusalem at the first Christian Pentecost ends with the quotation of Psalm 110:1 and the peroration based on it, calling on all the house of Israel to know assuredly that God has made the crucified Jesus "both Lord and Christ" (Acts 2:34-36).

To Paul, however (and to other early Christians), the acknowledgment of Jesus as Lord in the highest sense which that title can bear was far from being the result of a linguistic accident; it was far, too, from being but an *ex officio* designation of the Messiah. It was the most adequate term for expressing what he (and his fellow-believers) had come to understand and appreciate of Jesus' person and achievement and his present decisive role in the outworking of God's purpose of blessing for the universe.[9]

If it be asked if this use of the title "Lord" goes back to the earliest Aramaic-speaking phase of the church's life, the answer is Yes. The Aramaic equivalent of Greek κύριος is *mar*, as in the invocation *maranatha* ("Our Lord, come"), which found its way untranslated into the vocabulary of Greek-speaking Christians (1 Cor. 16:22)—more particularly, into the eucharistic liturgy (*Didache* 10:6).[10] That *mar* could be used (as κύριος was) to denote the God of Israel is shown by the targum on Job from Cave 11 at Qumran, where the form *mārē* appears as an equivalent of Shaddai, and in the Aramaic fragments of 1 Enoch from Cave 4, where *maranā* (9:4) and the emphatic state *maryā* (10:9) are used with reference to God.[11]

The title "Son of God" is also given to Jesus in a distinctive sense in resurrection: he was "designated Son of God in power, according to the Spirit of holiness, by his resurrection from the dead" (Rom. 1:4). In Paul's thought, of course, he did not *begin* to be Son of God at the resurrection: speaking of his coming into the world Paul says that "God sent forth his Son, born of a woman" (Gal. 4:4). But during his earthly life he was the Son of God, comparatively speaking, "in weakness";[12] as the risen Lord he is the Son of God "in power."[13]

Like the title "Lord," "Son of God" was also confirmed by an oracular *testimonium*—by Psalm 2:7, where Yahweh addresses his anointed one in the words: "You are my Son; today I have begotten you."[14] But (like the title "Lord") "Son of God" is for Paul much more than a designation which Jesus, as Messiah, bears *ex officio*;[15] it expresses the unique personal relation which Jesus bore to God, as indeed it appears to have done for Jesus himself.[16]

Luke seems to recognize the special place that the designation of Jesus as Son of God had in Paul's ministry, for whereas he makes other preachers of the apostolic message in its early days proclaim Jesus as Lord and Messiah, he sums up Paul's earliest public testimony to Jesus in the words, "He is the Son of God" (Acts 9:20). Perhaps the language in which Paul himself describes his call and commission, "God . . . was pleased to reveal his Son in me, that I might proclaim him among the Gentiles" (Gal. 1:15f.), implies that an appreciation of Jesus as the Son of God was inherent in his conversion experience.

Although Paul makes infrequent use of the metaphor "the right hand of God," he takes the oracle of Psalm 110:1 seriously as a messianic *testimonium,* and in fact in 1 Corinthians 15:24-28 he gives a fuller exposition of it than does any other New Testament writer. "Sit at my right hand," ran the oracle, "till I make your enemies your footstool"—and Paul undertakes to identify these enemies. They are not flesh-and-blood enemies; they are "principalities and powers," forces in the universe which work against the purpose of God and the well-being of man. It is to forces of this order that Paul has referred earlier in 1 Corinthians as the "rulers of this age" who, in ignorance of the hidden wisdom decreed by God from ages past for his people's glory, "crucified the Lord of glory" (1 Cor. 2:6-8). Pontius Pilate and others may have played their historic part in this, but without realizing it they were agents of those hostile forces in the spiritual realm. Now, thanks to the victory of the cross and the reign of the risen Lord, those forces are being progressively destroyed. The last and most intractable of those forces is death, which is to be destroyed at the final resurrection of which the resurrection of Christ is the first installment.

"Sit at my right hand," said the oracle, "till I make your enemies your footstool"—so, says Paul, "Christ must reign till God has put all his enemies under his feet" (1 Cor. 15:25). But when all those enemies are subjugated, including death itself, then the reign of Christ is merged in the eternal reign of God. The reign of Christ, "the age of the Messiah," is thus an intermediate phase between the present age and the endless age to come, or from certain points of view it may be regarded as the overlapping of the two, a phase in which the present age is not fully ended and the age to come has not been fully established.

A further word must be interjected here about those principalities and powers. A close examination of what Paul has to say about them shows that, to his way of thinking, they are largely those elemental forces which dominate the minds of men and women and are powerful so long as men and women believe in them and render them allegiance. But when their minds are liberated by faith in the crucified and risen Christ, then the bondage imposed by those forces is broken, their power is dissolved and they are revealed as the "weak and beggarly" nonentities that they are in themselves.[17] To mention two of the most potent, the strength of sin and the fear of death could bind men and women's lives in an iron grip, but those who enjoyed the liberation effected by Christ knew that sin had no more dominion over them and that even death, in advance of the coming resurrection, could be greeted as pure gain. The destruction of the principalities and powers may be expressed in figurative language, but the reality is the enjoyment of inward release and freedom experienced by the believer.

In the passage already quoted from Romans 8:34, where Paul seems to echo a primitive confession of faith in "Christ Jesus who died, yes, who was raised from the dead, who is at the right hand of God," he continues with the clause: "who indeed intercedes for us." The reigning Christ, that is to say, is not passively waiting for the Father to fulfill his promise to make his enemies his footstool; he is actively engaged on his people's behalf. The confessional words are placed by Paul in a forensic context, in imitation of a recurring Old Testament motif:[18] he begins with the challenge, "Who shall bring any charge against God's elect?" and affirms that no one will dare to fill the role of the Old Testament *śāṭān*[19] and attempt to prosecute them in the heavenly court because God himself is their justifier and the Christ who died and rose is present as counsel for their defense.

The ascription of an intercessory ministry to the ascended Christ may be based on Isaiah 53:12, where the humiliated and vindicated Servant of the Lord is said to have "made intercession for the transgressors";[20] it is not peculiar to Paul among the New Testament theologians, for in 1 John 2:1 "Jesus Christ the righteous" is presented as his people's "advocate with the Father," while the theme is elaborated by the writer to the Hebrews in his portrayal of Jesus as the enthroned high priest, who "is able for all time to save those who draw near to God through him, since he always lives to make intercession for them" (Heb. 9:25).[21]

In other words, Christ's active concern for his people is not exhausted by his death on their behalf; in his new order of existence he is still their friend and helper, supplying spiritual sustenance to meet their varied need.

III. THE GIFT OF THE SPIRIT

But when Paul deals with this supplying of the present spiritual need of the people of Christ, he does so for the most part in terms of the activity of the Spirit—to the point where much that he says of the ministry of the ascended Christ can be paralleled by what he says of the ministry of the Spirit.

Paul is by no means the only New Testament writer to speak of the Spirit as communicating to the people of Christ the living power of their risen Lord, although he develops this theme in his own way. It was a matter of common belief to Christians of the first generation that the special gift of the Spirit which they had received was the sign of the inbreaking of the new age.

Two strands of Old Testament prediction about the Spirit of God are depicted as fulfilled in the New Testament. One is the promise that the Spirit will be bestowed in unstinted measure on a servant-ruler to equip him for a ministry of mercy and judgment for Israel and the nations.[22] The other is the promise that in the latter days the same Spirit would be poured out "on all flesh."[23]

The earliest Christians recognized that the former strand of prediction had been fulfilled in Jesus, anointed at his baptism "with the Holy Spirit and power" (Acts 10:38). As for the latter-day outpouring of the Spirit, two of the evangelists (Luke and John) unambiguously make it depend on the prior passion and triumph of Jesus,[24] who is uniformly identified throughout the gospel tradition with the Coming One who, according to the preaching of John the Baptist, would baptize men and women with the Holy Spirit.[25]

This baptism with the Spirit, as Paul saw it, was not simply an experience of individual believers, but the means by which they were brought together into a corporate unity, which he calls the body of Christ: "in one Spirit we were all baptized into one body—Jews or Greeks, slaves or free—and we were all watered with one Spirit" (1 Cor. 12:13). His language may point to their baptism in water as the occasion of this experience, but insists on its inward and spiritual significance.

This corporate unity, in Paul's thought, is animated by the Spirit of God as the body of a living person is animated by the human spirit, and the individual believers who make up this corporate unity cooperate for the well-being of the whole just as the limbs and organs of a healthy body cooperate when they discharge their proper functions.[26]

Occasionally Paul expresses this corporate unity not in terms of a body but in terms of a temple: "Do you not know," he says to the church of Corinth, "that you are God's temple and that God's Spirit dwells in you?" (1 Cor. 3:16).[27] While the image of the body seems to be original with him, that of the temple has earlier antecedents: the Qumran community, for example, looked upon itself as a living temple.[28]

The temple image, moreover, is used by Paul not only for the community but also for the individual believer: "your body," he says, "is a temple of the Holy Spirit within you, which you have from God" (1 Cor. 6:19).

The distinctive mark of a Christian, indeed, is that within such a person the Holy Spirit dwells: "Any one who has not the Spirit of Christ," says Paul, "is none of his" (Rom. 8:9b). Again, in remonstrating with his Galatian converts for their readiness to seek security in legal observances, he assumes that when they believed the gospel they received the Spirit, and assumes that they know this to be so: "Did you receive the Spirit by works of the law, or by hearing with faith? . . . Having begun with the Spirit, are you now achieving completeness with the flesh? . . . Does he who supplies the Spirit to you and performs mighty acts among you do so by works of the law, or by hearing with faith?" (Gal. 3:2-5).

This receiving of the Spirit, which the Galatian Christians, for all their regrettable tendencies, are expected to acknowledge as a real experience of theirs, was no mere matter of logical conviction or of an inner glow: it was accompanied by more substantial evidences. Not only were there the tokens of divine power which attended their response to the preaching—miraculous healings, it might be, or glossolalic utterances—but there were the more durable tokens of changed lives, lives in which the fruit of the Spirit, a harvest of ethical graces, had begun to manifest itself. If in Galatians 5:22 love takes pride of place in the ninefold fruit of the Spirit, this is in keeping with Paul's emphasis elsewhere. "God's love," he reminds the Roman Christians, "has been poured into our hearts through the Holy Spirit who has been given to us" (Rom. 5:5), while, in writing to his friends at Corinth, he concludes his hymn in celebration of heavenly love by affirming that "faith, hope, love abide, these three; but the greatest of these is love" (1 Cor. 13:13).

Nor is this love, the primary fruit of the Spirit, an abstraction; the hymn describes it in almost personal terms, as though the character of Christ were being portrayed. This becomes especially clear in 2 Corinthians 3:18, where the primary function of the Spirit in believers is to transform them progressively into the image of Christ, "from one degree of glory to another; for this comes from the Lord who is the Spirit."

IV. THE LORD AND THE SPIRIT

This phrase, "the Lord who is the Spirit," is based on a midrashic interpretation which Paul has just been giving of the narrative in Exodus 34:29-35. Moses, his countenance shining from his confrontation with the divine glory, wore a veil to conceal the radiance from his fellow-

Israelites, but removed it when he "went in before the LORD." Paul takes this to mean that each time Moses went into the presence of God he was "re-charged" with the divine glory, and veiled his face when he went out so that the Israelites should not see that this glory was a fading one which required repeated renewal. The fading glory on Moses' face is contrasted, as we have seen, with the unfading "glory of God in the face of Christ" (2 Cor. 4:6), by way of pointing the contrast between the inferior glory of the law, introduced for a limited period and destined to pass away, and the surpassing glory of the gospel, "the dispensation of the Spirit" (2 Cor. 3:8).

But even in the Exodus narrative Paul sees the gospel age adumbrated: as Moses removed the veil from his face when he "went in before the LORD" (Exod. 34:34), so, "when one turns to the Lord, the veil is removed. Now [Paul adds] the Lord is the Spirit, and where the Spirit of the Lord is, there is freedom" (2 Cor. 3:16f.).[29] That is to say, "the LORD" in the Exodus narrative corresponds to the Spirit in this new order, and where the Spirit of the Lord is, there is freedom of access to the divine presence "with unveiled face."[30] Access to God in the dispensation of law, he implies, was difficult and hedged about with restrictions and inhibitions; access to God in the dispensation of the Spirit is free and unreserved.

This antithesis of the law, leading to bondage and death, and the Spirit, imparting liberty and life, is of crucial importance in Paul's understanding of the ways of God with men and women.[31] The dead letter has given way to the living Spirit, thanks to whom the law's requirements are now spontaneously fulfilled in those "who walk not according to the flesh but according to the Spirit" (Rom. 8:4).

The statement, "the Lord is the Spirit," has been taken to assert an identity between Christ as Lord and the Spirit of God, but this is probably not Paul's intention. The statement is rather Paul's interpretation of Moses' entering the divine presence, or his adaptation of Moses' experience to that of the believer under the new covenant. What the Lord was to Moses, the Spirit is to the believer; yet in saying "the Lord is the Spirit" and in his later reference to "the Lord who is the Spirit"—literally "the Lord the Spirit"—Paul suggests, not indeed the identity, but certainly the close association that exists between the ascended Christ and the Spirit in the believer. His language, in the circumspect words of George Smeaton, a nineteenth-century Scottish theologian, "shows how fully he apprehended their joint mission, and how emphatically he intimates that Christ is never to be conceived of apart from the Spirit, nor the Spirit conceived of apart from Him."[32] In our own day Ernst Käsemann is more forthright, if less circumspect, and describes the Spirit as "the earthly *praesentia* of the exalted Lord."[33]

But this is Professor Käsemann's comment not on "the Lord who is the Spirit" but on a statement to which we have already alluded: that Jesus in resurrection became "a life-giving Spirit" (1 Cor. 15:45). And whatever may be said of "the Lord is the Spirit," *prima facie* an identity of the risen Christ with the Spirit would seem to be affirmed in the clause: "the last Adam became a life-giving Spirit." Elsewhere Paul knows of only one life-giving Spirit, and that is "the Spirit of life in Christ Jesus" (Rom. 8:2), the Spirit whose indwelling power quickens mortal bodies (Rom. 8:11), the Spirit whose life-giving property is set in contrast with the death-dealing effect of the law (2 Cor. 3:6), the Spirit through whom the believer's inner being is renewed from day to day even while the outer being disintegrates (2 Cor. 4:16), the Spirit whose presence within is the guarantee of the believer's investiture with a heavenly and imperishable body (2 Cor. 5:5).

True, in using the phrase πνεῦμα ζῳοποιοῦν ("life-giving Spirit") of the last Adam, Paul may be moved by the desire to find an appropriately balancing phrase to the ψυχὴ ζῶσα ("living soul") predicated of the first Adam in Genesis 2:7. But the phrase chosen to describe the last Adam is particularly suitable in view of two crucial articles of faith which Paul repeatedly emphasizes: (i) that Christ, by his resurrection from the dead, is the first-fruits of the resurrection harvest in which all his people will share, and (ii) that the Spirit has been given to his people here and now as the pledge and first installment of their eventual participation in their Master's resurrection life and glory. Here and now "he who is united to the Lord becomes one Spirit with him" (1 Cor. 6:17). This is another balancing phrase, chosen by Paul as a counterpoise to the "one flesh" which man and woman become in marital union (Gen. 2:24), but it is not chosen for stylistic reasons only. It expresses a recurring theme in Pauline thought: "he who is united to the Lord" by faith derives from him eternal life now and the hope of glory to come; but since it is through the Spirit that the life and hope are mediated, "he who is united to the Lord becomes one Spirit with him"—and with all those who are similarly united to him.

V. PARALLEL MINISTRIES

Time and again in Paul we come upon parallel affirmations in which now the risen Christ and now the Spirit are spoken of as communicating to believers the blessings of salvation. "The Spirit conveys what Christ bestows."[34] But this close association of Christ and the Spirit, far from tending to depersonalize the risen Lord,[35] imparts a more personal quality to the Spirit.

For example, if the exalted Christ makes intercession for his people (Rom. 8:34), "the Spirit himself intercedes for us with sighs too deep for words" (Rom. 8:26). What Christ does on high the Spirit does within; we may recall that, while in 1 John 2:1 Christ is his people's "advocate (paraclete) with the Father," in John 14:16 he speaks of the Spirit as "another advocate (paraclete)" to be perpetually with them. Believers have been called by God "into the fellowship of his Son" (1 Cor. 1:8); they enjoy the "fellowship of the Spirit" (Phil. 2:1).[36] Perhaps there is a slight difference in meaning between these two genitives: the fellowship of the Son of God is their fellowship with him, their being his joint-heirs; the fellowship of the Spirit is, as the RSV puts it, their "participation in the Spirit." Again, Paul speaks of "the love of Christ" (Rom. 8:35; 2 Cor. 5:14, etc.) and of "the love of the Spirit" (Rom. 15:30);[37] but the former is the love lavished by Christ on his people while the latter is that same divine love implanted and fostered within them by the Spirit. When he speaks of "our freedom which we have in Christ Jesus" (Gal. 2:4) or the freedom for which "Christ has set us free" (Gal. 5:1), he has in mind the identical freedom which is present wherever the Spirit of the Lord is (2 Cor. 3:17).

If it is by the Spirit that the people of Christ know themselves to be sons of God (Rom. 8:14, 16), they are equally sons of God "in Christ Jesus, through faith" (Gal. 3:26). They are "sanctified in Christ Jesus" (1 Cor. 1:2) and "sanctified in the Holy Spirit" (Rom. 15:16).[38] But there is in essence no difference between the two concepts, as appears from Paul's more comprehensive statement in 1 Corinthians 6:11: "you were washed, you were sanctified, you were justified in the name of the Lord Jesus Christ and in the Spirit of our God." If the blessings secured by Christ are conveyed by the Spirit, it matters little whether Christ or the Spirit is named in relation to those blessings, or both Christ and Spirit together.

While Paul normally speaks of believers as being "in Christ," "in Christ Jesus" or "in the Lord" (especially when he has in mind their joint sharing in his risen life), he can when appropriate (e.g., by way of contrast with their former existence "in the flesh") speak of them as being "in the Spirit." Equally, it is immaterial whether Christ or the Spirit is said to be in them. "You are not in the flesh, you are in the Spirit," says Paul to the Romans, "if the Spirit of Christ really dwells in you. . . . But if Christ is in you, although your bodies are dead because of sin, your spirits are alive because of righteousness. If the Spirit of him who raised Jesus from the dead dwells in you, he who raised Christ Jesus from the dead will give life to your mortal bodies also through his Spirit which dwells in you" (Rom. 8:9-11).

In such statements, the indwelling Christ and the indwelling Spirit are practically interchangeable. The adverb "practically" is used here with its full force. Theoretically and in principle the indwelling Christ and the indwelling Spirit are distinguishable, but practically and in experience they cannot be separated. To obtain a rounded picture of Paul's doctrine of the Spirit, especially in relation to the ascended Christ, we must not concentrate on one set of texts and ignore the others but attain as comprehensive a conspectus as possible—primarily from his capital epistles. Paul was not a systematic theologian, and his thought and teaching cannot be organized into a neat and coherent system: attempts to do this regularly omit or do less than justice to features of value. Moreover, unlike Christian theologians of the post-Nicene era, he was free of all obligation to conform his language about Christ and the Spirit to established credal formulations.

Paul spoke of what he knew to be true in his own life and in the lives of his converts; and one of the most important things that he knew to be true was that the ascended Christ imparted his life and power to them through his Spirit. Dynamically, therefore, the ascended Christ and the indwelling Spirit were one, even if they were otherwise distinct. Paul plainly did distinguish them, as for example in the triadic benediction of 2 Corinthians 13:14, or in his discussion of the Spirit's distribution of gifts to the body of Christ in 1 Corinthians 12:4-11, which is introduced by the tripartite declaration that "there are varieties of gifts, but *the same Spirit*; and there are varieties of service, but *the same Lord*; and there are varieties of working, but it is *the same God* who inspires them all in every one."[39]

VI. ILLUMINATION AND PROPHECY

The Spirit, for Paul as for others before him, is the source of illumination, especially where the realities of the unseen world are involved. Quoting an extract from an unknown source—

> What no eye has seen, nor ear heard,
> nor the heart of man conceived,
> what God has prepared for those who love him[40]—

he adds that God has revealed all this to his servants through the Spirit, for "no one comprehends the thoughts of God except the Spirit of God" (1 Cor. 2:9-11). But Paul and others, who have received the Spirit of God, are enabled to "understand the gifts bestowed . . . by God" and to communicate them to those who have the spiritual wisdom to take them in. Without the Spirit it is impossible to appreciate the depths of the divine purpose, that "wisdom in a mystery" which God decreed before the ages for his people's glory.[41] No ordinary human intelligence is capable of grasping this, "for," asks Paul (quoting Isa. 40:13), "who has known the mind of the Lord so as to instruct him?" "But," he adds immediately, "we have the mind of Christ" (1 Cor. 2:16)—and in this context no sharp distinction can be drawn between the mind of Christ and the Spirit of God (cf. 1 Cor. 7:40b, "I think that I have the Spirit of God").

The illumination supplied by the Spirit of God is acknowledged in the Old Testament, as by Elihu (Job 32:8):

> it is the spirit in a man,
> the breath of the Almighty,
>   that makes him understand.

It forms an important aspect of the Qumran doctrine of the Spirit, as when the worshipper in one of the Hymns of Thanksgiving, speaking as a *maśkîl*, an instructor, says:

> I have come to know thee, O God, by the spirit which
>   thou hast placed within me,
> and by thy holy spirit I have listened faithfully
>   to thy wonderful secret counsel.[42]

But the distinctive feature of Paul's doctrine of the Spirit, in this as in other functions, lies in the emphasis which he places on the Spirit's inseparability from the living Christ.

Closely akin to the Spirit's gift of illumination is his gift of prophecy; it would be difficult, indeed, to say where the one gift ends and the other begins. Paul mentions a number of "spiritual gifts" which are exercised in the church—some relatively trivial, others of high importance[43]—but he plainly sets great value on prophecy, the declaration of the mind of God in the power of the Spirit. Such prophecy is not outside the intelligent control of the speaker;[44] mere ecstatic utterance, such as was quite familiar in paganism, was not necessarily genuine prophecy. Genuine prophecy could be recognized by its content: if it promoted the honor of Christ, then it was prompted by the Spirit of God. "No one can say 'Jesus is Lord' except by the Holy Spirit" (1 Cor. 12:3).[45]

According to the Qumran texts, it was their anointing with the Holy Spirit that enabled the prophets to foretell what God was going to do,[46] as it was by the aid of the same Spirit that the Teacher of Righteousness and his disciples interpreted the writings of the prophets, with special reference to the time at which their predictions would come to pass.[47] But here again, it is the close association of the Spirit of prophecy with the acknowledgment of Christ as Lord that distinguishes the Christian—more specifically the Pauline—understanding from that of the Qumran community.

VII. THE IMAGE OF GOD

Paul, as we have seen, associates "the light of the gospel of the glory of Christ" with the fact that Christ is "the image of God." If the former phrase recalls his Damascus road experience, what about the latter phrase? Was there something about the appearance of the risen Christ which instantaneously impressed him as being the image of God? We cannot be sure; it is difficult to know what meaning the expression "the image of God" would have had for Paul. Yet when he speaks of seeing "the light of the knowledge of the glory of God in the face of Christ" he uses language which practically amounts to seeing in Christ the image of God.[48]

Paul is not the only New Testament writer to present Christ in these terms: the Fourth Evangelist records the progressive revelation of God in the ministry of the incarnate Word, until it finds its climax on the cross; and the writer to the Hebrews speaks of the Son as God as "the effulgence of his glory and the very stamp of his being" (Heb. 1:3). But it is in Paul that the presentation of Christ as the image of God is worked out most fully and consistently, with its corollary of the increasing transformation of the people of Christ into the same image by the power of the indwelling Spirit,[49] until nothing remains of the earthly image in those who finally display the image of the heavenly man.[50]

Man, according to the Old Testament, was made in God's image (Gen. 1:26f.) and for his glory (Isa. 43:7): in the order of creation he is, as Paul says, "the image and glory of God" (1 Cor. 11:7).[51] It is difficult to dissociate Paul's portrayal of the risen Christ as the second man, the last Adam, from his view of Christ as the image of God and the revealer of his glory. What the first man was, imperfectly, in the old creation, Christ is, perfectly, in the new creation—the resurrection order.

It is tempting to go farther and relate another aspect of Paul's christology to this appreciation of Christ as the image of God. In the Alexandrian book of Wisdom, which was evidently known to Paul, wisdom is not only personified but described as the "image" (εἰκών) of God's goodness.[52]

One thing is certain: that Paul, in common with some of his fellow-theologians among the New Testament writers, identified Christ with the wisdom of God and ascribed to him certain activities which are predicated of personified wisdom in the wisdom literature of the Old Testament. When, for example, Paul speaks of the "one Lord, Jesus Christ, through whom are all things and through whom we exist" (1 Cor. 8:6), or describes him as "the image of the invisible God" in that "all things were created through him and for him" (Col. 1:15f.), this identification of Christ with divine wisdom underlies such statements, just as it underlies the affirmation of John 1:4 that "all things were made through him" (i.e., the pre-incarnate Word) and that of Hebrews 1:2 that the Son of God is the one "through whom also he made the worlds."[53] But here it is not particularly the *risen* Christ that is in view: it is the eternal Christ, whose entry into the world of mankind was no involuntary experience but a deliberate act of condescension: "being in the form of God, ... he emptied himself and took the form of a servant" (Phil. 2:6f.);[54] "though he was rich, yet for your sake he became poor" (2 Cor. 8:9).

If this aspect of Paul's christology is not related to his vision of Christ as the image of God, then it is difficult to relate it to Paul's subsequent personal experience of Christ. Before his conversion he probably identified divine wisdom with the Torah, the "desirable instrument"[55] by which God made the world, if not the goal for which he made it.[56] After his conversion the centrality of the Torah in Paul's thought and life was displaced by the centrality of Christ, and this might suggest the transference to Christ of properties and activities previously ascribed to the Torah. But this is less likely: Christ displaced the Torah in Paul's scheme of things, but, far from being its equivalent, he was for Paul "the end of the law" (Rom. 10:4).[57] But he was not the end of divine wisdom; he was its very embodiment.

It is probably significant, however, that the pre-existent Christ is not associated by Paul with the Spirit as the risen Christ is: for Paul, the Spirit is distinctively the herald and sign of the new age, coming into his purview first of all in relation to Christ's being "designated Son of God in power according to the Spirit of holiness by his resurrection from the dead" (Rom. 1:4). Why the phrase "Spirit of holiness" should be used here rather than Paul's more usual "Holy Spirit" is a matter for inquiry, but it is a literal translation of the Hebrew construction for "holy spirit"[58] and so cannot be distinguished in meaning from "the Spirit of him who raised Jesus from the dead," whose residence in the lives of the people of Christ is the pledge of their resurrection too (Rom. 8:11).

VIII. THE PLEDGE OF THE FUTURE

One of the most distinctive features of Paul's teaching about the Spirit is his presentation of the Spirit as the pledge of the future. At present the people of Christ have the "hope of glory,"[59] but not the glory itself; they have the promise of resurrection, but they are still subject to mortality. Thanks to the indwelling Spirit, however, the hope of glory and the promise of resurrection are present realities, in the good of which they can live.

In this regard the Spirit is described by Paul as the "firstfruits" and as the "seal" or the "guarantee."

As the "firstfruits" (ἀπαρχή), the Spirit conveys to those whom he indwells the assurance of coming resurrection with its attendant blessings. "We ourselves," says Paul, "who have the firstfruits of the Spirit, . . . wait for adoption as sons, the redemption of our bodies" (Rom. 8:23). Their "adoption as sons," as we have seen, is the climax of their salvation; but their present possession of the Spirit enables them to live as sons of God here and now. "All who are led by the Spirit of God are sons of God," for he is the "Spirit of sonship (adoption)" (Rom. 8:14f.). So, Paul adds, "when we cry 'Abba! Father!' it is the Spirit himself bearing witness with our spirit that we are children of God" (Rom. 8:15f.). So, calling God "Abba," like calling Jesus "Lord," is a token of the indwelling Holy Spirit.

This relation between the invocation of God as "Abba" and the indwelling of the Spirit is further clarified by the parallel passage in Galatians 4:4-6: "God sent forth his Son . . . so that we might receive adoption as sons. And because you are sons, God has sent the Spirit of his Son into our hearts, crying, 'Abba! Father!'" The point is that "Abba" was the distinctive term by which Jesus addressed God[60] and spoke of him, and when his people spontaneously invoke God in this way, that shows that they are inspired by the same Spirit as indwelt Jesus. Thus, while their manifestation in the glory which belongs to them as the children of God lies in the future, the relationship itself is made good to them already by the Spirit. Paul is here in complete agreement with John: "we are God's children now; it does not yet appear what we shall be, but we know that when he appears we shall be like him, for we shall see him as he is" (1 John 3:2).[61]

It is worth observing, in passing, that Christ is also called the firstfruits in relation to his people's resurrection—not in the sense in which the Spirit is so called, but in the sense that he, by his being raised from the dead, is "the firstfruits of those who have fallen asleep" (1 Cor. 15:20). As the firstfruits were presented in the sanctuary as the pledge of the harvest to follow, so is "Christ the firstfruits, then at his parousia those who belong to Christ" (1 Cor. 15:23).

When Paul speaks of God as having "sealed (σφραγισάμενος) us and given the guarantee (ἀρραβών) of his Spirit in our hearts"[62] (2 Cor. 1:22), he speaks very much to the same effect. In 2 Corinthians 5:1-5 he looks forward to the heavenly "housing" or "embodiment" waiting to be "put on" by the believer at death, and sums up his confident hope by saying that "he who has prepared us for this very thing is God, who has given us the Spirit as a guarantee." The same idea is expressed in Ephesians, where those who have come to faith in Christ are said thereby to have been "sealed with the Holy Spirit of promise, who is the guarantee of our inheritance until we acquire possession of it" (1:13f.), "sealed for the day of redemption" (4:30).[63] The Spirit, that is to say, is viewed as the first installment or initial down-payment of the inheritance of glory which lies in store for the people of God. "First installment" or "initial down-payment" may seem inappropriately commercial metaphors for a spiritual reality, but they are no more commercial than the Greek word ἀρραβών. The Spirit is well spoken of as "the Holy Spirit of promise," for his presence and power in the lives of believers here and now constitute an eloquent and valid promise. Some modern versions[64] give the rendering "the promised Holy Spirit" in Ephesians 1:14 but, while this is a possible interpretation of the genitive construction, the context suggests that he is here considered not as the Spirit who was promised but as the Spirit who is himself the promise.[65]

When the Spirit is further called in Ephesians 1:14 "the guarantee of our inheritance (κληρονομία)," we are brought back to his role as "the Spirit of sonship." In Galatians 4:6f. the Spirit-inspired cry "Abba!" is the token that, as Paul says, "you are no longer a slave but a son, and if a son then an heir (κληρονόμος)." Similarly in Romans 8:15-17 the same cry is the Spirit-borne witness that those who utter it "are children of God, and if children, then heirs (κληρονόμοι), heirs of God and fellow-heirs (συν-κληρονόμοι) with Christ, provided we suffer with him in order that we may also be glorified with him."

Of the role of the Spirit in the age to come Paul has nothing to say. The age to come is the resurrection age, introduced by the manifestation of Christ and leading on to the realization of God's eternal purpose "to unite all things in him, things in heaven and things on earth" (Eph. 1:9f.). The role of the Spirit with which Paul is concerned belongs to the present age, when Christ indeed is reigning, but reigning in a realm perceptible only by faith, to those who are quickened, enlightened and empowered by the Spirit. But the Spirit is not only the present pledge of the glory of the age to come; by his ministry in this period "between the ages" he keeps the hope of glory alive in the people of God and enables them to live in the good of it here and now. Not only so: by his daily renewal of their inner being he is creating that immortality which is to be consummated at the parousia—an immortality already enjoyed by them even while they live in mortal bodies. But their present hope and its future consummation spring from their participation in the risen Christ. The Spirit, as Albert Schweitzer put it, "is the life-principle of His Messianic personality";[66] it is the living Christ himself who is his people's hope of glory and it is in him that the hope is to be realized: "When Christ who is our life appears," says Paul, "then you also will appear with him in glory" (Col. 3:4). When the people of Christ in resurrection share fully in the glory of their exalted Lord, the Spirit's present ministry has been fulfilled. But the Spirit who fulfills this present ministry is the Spirit that came upon Jesus before he came upon his followers: for Paul, in other words, the exalted Lord whose risen life and power are conveyed to his people by the indwelling Spirit is identical and continuous with him who lived among men as a servant, the crucified one, the historical Jesus.

9. Chronological Questions in the Acts of the Apostles

I. CHRONOLOGICAL INDICATIONS

There are two main senses in which one may speak of the chronology of a historical document (or one which purports to be historical). On the one hand, one may speak of the date of its literary completion, or of the stages by which it reached completion; one may speak, on the other hand, of the dating of its contents, of the events which it records. It is with the latter sense—with the "dramatic" date of Acts, as it is called—that this lecture is concerned. All that need be said here about the date of the composition of Acts is that a sufficient time has elapsed for the author to look back in tranquillity over the course of events and present them in a more balanced perspective than would have been possible for one writing *in mediis rebus*. The outstanding personages of the narrative—Peter, Paul and James of Jerusalem—had all died (I think) by the time of writing,[1] and the author was able to stress their respective contributions to the rise and progress of Christianity rather than the temporary controversies in which they had been involved one with another.

But if the author wrote a decade or two later than the last events which he records, he was acquainted with the situation that he describes. Having examined Luke's presentation of such matters as Roman citizen-

A lecture delivered in the John Rylands University Library, Manchester, on Wednesday, 6 November 1985, and published in *BJRL* 68 (1985-86), pp. 273-295.

ship, the appeal to Caesar, judicial procedure and the tenure of magis-
tracies, A. N. Sherwin-White insists that his work is true to its dramatic
date: it does not reflect the conditions which obtained as little as a
generation later. "For Acts the confirmation of historicity is overwhelming . . . any attempt to reject its basic historicity even in matters of detail
must now appear absurd."[2]

There are many incidental chronological data in Acts. The "we"
sections or travel diaries provide a day-by-day record, so far as they go.[3]
Paul and Barnabas are said to have spent "a whole year" together in a
teaching ministry in Antioch (Acts 11:26). Later, Paul is said to have spent
"a year and six months" in Corinth (18:11), and between two and three
years in Ephesus (19:10; 20:31). He was kept for two years in custody at
Caesarea (24:27) and a further two years under house arrest in Rome
(28:30).

The book as a whole, however, exhibits no explicit chronological
framework. An implicit framework was postulated many years ago by
C. J. Cadoux.[4] He drew attention, as others had done, to the editorial
reports of progress which punctuate the narrative of Acts,[5] but struck
out on a new line by arguing that the intervals between them, six
intervals in all, represent a period of five years each, yielding a total of
thirty years. That the narrative of Acts does in fact cover a stretch of some
thirty years is certain, and it may well be true that each of the six intervals
represents a quinquennium, more or less, but it is unlikely that the
author intended them to have this chronological significance. Even more
unlikely is it that, as Cadoux further argued, each interval begins and
ends with a pentecostal festival. Moreover, there are one or two other
progress reports in Acts which cannot be stylistically distinguished from
those which Cadoux lists, but which he leaves unmentioned.[6]

A survey of studies of the chronology of Acts must go back to C. H.
Turner's magisterial article on "Chronology of the New Testament,"
published in 1898 in the first volume of *Hastings' Dictionary of the Bible.*
This article, which in itself is a small monograph, filling forty-three
columns of small print, includes a section on the apostolic age (c. A.D.
30-70). These forty years, said Turner, "are roughly coterminous with the
labours of St. Peter and St. Paul, and the principal documents concerned
are, on the one hand, their Epistles, on the other, the Acts, one half of
which book is in effect devoted to each of the two great apostles."[7]
Modern scholars would count it to Turner for righteousness that he
mentions the epistles, which provide first-hand evidence (so far as those
of undoubted authenticity are concerned), before the Acts. But neither
of these two bodies of literature presents any continuous system of
time-notes, and we must be grateful for the help given by their references

to contemporary events. Luke especially, because he sets his account of Christian beginnings in the context of world history, supplies indirectly some valuable chronological data.

Turner lists ten chronological data from apostolic history, eight of which are mentioned in Acts. They are:

1. The reign of King Aretas, mentioned not in Acts but in 2 Corinthians 11:32, but in connection with Paul's escape from Damascus through the city wall, to which reference is made also in Acts 9:23-25.
2. The reign and death of Herod Agrippa I (Acts 12:1-23).
3. The famine under Claudius (Acts 11:28-30).
4. The proconsulship of Sergius Paullus in Cyprus (Acts 13:7).
5. The expulsion of Jews from Rome under Claudius (Acts 18:2).
6. The proconsulship of Gallio in Achaia (Acts 18:12).
7. The reign of Herod Agrippa II, and the marriage of his sister Drusilla to Felix (Acts 24:24; 25:13–26:32).
8. The procuratorships of Felix and Festus in Judaea (Acts 21:38; 23:24-35; 24:10-27).
9. The days of unleavened bread (Acts 20:6f.).
10. The persecution of Christians under Nero, not explicitly mentioned either in Acts or in the epistles.

II. DATABLE EVENTS

It will be convenient to use this list of events as a basis for the next section of our study.

1. *The Reign of King Aretas*

Aretas IV was king of the Nabataean Arabs from about 9 B.C. to A.D. 40. It is widely supposed, though on doubtful grounds, that Damascus actually belonged to his kingdom for a few years before his death—perhaps through a change of imperial policy at the beginning of the principate of Gaius in A.D. 37.[8] His ethnarch who, according to 2 Corinthians 11:32, watched the gates of Damascus in an attempt to arrest Paul, was probably the head of the Nabataean colony in that city.[9] Paul's residence in Damascus, according to Galatians 1:17f., fell within the three years or so following his conversion, and that event must certainly be dated well before A.D. 40, the year of Aretas's death. Even if Aretas did control

Damascus from A.D. 37 until his death, Paul's escape from the city is probably to be dated before A.D. 37. It is only in a very general way that the reference to Aretas helps us in our chronological quest.

2. The Reign and Death of Herod Agrippa I

"Herod the king," as he is called in Acts 12:1, was raised to royal estate by Gaius when he become emperor in A.D. 37 and presented with the former tetrarchies of Philip (his uncle) and Lysanias, east and north of the upper Jordan valley.[10] Two years later he was also given Galilee and Peraea, the tetrarchy from which his uncle Antipas was deposed at that time; two years later still, the next emperor, Claudius, added Judaea to his kingdom.[11] He ruled Judaea for only three years[12] (A.D. 41-44), and it is within those three years that the events of Acts 12:1-23 (the execution of James the son of Zebedee and the imprisonment and escape of Peter) must be dated.

Luke's account of Herod Agrippa's attack on the apostles in Jerusalem is introduced by the vague phrase "about that time" (Acts 12:1). The year 42 or 43 is most probable for this attack. In A.D. 41 Agrippa was in Rome at the time of the assassination of Gaius on 24 January, and stayed there until Claudius's position as emperor was consolidated.[13] It took at least five weeks to travel from Rome to Jerusalem,[14] so he would not have reached Jerusalem long before Passover. It was at Passovertide that Peter was imprisoned, but when Agrippa arrived in his new capital he had more pressing matters to attend to than a campaign against the apostles. As for A.D. 44, he died in that year five days after taking ill at Caesarea while presiding at games in honor of the emperor which are usually identified with those celebrated quadrennially on the *dies natalis* of that city—that is, on 5 March.[15] If this identification is right, then Agrippa was dead by Passover of that year, so the Passover of Acts 12:4 must be that of an earlier year than 44.[16]

During an earlier persecution of the Jerusalem church—that which followed the death of Stephen—the apostles were apparently immune from molestation (Acts 8:1b). If a cause be sought for their loss of popularity (apart from which Agrippa would not have ventured to move against them), it is readily found in their fraternization with Gentiles, more particularly in Peter's paying a social visit to a Roman officer in Caesarea. It seems certain that the conversion of Cornelius must antedate the events of Acts 12, which (as we have just seen) must be placed between 41 and 44. But there is no certain indication, either in Luke's account or anywhere else, of the relative dating of the first Christian approaches to Gentiles—Philip's preaching Jesus to the homeward-bound Ethiopian (Acts 8:27-39), Peter's preaching Jesus in the house of Cornelius (Acts 10:24-48), and the unnamed Cypriots and Cyrenaeans' doing so to the pagan Greeks of Antioch (Acts 11:20). Probably all those approaches were made independently around the same time, to which the reign of Herod Agrippa I provides a *terminus ante quem.*

3. The Famine under Claudius

Some time after the establishment of the church in Antioch, it received a visit from prophets who had come from Jerusalem (Acts 11:27f.). One of them, Agabus by name, prophesied that a great famine would beset the whole world, the whole *oikoumenē* (by which the Roman Empire is probably meant, as in Luke 2:1)—and this, adds the narrator, took place under Claudius. Agabus may have thought of an impending famine as one of the woes to be unleashed at the end-time, but Luke historicizes his prophecy because he knows that the principate of Claudius (A.D. 41-54) was, in fact, marked by serious famines—by a persistent succession of droughts *(adsiduae sterilitates)*, as Suetonius says.[17] Serious scarcity is recorded at various times during those years in Rome, Greece and Egypt.[18] More particularly, Luke's reference should be taken along with the evidence of Josephus that under the procurator-ship of Tiberius Julius Alexander (*c.* 45-48), and possibly also under that of his predecessor Cuspius Fadus (*c.* 44-45), Judaea was hard hit by a famine.[19] At this time Helena, queen-mother of Adiabene beyond the Tigris and a proselyte to Judaism, bought grain in Egypt and figs in Cyprus for the relief of the people of Judaea, while her son King Izates, also a proselyte, sent money to the Jewish authorities in Jerusalem for distribution among the poorer citizens.[20] It was almost certainly at the same time that the church of Antioch, as Luke records, contributed a sum of money for the relief of the Christians of Jerusalem and sent Barnabas and Paul to hand it over (Acts 11:29f.). Attempts to make this occasion a redactional displacement of the famine-relief visit paid by Paul to Jerusalem later in his career are misconceived. There was an urgent need in Judaea between 45 and 48; that the Antiochene Christians should have done something to help their fellow-believers there is entirely credible. It has been conjectured that the Jerusalem church found it the more difficult to pay the high price of food in those conditions of short supply because its members had been encouraged some years before to put their capital into a common pool, which was now well-nigh exhausted. Joachim Jeremias made the further point that A.D. 47-48 (probably the year after the famine) was a sabbatical year, during which the fields were required by Jewish law to lie fallow; the scarcity was thus prolonged until the harvest of 49.[21] While this suggestion finds no explicit basis in either Luke or Josephus, it is perfectly probable; it fits in very well with the other chronological evidence.

4. The Proconsulship of Sergius Paullus in Cyprus

According to Acts 13:7, when Barnabas and Paul set out from Antioch on a missionary campaign which took them first to Cyprus and then into Central Anatolia, their preaching at Paphos came to the attention of Sergius Paullus, proconsul of Cyprus, and made a deep impression on him.

Sergius Paullus belonged to a noble Roman family which had a record of public service over several generations. We know, for example, of one Lucius Sergius Paullus who was a curator of the Tiber in the principate of Claudius,[22] and was therefore contemporary with our proconsul of Cyprus. Other members of the family held public offices in various parts of the Roman Empire until well into the second century. The Sergius Paullus of Acts has been widely identified with the curator of the Tiber (the two offices, of course, could not have been held simultaneously); but there is no evidence linking the curator of the Tiber with Cyprus. A more probable identification of our proconsul is with one Quintus Sergius Paullus, whose name appears in fragmentary form on a Greek inscription from Kythraia in North Cyprus; the name of his office is missing from the extant wording, but he is apparently said to have held it under Claudius (or, according to T. B. Mitford, Gaius).[23]

Another inscription from Soloi, on the north coast of Cyprus, mentions a proconsul named Paullus who held office in some emperor's tenth year.[24] The writing is said to be later than what we should expect under Claudius;[25] if the reference were, nevertheless, to Claudius's tenth year, A.D. 50/51 would seem to be too late for Barnabas and Paul's evangelization of Cyprus, in the light of the more precise evidence available for Paul's evangelization of Corinth (at which we shall look later). D. G. Hogarth was inclined to identify the Sergius Paullus of Acts with the proconsul mentioned on the Soloi inscription,[26] but few have followed him.

Thus far, then, Barnabas and Paul's evangelization of Cyprus cannot be certainly dated by external evidence.

5. Expulsion of Jews from Rome

When Paul arrived in Corinth for the first time, says Luke, he met "a Jew of Pontus, named Aquila, lately come from Italy with his wife Priscilla, because Claudius had commanded all the Jews to leave Rome" (Acts 18:2).

Such a clearance from Rome of people deemed to be undesirable immigrants was not unprecedented. A large-scale expulsion of Roman Jews had taken place in A.D. 19, under Tiberius, in consequence of the scandalous conduct of some members of the Jewish community in the capital. Josephus juxtaposes this earlier expulsion with severe action taken about the same time against Isis-worshippers in Rome.[27]

So far as Claudius's action is concerned, two references in classical literature are relevant. Dio Cassius, relating certain measures which Claudius took at the beginning of his rule, says that, because the number of Jews in Rome had increased unduly, "he did not indeed expel them, but forbade them to meet in their ancestral way."[28] Suetonius says that he expelled the Jews because they were persistently rioting "at the instigation of Chrestus."[29] The significance of this last phrase *(impulsore Chresto)* was discussed in a lecture on "Christianity under Claudius" delivered in this building in 1961.[30] What concerns us now is the chronological bearing of these references: in particular, are the two authors (Dio and Suetonius) speaking of the same occasion? On the face of it, it might appear that they are not: Dio says that Claudius did not expel the Jews of Rome, whereas Suetonius says that he did. Even so, it has been held that they do speak of the same occasion—that Suetonius is guilty of inaccuracy or exaggeration. Of those who see the same action referred to, some date it in A.D. 41 (Claudius's first year),[31] others in 49.[32] But it is more probable that two separate actions are in view. At the beginning of his principate Claudius tried to curb Jewish rioters in the capital by imposing limited restrictions on them; when, some years later, those limited restrictions proved to be insufficient, he took the more drastic step of banishing the Jewish community from the capital.[33]

The restrictions of A.D. 41 may have been less severe because of Claudius's friendship with Herod Agrippa I (although friendship with Agrippa would not have been allowed to interfere with the business of maintaining law and order in the capital). But by the time of the wholesale expulsion edict not only was Agrippa dead; a new factor had entered into the situation. The riotous tendencies of Roman Jews had been fanned by the recent introduction of Christianity into their community.[34]

If the expulsion edict is distinct from the measures mentioned by Dio, can it be dated? Orosius in his *Historiae adversus paganos* places it in Claudius's ninth year (A.D. 49/50). This is quite probably true, but one can place little confidence in Orosius's testimony in itself, because he claims Josephus as his authority for dating the expulsion edict in that year.[35] Nowhere in the extant writings of Josephus is there any allusion to Claudius's edict, and there is no reason to suppose that any such allusion ever found a place in his writings. Orosius may have quoted from an interpolated text of Josephus, or he may simply have made a mistake: either way, the error robs him of all title to be cited as an authority on this incident.

Even if the expulsion edict could be dated more accurately, it would not by itself give us a precise date for Paul's arrival in Corinth. Aquila and Priscilla had arrived "lately" from Italy when Paul met them in Corinth; but what period of time is indicated by "lately"? It has also been suggested[36] that the statement that they came to Corinth from *Italy* could allow for some time spent in another Italian city than Rome between their expulsion from Rome and their arrival in Corinth.

6. The Proconsulship of Gallio in Achaia

A more precise chronological indicator for Paul's stay in Corinth is provided by the incident of Acts 18:12-17, in which Paul was accused at Corinth before Gallio, proconsul of Achaia, of propagating an illegal religion. The record seems to imply that Gallio came to Achaia after Paul had already begun his missionary work in Corinth. When, not long after his arrival in Corinth, Paul found the synagogue doors barred against him, he was provided with a base of operations close by in the house of one Titius Justus, where he spent eighteen months "teaching the word of God" (Acts 18:11). It was while he was thus engaged that the unsuccessful attempt was made to prosecute him before Gallio's tribunal.

Since the late nineteenth century nine fragments have, from time to time, been identified of an inscription recording a rescript of Claudius to the people of Delphi.[37] The rescript is dated from the period of Claudius's twenty-sixth acclamation as *imperator*—a period known from other inscriptions to have covered the first seven months of A.D. 52.[38] In this rescript Claudius refers to a directive issued by "my friend Gallio, proconsul of Achaia," in terms which suggest that he *was* proconsul of Achaia, but is so no longer.[39] According to Dio Cassius, Claudius made provincial governors set out from Rome, year by year, not later than mid-April;[40] they would thus enter on their administrative duties in May. A date not later than May, A.D. 51, is indicated for Gallio's entrance on his proconsulship. Other evidence suggests that ill health prevented him from staying in the post long;[41] by the time of Claudius's rescript (possibly May or June, A.D. 52) he had demitted office. The narrative of Acts implies that Paul was accused before him shortly after his arrival as proconsul and stayed on in Corinth a good while after the case against him was dismissed. It is a near certainty, then, that Paul's eighteen months in Corinth lasted from the Fall of A.D. 50 to the Spring or early Summer of 52 (according to the Western text of Acts 18:21 he attended a festival in Jerusalem soon after leaving Corinth; probably Pentecost is meant).

7. The Reign of Herod Agrippa II

When Herod Agrippa I died in A.D. 44, he left three children—a son of seventeen, Agrippa the younger, and two daughters, Berenice, aged sixteen, and Drusilla, aged six.[42] Claudius was advised that it would not be wise to appoint the seventeen-year-old son as king of the Jews in his father's place, so Judaea reverted to administration by Roman governors.[43] Four years later, when his uncle Herod, king of Chalcis (in the Lebanon) died, the younger Agrippa was given that tiny kingdom; four or five years later he received from Claudius, in exchange for Chalcis, the former territories of Philip and Lysanias (which had constituted his father's first kingdom), and this territory was augmented when Nero, at the beginning of his principate (A.D. 54), gave him further lands both east and west of Jordan, including the cities of Tiberias and Tarichaeae on the west shore of Lake Tiberias.[44] He had no territory in Judaea, but as it was his privilege to appoint the Jewish high priest he was an influential person among the Jews. He figures briefly in the record of Acts when, coming to Caesarea to greet the new procurator Festus, he is invited by Festus to lend his aid in drafting the report to be sent to Rome about Paul, who has just appealed to Caesar (Acts 25:13–26:32).

His sister Drusilla figures earlier in the narrative as the wife of Felix, who was procurator of Judaea when Paul, during his last visit to Jerusalem, was charged with violating the sanctity of the temple.

At the age of fifteen Drusilla was given in marriage by her brother Agrippa to Azizus, king of Emesa in Syria, who was required to submit to circumcision in order to marry her.[45] But her marriage to Azizus did not last long. Felix, procurator of Judaea, fell in love with her, and promised her every *felicity* if she would leave her husband and become *his* wife.[46] She yielded to his persuasion, so we find Drusilla as Felix's wife when Paul is brought before him at Caesarea (Acts 24:24). Her marriage to Felix cannot be dated earlier than A.D. 54, which gives us one point within his term of office as procurator of Judaea.

8. The Procuratorships of Felix and Festus

But when did Felix become procurator of Judaea, and when was he

recalled and replaced by Porcius Festus (Acts 24:27)? The procuratorships of Felix and Festus, taken together, probably covered a period of
ten years. The duration of Festus's procuratorship is not actually stated,
but from Josephus's summary account of it in *BJ* 2.271 (amplified in *Ant.*
20.181, 185-197), it appears not to have lasted more than two or three
years when it was terminated by his death in office. His death was
followed by an interregnum of three months before the arrival of his
successor Albinus. It was during this interregnum that the illegal execution of James the Just took place.[47] The procuratorships of Albinus and,
after him, Gessius Florus were the last before the Jewish revolt of
September, A.D. 66. Four years would not be too much to allow to these
two last procuratorships, so that the generally accepted date of A.D. 62
for the death of James the Just (and therefore for the death of Festus a
few weeks previously) cannot be wide of the mark.

In deciding on the date of Felix's entry on his procuratorship, we
have to reckon with the discrepant evidence of Josephus and Tacitus.
Josephus (who had first-hand knowledge of the course of events) makes
Felix the successor of Ventidius Cumanus as procurator: Claudius apparently appointed him to this office shortly before he presented the
younger Agrippa with the former tetrarchies of Philip and Lysanias—
and that was "when he had completed the twelfth year of his principate"
(i.e., in A.D. 53).[48] Felix's appointment as procurator of all Judaea[49] may
thus be dated in 52, the year of Cumanus's deposition, according to
Tacitus.[50]

Tacitus, however, speaks of the province as having been divided
between Cumanus and Felix, so that Cumanus governed Galilee and
Felix Samaria.[51] (Then who, it might be asked, governed Judaea
proper?)[52] Tacitus's statement might be explained if Felix, before becoming procurator of Judaea, held a subsidiary post under Cumanus, with
special responsibility for Samaria.[53] Cumanus's procuratorship began
about A.D. 48: this is implied by Josephus when he brackets the younger
Agrippa's succeeding his uncle Herod as ruler of Chalcis—which he did
in the eighth year of Claudius[54]—with Cumanus's succeeding Alexander as governor of Judaea. When Tacitus, dealing with the events of
A.D. 52, says that Felix had been set over Judaea for a long time now *(iam
pridem Iudaeae impositus)*,[55] this can only be explained if Felix held a
subordinate office in the province since early in Cumanus's governorship. But one may wonder if Tacitus's sources misled him. He further
says that Felix was one of the judges appointed by Ummidius Quadra-
tus, legate of Syria, to help Claudius in reaching a decision in a quarrel
between Judaeans and Samaritans.[56]

According to Luke, Paul began his speech of defense before Felix with a reference to the "many years" during which Felix had been judge over the Jewish nation (Acts 24:10). This was two years before Felix was recalled from office, according to the most probable meaning of Acts 24:27 ("when two years had elapsed, Felix was succeeded by Porcius Festus"). The date of Felix's recall is debatable, but a change in the Judaean provincial coinage attested for Nero's fifth year (A.D. 58/59) may be a pointer: this coin issue, says Professor E. Mary Smallwood, "is more likely to be the work of a new procurator than of an outgoing one who had already minted a large issue."[57]

An earlier date for Felix's recall is defended by some on the ground that, when he was recalled, he was saved from the severest penalties which his misdemeanors in office merited by the interposition of his brother Pallas.[58] Pallas was one of the most influential of the imperial freedmen; he was head of the civil service *(libertus a rationibus)* under Claudius. Pallas's influence may well have had something to do with Felix's original appointment as procurator—an unprecedented honor for a freedman, normally reserved for a member of the equestrian order. (Josephus, however, says that the appointment of Felix was requested by the former high priest Jonathan, who had perhaps been impressed by his judicial handling of the quarrel between Judaeans and Samaritans.)[59] Pallas enjoyed the favor of Agrippina, Nero's mother, but was dismissed from his influential office when Agrippina forfeited her son's good will in A.D. 55.[60] Therefore, it is argued, he was in no position to protect his disgraced brother Felix after that year.

In fact, Pallas retained great power after his dismissal from the civil service; on that occasion, indeed, he stipulated that there should be no scrutiny of his conduct in office and that his accounts with the state should be treated as balanced.[61] His influence, based no doubt on his exceptional wealth, lasted till 62, when he fell victim to Nero's desire to lay hands on his wealth.[62] Nothing in the circumstances of Pallas's career for the years following his dismissal rules out 59 as the date of Felix's deposition.

Another argument for dating Felix's deposition in 55 is that Eusebius dates it in the second year of Nero.[63] But this is not easily reconciled with Josephus's statement that Nero appointed Felix (that is, confirmed him) as governor of all Judaea except those areas which he had given to the younger Agrippa.[64] (It has, in fact, been argued—but quite unconvincingly—that Eusebius was four years out in his estimate of Nero's regnal years, and that "second" here should be corrected to "sixth".[65])

9. *"The Days of Unleavened Bread"*

An attempt has been made to fix the year of Paul's last visit to Jerusalem on the basis of Acts 20:6f. There, in a "we" section, the narrator says, "we sailed away from Philippi [i.e., from Neapolis, the port of Philippi] after the days of unleavened bread, and in five days we came to . . . Troas, where we stayed for seven days. On the first day of the week . . . Paul conversed with them [the members of the church in Troas], intending to depart the next day."

The "days of unleavened bread" lasted from 14 to 21 Nisan. In five days (by inclusive reckoning) from 22 Nisan, Paul and his companions arrived at Troas, where they stayed seven days (26 Nisan to 3 Iyyar). The last full day they spent at Troas was a Sunday. In what year, then, around that time did 2 Iyyar fall on a Sunday—or (to put it otherwise) did 14 Nisan (Passover Eve) fall on a Thursday?[66] The answer is A.D. 57, which (as Sir William Ramsay confidently concluded) was accordingly the year of Paul's last journey to Jerusalem.[67]

I believe that A.D. 57 was indeed the year in question, but this cannot be established conclusively by Ramsay's argument. The party set out from Philippi "after the days of unleavened bread"—but how long after? Owing to a sudden change of plan, Paul's departure had been delayed, and he was anxious to lose no time; therefore, Ramsay argued, he and his friends must have set out immediately after the week of unleavened bread—the day after, in fact. But they would have had to wait until they could embark on a convenient ship. Further, Paul preached at Troas on the evening of the first day of the week, and "prolonged his speech until midnight" (Acts 20:7); but did Luke reckon that day as having started at sunset or at midnight? We cannot be sure, but again it could make a difference to the calculation.

Ramsay may be right in making Paul leave Philippi on Friday, 15 April, and preach at Troas on Sunday, 24 April, in A.D. 57; but the evidence is not firm enough to prove beyond question that the year was in fact 57.

Paul wished to be in Jerusalem for the Feast of Pentecost (Acts 20:16); in A.D. 57 it fell on 28/29 May. In the event, he and his fellow-travelers reached Judaea with time in hand; they were able to spend several days in Caesarea before going up to Jerusalem (Acts 21:10, 15). A week after Paul's arrival in Jerusalem he was arrested; a day or two later he was taken to Caesarea, where he was kept in custody for two years (Acts 21:27-34; 23:23-35; 24:11, 27).

At the end of those two years he set out from Caesarea on his voyage, under armed guard, to Italy. By the time he and his company reached Fair Havens, on the south coast of Crete, "sailing was now dangerous because the fast [i.e., the Day of Atonement] had already gone by" (Acts 27:9). The dangerous season for navigation in the Mediterranean lasted from 14 September to 11 November; from the latter date all navigation on the open sea ceased for the winter.[68] It may be inferred, then, that in this year the Day of Atonement (10 Tishri) fell after 14 September. In A.D. 59 it fell on 5 October, which was just about as late as it was possible for it to fall. So, if A.D. 57 suits the requirements for the journey from Philippi to Caesarea, A.D. 59, two years later, suits the requirements for the voyage from Caesarea to Italy. To that extent either date supports the other, but neither can be demonstrated to be the right one. Apart from other considerations, while the equivalences between the Jewish and the Julian calendars can be fixed with high probability, they cannot be determined with absolute certainty.

10. The Persecution under Nero

The tenth point of comparison listed by Turner, the persecution of Christians in Rome under Nero, need not detain us long. It is too late to have any bearing on the record of Acts. Tacitus makes it the sequel to the great fire of Rome, which raged for five days in July, A.D. 64.[69] How long after the fire the persecution broke out we cannot be sure. J. A. T. Robinson may be right, following G. Edmundson, in dating it not earlier than the spring of A.D. 65.[70]

Be that as it may, the end of the two years which Paul spent under house-arrest in Rome (Acts 28:30) cannot be dated later than A.D. 62. If the hearing of his appeal to Caesar ended in his conviction and execution, then he was not affected by the persecution. If, on the other hand, the tradition is right which makes his execution, like Peter's, an incident in the persecution, then he may have enjoyed a few years of liberty before being brought to trial again; but on these matters the available evidence is of the scantiest, and in any case is irrelevant to the chronology of Acts.

III. THE EVIDENCE OF PAUL'S LETTERS

There remains one body of literature which demands to be taken into consideration when the chronological data of Acts are compared with data from other sources: that is the Pauline corpus. Some comparison of these two sets of data has been offered more than once in this place.[71] If our present subject were the chronology of the life of Paul, then his own letters would provide us with our primary source; and even in an assessment of the chronological evidence of Acts they are by no means irrelevant.

About half a century ago a new approach was launched to Pauline chronology, which had radical implications for the chronology of Acts. The pioneer in this study was Professor John Knox, formerly of Union Theological Seminary, New York. Although the chronological indications in the Pauline letters are only occasional, Professor Knox has found them adequate for the construction of a coherent chronology of Paul's apostolic career, which (it is argued) deviates from that presented by Acts and must be accepted in preference to it because of its first-hand authority.[72]

The chronology constructed by Professor Knox and others is closely related to what Paul calls "the collection for the saints"—that is, the relief fund which he organized on behalf of the Jerusalem church towards the end of his ministry in the Aegean world. This fund is mentioned in 1 Corinthians 16:1-4 (where Paul tells the Corinthian church, as he had already told the Galatian churches, he says, how to set about collecting the money), 2 Corinthians 8:1–9:15 (where he encourages the Corinthians to complete the work so well begun), and Romans 15:25-29 (where he explains that he must go to Jerusalem to take part in the handing over of the money before he can fulfill his plan to visit Rome *en route* for Spain). The visit to Jerusalem on which he was about to set out when he sent his letter to the Romans is plainly to be identified with that of Acts 21–23.

How long did it take to organize and complete the collection? From internal evidence, not much more than two years. In 2 Corinthians 12:2 Paul tells the Corinthian Christians that he has been boasting about them to the Macedonian churches, saying, "Achaia has been ready since last year" (but that was an instance of hope outstripping experience: Achaia—meaning Corinth—was not ready even then).

At the meeting which Paul and Barnabas had with the leaders of the mother-church on a previous visit to Jerusalem, described in Galatians 2:1-10, the Jerusalem leaders, as their final request, urged Paul and Barnabas to "remember the poor"—the poorer members of the church of Jerusalem (and that meant most of them). The view of Knox and others is that Paul's organization of the great collection (the collection mentioned in the three places already cited) was his *immediate* response to this request: that, as soon as the request was made, he returned from Jerusalem to Antioch and then traveled through Asia Minor, Macedonia and Achaia to organize the collection, so that it was completed and delivered, probably, in four or five years after the request was made. This view telescopes the four "capital letters" (those to the Galatians, Corinthians and Romans) into a remarkably brief space of time.[73] Moreover, since the conference described in Galatians 2:1-10 took place fourteen years, probably (or seventeen years at most),[74] after Paul's conversion, his whole apostolic career must have been notably shorter than has been traditionally supposed, and the bulk of his activity must be assigned to the period before the conference.

When Paul says, in Galatians 1:21, that after this first postconversion visit to Jerusalem he "came into the parts of Syria and Cilicia," this (we are warned) must not be taken to mean that he remained there; in the interval between the visit of Galatians 1:18f. and that of Galatians 2:1-10 "we are at liberty to suppose that he went not only to Galatia but also to Macedonia, Greece and [proconsular] Asia before he returned to Jerusalem 'fourteen years later'," says Knox, and he goes on to argue that "he actually did so."[75]

In Paul's letters, mention is made of three occasions on which he visited Jerusalem in the course of his apostolic career. The first and second are referred to in the past tense ("I went up," Gal. 1:18; 2:1). The third is referred to in the future (1 Cor. 16:4; Rom. 15:25): he plans to go to Jerusalem with the representatives of the contributing churches. Further, it is maintained (by Knox and others), the logic of his successive references to the collection rules out the possibility of any other visit to Jerusalem within that period. But where Paul mentions three visits, Acts records five: those of Acts 9:26; 11:30; 15:4; 18:22 (where Jerusalem is implied, but not expressly mentioned); 21:15. Three of these (Acts 11:30; 15:4; 18:22) must therefore be triplicate accounts of one and the same visit, which actually took place at the point indicated in the narrative of Acts by 18:22.[76]

The proponents of this view agree with most students that Paul's conversion is to be dated in the early 30s, but hold that the greater part of his missionary work was done in the later 30s and the 40s, that he began organizing the collection about 47 (50 at the latest) and completed it and came to Jerusalem with it about 51 (55 at the latest).[77] By the year 60 he may well have been condemned and executed in Rome.

But in this reconstruction what is the relevance of Luke's reference to Gallio? Are we to abandon this fixed datum which Luke provides for Paul's evangelization of Corinth? The latest answer to this question has been proposed by Gerd Lüdemann. Luke, he says, tends to place all he wants to tell us about Paul's association with any one place in the setting of his first visit to that place. We need not abandon the Gallio reference: we must simply recognize that Paul's accusation before Gallio belongs to a later visit by Paul to Corinth—in fact, to his last visit.[78] If we were forced to this conclusion, we should, of course, have no option but to accept it. But there is no need to accept it. It is perfectly clear that, in Luke's understanding, Gallio's favorable verdict enabled Paul to prolong his evangelizing ministry in Corinth: it does not belong to the context of a later, consolidating, visit. The dating of Paul's first stay in Corinth between 50 and 52 cannot be so easily overthrown.

The flaw in the argument of Knox and those who take his line is their reading too much into Galatians 2:10. Paul concludes his account of the conversations which he and Barnabas held with the Jerusalem leaders by saying, "only they would have us remember the poor, which very thing I was eager to do." He does not necessarily mean "I proceeded at once to organize 'the collection for the saints'" (about which, in fact, nothing at all is said in Galatians). He may equally well mean "I made a special point of remembering 'the poor'"—with the possible implication that he had already paid attention to this matter[79] (as in the famine-relief mission from Antioch to Jerusalem, recorded in Acts 11:30).

It would not be surprising to learn that, however often or seldom Paul went to Jerusalem between receiving the leaders' request and paying his last visit to the city, he took with him on each occasion some token of his commitment to "remember the poor." The gift brought on his last visit was a special one, marking the completion of his ministry in the eastern Mediterranean.[80] C. H. Buck agrees that "without II Corinthians a reader would naturally assume that the collection was not a single event but a regular practice in Paul's ministry."[81] But even with the evidence of 2 Corinthians the assumption is quite a reasonable one to make. The climactic collection to which such importance is attached in 2 Corinthians (as in 1 Corinthians 16:1-4 and Romans 15:25-29) does not exclude earlier occasions when Paul may have had opportunity to "remember the poor" in response to the request made to him and Barnabas at the Jerusalem conference.

True, nothing is said in Acts of any delivery of money in connection with Paul's Jerusalem visits between the famine-relief visit from Antioch and the last visit he paid to Jerusalem—but only one very general allusion is made to the delivery of money in connection with his last visit (Acts 24:17), although his letters make it plain that the handing over of the collection was a prime purpose for this visit. True, nothing is said in Paul's letters of any delivery of money to Jerusalem before the handing over of the collection at his last visit—but the three capital letters (1 and 2 Corinthians and Romans) which mention that collection do so because they were written while it was being organized and got ready for transmission to Jerusalem. The other capital letter (Galatians) tells of the request to "remember the poor" but makes no reference to the collection as such. The Galatian Christians are not invited to contribute to it. The time came when Paul, either orally or in writing, gave directions to the Galatian Christians about their contributions comparable to those given in 1 Corinthians 16:1-4,[82] but those directions were not given in the canonical letter to the Galatians, but most probably some years later. There is no need to date Galatians in such proximity to the other capital letters as is required on the interpretation of John Knox and others—an interpretation which (in George Caird's words) "naturally avoids all the difficulties which beset those who take Acts more seriously, but . . . raises some very awkward problems of its own."[83] If Galatians is some years earlier than the Corinthian and Roman correspondence (as I have argued here before),[84] then we can continue to take the chronology of Acts seriously, without doing violence to the natural sense of Paul's language.

10. The Church of Jerusalem in the Acts of the Apostles

I. CHURCH OF APOSTLES AND ELDERS

When Luke speaks of "the church" with no qualification, geographical or otherwise, it is to the church of Jerusalem that he refers. In the earlier part of his second volume, the Acts of the Apostles, that is not surprising, since at that stage in his narrative there is no other church than the church of Jerusalem. The church of Jerusalem is the church *sans phrase;* the church universal is concentrated in one city. Not until the beginning of chapter 13 is the word "church" (ἐκκλησία) used of the followers of Jesus in another city than Jerusalem. There the history of the extension of Christianity from Antioch on the Orontes towards the west and north-west is introduced by a list of leaders "at Antioch, in the church that was there" (Acts 13:1).[1] The church of Antioch was, for Luke, the first of a succession of Gentile churches,[2] but he knows of only one Jewish-Christian church. Even in dispersion (on account of the persecution which broke out after Stephen's death) the church of Jerusalem remained "the church" in the singular. When the persecution died down with the conversion and departure of the leading persecutor, "then," says Luke, "the church had peace throughout all Judaea and Galilee and Samaria" (Acts 9:31).

This usage is different from Paul's: Paul speaks of "the churches of

---

A lecture delivered in the John Rylands University Library, Manchester, on Wednesday, 5 December 1984, and published in *BJRL* 67 (1984-85), pp. 641-661.

Judaea" in the plural (Galatians 1:22; 1 Thessalonians 2:14). For Luke, on the other hand, there is only one church in Judaea—the mother-church of the new society. Apart from the Jerusalem church, says Martin Hengel, "Luke ignores the communities in Judaea in an almost offensive way, not to mention those in Galilee, which are mentioned . . . only in passing."[3] He mentions "saints" both in Lydda and in Joppa (Acts 9:32, 41), but does not speak of a church in either of these places. The church of Jerusalem retains the primacy over the area of the Christian mission almost (but not altogether) to the end of the narrative of Acts, and in Palestine it enjoys not merely primacy, but monopoly.

Luke's account of the church of Jerusalem is derived from a variety of sources, but he handles his material (whencesoever derived) so that it serves his purpose in writing. He was indebted to more than one Jerusalem source and to at least one source which may provisionally be called Antiochene.[4] In his own handling of the material he presents the church of Jerusalem in two stages—first as the church of the apostles and then as a church ruled by elders. The two stages overlap: the elders appear (Acts 11:30) before the apostles leave the scene. The transition between the two stages is provided by the record of the Apostolic Council, where the responsibility for deliberation and decision is shared by "the apostles and the elders" (Acts 15:6, 22f.). In the church of the apostles Peter is the dominating figure; in the church ruled by elders, James. It is worth observing that Luke nowhere helps his readers to identify this James, whom he mentions in three places (Acts 12:17; 15:13; 21:18). This could be because James's identity was so well known in early Christian circles; others have discerned more tendentious reasons for Luke's reticence.[5] There is, in any case, no doubt at all that this is the James to whom Paul refers as "James the Lord's brother" (Galatians 1:19) and who is elsewhere called "James the Just."[6] Peter begins to be phased out at the time of his escape from prison under Herod Agrippa I (Acts 12:17).[7] His last appearance in Luke's record is at the Apostolic Council. There he makes a persuasive speech (Acts 15:7-11); but it is James who sums up the sense of the meeting, weaving Peter's testimony into his own argument (Acts 15:13-21).

II. HEBREWS AND HELLENISTS

The church, according to Luke, had its inception in Jerusalem on the day of Pentecost in the year of Jesus' death and resurrection. It was inaugurated by the descent of the Spirit, in fulfillment of Old Testament prophecy, and by the public proclamation of the gospel by Peter. It comprised the twelve apostles, the family of Jesus, and others associated with these (amounting in all to a hundred and twenty), together with those who believed and were baptized in response to Peter's preaching that day—a total of three thousand (Acts 2:41). In a few weeks the number had increased to five thousand—five thousand *men,* says Luke, apparently not including women and children (Acts 4:4). (This figure of five thousand *men,* which is reminiscent of the narrative of the feeding of the multitude in Mark 6:44, has been ascribed to a different source from the earlier figure of three thousand *persons.*)[8] A quarter of a century later, the number of church members in Jerusalem has risen to many "myriads" (Acts 21:10)[9]—a figure which should not be pressed too literally, especially if Joachim Jeremias was even approximately correct in his estimate of up to 30,000 for the normal population of the city at that time.[10]

The picture of the church of Jerusalem in the first five chapters of Acts is that of a community of enthusiastic followers of Jesus, growing by leaps and bounds, and enjoying the goodwill of its neighbors. Its members practice community of goods voluntarily and spontaneously, delighting in this way to manifest their conscious unity and charity. True, the serpent which lurks at the heart of every utopia revealed its presence in the sad incident of Ananias and Sapphira, who tried to get credit for being more generous than they were (Acts 5:1-11); but the chapter which records their disastrous lapse ends with a description of the increasing activity of the church's apostolic leaders, "teaching and preaching the gospel of Jesus as the Messiah" (Acts 5:42).

It is, then, a complete surprise for the reader to be introduced at the beginning of the next chapter to two rather sharply differentiated groups in the church—the "Hebrews" and the "Hellenists."[11] The members of both these groups were Jewish by birth (except for those Hellenists who were proselytes, converts to Judaism from paganism); they were distinguished from other members of the Jewish religious community by their recognition of Jesus as the Messiah of Israel. The difference between the two groups, it appears, was mainly linguistic: the Hebrews were Aramaic-speaking while the Hellenists were Greek-speaking. To which group would speakers of both languages be assigned? It would depend, probably, on the kind of synagogue they attended. The Hebrews would attend synagogues where the scriptures were read and the prayers said in Hebrew; the Hellenists would attend synagogues where the whole service was conducted in Greek.[12] Here and there throughout the Graeco-Roman world we find reference made to a "synagogue of Hebrews";[13] unless "Hebrews" in such a context is simply a synonym for "Jews," a synagogue so designated might be one where, even in lands of the dispersion, a pious Jew might hear the lessons and the prayers in the sacred language. On the other hand, even in Jerusalem people who knew no language but Greek could attend a synagogue where the service was conducted in that tongue: such was the "synagogue of the Freedmen" mentioned in Acts 6:9 or the synagogue referred to in the Theodotus inscription (discovered in Jerusalem shortly before the outbreak of World War I).[14]

If the basic distinction between the two groups was linguistic, there were other differences of a cultural kind sufficient to give each of them a sense of separate corporate identity. Any real or imagined discrimination which seemed to favor one would be resented by the other. Luke (drawing, it appears, on a new source, different from those which he may have used for the earlier part of his narrative)[15] records one instance of alleged discrimination in the preferential treatment which the Hellenists believed the Hebrew widows were receiving over theirs when daily distribution was made from the common fund to needy members of the community. There may have been other points at issue between the two groups, some of them theological in character, but Luke concentrates (and not here only) on a nontheological area of dispute.[16] He shows true understanding of human nature in this: leaders and teachers of religious bodies may insist on points of theological disagreement, but the rank and file will more readily begin to show an interest when the disagreement affects them in a practical way.

We are dealing here with a situation which may have arisen not more than five years after the death of Jesus and the foundation of the church—probably less than that. What, then, was the origin of this Hellenistic group in the Jerusalem church?

Some scholars have wisely insisted in recent years that the distinction between Palestinian and Hellenistic Judaism should not be overpressed.[17] Palestine had been part of the Hellenistic world since its incorporation in Alexander's empire in 332/1 B.C. Even if there was a violent reaction on the part of many Palestinian Jews against assimilation to Hellenism (especially when such assimilation was forcibly imposed, as it was under Antiochus Epiphanes), those who reacted violently were themselves influenced by other forms of Hellenistic culture than those which they consciously resisted. In Palestine students of religious law received the "tradition of the elders" which was handed down orally in Hebrew from one generation to another, but there is evidence to suggest that even in rabbinical academies in Palestine provision was made for instruction in Greek.[18]

As for the Jews of the dispersion around the eastern Mediterranean, they were predominantly Hellenists. Even Paul, who insists that he is "a Hebrew of Hebrews"[19]—a Hebrew born and bred—might equally well have been called a Hellenist. Not only was he a native of Tarsus, a Greek-speaking city, but his mastery of Greek shows that it was no foreign language to him. No doubt he was thoroughly bilingual. It has been argued with some probability that, while many Hebrews spoke Greek as well as their Semitic tongue, Hellenists normally knew Greek only.[20] Barnabas, the Levite from Cyprus, a member of the Jerusalem church from early days,[21] was presumably a Hellenist, as was his fellow-Cypriot Mnason, described in Acts 21:16 as ἀρχαῖος μαθητής (which probably means a foundation-member of the church).

There may well have been Hellenists among Jesus' followers in Jerusalem before his crucifixion; if so, their number was augmented from Pentecost onwards. It was among such Hellenists, rather than in the ranks of the twelve apostles and their close associates, that Jesus' more radical utterances about the temple were cherished and repeated, especially his words about destroying the temple and rebuilding it in three days, which were flung back at him in mockery by passers-by when he was exposed to public derision on the cross.

When the complaint about the unfairness shown to Hellenistic widows was met by the apostles with the advice to choose seven men to supervise the daily distribution, the men appointed to this responsibility all bore Greek names. This in itself does not prove that they were Hellenists: should we conclude that Andrew and Philip among the apostles were Hellenists? Perhaps they were; it is even conceivable that Andrew's parents deliberately brought him up as a Hellenist while they brought his brother Simon up to be a Hebrew. (A twentieth-century parallel comes to mind: I knew a family in Bratislava in the 1930s of which one son was sent to a German-speaking school and his brother to a Slovak-speaking school.) But, over and above their Greek names, the general context suggests that the seven men were all Hellenists. This was indubitably true of one of their number, Nicolas the proselyte of Antioch,[22] and it was probably true of them all. The narrative implies, indeed, that they were leaders of the Hellenistic group in the primitive church, fulfilling a much wider ministry than that of *septem viri mensis ordinandis,*[23] to which they were appointed on the occasion described by Luke. When the apostles invited the complainants to select seven men to take charge of the allocation of charity, they responded to the invitation by selecting those whom they already recognized as their leaders.

As Luke develops this phase of his narrative, one point of theological significance which emerges is the different attitude shown to the temple by the leaders of the church as a whole and by the leaders of the Hellenistic group—especially if Stephen's attitude be taken as characteristic of the latter. The apostolic leaders attended the temple at the customary times of prayer and preached in the outer court as Jesus had done, while the members of the church came together daily in Solomon's colonnade, on the east side of the temple area.[24] Stephen, on the other hand, declared that God never desired a permanently fixed dwelling-place like the temple, that a movable shrine was more suitable for a pilgrim people.[25]

Both sides could appeal to the authority of Jesus for their attitude to the temple. Jesus, on the one hand, defended the sanctity of the temple, calling it "my Father's house" (Luke 2:49; John 2:16), and endorsing the prophet's description of it as "a house of prayer for all the nations" (Mark 11:7, quoting Isaiah 56:7). On the other hand, he not only predicted the demolition of the temple structure (Mark 13:2) but also announced its abandonment by God—"your house is forsaken and desolate" (Matthew 23:38)—and its replacement by a new temple "not made with hands" (Mark 14:58).[26] The tension between these two attitudes is resolved by Luke later in the narrative of Acts.[27]

Luke's assessment of the temple is more positive than Stephen's, but he has a lively sympathy with the Hellenistic group of which Stephen was so forthright a spokesman. Naturally so: it was members of that group who, forced to leave Jerusalem because of the persecution that followed Stephen's death, carried the gospel north to Antioch. Antioch, according to tradition, was Luke's native city;[28] in any case, he was keenly interested in Antiochene Christianity and the part it played in the further expansion of the gospel along the road which led ultimately to Rome.

When Jesus was being judicially examined by the high priest and his colleagues, an attempt was made to convict him of a threat to destroy the temple.[29] The attempt failed because the witnesses could not agree on the precise wording of his alleged threat; that he had said something about the destruction of the temple was undoubted. If he had been successfully convicted on this charge, he could perhaps have been sentenced and executed without reference to the Roman governor; violation of the sanctity of the temple was the one area in which the Romans allowed the Jewish authorities to exercise capital jurisdiction. But there was no difficulty about convicting Stephen: when witnesses alleged that he had committed blasphemy against the temple, he effectively convicted himself (in his judges' eyes) by denying that the temple had any place in the divine purpose for Israel. Execution by stoning was the inevitable outcome of the case, the first stones being thrown, in accordance with the ancient law, by the witnesses for the prosecution.[30]

The apostles and their followers enjoyed the goodwill of the people of Jerusalem, who would, however, resent any attack on the temple or disparagement of its sanctity. When, then, the chief priests launched an attack on Stephen's associates, they could be sure of popular support. Luke uses generalizing terms when he speaks of a "great persecution" breaking out against the church of Jerusalem or of Saul of Tarsus, the chief priests' agent, as "breathing threats and slaughter against the disciples of the Lord" (Acts 8:1; 9:1), but when one reads his narrative carefully, it emerges that the Hellenists bore the brunt of the attack. The apostles are specifically excluded when "all" the members of the church are said to have been scattered throughout Judaea and Samaria.[31]

We should envisage the believing community in Jerusalem as organized in a number of household groups. Those groups closely associated with the apostles (and, it may be surmised, with James and other members of the holy family) seem to have remained *relatively* undisturbed. Paul indeed, when he refers to his active participation in the campaign of repression, says that he "persecuted the church of God" (Galatians 1:13; 1 Corinthians 15:9; cf. Philippians 3:6). Before his conversion he probably saw no difference in principle between the Hebrews and the Hellenists in the church: in his view it was the insistence that the crucified Jesus was the Messiah, not the disparagement of the temple, that was the head and front of the offending. But the tactics dictated by the chief priests, who had no desire to outrage public opinion, confined the attack in the main to the Hellenists. It was the Hellenists who were dispersed; it was they who carried the gospel far and wide as they moved from place to place. The reader of Acts may get the impression that, after their departure, the church of Jerusalem was more monochrome, more consistently and even conservatively "Hebrew," than it had been before. There were, to be sure, a few Hellenists left, like Mnason the Cypriot, who was host to Paul and his companions when they visited the city in A.D. 57; but had there still been a substantial number of them, the members of the mother-church could not have been described, as they were in that year, as "all zealots for the law" (Acts 21:20).[32]

III. PAUL'S FIRST CONTACT WITH THE CHURCH OF JERUSALEM

It is difficult to be sure what impact Paul's conversion made on the church of Jerusalem, apart from the fact that, deprived of his leadership, the persecution died down. Paul's contact with the mother-church was minimal in the earlier years of his Christian career (even in the later years it was not very close or frequent). Luke says that, some time after his conversion, he came to Jerusalem "and tried to join the disciples, but they were all afraid of him and would not believe that he was a [true] disciple." Barnabas, however, took him to the apostles and vouched for his *bona fides,* and he remained in their company, boldly proclaiming his new-found faith, especially to the Hellenists (that is, the non-Christian Hellenists), so that his life was endangered and he had to be got away from Jerusalem in a hurry: "the brothers took him down to Caesarea and sent him off to Tarsus" (Acts 9:26-30).

This narrative makes a different impression from Paul's own account of the same visit in Galatians 1:18-20,[33] according to which he went up to Jerusalem (from Damascus) three years after his conversion and spent fifteen days with Peter, seeing none of the other apostles during his visit except James, "the Lord's brother." Paul minimizes his contact with the Jerusalem leaders, and calls God to witness that his account is true, in terms which suggest that he is anxious to refute another account which had come to the ears of his converts in Galatia. It has been suggested, notably by the late Olof Linton of Copenhagen, that the other account which Paul is anxious to refute is the account reproduced by Luke in Acts 9:26-30.[34] But this is unlikely. Luke's information about this visit is scanty, and his filling out of that information is mainly redactional. He uses the generalizing plurals "the disciples," "the apostles," "the brothers"; whereas Paul makes it plain that he saw no more than two apostles (and one of these, James, was not an apostle in Luke's understanding of the term).[35] If other apostles were around in Jerusalem at that time, then Paul's visit to Peter must have been a very private one. We cannot be sure, indeed, what opportunity the church of Jerusalem had had to reorganize itself after the persecution.

But Luke does not suggest that during this visit the church of Jerusalem or its leaders conferred any authority on Paul, and that is the suggestion which Paul is at such pains to deny in Galatians 1:18-20. Those disciples in Jerusalem whom Paul met on this occasion recognized him, after initial misgivings, as a fellow-disciple. They looked after him and took steps for his safety, but even in Luke's account he appears to have acted independently in his witness to Hellenistic Jews during those days. We can easily recognize Paul's motives in relating the visit as he does; it is difficult to recognize any "tendency" in Luke's generalizing narrative. The church probably breathed a collective sigh of relief when Paul set sail for Tarsus; it then got down to the task of rebuilding its communal life.

IV. THE APOSTLES UNDER ATTACK

A greater shock to the life of the Jerusalem church was administered by

Peter's visit to the house of the Roman centurion Cornelius at Caesarea and its sequel.

According to Luke's arrangement of his narrative, it was not long after Paul's departure for Tarsus and the restoration of peace to the church that Peter visited this Gentile and was invited to preach the gospel to him and his family and friends. Their reception of the message was attended by signs which left Peter with no option but to have Cornelius and the others baptized.[36] This fraternizing with Gentiles caused misgivings among Peter's associates back in Jerusalem, but when Peter gave them a full account of the matter the evidence of divine guidance was such that objections were silenced: the other apostles acquiesced in his action.[37]

In one respect the misgivings were well founded: Peter's action and his colleagues' acquiescence in it lost them much of the popular good-will which they had enjoyed until then. It is not surprising that, shortly after this, an attack was launched on the church leaders by Herod Agrippa I, king of the Jews by grace of the Emperor Claudius. Instead of being exempt from molestation, as they had been in the persecution which followed Stephen's death, the apostles were now the principal targets for attack. James the Zebedaean was executed, and Peter would have suffered the same fate, but he was kept under armed guard until the passover season was over and was helped to escape just before the day appointed for his public execution. The attack did not last long—a consequence, probably, of Agrippa's unexpected death in March, A.D. 44—but while it lasted it had the approval of the Jewish leaders.[38]

From this time onwards the undisputed leadership of the church was exercised by James the Just, who continued to enjoy public esteem after Peter and his fellow-apostles lost it. He at any rate was known to have nothing to do with the recent scandalous approach to Gentiles.[39] The transition from the leadership of Peter to the primacy of James is indicated indirectly by Luke when he tells how Peter, on his escape from Agrippa's prison, reported his deliverance to the group that met in the house of Mary, the mother of Mark, and, with the words "Tell this to James and to the brothers," went off to "another place" (Acts 12:17).

V. JERUSALEM AND THE GENTILE MISSION

The first presentation of the gospel to Gentiles, however, took place informally and almost accidentally in places remote from Jerusalem. One result of the dispersion that followed the death of Stephen was that now, in every region of Palestine and in the adjoining provinces, there were groups of believers in Jesus who had once lived in Jerusalem and were still regarded by the church leaders there as subject to their authority. Such were the groups in Lydda and Joppa which received a visit from Peter when peace returned to the church (Acts 9:32-43).

When the gospel was carried into neighboring provinces by some of the dispersed Hellenists, the leaders of the Jerusalem church held themselves responsible to supervise its progress. When some of the Hellenists began to evangelize pagans in the North Syrian city of Antioch, they treated the news of this innovative advance so seriously that they sent Barnabas to Antioch to investigate and report back. Barnabas was so impressed by what he found in Antioch that he stayed on there to give the new movement the direction and encouragement which he saw it needed. But in Antioch, and even farther afield, Barnabas was an emissary (an ἀπόστολος) of the Jerusalem church.[40]

The desire of the Jerusalem church to maintain control over the extension of the Christian way, and Luke's understanding of its authority, may be gathered from his record of the "Council of Jerusalem" in Acts 15:6-29. The designation "Council of Jerusalem" could be misleading if it suggested an ecumenical synod; it was a meeting of the apostles and elders of the church of Jerusalem to consider what policy should be adopted with regard to the rapidly advancing Gentile mission in Antioch and neighboring parts of the united province of Syria and Cilicia. A few representatives of the church of Antioch were present, but they took no part in deciding on an appropriate policy: their role was confined to the supplying of evidence which the apostles and elders could take into consideration in reaching their decision.

According to Luke's presentation of the order of events, Barnabas and Paul had recently been released by the church of Antioch for missionary work beyond the province of Syria and Cilicia—more particularly, in Cyprus and South Galatia. The fact that they undertook this work as emissaries of the Antiochene church did not deter the Jerusalem authorities from paying serious attention to its wider implications.

The special status of the church of Jerusalem as the mother-church of the expanding Christian mission was recognized outside the bounds of that church. Even Paul, who stoutly resisted any attempt to impose the authority of Jerusalem over his Gentile churches, took care to maintain as friendly relations as possible with Jerusalem. He knew that his apostolic ministry would be abortive if any attempt were made to carry it on in isolation from Jerusalem.

The increase in the number of Gentile converts, even at a considerable distance from Jerusalem and Judaea, made the Jerusalem church give more urgent thought than previously to the conditions on which

Gentiles might be recognized as full members of the believing community. If no controls were imposed, the community could be swamped by the influx of new converts from a pagan background, and its whole ethos would be changed—for the worse. Luke's account of the conversion of Cornelius does not suggest that anything was said to him about circumcision or submission to the law of Moses. But Cornelius was no idolater at the time of his conversion: he already regulated his life by Jewish standards of morality and worship.[41] What was to be done, however, with converts from raw paganism? Cornelius, with his family and friends, formed a small group, in whose favor an exception could easily be made, but Gentile converts in Syria, Cilicia and farther afield were increasing in number all the time. It is not surprising that some members of the Jerusalem church argued that they should be treated in the same way as proselytes from paganism to the Jewish religion—that is, they should be circumcised and charged to keep Moses' law.[42] They should, in other words, become Jews first in order then to receive recognition as Christians by virtue of their belief in Jesus. This view was pressed not only in Jerusalem but also in the church of Antioch.

Those who pressed this view at Antioch were visitors from Jerusalem. It is natural to link them with the "certain persons from James" whose arrival in Antioch led to controversy there over the seating of Jewish and Gentile Christians at separate tables—the controversy described by Paul in a vivid passage in his letter to the churches of Galatia (Galatians 2:11-14). Be that as it may, the situation had to be discussed and resolved at the highest level. The church of Antioch, says Luke, sent a deputation to Jerusalem, headed by Barnabas and Paul, to raise the matter with the apostles and elders. But when this deputation had discussed the matter informally with the Jerusalem leaders, it was the Jerusalem leaders who met to settle the question. Their decision, summed up and put to the meeting by James, was that Gentile converts should not be required to become proselytes to Judaism, but that they should undertake to observe the Jewish code of sexual ethics and the most important Jewish food-restrictions (avoiding in particular the eating of meat from which the blood had not been completely drained and of the flesh of animals which had been sacrificed to pagan divinities).[43]

In view of the pressure to insist on circumcision and submission to the "yoke of the commandments," the Jerusalem decree (as it is called) was a remarkably liberal document.[44] We need not deal here with the literary-critical judgment that two distinct meetings have been fused into one in Luke's narrative at this point.[45] It is certain, at least, that the decree was issued by the authority of the church of Jerusalem. It was embodied in a letter addressed to the "brothers of Gentile origin" in

Antioch and the province of Syria and Cilicia. It claimed even higher authority than that of the church of Jerusalem: "The Holy Spirit has resolved, and so have we," the apostles and elders wrote, "to lay on you no other burden than the following: you must abstain from food sacrificed to idols, from blood and strangled meat, and from fornication" (Acts 15:28f.).

Luke implies that the letter was circulated beyond the frontiers of its stated address, in Syria and Cilicia: he represents Paul and his Jerusalemite colleague Silas as communicating its terms to the recently founded churches of South Galatia.[46] When, however, Paul deals in his letters with the issues covered by the Jerusalem decree (especially the issue of food which has been sacrificed to idols), he never appeals to the decree—he does not even mention it—but argues from first principles. The claim implicitly made by the Jerusalem leaders to impose their authority over Gentile Christians—a claim tacitly conceded by Luke— was not allowed by Paul.

VI. PAUL'S LAST VISIT TO JERUSALEM

According to Luke, Paul visited the Jerusalem church at the end of each phase of his apostolic mission.[47] This is quite in line with Paul's desire to maintain good relations with the mother-church. If on each of those visits he reported to the church what had been accomplished through his ministry during the preceding phase (cf. Acts 15:12; 21:19), this was by way of engaging the Jerusalem believers' interest in his ministry, not by way of rendering an account of a commission which he had received from them. Luke himself nowhere suggests that Paul had received any commission from Jerusalem. At the end of his evangelization of Corinth, Paul is said by Luke to have paid a brief visit to Judaea and Syria: "putting in at Caesarea he went up and greeted the church and then went down to Antioch" (Acts 18:22). The church which he greeted was certainly the Jerusalem church (to which one would necessarily "go up" from Caesarea and from which one would "go down" to Antioch).[48] There was no doubt by this time (A.D. 52) a church at Caesarea, but if Luke had meant that Paul on this occasion greeted the Caesarean church, he would have said something like "the church that was there" (τὴν οὖσαν ἐκκλησίαν) and not simply "the church" (τὴν ἐκκλησίαν)[49]—which, especially in a Judaean context, could only be the church of Jerusalem. So the Western text of Acts 18:21 understands the situation: it makes Paul say to the members of the synagogue at Ephesus when he visits them briefly on his way from Corinth, "I must by all means keep the coming festival in Jerusalem"—the festival of Pentecost, probably. Here the Western text anticipates the situation a few years later, when Paul, according to the undisputed testimony of Acts 20:16, "made haste to be in Jerusalem, if possible, for the day of Pentecost."

It is this later occasion, sometime after the end of Paul's Ephesian ministry, that provides the final and crucial phase of Luke's history of the Jerusalem church. On this, his last, visit to Jerusalem Paul was accompanied by a number of Christians from churches which he himself had planted. The reader of Paul's letters knows why those representatives of Gentile churches came with Paul on this occasion: they were carrying their respective churches' contributions to the relief fund for the Jerusalem church which Paul had been organizing in his mission-field for two or three years back. It may be said that our knowledge of this fact (which may not have been so directly accessible to Luke's first readers as it is to us) should not influence overmuch our appraisal of Luke's narrative of Paul's last visit to Jerusalem. It does, however, compel us to wonder why Luke is so reticent about Paul's Jerusalem relief fund, which cannot have been unknown to him.[50] His one reference to it comes in his report of Paul's defense before Felix, procurator of Judaea: "After many years," says Paul, "I came to bring alms and offerings to my nation" (Acts 24:19). The explanation of Luke's reticence in this regard must be attempted elsewhere;[51] here it is Luke's positive picture of the Jerusalem church on this occasion that invites examination.

This time there is no word of Peter or any other of the twelve apostles in Jerusalem. They appear to be no longer based in the city; the church is administered by a body of elders, among whom James is *primus inter pares,* the acknowledged leader. Hospitality in Jerusalem has been arranged in advance for Paul and his companions in the house of Mnason, with whom they would feel at home. The day after their arrival, they were received by James and the elders. Paul gave them an account of the progress of the Gentile mission in the period that had elapsed since his last visit, and they were evidently pleased by what they heard.[52] But they were worried by exaggerated rumors about Paul's liberal policies which were circulating in Jerusalem both inside and outside the church. They had agreed that circumcision and submission to the law of Moses were not to be imposed on Gentile converts, but Paul (it was reported) was telling *Jews*—Jewish Christians, presumably—that they should give up circumcising their sons and observing the other ancestral customs.

These rumors were bound to excite the hostility of the many "zealots for the law" among the believing Jews of Jerusalem (not to mention the Jews of the city as a whole).[53] Something should be done to allay their suspicions: Paul should do something publicly to show that he was still a practicing Jew. An opportunity presented itself: four members of the church had undertaken a Nazirite vow and were about to complete certain purificatory rites in the temple in the course of discharging the vow. If Paul were to associate himself with them, accompany them into the temple and pay their dues, then (the elders argued) everyone would recognize that Paul was a pious and observant Jew.[54]

There was an engaging naïveté about their professed expectation, but if that would make life easier for them, Paul would go along with their plan. He knew that his presence in Jerusalem must be an embarrassment to the church and its leaders; he would do anything reasonable to relieve their embarrassment. The action they urged upon him involved no compromise of principle: it was his settled policy to conform to Jewish ways when living among Jews.[55] But the outcome of their plan was disastrous. Some Jews from the province of Asia, who were in Jerusalem for Pentecost, recognized Paul in the temple precincts and raised a hue and cry against him, charging him with violating the sanctity of the place by bringing into it one or more of his Gentile friends whom they had seen with him in the city.[56] Paul was set upon, and rescued from being beaten to death by the timely arrival of Roman soldiers from the adjoining Antonia fortress. The sequel is well known: Paul was arraigned before the Roman procurator, appealed to Caesar, was sent under guard to Rome and was detained there for two years while he waited for his appeal to come up before the supreme court.

VII. JERUSALEM AND ROME

Luke, describing how Paul's assailants dragged him into the outer court of the temple, adds "and immediately the gates were shut" (Acts 21:30).[57] In this detail the Bampton Lecturer for 1864 saw symbolic significance:

> "Believing all things which are written in the Law and in the Prophets," and "having committed nothing against the people or customs of [his] fathers," he and his creed are forced from their proper home. On it as well as him the Temple doors are shut.[58]

This was the moment when, in Luke's eyes, the temple ceased to fill the role allotted to it in his history up to this point. The exclusion of God's message and his messenger from the house formerly called by his name sealed its doom: it was now ripe for the destruction which overtook it not many years later. Luke does not say so in express words, but he implies it. Here is the resolution of the tension referred to above between two attitudes to the temple—that reflected in Jesus' proclamation of the temple's doom and that reflected in the apostles' continued respect for the building and its services.[59]

But the material temple was to be replaced by a new temple, "not made with hands."[60] There are hints of an early tradition identifying the church of Jerusalem with this new temple, and James the Just as its high priest. (This could explain, for example, the curious statement of Hegesippus that "to James alone it was permitted to enter the sanctuary, for he did not wear wool but linen."[61]) This concept finds no place in Acts. But what is the place of the church of Jerusalem in Paul's expulsion from the temple precincts and its aftermath?

The hope of James and his fellow-elders that Paul's public involvement in a ceremony of purification in the temple would disarm suspicion and hostility was so unrealistically optimistic that doubts have been raised about their sincerity in proposing the scheme. Did they really expect their plan to work? According to some readers of Acts, they did not, and Luke knew that they did not. A few go so far as to suggest that, by this plan, they deliberately lured Paul into a trap which, they hoped, would relieve them of his embarrassing presence.[62]

Luke can be quite selective in his presentation of evidence, but there is no need to charge him with such a *suggestio falsi* as this suggestion implies. Luke leaves the ordinary reader of his account with the impression that James and his colleagues were a body of well-meaning but deeply troubled men. But even if their scheme was well-intentioned and put forward in all good faith, they could not so easily be absolved from responsibility for Paul's exposure to danger and loss of liberty. Luke's last portrayal of the church of Jerusalem in Acts brings it little glory. Like the Jerusalem temple, the Jerusalem church had outlived its role in the divine purpose. As the temple was to be destroyed, so the church was to be uprooted and scattered in a few years' time. By the time Luke wrote, both events had taken place, and he had pondered their significance.

What now was to replace the church of Jerusalem in the outworking of the divine purpose?

In the Manson Memorial Lecture for 1981 it was argued (in pursuance of a thesis earlier defended by Henry Chadwick)[63] that in Paul's eyes Rome was designed to replace Jerusalem as the center of the Christian mission (and to inherit his own apostolic responsibility).[64] Luke's perspective was different from Paul's, but from Luke's perspective too, as Jerusalem Christianity was henceforth unable to fulfill God's saving purpose in the world, it was for Roman Christianity to take up the task and carry it forward. Rome is the goal of Luke's narrative, as he indicates in advance towards the end of his record of Paul's Ephesian ministry when he tells how Paul announced his intention of paying a visit to Jerusalem, adding, "After I have been there, I must also see Rome" (Acts 19:21). The remainder of Acts shows how this plan of Paul's was realized, and Luke rests content when he has brought Paul to Rome and leaves him there, at the heart of the empire, preaching the gospel without let or hindrance (Acts 28:30f.). "Victory of the word of God," comments J. A. Bengel on the closing sentence of Luke's narrative: "Paul in Rome, the capstone of the gospel, the end of Acts. . . . It began in Jerusalem; it ends in Rome."[65]

Christianity has come to Rome and found a secure lodgment there: now let it work. But during the preceding twenty-five to thirty years the church of Jerusalem had served as the fountainhead on earth from which the gospel flowed forth,[66] and by virtue of its prestige as the mother-church it exercised supervision over the continuous expansion of the new community first into the adjoining regions and then into territories more remote.[67]

11. Paul's Apologetic and the Purpose of Acts

The speeches in the Acts of the Apostles are generally held to have been included by Luke because of the contribution they make to the purpose and plan of his work. How far they represent the mind of the various speakers to whom they are attributed is a disputed question. The view taken here is that Luke followed the precedent of Thucydides, who says that he himself composed the speeches which form such a notable feature of his History but endeavored at the same time to reproduce the general purport of what was actually said.[1]

The speeches to be considered in this paper are those delivered by Paul in his own defense in the last quarter of Acts (chs. 22–28).[2]

I. PAUL'S PLAN TO SEE ROME

In Acts 19:21 Paul, towards the end of his ministry in Ephesus (A.D. 52-55), announces his intention of seeing Rome, after briefly returning to his former mission-field in Macedonia and Achaia and then visiting Jerusalem. To Paul himself we owe the further information that he planned, after seeing Rome, to go on to Spain and launch a campaign of evangelization there (Rom. 15:22-29), and also that the purpose of his visiting Jerusalem first was to deliver the proceeds of a collection which

---

A lecture delivered in the John Rylands University Library, Manchester, on Wednesday, 12 November 1986, and published in *BJRL* 69 (1986-87), pp. 379-393.

he had organized among his Gentile converts for the relief of poverty in the mother-church.[3] Luke's purpose in writing Acts, however, must be inferred mainly from what he himself tells us rather than from what someone else tells us—even when that someone else is such an eminent first-hand authority as Paul—but Luke's silences also constitute evidence in their own right, and Paul's letters provide the reader of Acts with some help in identifying and interpreting those silences.

The remainder of Luke's narrative tells how Paul's purpose of seeing Rome was realized, in spite of many unforeseen obstacles which might have prevented his ever getting there.[4]

After his visit to Macedonia and Achaia Paul takes ship for Judaea, along with a number of fellow-travelers.[5] The voyage to Judaea is recorded in day-by-day detail in one of the "we" sections of Acts (20:5–21:18). As the voyage proceeds, ominous predictions of threats to Paul's liberty and to his life itself are made in one port after another. But Paul refuses to be turned aside from his determined course, and at last he and his friends arrive in Jerusalem.

There they have a meeting with James the Just and other leaders of the church. These are deeply worried men: for them to receive Paul will inevitably compromise them in the eyes not only of the general Jewish population of Jerusalem but also of many members of the church, described as "all zealots for the law" (Acts 21:10). In Jerusalem Paul is widely regarded as an apostate from Israel's true religion and as an agent of apostasy among other Jewish Christians throughout the Roman Empire. The leaders of the church of Jerusalem urge him to demonstrate his Jewish orthodoxy and loyalty by associating himself with four of their number who have to complete a purification ceremony in the temple in connection with the discharge of a Nazirite vow. Paul consents to go along with this suggestion, which indeed chimes in well enough with his own stated policy of being "all things to all men" for the gospel's sake (1 Cor. 9:22f.). But with his appearance in the temple precincts trouble breaks out: he is spotted there by some of his old opponents from the province of Asia, who have come to Jerusalem for the feast of Pentecost, and they raise a hue and cry against him, charging him with violating the sanctity of the temple by bringing Gentiles into it. The crowd of worshippers turns on Paul, drags him down the steps into the outer court and begins to beat him up. He is saved from death at the hands of his assailants by a detachment of Roman soldiers from the garrison in the Antonia fortress (northwest of the temple area); they rescue him and carry him on their shoulders up one of the two flights of steps connecting the outer court with the fortress. Paul is placed under formal arrest by the commanding officer of the garrison, and from then to the end of Acts he remains in Roman custody, no longer a free agent.

II. PAUL'S LAST SPEECHES

From this point on Luke's record is punctuated by a succession of speeches in which Paul defends himself before varying audiences against the charges laid against him. These speeches are addressed:

1. to the Jewish crowd in the temple precincts (Acts 22:1-21);
2. to the Sanhedrin (Acts 23:1-6);
3. to Felix, procurator of Judaea (Acts 24:10-21);
4. to Festus, Felix's successor as procurator (Acts 25:8, 10f.);
5. to Agrippa the younger (Acts 26:2-23);
6. to the leaders of the Jewish community in Rome (Acts 28:17-28).

1. To the Jerusalem Crowd

The crowd in the outer court of the temple, to whom Paul spoke in the Aramaic vernacular from the top of the steps leading up to the Antonia fortress, was fiercely hostile to him and had to be conciliated. The first attempt at conciliation was his speaking in Aramaic, not Greek. "When they heard that he was addressing them in the Aramaic speech, they were the more quiet" (Acts 22:2).

Then he told them of his early life and upbringing as an orthodox Jew: although born in Tarsus, he was brought up in Jerusalem and educated in the academy of Gamaliel;[6] he was, like his hearers, a zealot for the God of Israel. It was his zeal that impelled him to lead the campaign of repression against the followers of Jesus. Nothing but a compulsion too great to be resisted could have turned him from his career as a persecutor. But this compulsion came when the risen Lord appeared to him on the Damascus road and called him to be his servant and messenger. In the interpretation of this call an influential part was played by "a devout man according to the law," highly respected by the Jewish community of Damascus, Ananias by name. So Paul had become a follower of Jesus in circumstances which left him with no choice to do anything else.

But later, in Jerusalem, he went on to tell them, he had a further vision of Christ in the temple, not unlike the vision which inaugurated Isaiah's prophetic ministry (Isa. 6:1-10), and was commissioned expressly as his messenger to the Gentiles. The mention of Gentiles reminded his hearers of their original grievance against him and, whereas they had thus far given him a quiet enough hearing, their fury now burst out afresh: Paul's attempt at conciliating them was frustrated.

2. To the Sanhedrin

Since Paul had been accused in the first instance of an offense against the temple, this made him liable to the jurisdiction of the Sanhedrin, the supreme court of Israel.[7] If a prima facie case could have been made out, the commanding officer would have handed him over to the Sanhedrin for trial; until then, he was responsible for this Roman citizen's safety. A preliminary appearance before the Sanhedrin was desirable in order that the officer might be satisfied that there was (or was not) a prima facie case. So Paul was brought before the Sanhedrin, over which the high priest presided *ex officio,* and introduced his case with a protestation that he had maintained a good conscience before God throughout his life up to the present moment. For this protestation the high priest—Ananias, an impetuous and thoroughly deplorable character, according to Jewish tradition—ordered him to be struck in the face. This illegality on the part of the president of a court of justice drew forth an indignant retort from Paul.

Then he made a second beginning: he asserted that his whole case rested on the resurrection hope, a hope maintained especially by the Pharisaic party. The Sanhedrin comprised an influential minority of Pharisees alongside its Sadducean majority.[8] Paul addressed the court as a Pharisee himself, and immediately divided his hearers—some of them supporting a man who, being so sound as he evidently was on the doctrine of resurrection, could not be far wrong in general, while others treated his commitment to that doctrine as another black mark against him. "What if he has really seen an angelic vision?" said some of the Pharisees. The result was that the court dissolved into disorderly wrangling, and the commanding officer had Paul taken back to the fortress. His attempt to get some kind of authoritative ruling from the Sanhedrin had evidently come to nothing.

There was no more that he could do along that line, and as Paul had so many enemies in Jerusalem, he decided to remit the problem to the procurator of Judaea, Felix. He therefore sent Paul under armed guard to the procurator's headquarters in Caesarea, with a covering letter setting out the circumstances of his arrest and the subsequent inquiry.

3. To Felix

Paul's defense before Felix (Acts 24:10-21) is the most directly forensic of his speeches. In its context it is his reply to the accusations voiced by one Tertullus, an orator who delivered the speech for the prosecution on behalf of the high priest and some other members of the Sanhedrin. There are three points in their indictment, two general and one particular: (1) Paul is a perfect pest, stirring up unrest in Jewish communities throughout the empire; (2) he is a ringleader of the sect of the Nazarenes; (3) in particular, he was caught in the act of trying to defile the temple.

Paul replies to this particular charge first and again last: he has committed no act against the temple, but on returning to Jerusalem on pilgrimage after several years' absence he was going about his religious duties in the sacred precincts when he was accused of sacrilege by some Jews from Asia; let them be called as witnesses. But in fact they made no appearance in court: they had no evidence to give. To the general charge of causing trouble throughout the Roman provinces Paul makes no specific reply: Felix in any case would be more concerned with what had been done in his own province. As for his being a ringleader of the sect of the Nazarenes, this is described by Paul in terms of his practicing the ancestral worship of God according to "The Way," as he and his fellow-Christians called it—"sect" was their opponents' term for it. As to the crowd in the temple court and to the Sanhedrin, so to Felix he affirms that he is a loyal Jew; as before the Sanhedrin, so now he maintains that he shares and proclaims Israel's traditional resurrection hope. He credits his prosecutors with cherishing the same hope, although the chief-priestly members of the Sanhedrin delegation and in particular the high priest Ananias, being Sadducees, presumably did not accept it. It is a matter of interest that Paul is here represented as speaking of a resurrection "both of the just and of the unjust." He may well have been brought up to believe, with most other Pharisees, that the wicked as well as the good would be raised from death, but in his letters he refers only to the resurrection of "those who belong to Christ" (1 Cor. 15:23), treating it as their participation in the resurrection of Christ, related to it as the full harvest is related to the firstfruits.

There is one point in Paul's defense before Felix that calls for special attention: this speech contains the only allusion in Acts to the Jerusalem relief fund which, as we know from Paul's letters, played such a large part in his policy at this time.[9] "After several years," he said to Felix, "I came bringing alms and offerings to my nation, and it was while I was engaged in [presenting] these that they found me purified in the temple" (Acts 24:17f.).

Here we have an instance of the kind of help which (as was said above) Paul's letters provide for the interpretation of Luke's silences. Why is Luke so reticent about the collection for Jerusalem to which Paul, at that very time, attached so much importance? And why, in Paul's one allusion to it in Acts, is it spoken of not as a contribution for the relief of the church of Jerusalem, and more especially for its poorer members, but as "alms and offerings" for the "nation" in general?[10]

We do not know the answer to these questions: we can but speculate. Two possible answers, for either of which much can be said, seem to be mutually exclusive.

One is that the relief fund was misrepresented by Paul's accusers as an attempt to divert money which was due to the Jerusalem temple, and that this charge was pressed against him at his hearing before Caesar. But how could an offering made by Gentiles be treated as a diversion from funds which should have gone to swell the temple tax, the half-shekel levied annually, with the permission and indeed the protection of Rome, on all Jews throughout the world between the ages of twenty and fifty? It was argued, perhaps, that Paul's Gentile converts, especially those of them who had belonged to the fringe of Gentile adherents of the synagogue[11] in cities of the *diaspora,* were potential proselytes to Judaism, and that, but for Paul's intervention, they might have been expected to become in due course converts to the synagogue and hence contributors to the temple tax. If this was one of the planks in the indictment brought against Paul in the imperial court, it could have been regarded as a charge of temple profanation less easily rebutted than the charge that Paul had taken a Gentile with him on to forbidden territory. Luke, it might be further suggested, was aware that this more subtle charge was brought against Paul before Caesar; he may even have been aware that it was effective enough to lead to his conviction. At any rate, it was a sufficiently delicate issue for Luke to judge it best to say as little about it as possible.

But all this is quite uncertain. The other, and more probable, answer is that the relief fund failed to achieve Paul's purpose in organizing it. It did not promote a spirit of unity between the church of Jerusalem and Paul's Gentile churches. It has been questioned, indeed, whether the money brought by Paul and his companions was accepted at all by the Jerusalem church.[12] Luke gives the impression that it *was* accepted; but it was hazardous for the elders of the Jerusalem church to accept anything from such a suspect source as Paul and his Gentile mission. Could their reputation in the eyes of their fellow-Jerusalemites (or indeed in the eyes of some of their own fellow-churchmen) survive any appearance of fellowship with Paul? Their suggestion that Paul should participate in the four Nazirites' purification ceremony was probably designed to make it easier for them to accept what he brought; if part of the gift was sanctified by being used to pay the Nazirites' expenses, they could more safely receive the rest of it.[13] But their well-meant suggestion turned out disastrously. Any further association on their part with Paul was now out of the question. Since the relief fund, for all the high hopes which Paul placed in it, was in the event a fiasco, Luke preferred to forget it. In retrospect, it was an abortive enterprise and was best left unmentioned.[14]

4. To Festus

Felix might have discharged Paul for lack of positive evidence against him, but he kept on deferring a decision for two years, and then he was recalled to Rome. Not wishing to add to the abundant offense which he had already given to the Jewish authorities in the province, he left Paul in prison instead of releasing him; and when his successor Festus arrived, he found this item of unfinished business awaiting his attention. The Sanhedrin lost no time in bringing it up, and sent a deputation to Caesarea to restate the charges against Paul. Luke reports the hearing before Festus quite summarily: on the one hand, he says, Paul's accusers brought many grave charges against him which they could not substantiate, while on the other hand Paul replied to each of the three main charges with a direct negative: "I have committed no offense against the iaw of the Jews, nor against the temple, nor yet against Caesar" (Acts 25:8). His denial of having committed any offense against Caesar must refer to the charge of being a disturber of the peace throughout the Roman world (cf. Acts 24:5a).[15]

But Festus was new to the office of procurator, and naturally wished to est.:blish good relations with the Jewish authorities at the beginning of his governorship, so he spoke of taking Paul to Jerusalem and conducting his trial there. Paul, seeing that he was likely to be put in jeopardy all over again through Festus's inexperience, exercised his right as a Roman citizen and appealed to Caesar—appealed, that is to say, to have his case transferred from the jurisdiction of the provincial court to the supreme tribunal of the empire. Festus was relieved, because he no longer had to reach a decision in a matter where he felt himself to be out of his depth; his only problem now was the drafting of a report, the *litterae dimissoriae*, to be sent to Rome on the conduct of the case thus far. He no doubt had the court records of Felix's proceedings to help him in the task, but these were perhaps not sufficiently explicit with regard to this man "Jesus, who was dead, but whom Paul affirmed to be alive" (Acts 25:19).

Happily, Festus was able to draw on the superior knowledge of Agrippa the younger, ruler of a client kingdom on the northeastern frontiers of his own province, who came to Caesarea at this time on an official visit to congratulate him on his arrival in Judaea as the emperor's representative. Agrippa, a member of the Herod family, was reputed to have expert knowledge of all matters related to the Jewish religion—among other things, he enjoyed the privilege of appointing (and, where he thought fit, deposing) the high priest of Israel. Festus therefore told him of his problem. Agrippa was interested in what Festus had to say about Paul, and expressed the wish to meet this man for himself. An early opportunity for this was arranged, and Paul was invited to give an account of himself to Agrippa.

This was no formal speech for the defense. By appealing to Caesar, Paul had effectively removed his case from any lower jurisdiction, and Agrippa could in any case have had no jurisdiction over him at all. But if Agrippa was to help Festus in drafting his report, he would be in a better position to advise him if he heard Paul's account of the matter, and he called on Paul to tell his story.

5. To Agrippa the Younger

Paul's speech before Agrippa, as Luke reports it, is a carefully constructed *apologia pro vita sua*. Like the address to the crowd in the outer court of the temple, it is autobiographical in character, laying special weight on Paul's call and commission; but it is specially adapted to a very different audience and setting. Its language is studiously classical, as befitted the circumstances of its delivery. After a complimentary exordium (Acts 26:2f.), Paul speaks of his early upbringing as a Pharisee and his devotion to the resurrection hope (vv. 4-8), his campaign of repression against the followers of Jesus (vv. 9-11), his confrontation with the risen Christ on the Damascus road (vv. 12-18), his life of obedience to the commission received then (vv. 19f.) and his arrest in the temple (v. 21). A summary of his preaching forms the peroration to his speech (vv. 22f.).

The main emphasis throughout the speech is laid on the loyalty of Paul and his message to Israel's ancestral religion. His preaching, he affirms, contains nothing but what Moses and the prophets said would happen—especially the death and resurrection of the Christ and the proclamation through him of "light both to the people [of Israel] and to the Gentiles" (v. 23).[16] As in the speeches before the Sanhedrin and before Felix, special weight lies on the resurrection hope and its realization in Jesus. "Why should it be thought incredible by any of you," Paul asks, "that God should raise the dead?"—the dead in general, and Christ in particular, for his resurrection, having already taken place, is the guarantee that God will fulfill his promise by raising the rest of the dead.

6. To the Leading Jews in Rome

The same emphasis appears in Paul's last apologetic speech in Acts: his address to the leaders of the Jewish community in Rome.

When, in consequence of his appeal to Caesar, Paul arrived in Rome to await his hearing in the supreme court, he was kept under house arrest. Some three days after he settled in his lodgings, he invited the leaders of the local Jewish community to pay him a visit and he acquainted them with his arrival in the city and the circumstances of his being there. He could not be sure if they had already had some communication from Jerusalem about him; the Roman community's links with the Judaean authorities were close. But it was important that they should hear Paul's own account of events as soon as possible. He assures them that he has no complaint to make against the Jewish nation or its leaders, but insists that he has "done nothing against the people or the ancestral customs." It is his loyalty to Israel's true religion that has brought him to his present situation: "it is because of the hope of Israel that I am bound with this chain" (Acts 28:20)—a reminder that one of the conditions of his house arrest was his being chained by the wrist to the soldier who guarded him.

This first visit to Paul by the Jewish leaders in Rome was followed by a second, on an appointed day, when more members of the community came to his lodgings to hear him expound his message. As he spent a whole day "testifying to the kingdom of God and trying to convince them about Jesus both from the law of Moses and from the prophets" (Acts 28:23), some were persuaded by his arguments but others were not. The latter were evidently in the majority, for Luke treats their skepticism as the definitive instance of Jewish rejection of the gospel (of which earlier instances have been given throughout his record), quoting Paul's final word to them as one of the *Leitmotivs* of Acts: "Let it be known to you, then, that this salvation of God has been sent to the Gentiles: *they* will listen" (28:28). Henceforth, the gospel is expressly for the Gentile world.

Yet Luke is not anti-Jewish; least of all is he anti-Pharisaic. In his portrayal, Paul is the ideal Jew, "believing everything laid down by the law or written by the prophets" (Acts 24:14), and finding the fulfillment of all in Jesus. The gospel, for Luke, is the crown and climax of Israel's faith: that is the dominant emphasis of these apologetic speeches.

III. LUKE'S APOLOGETIC CONCERN

Luke's purpose in writing his history is not *primarily* apologetic. He writes in order to provide his readers with an orderly account of the rise and progress of Christianity.[17] But since this movement was "everywhere spoken against" (Acts 28:22), it seemed desirable to refute some of the current objections to it. The first Christian historian found himself accordingly obliged to be the first Christian apologist. Of three main types of Christian apologetic in the second century Luke provides first-century prototypes: apologetic in relation to pagan religion (Christianity is true; paganism is false); apologetic in relation to Judaism (Christianity represents the fulfillment of true Judaism); apologetic in relation to the political authorities (Christianity is innocent of any offense against Roman law).

As for apologetic in relation to pagan religions, that figures earlier in Acts—in Paul and Barnabas's protest to the people of Lystra who were about to pay them divine honors (14:15-18) and in Paul's address to the court of the Areopagus in Athens (17:22-31)—but it plays no part in Paul's apologetic in the closing chapters of the book.

It is otherwise with apologetic in relation to Judaism. This is prominent in one of Paul's defense speeches after another. One might put a marginal question-mark against some elements in Paul's repeated claim to be an exemplary Jew, living according to the ancestral customs. He did live according to these when he was in Jewish company, but when he lived in a Gentile environment he was happy to live like a Gentile, eating Gentile food and conforming in general to the Gentile way of life (but not to Gentile morals). When he told the leading Jews of Rome that he was loyal to the customs, did some of them compare him with other Jews who were taken to Rome as prisoners around the same time and who showed their adherence to the "customs" by restricting their diet to figs and nuts, sooner than risk eating food which was forbidden to pious Jews?[18] Luke relates earlier in Acts how Peter learned to call no food common or unclean (non-kosher), and certainly he knew that Paul had learned the same lesson and practiced it even more thoroughly than Peter did: why then does he not indicate that Paul's alleged devotion to the "customs" was subject to wholesale modification as expediency directed?

If, in representing Paul's claim in such terms, Luke has in view not Paul's defense before Caesar (which was past by the time he wrote) but the ongoing defense of Christians in the Roman Empire, his purpose seems to be to maintain that Christianity, far from being a novel and illicit cult, was in fact the full flowering of Judaism, which had for a long time now been a recognized and protected religion; he stresses the continuity of the old and the new. The recognition given by Roman law to Judaism ought *a fortiori* to be granted to Christianity. Christianity goes back beyond Moses and the law to Abraham and the patriarchs. Points in which it differs from traditional Judaism are due to the impact made by the Christ-event, and these, like the Christ-event itself, were divinely foreseen and designed.

In Paul's insistence that he is a loyal Jew he repeatedly lays special weight on his lifelong commitment to the crucial doctrine of resurrection. We know from Paul's own writings that in his eyes the general resurrection, which still lay in the future (and to which Pharisees looked forward), was all of a piece with the particular resurrection of Jesus, which had already taken place. Therefore to deny the one was to deny the other; to believe that Jesus had risen logically involved belief in the general resurrection (1 Cor. 15:12f.). This same conviction underlies Paul's insistence in these speeches that the doctrine of resurrection is the key issue in the case against him: "It is for the hope of the resurrection of the dead that I stand on trial," he said to the Sanhedrin (Acts 23:6); "it is for this hope that I am accused by Jews (of all people)," he said to King Agrippa (26:7). Why, he went on to ask, was it deemed incredible that God should already have done something (in the case of Jesus) which many of his accusers believed he would one day do (in the case of the rest of the dead)?

It has been questioned if Luke does justice to the true force of Paul's resurrection doctrine when he represents Paul as arguing thus. Probably he does; but his aim, as has been said, is to present Christianity as the fulfillment of Judaism and therefore as entitled to share in the liberty which the empire accorded to the practice of Judaism. Paul—whether the Paul of Acts or the Paul whom we know from his letters—could defend his case on biblical and theological grounds: the great prophets of Israel had looked forward to the day when Israel would be a light to the nations, and he sees the gospel as the realization of this hope. But this meant in practice that Christianity became predominantly a Gentile faith, and it was unrealistic to expect the state to recognize it as a variety of Judaism, let alone as the truest Judaism of all.

As for apologetic in relation to the state, some scholars have argued that Acts (or even Luke-Acts as a whole) was written to provide the counsel for Paul's defense before Nero with information which would be useful to him as he presented Paul's case in court.[19] This view, as maintained by those scholars, cannot well be sustained and has not been generally accepted. There is much in Acts that would be irrelevant for forensic purposes. It is conceivable, however, that Luke had at his disposal some document which played a part at Paul's trial.

The charges brought against Paul before Felix (and Festus) would be repeated before Nero, and Paul's replies in the procurator's court would be relevant to his defense in the supreme court. The charge of stirring up unrest in the Jewish communities throughout the empire (Acts 24:5) would be even more relevant in the imperial court than it was before Felix: indeed, it was probably the main plank in the indictment when his prosecutors gave evidence against him in Rome and would certainly have attracted the death penalty if it could have been proved. Luke seems definitely to have had this charge in mind in his narrative of Paul's missionary activity. He does not deny that Paul's presence was the occasion of rioting in one place after another, but tries to show that Paul was not responsible for this: the responsibility, according to Luke's account, lay with others—sometimes with property interests which felt themselves threatened by the gospel[20] but frequently with the leaders of local Jewish communities.

If Paul's appeal to Caesar had been heard by the time Acts was written (as no doubt it was), this apologetic was still necessary: the charge of subversive activity pressed against him continued to be pressed against Christians in general, and Paul's defense was relevant to their situation.

One writer has argued that Luke wrote not only to commend Christianity to the favorable attention of the Roman state but also to commend the Roman state to Christian readers.[21] This thesis can scarcely be upheld in an unqualified form. But Luke's attitude to the Roman state and to the imperial authorities throughout the provinces is quite positive. After the favorable judgments of Gallio and others earlier in the narrative, the reader is quite prepared for a favorable outcome in Paul's appeal. When Paul made his appeal, there was nothing in Nero's record that made an appeal to him exceptionally risky. If Luke wrote, as is probable, a decade or two later, he wrote for people who knew much more about Nero than was known in A.D. 59, the probable year of Paul's appeal, towards the end of the enlightened administration of the *quinquennium Neronis*. If, in the event, the outcome of the appeal was indeed favorable, then Luke's picture of Roman justice would be reinforced by what his readers knew. If, on the other hand, it led to Paul's conviction and execution then the implication would be that this was an instance of Nero's deviation from Roman standards, which led in due course to the reprobation of his memory. What Tertullian was later to call an *institutum Neronianum*, a precedent set by Nero,[22] was *ipso facto* an infringement of the tradition of Roman justice.

The note of cautious optimism on which Acts ends is not unlike that heard in Paul's letter to the church of Philippi—if that letter, or at least this part of it, is to be dated (as I think it is) towards the end of his two years of Roman imprisonment. There he does not know how his hearing will turn out, but thinks it more likely than not that he will be set at liberty and be able to continue his apostolic ministry (Phil. 1:19-26). It says something for Luke's quality as a historian that, writing as he probably does several years later, he is able at the end of Acts to recapture so accurately the atmosphere of this period of Paul's house-arrest.

IV. EARLY CHURCH

12. *Antichrist in the Early Church*

I. THE WORD "ANTICHRIST"

The biblical occurrences of the term "antichrist" (Gk. *antichristos*) are very few. It does not appear in the Septuagint, and in the New Testament it is found only in two of the Johannine Epistles. The relevant passages are these:

> Children, it is the last hour; and as you have heard that *antichrist* is coming so now many *antichrists* have come; therefore we know that it is the last hour. They went out from us, but they were not of us; for if they had been of us, they would have continued with us; but they went out, that it might be plain that they all are not of us. . . . Who is the liar, but he who denies that Jesus is the Christ? This is the *antichrist*, he who denies the Father and the Son (1 John 2:18f., 22).

> Beloved, do not believe every spirit, but test the spirits to see whether they are of God; for many false prophets have gone out into the world. By this you know the Spirit of God: every spirit which confesses that Jesus Christ has come in the flesh is of God, and every spirit which disunites[1] Jesus is not of God. This is the spirit of *antichrist*, of which you heard that it was coming, and now it is in the world already (1 John 4:1-3).

> For many deceivers have gone out into the world, men who will not acknowledge the coming of Jesus Christ in the flesh;[2] such a one is the deceiver and the *antichrist* (2 John 7).

A paper read on April 2, 1959, to a meeting of the Prophecy Investigation Society (London), and published by the Society as Aids to Prophetic Study, No. 92.

181

The parallel term *pseudochristos* ("false Messiah") appears in our Lord's Olivet discourse, where he says, in reference to the period of the great tribulation:

> And then if any one says to you, "Look, here is the Christ!" or "Look, there he is!" do not believe it. *False Christs* and false prophets will arise and show signs and wonders, to lead astray, if possible, the elect (Mark 13:21f.; cf. Matt. 24:23f.).

Like the Antichrist of 1 John 4:3, the false Christs here are linked with false prophets; like the Antichrist of 2 John 7, the false Christs here are deceivers (in 2 John the noun *planos* is used; in the Gospels the cognate verb *planaō* or its compound *apoplanaō*). We conclude, then, that *antichristos* and *pseudochristos* are synonyms, although *antichristos* has a wider range of meaning. It may mean "a substitute Christ," "a rival Christ" or "an opponent of Christ." And therefore a study of the history of the idea of Antichrist may lead to confusion, unless we distinguish the sense in which the term is understood by those who use it. It includes the idea of a false Messiah *(pseudochristos)*, but it includes other ideas too. In particular, we must distinguish between the Antichrist who seduces the believing community from within, and the Antichrist who assails it from without.

When John speaks of the "many antichrists" who have arisen in his time (say the last decade of the first century A.D.), he has in mind false teachers whose doctrines undermine the foundations of the gospel, and more particularly those called Docetists, who by their denial of our Lord's real manhood nullified such cardinal articles of the apostolic faith as his incarnation, passion and resurrection. This usage persists in John's disciple Polycarp; in his *Epistle to the Philippians* (c. A.D. 120) Polycarp says:

> Everyone who does not confess that Jesus Christ has come in the flesh is *antichrist.* And whosoever does not confess the testimony of the cross is of the devil; and whosoever perverts the oracles of the Lord to his own lusts and says that there is neither resurrection nor judgment—he is Satan's firstborn.[3]

By "the testimony of the cross" he probably means the witness which our Lord's suffering and death bore to his real manhood (cf. John 19:35; 1 John 5:8). And the reference to "Satan's firstborn" reminds us of Polycarp's retort to Marcion, several years later, when Marcion invited the aged bishop to recognize him: "I recognize—Satan's firstborn!"[4] Any heretic in Polycarp's eyes was an antichrist; but a heresiarch like Marcion was *the* Antichrist himself, the firstborn of Satan as Christ was the first-begotten of the Father.

Other New Testament writers use language which suggests that they regarded false teachers as so many antichrists. For example, when it is said of the false teachers denounced by Jude that "their mouth speaks great swelling words" (v. 16), there is probably an allusion to the "little horn" of Dan. 7:8 with "a mouth speaking great things" and to the "willful king" of Dan. 11:36 who "shall speak astonishing things against the God of gods" (the Theodotionic Greek text of Daniel uses the same adjective *hyperonkos* here as is rendered "great swelling words" in Jude 16 and 2 Pet. 2:18). And, as we shall see, the little horn and the willful king of Daniel (two figures which were identical from the start) are regularly equated with the Antichrist in early Christian literature.

II. THE ANTICHRIST IDEA AND ITS BACKGROUND

Although the word *antichristos* does not appear in Greek literature before its appearance in John's letters, it was evidently current among Christians before John wrote. "You have heard," he tells his readers, "that antichrist is coming" (1 John 2:18). Where and when had they heard this? From those who preached the gospel to them and instructed them in the faith, no doubt; but those men did not invent the doctrine. They delivered to their hearers what they themselves had first received. This delivering and receiving in New Testament usage implies a Christian tradition which can be traced back through the apostles to Christ himself; and so it is with regard to the teaching about Antichrist.

About A.D. 50, shortly after his arrival in Corinth, Paul wrote two letters to the Christians in Thessalonica, where he had preached the gospel and planted a church only a few weeks previously. In the second of these two letters he finds it necessary to warn his Thessalonian converts against unsettling eschatological expectations which lack any foundation, and writes to them thus:

> Now concerning the coming of our Lord Jesus Christ and our assembling to meet him, we beg you, brethren, not to be quickly shaken in mind or excited, either by spirit or by word, or by letter purporting to be from us, to the effect that the day of the Lord has come. Let no one deceive you in any way; for that day will not come, unless the rebellion comes first, and the man of lawlessness is revealed, the son of perdition, who opposes and exalts himself against every so-called god or object of worship, so that he takes his seat in the temple of God, proclaiming himself to be God. Do you not remember that when I was still with you I told you this? And now you know what is restraining him[5] so that he may be revealed in his time. For the mystery of lawlessness is already at work; only he who now restrains

it will do so until he is out of the way. And then the lawless one will be revealed, and the Lord Jesus will slay him with the breath of his mouth and destroy him by his appearing and his coming. The coming of the lawless one by the activity of Satan will be with all power and with pretended signs and wonders, and with all wicked deception for those who are to perish, because they refused to love the truth and so be saved. Therefore God sends upon them a strong delusion, to make them believe what is false, so that all may be condemned who did not believe the truth but had pleasure in unrighteousness (2 Thess. 2:1-12).[6]

We need not suppose that John's readers had read these words of Paul, but we may be sure that they had received instruction to much the same effect. That is to say, a day would come when the restraint on lawlessness at present exercised by the power of law and order would be removed, and lawlessness would manifest itself in all its evil. It would be practically incarnated in a sinister personage called "the man of lawlessness" (a better reading than "the man of sin") or "the lawless one"—a personage appointed to final destruction, which would be effected by the appearing of the true Christ in glory. But during the heyday of the lawless one's power he would claim divine honors, and so skillfully would he hoodwink men by impressive signs, performed by Satan's aid, that they would acknowledge his claims and follow him blindly to perdition. This being is regularly identified by early Christian writers with the Antichrist, and it is to him that John probably refers when he says: "you have heard that antichrist is coming."

But when Paul writes to the Thessalonians in the language quoted above, he is not telling them all this for the first time. He is reminding them of what he had told them by word of mouth a short time before when he paid his first visit to their city. Nor was the teaching new then. Paul's description of the lawless one "setting himself forth as God" in the very temple of God recalls the words of our Lord about "the abomination of desolation standing where he ought not" (Mark 13:14). It is important to note the RV rendering "where *he* ought not"; a personal abomination of desolation is implied in the Greek text (a point which is overlooked both by the AV/KJV and by the RSV).[7]

I do not stop here to argue that these words, together with their context, are actual words of Christ; those who are interested in the question of their authenticity are referred to two earlier works by Dr. G. R. Beasley-Murray, *Jesus and the Future* (1954) and *A Commentary on Mark Thirteen* (1957). But I do suggest that ten years after they were reportedly uttered a situation arose in which the disciples may well have thought that they were on the point of being fulfilled—when the Emperor Gaius ordered his image to be set up in the temple at

Jerusalem.[8] It seems probable to me that it was then that this part of the eschatological discourse was put in written form and circulated among Christians, so that they would know what to do when the appalling horror took shape before their eyes. In the event, of course, the imperial image was not set up after all; but the terror and anxiety of those days must have remained long in the minds of Palestinian Christians and colored their views of what would happen when at last the abomination of desolation did indeed stand "where he ought not." In fact, some of Paul's language in 2 Thess. 2:1-12 may reflect the crisis of ten years before. And in any case the Emperor Gaius made his own contribution to the picture of Antichrist which grew up in the early Christian generations.

(A Roman Antichrist is found in Jewish rabbinical tradition, under the name of Armillos or Urmillos—a corruption of Romulus, the eponymous first king of Rome. Thus in Isa. 11:4, where it is said of the Davidic Messiah that "with the breath of his lips he shall slay the wicked," the Targum treats the generic singular "wicked" as an individual singular, and renders it "the wicked Armillos." This, incidentally, presents an interesting parallel with 2 Thess. 2:8, where the Lord Jesus slays the man of lawlessness "with the breath of his mouth," and with Rev. 19:15, 21, where the warrior Messiah smites his enemies with the sharp sword which comes forth from his mouth.)

But an earlier claimant to divine honors than Gaius made a still more potent contribution. This was Antiochus IV, Seleucid king of Syria from 175 to 164 B.C., whose title Epiphanes ("manifest") recalls his claim to be the manifestation on earth of Olympian Zeus, identified with the Syrian Ba'al Shamen ("lord of heaven"). When, towards the end of 167 B.C., he replaced the worship of the God of Israel in the temple at Jerusalem by the cult of Olympian Zeus, and set up an idolatrous altar on the great altar of burnt-offering, pious Jews referred to this pagan installation by a derogatory pun on the Syrian name Ba'al Shamen, which (through Greek) gives us the English expression, "the abomination of desolation."[9] Thus the author of 1 Maccabees, recording the event, says, "they built an abomination of desolation on the altar" (1:54), harking back to the passages in Daniel where this and related expressions are found (8:13; 9:27; 11:31; 12:11).

In the New Testament, however, these passages in Daniel are given a future reference. This is evident from Mark 13:14, which we have already quoted, and the point is made more explicit in the parallel passage in Matt. 24:15: "When therefore you see the abomination of desolation, which was spoken of by Daniel the prophet, standing in the holy place. . . ." Here the abomination of desolation is neuter; in the eyes of some ancient (and some less ancient) commentators the reference here is to the Roman military standards bearing the imperial image, to which worship was offered. (It will be remembered how the legionaries who captured the temple area in A.D. 70, according to the narrative of Josephus, brought their standards into the temple court and offered sacrifices to them over against the east gate.)[10]

Another passage in Daniel which has profoundly influenced the conception of Antichrist is the description in 11:36-45 of "the king" who "shall do according to his will," and "shall exalt himself and magnify himself above every god, and shall speak astonishing things against the God of gods." If we take these verses to be a continuation of the account of Antiochus IV given in the preceding verses, it must be recognized that it is difficult to relate them to that king's historical career, whereas the account in vv. 21-35 can be confirmed clause by clause from our other sources of information about him. Father Lattey, indeed, in his fine commentary on Daniel, sees in vv. 36-45 a more general description of the conduct of Antiochus, leading up to his end, and holds that the gaps in our knowledge of his closing years preclude us from saying too emphatically that he did not invade Egypt once more (v. 40).[11] But most commentators would disagree with him here, and many see in the transition from v. 35 to v. 36 a clue to the dating of the prophecy.[12] Calvin interpreted the passage from v. 36 onward of the Roman Empire.[13] Philip Mauro (anticipated independently by a Scottish writer named James Farquharson in 1838) identifies the "willful king" with Herod the Great.[14] (Mauro's study, *The Seventy Weeks and the Great Tribulation,* came under my observation in my earliest teens, and made a deep impression on my mind which has not yet been completely effaced.)[15] The Qumran community's *Rule of War* is in some degree a *midrash* on these verses and their sequel, and shows the way in which they helped to mold the community's eschatological hope. But the dominant Christian tradition, from Hippolytus (if not earlier) and Jerome to Edward J. Young (if not later), identifies the "willful king" with the Antichrist of the last days, an identification which requires an ever-lengthening chronological gap between verses 35 and 36.[16]

III. ANTICHRIST IN THE APOCALYPSE

Antichrist appears again in the New Testament in the Apocalypse, although the actual title is not found in that book. The beast from the abyss which kills the two faithful witnesses in Rev. 11:7 is introduced more formally in chapter 13. In the first ten verses of this chapter we can scarcely doubt that we have a more detailed description of the man of lawlessness depicted in 2 Thess. 2, although in Revelation there is an oscillation between the antichristian power itself and the individual in whom that power is vested for the time being. But whereas in Paul's day the forces of lawlessness that would have tried to overwhelm Christ and his people were held in check by the imperial power, as Paul himself had good reason to acknowledge with gratitude, the situation has changed: the imperial power itself has become the incarnation of lawlessness by setting itself against Christ and his people. Had Gaius had his way in A.D. 40, the mystery of lawlessness would have been revealed then; but the forces of law and order were too strong for Gaius and brought him down. It was during the reign of his successor Claudius, and during the golden age of Nero's first five years, that Paul accomplished most of his apostolic ministry, protected by the representatives of the empire. But Nero's assault on the Christians of Rome in the aftermath of the great fire of A.D. 64 marked a change in the relations between church and empire. Nero now emerged as the incarnation of lawlessness. To be sure, many of his pagan subjects thought him so as well, and the forces of law and order, which had brought Gaius down in A.D. 41, brought Nero down in A.D. 68. For a year after that it looked as if the empire would dissolve in anarchy, but law and order triumphed with the accession of Vespasian, first emperor of the Flavian dynasty, in A.D. 69. The Flavian dynasty, however, brought no advantage to the Christians of Rome or elsewhere in the empire; the imperial power continued to repress them.

But the mere fact that the imperial power persecuted them would not have sufficed to equate it with Antichrist in their eyes. Nero's attack upon them may have been capricious, but the real issue between church and empire for the next two and a half centuries was a religious one. The imperial power claimed divine honors which the Christians could not conscientiously accord it. When the emperor claimed the title "Lord" in a divine sense, Christians were bound to refuse it; to them there was one Lord, Jesus Christ, and to grant that title to anyone else in the sense in which they used it of Christ would have been high treason to Christ. The fact that the emperor claimed it in that sense made him *Antichrist*, a rival Christ, who treated the refusal of the divine honors which he claimed as high treason against him.

This state of affairs had developed to a considerable degree by the time of John's Patmos visions, and he sees it developing further until it reaches its climax in the first beast of Rev. 13, the ultimate Antichrist. This beast represents a conjunction of ancient symbols. Some of these go back to very early times, such as the seven heads, which link him with Leviathan, the monster which represents the unruly deep, curbed by the

Creator's fiat.[17] The ten horns link him with Daniel's fourth beast (Dan. 7:7). (The fact that the great red dragon of Rev. 12:3 also has seven heads and ten horns indicates that the first beast of Rev. 13 is energized by the devil, the perennial enemy of God and man.) But it is not only with Daniel's fourth beast that the first beast of Rev. 13 is linked; he combines features of all four of Daniel's beasts, and also of the little horn which came up among the ten horns of the fourth beast. For, like the little horn, the first beast of Rev. 13 makes war with the saints and prevails against them. And, like the man of lawlessness in 2 Thess. 2, he receives all but universal worship. The duration of his rule (42 months) is probably based on Dan. 7:25; 9:27; 12:7.

In the receiving of worship he is greatly assisted by the second beast of Rev. 13. It is he who performs the "mighty works and signs and lying wonders" by which, according to 2 Thess. 2:9f., men are beguiled into worshipping the man of lawlessness. The second beast is not the Antichrist in person; he is rather his public relations officer, or minister of propaganda, the "false prophet" of a false god. John may very well have had in mind the emperor-worship which had been established as a popular cult since the reign of Augustus in the province of Asia, and preeminently in the city of Pergamum, "where Satan's throne is" (Rev. 2:13). This would be its end-product: a social and economic boycott of all who refused to conform to the worship of the Antichrist, cutting them off from access to the necessities of life. But as in 2 Thess. 2:8 the man of lawlessness is destroyed by the advent of Christ, so in Rev. 19:20 the beast and the false prophet are seized and consigned to perdition by the victorious Word of God at his appearing.

The beast of Rev. 17 is not the personal Antichrist, but the Roman Empire; the woman seated on the beast is the city of Rome. Antichrist in this chapter is one of the beast's seven heads. The seven heads are seven emperors, the first five of whom (Augustus, Tiberius, Gaius, Claudius and Nero, most probably) "have fallen." When all seven have come and gone, one of them (evidently one of the first five) will return as the last Antichrist. This is the head which was "smitten to death," according to Rev. 13:3, where we are told further that "his death-stroke was healed." Those commentators are probably right who see here a reflection of the belief in a *Nero redivivus.*[18] The last Antichrist will be a veritable Nero returned to life again. Many ancient commentators viewed the Emperor Domitian, brother and successor of Titus, as the second Nero;[19] it is by no means certain that this was John's own view. Unfortunately the secret of his cipher 666 has been kept so well that we cannot say which name he had in mind when he expressed its number thus (Rev. 13:18). A Hebrew writing of "Nero Caesar" is possible;[20] on the other hand

Professor Ethelbert Stauffer refers to a coin of Domitian where the letters recording that emperor's designation are said to yield a total of 666.[21]

IV. THE POST-APOSTOLIC AGE

In an early Christian document, *The Testament of Hezekiah*, which has been incorporated in *The Ascension of Isaiah*, the ultimate Antichrist is portrayed as an incarnation of Beliar (the Greek spelling of Belial, as in 2 Cor. 6:15). Beliar figures in postbiblical Jewish literature as the spirit of evil in the world. But in this work the incarnate Beliar of the end-time is clearly identified with the returning Nero. In the eyes of many, Nero's culminating crime was the murder of his mother Agrippina. So King Hezekiah is represented as foretelling the end-time thus:

> Beliar the great ruler, the king of this world, will descend, who hath ruled it since it came into being, yea, he will descend from his firmament in the likeness of a man, a lawless king, the slayer of his mother: who himself, even this king, will persecute the plant which the Twelve Apostles of the Beloved have planted. . . . This ruler in the form of that king will come, and there will come with him all the powers of this world, and they will hearken unto him in all that he desires.[22]

Some of the *Sibylline Oracles* from about the same period (towards the end of the first century A.D.) foretell the return and reign of Beliar, who will be consumed with all the men of pride, and also predict the return of Nero; but they do not identify the two, for Beliar is here presented as a false prophet, and the returning Nero as an impious tyrant.

Both these forms of Antichrist are found in early Christian literature from the beginning of the second century onwards, but it is the imperial Antichrist that predominates.

A good example of the former concept is provided in the closing section of the *Didache:*

> In the last days the false prophets and the corrupters will be multiplied, and the sheep will be turned into wolves, and love will change to hate, for as lawlessness increases they will hate one another and persecute and betray, and then the deceiver of the world will appear as a son of God, and will do signs and wonders, and the earth will be given over into his hands and he will commit iniquities which have never been since the world began. Then will the creation of mankind come to the fiery trial and many will be offended and be lost, but they who endure in their faith will be saved by the curse itself. And then will the signs of the truth appear. First

the sign spread out in heaven, then the sign of the sound of the trumpet, and thirdly the resurrection of the dead—but not of all the dead, but as it was said: "The Lord will come and all his saints with him." Then will the world see the Lord coming on the clouds of heaven.[23]

The biblical references in this quotation are lucid enough for the most part, but it is as a deceiver that the Antichrist is pictured. On the other hand, the *Epistle of Barnabas,* which may be dated shortly before A.D. 96, envisages the final stumbling-block *(skandalon)* in terms of an imminent fulfillment of Daniel's vision of the little horn and related prophecies:

> The final stumbling-block is at hand, of which it was written, as Enoch says: "For to this end the Lord has cut short the times and the days, that his Beloved should make haste and come to his inheritance." And the prophet also says this: "Ten kingdoms will reign on the earth and there will rise up after them a little king, who will subdue three of the kings under one."[24] Daniel says likewise concerning the same: "And I beheld the fourth beast, wicked and powerful and fiercer than all the beasts of the sea, with ten horns springing from it, and out of them a little excrescent horn, which subdued three of the great horns under one."[25] You ought then to understand.[26]

The three kings are probably interpreted here of the three emperors of the Flavian dynasty—Vespasian (69-79), Titus (79-81) and Domitian (81-96)—who are to be overthrown by the imperial Antichrist. This is evidently the interpretation of the three horns adopted in the fifth book of the *Sibylline Oracles,* where the conqueror who tears them out by the roots is identified with the returning Nero[27]—an identification which may also have been in the mind of the writer of the *Epistle of Barnabas.* But whether Antichrist was identified with the returning Nero or not, it was natural that he should be viewed as a Roman Emperor so long as the empire maintained its repressive policy against Christianity. When persecution was especially severe, then its climax under Antichrist seemed most imminent. Thus Eusebius[28] tells us of a Christian writer named Judas, who at the height of the persecution under Septimius Severus (A.D. 202) brought down the chronology of Daniel's seventy heptads to that very year, and calculated accordingly that Antichrist was on the point of appearing.

This may be the reason why Justin Martyr, foretelling the triumph of Christ in his *First Apology* addressed to the Emperor Antoninus Pius (139-161), tactfully says nothing about the rise and fall of Antichrist. In his *Dialogue with Trypho the Jew,* however, he has no need to inhibit himself, and quotes a considerable part of Daniel's vision of the four beasts. Trypho agrees with him in his interpretation, except that Trypho cannot allow that the glorious being who receives dominion from the Ancient of Days can be the crucified Jesus, and understands the "time and times and half a time" of Dan. 7:25 as 350 years.[29] Later, Justin distinguishes the two advents of Christ—the first in humiliation, the second in glory—and says that the second will follow the rise of the "man of apostasy" and his assault upon the Christians on earth.[30]

V. THE EARLY CHILIASTS

We come now to an important group of writers who, in eschatology at any rate, all belonged to the same school—Irenaeus of Lyons, Hippolytus of Rome and Victorinus of Pettau. All three were chiliasts, and developed views which were held and expressed in the earlier part of the second century by Papias of Hierapolis. Unfortunately Papias's work survives only in fragments, so that we cannot quote him directly on the subject of Antichrist. But one wonders whether he may not be responsible for the interesting theory that the last Antichrist would be a Jew, a member of the tribe of Dan.

As it is, this theory is extant first of all in the fifth book of Irenaeus's treatise *Against Heresies* (c. A.D. 180). The Roman Empire, he says, is to be partitioned among ten kings, in whose days Antichrist will arise and lead the great apostasy of the end-time. Antichrist is identified with the man of lawlessness (2 Thess. 2:3), the abomination of desolation (Matt. 24:15), the little horn (Dan. 7:8), the "king of fierce countenance" (Dan. 8:23), the deceiver who is to "come in his own name" (John 5:43), the beast from the abyss (Rev. 17:8, etc.). Antichrist's rule would mark the culmination of six millennia of world history, and his overthrow would be followed by the establishment of the seventh sabbatic millennium; for world history (as Irenaeus and others held) was a recapitulation of the creative week of Gen. 1:1–2:4a, on the scale of a thousand years to one day. He makes various attempts at unriddling the riddle of the number of Antichrist: *Euanthas*, *Lateinos* and *Teitan* are put forward as possible solutions, but he wisely refuses to dogmatize.[31]

Antichrist's derivation from the tribe of Dan is based by Irenaeus on Jer. 8:16, which he quotes in the Septuagint version and applies to Antichrist:

> From Dan we shall hear the noise of his swift horses; at the sound of the neighing of his cavalry the whole earth is shaken; he will come and devour the earth and its fulness, the city and those who dwell therein.[32]

To Irenaeus this indicates clearly that Antichrist is to come from Dan, and he adds that this is the reason why the tribe of Dan is not included in the list of tribes from which the 144,000 are sealed in Rev. 7:5ff. Antichrist is thus envisaged as an apostate Jew, sitting enthroned in the temple at Jerusalem, and claiming divine honors for himself there. By Tertullian, however, who in many of these respects dots Irenaeus's *i*'s and crosses his *t*'s, Antichrist is not envisaged as a Jew, and the temple of God in which he sits is the church.[33]

Hippolytus of Rome (*c.* A.D. 217), the greatest scholar of his age in the Christian West, has left a complete treatise *On Christ and Antichrist.* In essence this is an elaboration of the ideas already familiar to us from Irenaeus, including the derivation of Antichrist from Dan. If Jacob says "Judah is a lion's whelp" (Gen. 49:9), referring, of course, to Christ as the lion of the tribe of Judah, Moses says "Dan is a lion's whelp" (Deut. 33:22), referring to Antichrist as a counterfeit imitation of the true Christ. And when Jacob says "Dan shall be a serpent in the way" (Gen. 49:17), the allusion to the serpent of Eden (Hippolytus thinks) is too evident to be missed. But Jacob also said "Dan shall judge his people" (Gen. 49:16). True, says Hippolytus, but this is not a reference to Samson, the judge from the tribe of Dan, but to Antichrist as the unjust judge,[34] in which role he also figures in one of our Lord's parables (Luke 18:1ff.).[35]

He repeats all the usual identifications of Antichrist—with the little horn, the man of lawlessness, the beast from the abyss, and so forth—and identifies him further with Daniel's "willful king." The three horns which the little horn tears out by the roots are said to be Egypt, Libya and Ethiopia—an inference, probably, from Dan. 11:43.[36] But he finds Antichrist in a variety of other Scriptures: he is, for example, the Assyrian of Isa. 10:12ff., the king of Babylon of Isa. 14:4ff., the prince of Tyre of Ezek. 28:2ff. This lumping together of distinct enemies of Israel in earlier days and giving them a unitive eschatological interpretation reminds one of the Old Testament exegesis attested in the Qumran texts. Antichrist, according to Hippolytus, is also the partridge of Jer. 17:11 (here he gives a brief excursus on the natural history of the partridge), and the sender of ambassadors in vessels of papyrus of Isa. 18:2, carrying his directives against the saints.[37] Plainly exegesis here has slipped its moorings to drift in the sea of imagination.

Victorinus of Pettau, who was martyred in the last imperial persecution (A.D. 304), is the earliest Latin commentator on the Apocalypse whose commentary has survived.[38] He is important not only in his own right but also for his indebtedness to earlier commentators whose writings are no longer extant, to Papias in particular. "His value," says J. Rendel Harris, "lies in the fact that he was the most unblushing of the patristic plagiarists, and he was in the habit of transcribing his favorite authors with the minimum of modification, or of literally translating them from Greek into not very polished Latin and re-issuing his transcriptions and translations under his own name."[39] This may be somewhat exaggerated, and is certainly rather unfair, for it judges Victorinus by the standards of a day when ideas of literary copyright are very different from what they were in his day. R. H. Charles redresses the balance by calling him "the most scientific and original representative" of the early chiliastic interpreters of Revelation, particularly in his adoption of the recapitulatory principle in interpreting the book.[40]

On Rev. 11:7, where "the beast that comes up out of the abyss" first appears, Victorinus explains this designation in terms of Ezek. 31:3ff., which he mistakenly ascribes to Isaiah (perhaps by confusion with Isa. 10:34). There, in the Septuagint text, Asshur (the Assyrian) is a cypress in Lebanon nourished by the waters ("the many millions of men who will be subject to him") and caused to grow by the abyss (which "belched him forth"). Victorinus then quotes 2 Thess. 2:7ff., saying that Paul's words, "the mystery of lawlessness is already at work," were intended to teach his readers that the coming Antichrist was the man who was then emperor (i.e., Nero).[41]

On the expulsion of Satan from heaven in Rev. 12:9 Victorinus says:

> This is the beginning of the advent of Antichrist. However, Elijah must first prophesy and there must be times of peace then; so it is afterwards, when the three years and six months of Elijah's prophesying have been fulfilled, that Antichrist is to be cast out of heaven (to which hitherto he has had the right to ascend), together with all the renegade angels. That Antichrist is thus raised up from hell is further attested by the apostle Paul when he says: "unless first there come the man of sin, the son of perdition, the adversary, who will raise himself above everything that is called god or is worshipped."[42]

There is some confusion here between Antichrist, who is energized by Satan, and Satan himself, and it is curious to be told that Antichrist is both cast down from heaven and to be raised up from hell.

Chapters 13 and 17 of Revelation are combined in Victorinus's commentary. Following Irenaeus,[43] he believes Revelation to have been written under Domitian; therefore Domitian is the sixth emperor of Rev. 17:10. The preceding five are Galba, Otho, Vitellius, Vespasian and Titus; the seventh who is to come is Nerva (A.D. 96-98), and the eighth is the returning Nero, although Nero is not one of the seven according to Victorinus's computation. Nero is the head that was wounded to death and healed (Rev. 13:3):

It is well known that when the horsemen sent by the senate were in hot pursuit of Nero, he cut his own throat. But after his restoration to life God sends him to the Jews, the persecutors of Christ, a fit king for fit subjects, just such a "Christ" as persecutors and Jews have deserved. Since he is to bear another name, he will enter upon another life, that so they may receive him as their "Christ" (Messiah). . . . For he will not be able to seduce people to circumcision, if he himself is not a champion of the law. Indeed, the only compulsion he will impose on the saints will be to submit to circumcision, if perchance he can seduce any. Thus he leads them to put their trust in him, so that they call him the Christ.[44]

This is a valiant attempt to combine the two identifications of the Antichrist—with *Nero redivivus,* and with a Jewish false Messiah. Nero is to be reborn as a Jew, and it is the new name that he will bear in his reincarnation which is denoted by the number 666. This will enable the wise to recognize his true identity when he appears. He will erect a golden image and require it to be worshipped, as Nebuchadnezzar did. This image, the abomination of desolation, will be placed in Jerusalem, "in his temple between the mountain of the sea and the two seas" (so Victorinus renders Dan. 11:45).[45] But he will meet his doom at the advent of Christ, and his dominion will be replaced by the millennial reign of the saints.

With the peace of the church, which began ten years after the death of Victorinus, the line of interpretation which he represents died out. But it was this line of interpretation, by and large, which was revived by Francisco Ribeira and other Jesuit exegetes in the sixteenth and seventeenth centuries, and again in a fresh form by the latter-day futurism which arose at the end of the eighteenth and beginning of the nineteenth centuries. It may be pointed out, however, that a line of interpretation which was reasonable while the Roman Empire was still in being loses something of its persuasive power when it has to be stretched on a Procrustean bed in order to make room for an indefinite gap of many centuries between the fall of that empire and its putative resurgence in the end-time.

VI. LATER INTERPRETATIONS

With the empire's recognition and subsequent acceptance of Christianity the form of the expectation of Antichrist was inevitably modified. He was envisaged as an enemy of the Christendom which now comprised church and empire together, but opinions continued to differ on whether he would arise from without or within. On the one hand he was envisaged as an avowed enemy assaulting Christendom from without, like Genseric the Vandal king in the fifth century (whose name in Greek could be spelled so as to yield the total 666), or Muhammad in the seventh century. On the other hand he was envisaged as an apostate individual or group arising within Christendom. This is the view to which Augustine apparently inclines, although he does not speak with assurance. Thus, mentioning various interpretations of the "man of lawlessness" in 2 Thess. 2, he goes on:

> Some think that in this passage Antichrist means not the prince himself alone, but his whole body, that is, the mass of men who adhere to him, along with him who is their prince; and they also think that we should render the Greek more exactly if we read, not "in the temple of God" but "for" or "as the temple of God," as if he himself were the temple of God, the church.[46]

Pope Gregory the Great (590-604) saw a foreshadowing of the rise of Antichrist when the Patriarch of Constantinople assumed the distinctive title "Ecumenical Bishop" (to the present day the Patriarch of Constantinople is known as the Ecumenical Patriarch). But he expected an individual Antichrist to arise in due course from the tribe of Dan, although he believed Antichrist to be alive and operative already in his members, among whom the Patriarch of Constantinople and those who acquiesced in his new title were in danger of being numbered. But Pope Gregory's next successor but one, Boniface III (607-608), accepted from the Eastern Emperor Phocas the very title which Gregory had deprecated when the Constantinopolitan Patriarch accepted it; and to this day his successor includes among his titles that of "Universal Bishop." We may say, then, that on this score the honors are even between the bishops of the old Rome and the new Rome.

From time to time in the Middle Ages Antichrist was identified with an outstanding individual in Western Christendom—a pope, like the delinquent John XII (956-964), or an emperor, like Friedrich Barbarossa (1155-90). As regards Barbarossa, the popular expectation of his return to life and power is reminiscent of the similar expectation of *Nero redivivus*. As for the identification of Antichrist with an individual pope, this implied that the individual in question was the unworthy occupant of an office which in itself was holy. On the other hand, from the twelfth century on we can trace the rise of the opinion that the papal institution itself was the predicted Antichrist—for example, among the followers of Joachim of Floris, among the Hussites, and preeminently in Luther and the Reformers. The identification of Antichrist with the Papacy attained confessional status in many churches of the Reformation: as late as 1646, for example, the Westminster Confession of Faith speaks of "the Pope of Rome" as "that Antichrist, that man of sin, and son of perdition, that exalteth himself, in the Church, against Christ and all that is called God."[47] The first Reformed exegete to abandon the identification of Antichrist with the Papacy appears to have been the Dutch scholar Hugo Grotius in 1644.[48]

Those who adhered to the old religion, in their turn, were not slow to fix the label of Antichrist on Luther and the Reformers. And Luther, to be sure, is another name which with a modicum of ingenuity and resolution can yield the sum of 666.[49] But both sides in this dispute might be charged with attaching too great an importance to Western Christendom and the part it plays in the eternal purpose.[50] Since then many other candidates have been nominated—among them, Archbishop Laud, Napoleon, Mussolini, Hitler, Stalin, international Communism, the World Council of Churches, the General Assembly of the Church of Scotland, and perhaps (for aught I know to the contrary) the Prophecy Investigation Society!

VII. CONCLUSION

The fact is, people tend to make the identification of Antichrist with some person or movement that they dislike or fear. It is relatively easy, indeed, to recognize the Antichrist from without when, in the guise of an absolute monarch or a totalitarian state, he demands the obedience which is due to Christ alone, and penalizes those who refuse to render to Caesar the things which belong to God. But the Antichrist from within is the deadlier menace, precisely because he is not a person or movement that we dislike or fear. He is attractive, plausible, convincing.[51] In whatever form we may expect a final manifestation of his power on the eve of the Second Advent, a consideration of the history of interpretation will warn us not to dogmatize. The serious student of Scripture can never afford to ignore what was thought of its meaning by serious students of earlier days. For the present, we may recall the solemnizing lesson which Provost Salmon learned when he remarked to Bishop FitzGerald that neither his own name nor the bishop's would fit the cryptogram 666; he received a letter pointing out that "Mr. Salmon" in Hebrew letters fitted the cryptogram exactly![52] When we speculate on the identity of Antichrist, our best policy might be for each one to ask the question which the disciples asked when Jesus told them that one of their number was a traitor: "Lord, is it I?" The spirit of Antichrist will be strengthened if we allow ourselves to be seduced by it and to foster it in our hearts; it will be diminished and weakened if we individually watch for every manifestation of it within ourselves, cast it out and wage unceasing war against it, confessing Jesus as Lord and Christ, not in word only but in deed and in truth.

13. The Earliest Latin Commentary on the Apocalypse

I. VICTORINUS OF PETTAU

The Book of the Revelation was widely recognized by the churches of the West long before the eastern churches made up their minds to accept it as canonical. Various reasons might be suggested for this: at any rate there was something about the book which immediately appealed to the souls of the western Christians and convinced them of its divinity. It might have been thought that its peculiar Greek would not lend itself readily to translation into Latin; but, as a matter of fact, the Vulgate Apocalypse is a masterpiece of literature and comes home to the reader with a charm and a vigor all its own. It is quite in keeping with these facts that the earliest complete commentary on the Apocalypse which has come down to us should be in Latin. Its author was Victorinus, bishop of Poetouio in Upper Pannonia, now Ptuj on the Drava in Yugoslavia (German *Pettau*). Victorinus suffered martyrdom under Diocletian, probably about the year 304.

Before his day others had commented on the Apocalypse, but in Greek. Fragments of exposition appear in the works of Justin Martyr and Irenaeus; Melito of Sardis and Hippolytus of Rome wrote complete commentaries on it (both, unfortunately, lost); while Clement of Alexandria and Origen are also said to have commented on it. So, apart from Clement and Origen, even the earliest *Greek* commentators on the Apoc-

Published in *The Evangelical Quarterly* 10 (1938), pp. 352-366.

alypse represent the western churches and the churches of the province of Asia. The latter churches, for obvious reasons, did not regard the Apocalypse with the indifference of many of the eastern churches. Justin lived at Ephesus before he went to Rome; Irenaeus, bishop of Lyons, had as his master Polycarp, the martyr-bishop of Smyrna; while Melito represented yet another of the seven churches. Hippolytus (died *c.* 236) was for a time bishop of a schismatic group in Rome (the first antipope).

The first commentators interpreted the Apocalypse more literally than their successors: in particular, they accepted the "chiliastic" view of the millennial reign of chapter 20.

> These writers were acquainted with the original interpretation of this chapter. But this interpretation was soon displaced by the spiritualizing methods of Alexandria. Tyconius, adopting these methods, rejected the literal interpretation of chapter xx., treated the millennium as the period between the first and second advents of Christ. Jerome and Augustine followed in the footsteps of Tyconius, and a realistic eschatology was crushed out of existence in the Church for full 800 years.[1]

Justin, Irenaeus and Hippolytus all belonged to this school, and Victorinus followed in their steps.

> Like them he was a Chiliast, and still preserved elements of the true and ancient interpretation of the Apocalypse according to the Contemporary-Historical Method. Thus Nero *redivivus* is the first Beast, and the False Prophet is the second. But his most important contribution historically is his Theory of Recapitulation. This is, that the Apocalypse does not represent a strict succession of events following chronologically upon one another, but under each successive series of seven seals, seven trumpets, seven bowls, the same events are dealt with.[2]

Of the life of Victorinus we know almost nothing. He seems to have come originally from a Greek-speaking part of the Empire. According to Jerome,

> he did not know Latin as well as he knew Greek. As a result, his works, while important in sense, appear less important because of his way of putting words together. They are as follows: commentaries on Genesis, Exodus, Leviticus, Isaiah, Ezekiel, Habakkuk, Ecclesiastes, the Song of Songs, the Apocalypse of John; a work *Against all Heresies* and many others. At the end he was crowned with martyrdom.[3]

Jerome's witness to his imperfect knowledge of Latin is decidedly justified by his writings that remain. While his meaning is usually quite plain, his grammatical constructions are the reverse. In many places they conform to no known rule of Latin syntax, classical or postclassical. He makes frequent use of the infinitive in independent clauses, the subject being sometimes in the nominative, sometimes in the accusative. He inverts the normal usages of *in* with the accusative and *in* with the ablative. An *Index Verborum et Elocutionum* will be found in Haussleiter's edition of his extant works.[4]

To the list of his works given by Jerome in the above citation we must add a commentary on Matthew (referred to by Jerome himself in two or three other places, and by Cassiodorus), and a tractate on the creation, *De fabrica mundi*, mentioned by no ancient author, but extant in a Lambeth manuscript, from which it was first published in 1688. Apart from this tractate, the only one of his works which has come down to our day is his commentary on the Apocalypse. This commentary was edited and re-edited after its author was dead, and most of the manuscripts in which it has been preserved give us not the original edition of Victorinus, but one or other of these posthumous recensions. It was believed for long that the original work of Victorinus was quite lost. Thus H. A. Wilson, writing in 1887, says of *De fabrica mundi*:

> It is possible that it may be a portion of the commentary on Genesis, but it is perhaps more probable that both this fragment and the scholia on the Apocalypse are the work of another Victorinus, and that all the works of the bishop of Pettau have been lost.[5]

II. TEXTUAL HISTORY

The credit for establishing and editing the text of the original commentary must go to J. Haussleiter, whose *Victorini episcopi Petauionensis opera* appeared in 1916 as the forty-ninth volume of the Vienna *Corpus Scriptorum Ecclesiasticorum Latinorum*. Haussleiter distinguishes three later recensions of the work. The first and most important of these was made by Jerome. A certain Anatolius sent Jerome a copy of Victorinus's exposition and asked him to say what he thought of it. Jerome returned it with a covering letter, in which he said that he had made what seemed to him necessary corrections and that in particular he had removed passages in which the author had expressed chiliastic views, substituting instead excerpts from other writers, who had interpreted the millennium more in accordance with his own views.[6]

This Hieronymian recension is extant in seven MSS of the tenth, eleventh, twelfth and fifteenth centuries, and Haussleiter prints it on the odd-numbered pages of his edition, from 17 to 153. By comparing this with the original edition, we can see how Jerome set about his work of emendation. He improved Victorinus's language, changed words and phrases here and there, revised the text of the biblical quotations, omitted what he disagreed with, transposed sections of the commentary, and added excerpts from other writers, especially Tyconius, as well as comments of his own. This recension is referred to by Haussleiter as Y.[7]

The second recension, to which Haussleiter assigns the symbol, Φ, augmented Jerome's by inserting a text of the Apocalypse (the same as Augustine used in his *De ciuitate Dei* and after him Primasius), and some further exposition. This edition was used by Beatus (eighth century). The third recension, referred to as S, represents a mixture of the previous recensions, and adds citations from the Vulgate. It appears to have been made before the year 452.

The original edition of Victorinus was for long superseded by these recensions, particularly by Jerome's. References to "Victorinus" in most works on the Revelation refer to this recension. The original edition is extant in three MSS only, first mentioned in 1828 by Cardinal Angelo Mai, who found them in the Vatican library. They are the Ottobonian MS. 3288A (fifteenth century), Ottobonian 3288B (sixteenth century), a copy of the preceding, and the Vatican MS. 3546 (sixteenth century), a copy of one or other of the former two. There is hardly any difference between the three MSS. They contain, in addition to Victorinus on the Apocalypse and Jerome's covering letter to Anatolius, the commentaries on Galatians, Ephesians and Philippians by our author's more illustrious namesake, Victorinus Afer[8] (who must have been born about the time when Victorinus of Pettau died), together with three short works sometimes, though erroneously, attributed to Victorinus Afer.[9] These three MSS are referred to respectively by Haussleiter by the symbols *A, a* and *a*. He prints the true Victorinian text, obtained from these MSS, on the even-numbered pages of his edition, from 16 to 154. The letter to Anatolius is printed on pp. 14f.

III. THE EXPOSITION

Victorinus did not provide a verse-by-verse exposition of the whole Apocalypse: in the words of Cassiodorus, "he gave a brief treatment of some of the most difficult places."[10] Some authors refer to his comments as *scholia*. He quotes a longer or shorter passage which seems deserving of comment, frequently in the accusative and infinitive construction of an indirect statement, and then adds his interpretation. This is usually highly allegorical, though Jerome found it at times excessively literal. He is not diffuse; he says what he has to say and passes on to the next question without more ado. He quotes freely from other parts of Scripture: Genesis, Exodus, Numbers, Job, Psalms, Proverbs, Ecclesiastes, Isaiah, Jeremiah, Ezekiel, Daniel, Joel, Micah, Zechariah, Malachi, the four Gospels (especially Matthew), Acts, Romans, 1 and 2 Corinthians, 1 and 2 Thessalonians, 1 Timothy, Hebrews, 1 Peter and Jude are all laid under contribution. In his quotations he uses the parenthetic *ait* or *inquit* with unnecessary frequency.

Charles, as we have seen, finds the chief importance of Victorinus in the history of the interpretation of the Apocalypse in his initiation of the Theory of Recapitulation. While some forms of this theory suppose, as Charles says, that "under each successive series of seven seals, seven trumpets, seven bowls, the same events are dealt with," Victorinus does not seem to have developed the theory so far as this, but to have regarded only the trumpets and the bowls as portraying the same events. He states the theory in the course of his comments on chapter 8, as follows:

> Now "trumpet" is a word of power, and though he repeats it by means of the "bowls," his telling it twice indicates not that it has already happened once, but that it has once been decreed that what is to take place among them shall indeed happen to them. Therefore whatever he said less plainly in the "trumpets," he said more emphatically in the "bowls." Nor is the order of the sayings to be regarded, since the sevenfold Holy Spirit, after going right through to the last time and to the end, returns again to the same times and supplies what he has said less fully. It is not order but meaning that should be looked for in the Apocalypse; for there is also a false prophecy. The things then which are written in the "trumpets" and in the "bowls" are either disastrous plagues sent on the earth, or the fury of Antichrist himself, or the diminution of peoples, or different plagues, or hope in the kingdom of the saints, or the fall of cities, or the fall of Babylon, that is, the Roman city.

The seven alternatives in the last sentence correspond one by one to what the seer saw when the seven trumpets were sounded and the seven bowls emptied. A comparison of the two series has persuaded several expositors that Victorinus was on the right lines here. Both the seventh trumpet and, after the parenthesis of chapters 18 and 19, the seventh bowl are followed by the advent of Christ to judge and reign. And a consideration of the scene which follows the opening of the sixth seal—the advent of the *Dies Irae*—has led some to extend the recapitulatory theory to include the seals as well.[11] (The seventh seal serves mainly to introduce the seven trumpets.)

Victorinus's exegesis, as we have said, is for the most part allegorical. But what we do find of the contemporary-historical method of interpretation is very interesting. We find it chiefly in his combined notes on chapters 13 and 17:

> *The seven heads are seven hills, on which the woman sits* (that is, the Roman city); *and they are seven kings: five have fallen, one is, and another has not yet come; and when he comes, he will be for a short time. And the beast which you saw is of the seven, and is the eighth.* Therefore we must understand that time at which the Apocalypse was written, for Domitian was then emperor. Now before him had been his brother Titus and their father Vespasian; Otho, Vitellius and Galba. These are the "five" who "have fallen"; "one is," he says, under whom the Apocalypse is said to have been written, namely Domitian. "Another has not yet come": he means Nerva; "and when he comes, he will be for a short time"—for he did not complete two years. "And the beast which you saw," says he, "is of the seven": for before these kings Nero reigned; "and is the eighth": when that one arrives, he will be counted in the eighth place. And since the end will take place in his reign, he added: *and he goes into destruction.* For *ten kings have received royal authority:* when he moves from the east, they will be sent from the Roman city with their armies. These he calls *ten horns* and *ten diadems.* Daniel shows this too: *three of the former will be rooted up;*[12] that is, three of the foremost leaders are killed by Antichrist. The other seven give him *glory and honour and a throne and authority.* Of them he says: *these will hate the harlot* (he means the city) *and will burn her flesh with fire.*
>
> *Now one of the heads was wounded to death, and its wound of death was healed.* He refers to Nero. For it is well known that when the horsemen sent by the Senate were coming upon him, he cut his own throat. He then is raised from the dead and sent by God to the Jews and persecutors of Christ, a worthy king to worthy subjects, and a Messiah such as persecutors and Jews deserved. And as he is to bear another name, he will also enter upon another life, that so they may receive him as their Messiah. Daniel says: *he will not recognize the desire of women*—since he himself is most filthy—*and will recognize no god of his fathers.*[13] For he will not be able to seduce the people to circumcision unless he is a defender of the law. He will lay no compulsion upon the saints except to receive circumcision, if he can seduce any. Thus at length he makes them believe in him, so that they call him Christ. Now that he rises from hell we have also said above in the words of Isaiah:[14] *the water nourished him and the abyss gave him increase* (that is, belched him forth). However, though he comes with changed name, the Holy Spirit says: *His number is six hundred and sixty-six.* He will fulfil this number according to the Greek lettering.

The dating of the Apocalypse in the principate of Domitian was taken over by Victorinus from his predecessors, primarily no doubt from

Irenaeus.[15] But this landed him in difficulties when he came to identify the seven emperors referred to in Rev. 17:10. He naturally took Domitian to be the one who currently "is," and then, counting back, he came to Galba as the first of the "five" who "have fallen"—that is, the first of the seven. But the "eighth" emperor, the personal Antichrist, is the resuscitated Nero, and since he was one of the seven, it is odd that Nero should be excluded from the seven whom Victorinus lists by name, the first of the seven being Nero's successor. He makes no attempt to resolve this discrepancy. Again, he identifies the seventh, who "will be for a short time," with Domitian's successor Nerva, who ruled for two years only (A.D. 96-98). It might then have been supposed that Nerva's successor Trajan should be identified with *Nero resuscitatus,* but this would have been deemed absurd, so an indefinite interval in the fulfillment of the prophecy must lie between the death of Nerva and the rise of Antichrist (the sort of interval which figures even today in some ingenious schemes of prophetic interpretation).

Victorinus did not attempt to explain the number 666. But the authors of the later recensions were not so cautious. We find the suggestions TEITAN,[16] GENSERIKOS,[17] ANTEMOS[18] (these to be numerically assessed according to the values of the Greek letters); and, most curious of all, recension Φ gives us a word DICLVX, supposed to be the Latin for TEITAN. DICLVX is, of course, DCLXVI (666) with the order of the letters changed. But why should it refer to Antichrist? "Because he changes himself into an angel of light, *audens se DICere LVcem*" (from *LVX*)! An excellent example of ancient classical etymology!

There are two other historical notes on Revelation 10:11 and 11:1:

> *You must preach again* (that is, prophesy) *among peoples, tongues and nations:* that is, because when John saw this he was on the island of Patmos, condemned to the mine by the Emperor Domitian. So we see that John composed the Apocalypse there; and when he thought that now, being an old man, he might be received (*sc.* into heaven) after suffering, on the death of Domitian all his judgments were declared null and void, and John was released from the mine and thus afterwards handed on this same Apocalypse which he had received from the Lord. This is the meaning of the words, *You must prophesy again.*
>
> Moreover, he received *a reed like a rod,* in order to *measure the temple of God and the altar and those who worship at it.* This signifies the authority which he subsequently exhibited to the churches on his release. For afterwards he also wrote the Gospel. For when Valentinus and Cerinthus and Ebion and the rest of Satan's school were dispersed throughout the earth, the bishops of the neighboring cities came together to him and compelled him to write his testimony to the Lord. Now the *measure* of faith

is the commandment of our Lord, to confess the Father Almighty, as we have been taught, and His Son Jesus Christ our Lord, begotten spiritually by the Father before the creation of the world, who became man and after vanquishing death was received bodily into the heavens by the Father, the holy Lord and pledge of immortality, who was foretold by the prophets and written of in the law; he is the hand of God and the Word of the Almighty Father, the creator of the whole sphere of the world. This is the *reed* and *measure* of faith, that none should worship at the holy altar, save the one who makes this confession: *the Lord and His Christ.*

Apart from the historical comment, the credal statement is interesting, in that there is no reference to the Holy Spirit. Jerome omits the final phrase, *the Lord and His Christ,* no doubt as being too explicitly "binitarian." The Latin of part of this creed is very obscure: it seems to say that our Lord is *by* the hand of God and *by* the Word of the Almighty Father *(hunc per manum dei et per uerbum patris omnipotentis),* perhaps because of a mechanical carrying on of the preposition *per* from the preceding phrases: "foretold by *(per)* the prophets and written of by *(per)* the law." Jerome's recension quotes the wording as "he is the hand of God, the word of the Father, the creator of the world" *(hunc esse manum dei et uerbum patris et conditorem orbis),* where "creator" denotes Christ, not (as in the manuscripts) the Father.[19]

The Nicolaitans are also explained historically. In his comments on the letter to Ephesus Victorinus says:

> Before that time factious and pestilential men had made themselves a heresy in the name of the deacon Nicolaus, teaching that meat offered to idols *(delibatum)* could be exorcised, so that it might be eaten, and that one who had committed fornication might receive peace *(pacem acciperet)* on the eighth day.[20]

Pax here seems to have the sense of "absolution." We come across this usage again in his exposition of the letter to Thyatira.

> He shows that there too there are men prone to grant unlawful absolutions *(faciles homines ad inlicitas paces dandas)* and to listen to new prophecies.

He does not mention the woman Jezebel by name, but one gathers that he considers those who tolerate her to be much the same as those who hold the doctrine of Balaam and of the Nicolaitans, i.e., those who are guilty of undue laxity in church discipline and who disregard the instructions of the Apostolic Decree in Acts 15:29.

The contemporary-historical interpretation is not incompatible with the eschatological. The former passes over into the latter. We see this particularly in Victorinus's references to Nero. He treats him at first historically, but then uses the current belief that Nero was still alive and would return from the East to take vengeance on Rome as a basis for his eschatological exposition, in which the Antichrist is identified with Nero *resuscitatus.*

Victorinus's literal interpretation of the first resurrection and the millennial reign plainly appears in his comments on chapters 19, 20 and 21. Our Lord arrives with his heavenly host, the nations gather to oppose him, and fall by the sword. Some of them survive, to act as servants to the reigning saints during the millennium; these in turn are to be slain when the devil is let loose at the end of the thousand years and they allow themselves to be deceived by him. This much we learn from the commentary on chapter 19, and "on all these things," he says, "the prophets similarly agree." The holy city of the millennial age, depicted in chapter 21, is more than a city in the strict sense: it embraces all the territory promised to Abraham in Genesis 15:18, *from the great river Euphrates to the river of Egypt;* and to the Messianic king of Psalm 72:8, *from sea to sea* ("that is, from the Red Sea to the sea of Arabia, and from the sea of the northeast to the sea of Phoenicia") *and to the ends of the earth* ("they are the parts of greater Syria").

By way of illustrating the two resurrections he quotes 1 Thessalonians 4:15-17 and 1 Corinthians 15:52. The *trump of God* of the former passage—the signal for the first resurrection—is contrasted with the *last trump* of the other: this, he says, is sounded after the millennium and heralds the second resurrection. But his exposition of Revelation 20 is worth quoting in full.

> Now let no one be ignorant that the scarlet devil is shut up with all his apostate angels in the Tartarus of Gehenna at the advent of the Lord, and let loose after a thousand years on account of the nations which have served Antichrist, that they alone may perish, because they have deserved this: then comes judgment generally. Therefore he says: *And the dead* ("those written in the book of life") *lived and reigned with Christ a thousand years. This is the first resurrection. Blessed and holy is he who has part in the first resurrection: against him the second death has no power.* Concerning this resurrection he says: *And I saw the Lamb standing and with him a hundred and forty-four thousand,* that is, standing with Christ, namely those who are to believe at the last time from among the Jews through the preaching of Elijah, to whom the Spirit bears witness not only for their virgin body but also for their speech. Therefore he mentions previously that the twenty-four elders said: *We give thee thanks, Lord God, who hast reigned; and the nations were angry.*
>
> In this same first resurrection also a beautiful city to come is described by this scripture. Of this first resurrection Paul also spoke to the Macedonian church, as follows: *For this we tell you thus, by the word of God, that*

the Lord himself will descend from heaven with the trump of God to raise (sc. the dead); and the dead in Christ will stand up first: then we who live shall be caught away with them in the clouds to meet the Lord in the air, and so shall we ever be with the Lord.[21]

We have heard a "trump" mentioned; this is to be observed: in another place the apostle mentions another trump. He says to the Corinthians: *At the last trump the dead will rise*—they will become immortal—*and we shall be changed.*[22] He said that the dead for their part would rise immortal for the punishments which they must bear, but it is manifest that we shall be changed and clothed with glory. When therefore we have heard that there is a *last trump,* we must understand that there is a first one also. Now these are the two resurrections. As many therefore as have not risen beforehand in the first resurrection and reigned with Christ over the earth—over all nations—will rise *at the last trump* after a thousand years, that is, in the last resurrection, among the impious and sinners and evildoers of various kinds. Rightly did he go on to say: *Blessed and holy is he who has part in the first resurrection: against him the second death has no power.* Now the *second death* is punishment in hell.

All this passage disappears in later recensions, which explain the first resurrection in the sense of Colossians 3:1, as "the present resurrection of souls by faith, which does not allow men to pass over to the second death," and allegorize the millennial reign. Jerome, for example, substitutes a spiritualizing exegesis, according to which the reign is to be understood as heavenly, not earthly. The thousand years are not to be taken literally, for "if we must understand them thus, the saints cease to reign when the thousand years are completed." The number 1,000 is, of course, the product of 10 and 100; and "the number 10 signifies the decalogue, and the number 100 indicates the crown of virginity." So, he argues, those who keep the ten commandments and guard themselves from impurity are priests of Christ and reign with him, for in them the devil is bound, whereas he is let loose in those who are guilty of evil behavior and false doctrine. The end of the thousand years signifies the completion of the number of the saints, when the devil and his followers will be consigned to the lake of fire. Then takes place the resurrection of the bodies of all sleeping saints. Jerome's own account of this alteration of the original commentary is given in his letter to Anatolius:

> So as not to spurn your request, I immediately opened the books of former writers, and what I found in their commentaries concerning the millennial reign I added to the work of Victorinus, removing from it what he understood literally.

Anatolius, it appears, finding in his copy doctrines which were beginning to be regarded as heretical, thought his safest plan was to get the great Doctor to remove the dangerous passages and substitute whatever was considered the orthodox view.

We may now go through the commentary, noting briefly some interesting points other than those we have already mentioned. He emphasizes the word *like* in *one like a son of man* (1:13), because while the title "Son of Man" was appropriate for our Lord when he was on earth, in his present glory he is more suitably called "Son of God." The *two-edged sword* (1:16) is the Word of God, the two edges being the Old and New Testaments respectively. The two Testaments, he says, are also indicated by the *things new and old* of Matthew 13:52 and by the *stater* (two *denarii*) which Peter found in the fish's mouth (Matt. 17:26). The *feet* of Christ (1:15) are the apostles; "for those by whom the preaching proceeds are rightly called feet."[23]

The seven Spirits (1:4, etc.) are gifts of the one Holy Spirit: he compares Isaiah 11:2 (his Old Latin text follows the LXX): *the spirit of wisdom and understanding, of counsel and might, of knowledge and piety, the spirit of the fear of God*. As for the *seven churches*, all the churches are embraced in the perfect number. The seven letters apply to seven types of churches. Paul, he remarks, also addressed letters to seven churches and no more, so as not to outstep the perfect number (whatever else he had to say he said to individuals);[24] and similarly the *seven women* of Isaiah 4:1 who *take hold of one man* are seven churches (i.e., the complete church) taking hold of Christ!

The morning star (2:28) is the first resurrection. The *jasper* and *sardius* (4:3), being the color of water and fire respectively, represent the watery judgment of the Old Testament and the fiery judgment foretold in the New. The *rainbow round about the throne* reminds us that the former judgment is past, never to return, and that we "should no longer fear water, but fire." The four living creatures represent the four Gospels, and here follows an excursus on the Gospels based on the well-known passage of Irenaeus.[25] As each creature has six wings, there are twenty-four wings in all: these are the books of the Old Testament according to the Hebrew enumeration, which bear up the Gospels. This refers to the importance of O.T. prophecy for the attestation of the Gospel. The *twenty-four elders seated on thrones* also represent the Law and the Prophets, "bearing the testimonies of judgment"; but Victorinus more usually regards them as the twelve patriarchs and the twelve apostles.

In 5:1, his text represents the *book* as being *written on the inside* only: *in manu sedentis super tribunal librum scriptum deintus, signatum sigillis VII*. The evidence for retaining "and on the back" (καὶ ὄπισθεν) is overwhelming, but Victorinus's reading adopts the punctuation after "on the inside" (ἔσωθεν) which implies the construction of "on the back" with "sealed" (κατεσφραγισμένον)—"sealed on the back with seven seals."[26] The "book" is the Old Testament: Christ had authority to open it because the Father had committed all judgment to him.[27] "To open the testament is to suffer and vanquish death on man's behalf." He had to die ere his testament could be opened: he could open it himself because he had *prevailed*, i.e., "crushed death like a lion." The *harps* (5:8) with their strings stretched on wood speak of the body of Christ on the cross.

Although the seals are opened one after another, they portray contemporaneous events. The four horsemen (6:2ff.) represent the gospel, famine, wars, pestilence. The *altar* (6:9) is the earth: the brazen altar of burnt-offering and the golden altar of incense in the Tabernacle correspond to earth and heaven respectively. The *souls under the altar,* therefore, are in Hades, in that department of it which is "remote from pains and fires, the rest of the saints." The *white robes* (6:11) are described as "the gift of the Holy Spirit."

The *angel descending from the sun-rising* (7:2; Victorinus reads *descending* for *ascending:* Jerome corrects him) is Elijah, as is also the angel proclaiming *an eternal gospel* in 14:6. Under his preaching a number of Jews will believe, and *a great multitude from all nations.* The seven angels who pour forth the bowls of wrath fulfill our Savior's words in Matthew 13:41; 24:31, as well as such O.T. prophecies as Micah 5:6, which he reads: *they will chase Assur in* (or *into*) *the ditch of Nebroth.*[28] *Assur* is the Antichrist and *the ditch of Nebroth* "the damnation of the devil." The *eagle flying in the mid heaven* (8:13) is the Holy Spirit; the *strong angel with the rainbow upon his head* (10:1) is our Lord. The book in the angel's hand is the Apocalypse. By taking and eating it John commits it to memory.

The *two witnesses* (11:3) are not, as many have said, Elijah and Enoch or Elijah and Moses, but Elijah and Jeremiah. These two are also represented by *the two wings of the great eagle* which carry the woman into the wilderness (12:14), and by the two angels of 14:6 and 14:8. Of these two angels the former, as we have seen, announces the *eternal gospel;* while the latter proclaims the imminent fall of Babylon, in words reminiscent of Jeremiah 51:8. After these two have prophesied for three and a half years, they are killed by *the beast which comes up from the abyss,* and rise again *after three days and a half,* i.e., "on the fourth day," not on the third, "that none might be found equal to God." The beast or Antichrist, who then proceeds to reign for a further period of three and a half years, Victorinus finds foretold by Isaiah (8:7) and Ezekiel (31:3) as *the king of Assyria* or *the Assyrian,* and by Paul (2 Thess. 2:3-10) as *the man of lawlessness* or *the lawless one.* He supposes that Paul meant his readers to understand that "the lawless one" was one of the Caesars, i.e., Nero *(resuscitatus)*. If this were so, it would account for the obscurity of the apostle's language; but this interpretation can only with difficulty be maintained. The meaning of 2 Thessalonians 2:7 is not plain, but if (as is probable) the power that restrains the lawless one is the Roman emperor, he can scarcely be identified at the same time with the lawless one of verse 8. (John's perspective in the Apocalypse is different from Paul's: for John the Roman Empire, and one individual emperor in particular, is the embodiment of unrestrained God-defying lawlessness.)[29]

The opening of the temple (11:19) is the manifestation of Christ (did he not speak of *the temple of his body?*)[30] and *the ark of his testament* is the gospel. The woman (12:1) "is the ancient church of the fathers and prophets and holy apostles": her *twelve stars* are the patriarchs. The dragon's *seven heads* (12:3) are "seven Roman kings, one of whom also is Antichrist: the *ten horns* are ten kings at the last time." *The third part of the stars of heaven* (12:4) are the apostate angels. Victorinus disagrees with other expositors, who refer to them as the third part of believing men, who are seduced by the devil. The *scarlet* color is appropriate to him who *was a murderer from the beginning.* The woman's flight (12:14) is made in accordance with the instructions of Christ in Matthew 24:16: *then let those who are in Judaea flee into the mountains.*

The image of the beast is a golden image of Antichrist, set up by the false prophet in the temple at Jerusalem and indwelt by a fallen angel, who speaks from within it. This is the idolatrous object, *spoken of by Daniel the prophet,*[31] which Victorinus renders *aspernationem euersionis,* "the contempt of subversion," because it "contemns" God and "subverts" men. (Our familiar rendering, *the abomination of desolation,* is derived from the Vulgate *abominationem desolationis.*)

He has some interesting remarks to make about the *great harlot:*

> And, says he, *I saw the woman drunk with the blood of the saints and the blood of the witnesses of Jesus Christ.* For all the sufferings of the saints were always carried out by the decree of her Senate, and she herself made every decree among all the nations against the preaching of the faith, leaving no room for mercy.
>
> Now *the woman sits upon a rose-colored beast,* murderess that she is; the beast has the image of the devil.[32] There also are these *heads,* which we have already mentioned and expounded. In the Apocalypse and in Isaiah she is called *Babylon* on account of the dispersion of the peoples, but Ezekiel called her *Sor.* And indeed, if you compare what is said of *Sor* with what Isaiah and the Apocalypse have said of *Babylon,* you will find that they are all one.

Sor is Tyre (Heb. *ṣôr,* LXX Σόρ, Vg. *Tyrus*). It is highly probable that Victorinus did not use an Old Latin text already existing, but made his own translation from the Greek. *Sor* has been corrupted in many of the MSS; in the MSS in which the original commentary is preserved we find *sorech* (cf. Judges 16:4): *Sor* was a name unknown to readers of the Latin Bible.

The commentary closes with several quotations describing the millennial kingdom from the Psalms, Prophets, Gospels and Epistles. Among many interesting points raised here, we may mention one, in the first sentence of the last paragraph.

> The Lord made mention of this kingdom before he suffered, saying to the apostles: *I will no longer drink of the fruit of this vine, except when I drink it new with you in the coming kingdom,* which is *a hundred times as much,* ten thousand times greater and better *(quod est centum partibus multiplicatum, decies millies ad maiora et meliora).*

The first quotation, of course, is from Matthew 26:29, from the narrative of the Last Supper; *a hundred times as much* may be a reminiscence of Matthew 19:29 or 13:8, 23; the concluding phrase alludes to one of our Lord's *agrapha* or sayings unrecorded in the Bible, preserved for us by Irenaeus in a quotation from Papias.[33] Irenaeus in the last book of *Aduersus Haereses* contends for a temporal and earthly kingdom of the saints, and cites Matthew 26:29 as a prophecy thereof. Then, enlarging on the topic of the vine, he goes on:

> The elders who saw John, the disciple of the Lord, related that they had heard from him how the Lord used to teach in regard to these times, and say: The days will come, in which vines shall grow, each having ten thousand branches, and in each branch ten thousand twigs, and in each true twig ten thousand shoots, and in each one of the shoots ten thousand clusters, and on every one of the clusters ten thousand grapes, and every grape when pressed will give twenty-five measures of wine. . . . In like manner a grain of wheat would produce ten thousand ears, and every ear would have ten thousand grains, and every grain would yield ten pounds of clear, pure, fine flour. . . .
>
> And these things are borne witness to in writing by Papias, the hearer of John, and a companion of Polycarp, in his fourth book.[34]

Papias seems to have connected this *agraphon* with Matthew 26:29. Victorinus probably owed his knowledge of the *agraphon* to Papias, on whose writings he also drew elsewhere.[35] Jerome, in his letter to Anatolius, mentions Papias, bishop of Hierapolis (in Asia Minor), and an Egyptian bishop Nepos as early exponents of millenarian views.[36]

According to a foremost authority on the writings of the Latin Fathers, "it can never cease to be of moment to the real lover of Scripture what was thought of its meaning by any patient investigator in any country or in any age."[37] This is doubly true when the expositor is specially qualified to appreciate with sympathetic insight the words which he seeks to interpret. Such an expositor was our Victorinus. Himself a sufferer in the last and fiercest persecution of the church by the Roman Empire, he was able to enter with the seer of Patmos into the fellowship of Christ's sufferings: though separated by two centuries, each was to the other a *companion in tribulation, and in the kingdom and patience of Jesus Christ.* In more comfortable times, the Revelation may be degraded to the unworthy status of a book of puzzles, a battleground for conflicting schools of interpretation. But *when tribulation or persecution arises because of the word,* the book becomes once more what it really is, a living word from God, full of encouragement and strength to those who are proving the truth of the apostolic words: *All who would live godly in Christ Jesus shall suffer persecution.*[38] Christians at the present day who have to suffer *for the word of God and the testimony of Jesus* under a regime which, on its own admission, sets itself *against the Lord and against his Christ,* find no difficulty in identifying Antichrist and in seeing themselves in the company of those who *come out of the great tribulation.* Nor should we think that they are wrong, if there is any substance in Francis Bacon's dictum that divine prophecies "are not fulfilled punctually at once, but have springing and germinant accomplishment throughout many ages, though the height or fullness of them may refer to some one age."[39]

14. *Marius Victorinus and His Works: In Memory of Alexander Souter (1872-1948)*

I. LIFE AND TIMES

Gaius Marius Victorinus was a native of the Roman province of Africa, who achieved great eminence as a teacher of rhetoric at Rome about the middle of the fourth century A.D. A century and a half later, the great statesman and author Boethius could look back upon him as "almost the most learned orator of his time."[1]

Our chief source of information about Victorinus is the eighth book of Augustine's *Confessions,* where we read how Augustine, after reading some Platonic books translated into Latin by this Victorinus, betook himself to Simplicianus (later Bishop of Milan), an older Christian who in his younger days had been intimate with Victorinus, and who told the young Augustine the story of the great rhetorician's conversion to Christianity. This narrative made a deep impression on Augustine, and led him farther along the road to his own conversion. The relation between the thought of Victorinus and that of Augustine has also been, and still is, a fruitful field of study. At any rate, there can be no doubt of the profound admiration which Augustine had for the memory of Victorinus, and he describes his eminence as a scholar and philosopher in the most generous language:

Published in *The Evangelical Quarterly* 18 (1946), pp. 132-153.

that most learned old man, most skilled in all the liberal arts, who had read and evaluated so many works of the philosophers, the teacher of so many highly born senators, who had both merited and received a statue in the Roman forum (which citizens of this world deem the highest honour) in recognition of his distinguished career.[2]

After Victorinus became a Christian, he proceeded to devote his talents to the defense of the Catholic faith, and to dedicate to the advancement of Christian learning the erudition which he had amassed in his pagan days. The value of such erudition to the Church was appreciated by Augustine, as we may see in that section of his *De Doctrina Christiana* which defends the proposition that "anything rightly said by Gentiles is to be turned to our use." "Do we not see," he asks, "with what a weight of gold, silver and apparel Cyprian, that most persuasive teacher and most blessed martyr, came out of Egypt? Or how much was brought out by Lactantius, or—to say nothing of those still alive—by Victorinus, Optatus and Hilary?"[3]

Of ancient scholars Jerome seems to have been the only one who did not appreciate the qualities of Victorinus.[4] If Augustine considered that his classical training was an advantage to him, Jerome considered it a hindrance, because, he said, his occupation with secular learning led him to neglect the holy Scriptures—a totally unjustified criticism. Not only have we Augustine's testimony to Victorinus's study of the Scriptures even before his public confession of Christianity;[5] his own writings also bear witness to his close acquaintance with them. But even Jerome included him among the number of illustrious men, and devotes the hundred and first chapter of his *De Viris Illustribus* to a brief account of him, of which we shall have more to say anon.[6]

We know neither the year when Victorinus was born nor the year of his death, but we can say with considerable probability that 300 and 370 respectively are sufficiently approximate dates. Augustine and Jerome concur in saying that he was already an old man *(senex)* at the time of his conversion, which must be dated between 353 and 359; while at the time when Simplicianus told Augustine the story of Victorinus, that is to say in 386, he seems to have been dead for several years.

We can fix with practical certainty three dates in his life:

(a) 353, the year in which his eminence as a rhetorician was recognized by the erection of a statue to him in the *Forum Romanum,* according to Augustine, or the *Forum Traiani,* according to Jerome. "Victorinus the rhetorician and Donatus the grammarian, my own teacher, are publicly honoured in Rome: Victorinus was even deemed worthy of a statue in the forum of Trajan," he says, with reference to that year.[7]

(b) 359, about which date he was engaged in the composition of his work against Arius. In it he refers to the excommunication of Valens and Ursacius in language which must mean that it had just taken place: "*Now* Valens and Ursacius have been deposed. . . . Valens and Ursacius, the remnants of Arius."[8] The excommunication of these two bishops occurred at the Council of Ariminum in this year.

(c) 362, the year of Julian the Apostate's educational rescript, as a result of which Victorinus was obliged to relinquish his public professorship of rhetoric at Rome: "In the time of the Emperor Julian," says Augustine, "a law was passed by which Christians were prohibited from teaching literature and rhetoric. Victorinus submitted to this law and chose rather to abandon the school of talk than to abandon your word [O God], by which you make the tongues of infants eloquent."[9]

Within this framework we can give the following skeleton chronological table of the life and times of Victorinus:

c. 300.	Birth of Victorinus.
313.	Edict of Milan.
325.	Council of Nicaea.[10]
337.	Death of Constantine.
c. 340.	Victorinus leaves Africa for Rome.
c. 340-355.	Works on grammar, rhetoric and logic, and metaphysics.
341.	Council of Antioch.
343.	Council of Sardica.
347.	Birth of Jerome.
353.	Constantius reigns alone; statue of Victorinus erected in Forum.
354.	Birth of Augustine.
355.	Council of Milan.
c. 355.	Conversion of Victorinus, followed immediately by his earlier Christian works.
357.	Sirmian manifesto.
359.	Council of Ariminum; excommunication of Valens and Ursacius, about the time when Victorinus was writing *Aduersus Arium;* Council of Seleucia.
361.	Death of Constantius; accession of Julian.
362.	Julian's educational rescript; Council of Alexandria.
366.	Death of Hilary of Poitiers.
c. 370.	Death of Victorinus.
386.	Augustine's conversion with Simplicianus; Victorinus dead a considerable time. Conversion of Augustine.

II. WORKS

The extant works of Victorinus are as follows, in what appears to be their chronological order:

A. Pre-Christian

1. An *Ars Grammatica (AG)* in four books, to which are appended three small works, viz., *De Metris Horatianis (M. Hor.)*, a shorter *Ars Grammatica (AG min.)*, and *De Metris et de Hexametro Versu (M. Hex.)*. A critical edition of these is to be found in H. Keil, *Grammatici Latini (GL)*, VI (Leipzig, 1874), pp. 3-215. References to these writings are here given by page and line of Keil's edition.

2. Fragments of a translation of Porphyry's introduction to the Aristotelian categories, Εἰσαγωγὴ τῶν πέντε φωνῶν[11] *(Isag.)*, preserved in the two dialogues of Boethius *In Porphyrium a Victorino translatum*, edited by S. Brandt in *Corpus Scriptorum Ecclesiasticorum Latinorum* (CSEL) 48 (Vienna, 1906), pp. 1-132 passim.

3. A small treatise *De Definitionibus (Def.)*, formerly ascribed to Boethius, but shown to be the work of Victorinus by H. Usener in *Anecdoton Holderi* (Bonn, 1877). It has been critically edited by Th. Stangl in *Tulliana et Mario-Victoriniana* (Munich, 1888), pp. 17-48.

4. *Explanationes in Ciceronis Rhetoricam (Rhet.)*, a commentary on Cicero's two books *De Inuentione*. The best critical edition is by C. Halm, in *Rhetores Latini Minores* (Leipzig, 1863), pp. 153-304.[12]

B. Christian

i. Christological and Trinitarian

The text of these works in J.-P. Migne's *Patrologia Latina (PL)* 8 (Paris, 1844) is a reprint of that in A. Galland, *Collectio noua ueterum patrum* VIII (Venice, 1772), pp. 133ff. There are critical editions by P. Henry and P. Hadot in "Sources chrétiennes," nos. 68, 69 (Paris, 1960)[13] and in CSEL 83 (Vienna, 1971-), and by A. Locher in Bibliotheca Teubneriana (Leipzig, 1976).

5. *De Generatione Verbi Diuini (GVD)*, a short but highly technical treatise addressed ostensibly to one Candidus the Arian in reply to the latter's *Liber de Generatione Diuina (PL 8, 1019c-1036a)*.[14]

6. Four books *Aduersus Arium (Ar.)*, the books described by Jerome as "very obscure," also addressed to Candidus (*PL* 8.1039b-1138b).

7. *De* ὁμοουσίῳ *recipiendo (HR)*, a synopsis of the argument of *Aduersus Arium (PL* 8.1137c-1140d).

8. Three *Hymns on the Trinity (Hy.)*, in the style of the theological works listed above (*PL* 8.1139d-1146d).

ii. Commentaries on Pauline Epistles

The text of these commentaries in *PL* 8 is a reprint of the *editio princeps* of A. Mai in *Scriptorum ueterum noua collectio e Vaticanis codicibus edita*, III/2 (Rome, 1828), pp. 1ff.[15] While Mai and Migne print the three commentaries in the order Galatians-Philippians-Ephesians, a back-reference to the commentary on Ephesians in the note on Phil. 2:6-8 (1207b) shows that the chronological order is Galatians-Ephesians-Philippians. There is a critical edition by A. Locher in Bibliotheca Teubneriana (Leipzig, 1972).[16]

9. *In Epistulam Pauli ad Galatas libri duo (Gal.)*, in *PL* 8.1145d-1198b.

10. *In Epistulam Pauli ad Ephesios libri duo (Eph.)*, in *PL* 8.1235a-1294d.

11. *In Epistulam Pauli ad Philippenses liber unicus (Phil.)*, in *PL* 8.1197c-1236a.

iii. False Attributions

Other works attributed to him in the manuscript tradition, but with little or no plausibility, are the *Liber ad Iustinum Manichaeum (IM)*, in *PL* 8. 999-1010 (reprinted from Galland); *De Verbis Scripturae: "Factum est uespere et mane dies unus" (VS)* in *PL* 8.1009-14 (reprinted from Galland); *De Maccabaeis Carmen* (Herold, *Haeresiologia*, pp. 241f., and *Bibliotheca ueterum Patrum Lugdunensis*, pp. 297f.); and *De Physicis (Phys.)*, a charming little treatise on the Creation and Fall, and the restoration effected by Christ in the Incarnation and Passion (*PL* 8.1295d-1301c, reprinted from Mai). Considerations of style, vocabulary, thought and biblical text forbid us to consider these as works of our Victorinus.[17]

Victorinus's literary output is not exhausted by his extant works. Evidence for the existence of works of his no longer extant is to be found in remarks of Jerome, Augustine, Cassiodorus, Boethius and Isidore of Seville.[18] P. Henry has argued persuasively that the "Platonic books" translated by Victorinus which made such a deep impression on Augustine were the *Enneads* of Plotinus.[19] F. Bömer has similarly argued that Victorinus also translated Porphyry's *De Regressu Animarum*, and that his translation lay before Augustine.[20]

Apart from these and possibly other Neoplatonic translations, other works attributed to him which are not now extant include, from his pagan period (*c.* 340-355), commentaries on Cicero's *Topica* and dialogues, and a treatise *De syllogismis hypotheticis,* and from his Christian period (*c.* 355-370), works on the Trinity, the Logos and the Holy Spirit, and commentaries on other Pauline epistles than the three which have survived.

III. THE PROBLEM OF APHTHONIUS

P. Monceaux and M. Schanz, both of whom discuss the works of Victorinus in the context of Latin literary history,[21] disagree with each other on one critical point.

The bulk of the larger *Ars Grammatica* is a treatise on meter, which closes with the words: "Aelii Festi Aphthonii V.P. de metris omnibus explicit liber iiii." Keil concludes from these words that all that lies between *AG* I, p. 31, line 17 and IV, p. 173, line 31 (where the above note is appended) is the work of an otherwise unknown author named Aphthonius, which was adapted and incorporated by Victorinus in his own work. Keil allows that Victorinus himself was the author of *AG* as far as p. 31, line 16 (i.e., of the section *De Orthographia* together with a few metrical notes), of *M. Hor., AG min.,* and *M. Hex.*[22]

The majority of later writers have taken Keil's view. Schanz, for example (§ 829), says of *AG:*

> In this work we are not dealing with an expert and independent writer. His dependence is indicated especially by the fact that he simply took over the metrical handbook of Aelius Festus Aphthonius with some minor changes and additions; but he acted in this matter as an honest man, for, as we can conclude from the tradition, he did not publish the other man's property as his own, but introduced the borrowed part to the reader under its author's name, as Charisius also did. To Victorinus should be attributed only the grammatical introduction, and most probably also the appendix dealing with the metre of Horace. Thus the *Ars* of Marius Victorinus belongs to Aphthonius, as regards the body of the work, and we must always remember this when we look up our grammarian.[23]

Monceaux, however, warns us against following Keil and Schanz too uncritically. He suggests that, far from Victorinus mutilating the work of Aphthonius, it is more likely that Aphthonius mutilated the work of Victorinus. Here are his words:

> The MSS, like several grammarians of antiquity, attribute the whole of the work to Victorinus, and yet these same MSS attribute the metrical treatise separately to a certain Aelius Festus Aphthonius, otherwise unknown. All

this is remarkably inconsistent. It is supposed to-day that for the metrical part Victorinus was content to reproduce the manual of Aphthonius, with some changes and additions. He would thus himself be the author only of the grammatical introduction and of the statistical appendix on the metres of Horace. This hypothesis is far from explaining everything. In any case, this formless compilation seems to us unworthy of Victorinus, as we know him from his other works. All the evidence leads us to believe that his *Ars Grammatica* was disfigured by some grammarian, perhaps the Aphthonius of the MSS, and that it originally had quite a different appearance.[24]

The evidence is too scanty and the question too complicated to permit of a definite pronouncement. The language alone does not help us to distinguish between two authors in *AG*. Sometimes we find language in the appendix on the Horatian meters identical with that in "Aphthonius." For example, *M. Hor.* 175.30f. ("quod metrum uocatur dimoeron epicon, ideo quod duos pedes heroos accipit, dactylum et spondeum") repeats the wording of *AG* 161.28f. and 167.16f., except that the *AG* passages have "accipiat" instead of "accipit"; and five lines commencing at *M. Hor.* 176.17 are almost identical with five commencing at *AG* 163.11. But *M. Hor.* is admitted by all to be the work of Victorinus. In the present state of uncertainty, the uniformity of style and language seems to justify us in treating the whole of *AG* as the work of Victorinus.

IV. SIGNIFICANCE

Victorinus certainly enjoyed great esteem in his own day and for many years after his death. He has now been almost entirely forgotten. Deservedly so, in the opinion of many. "Through his midway position between Paganism and Christianity, through his rhetorical and grammatical studies on the one hand and theological studies on the other hand, Victorinus acquired for a long time a reputation hardly merited by his contributions to learning, which did not rise above the mediocrity of his period." That was the judgment of W. S. Teuffel.[25] A far cry from the estimate of Boethius! And yet Boethius and Cassiodorus and, above all, Augustine could not have been so seriously misled about his quality.

Of recent years, however, there has been a closer study of the work of Victorinus, and, as a result, a greater appreciation of his worth. His function as a mediator of Neoplatonic thought to the Western world has been emphasized, and in consequence his significance has been better understood.

In grammar, logic and rhetoric he was not only a prominent leader of contemporary culture, but also exercised an influence on medieval study. He treated these disciplines not merely from an objective viewpoint, but sought to place them on a philosophical basis and thus give a new direction to their study. He is theologically significant because of his presentation of the main doctrines of Christianity in terms of Neoplatonism, and also by reason of his influence on Augustine.[26]

In particular, his linguistic significance must not be underestimated. He is worthy to stand alongside Cicero and Tertullian as creator of a new Latin vocabulary; for, as Cicero created a philosophical terminology for the Latin expression of Greek thought, and Tertullian was largely responsible for the vocabulary of Latin Christianity, so Victorinus was in considerable measure the author of the vocabulary of the schoolmen.

By translating and commenting on the writings of Aristotle, he provided the Middle Ages, through Boethius, with a technical vocabulary for expressing the niceties of logic. By his translations from Plotinus and other Neoplatonists, he introduced into the Latin language the terminology of a transcendental metaphysic. And by expounding Christian doctrine in this terminology, he laid the foundation of a dogmatic vocabulary, more advanced and scientific than the vocabulary of Tertullian and the Latin Bible. It is in his writings, for example, that we first meet the participle *ens*, in the sense of Gk. τὸ ὄν. (According to Priscian, the word was invented by Julius Caesar as the equivalent of ὤν.) It appears, too, that Victorinus first used *indiuiduum* with the meaning "an individual"; Cicero had used it in the sense "atom." To Victorinus we owe a multitude of abstract nouns in *-tio, -tas, -ntia, -tus, -mentum;* adjectives in *-alis, -iuus, -osus;* forms compounded with *prae-* (expressing transcendental qualities), with *omni-* (expressing perfection in qualities and activities), and with the negative *in-* (defining the divine by negation); as well as a host of words derived from Greek. According to Benz and others, these facts justify us in claiming Victorinus as the first scholastic theologian, a claim supported besides by his unique intellectual position, in which a synthesis of Aristotelian logic and dialectic with Neoplatonic metaphysics and Ciceronian rhetoric formed the foundation for the interpretation of Christian dogma.

V. VOCABULARY

There follows a list of words or usages which occur in the writings of Victorinus and which, so far as I am aware, are not found in Latin literature before his time:[27]

accidentalis, actualis, adintellegentia, adsequella, alsito, alteritas, altifico, amplexio, animaliter, antecantatiuus, apostrofo, aspargen, astrologice, astructio, biduanculus, bigeminus, bipotens, blasphemiter, calculatio, christianitas, circumformo, circuminspector, circumpungo, circumtermino, circumuitalis, coaedificatio, coexsisto, cognoscentia, completiuus, condoctor, confragose, connaturalis, conseruio, consistentia, constitutiuus, corrationaliter, counio *(verb)*, counitio, declaratiuus, decurtatio, depositio, discernibilis, disertitudo, dualiter, effatio, effluentia, effulgenter, effulgentia, elambo, elucescentia, ens, enuntiatus *(4th declension)*, erector, essentialitas, essentitas, explanatiuus, exsequenter, exsistentialis, exsistentialitas, exsistentialiter, exterminatio, filiatio, filietas, gignibilis, grammaticalis, identitas, imaginalis, immaculatio, imparticipatus, impassiona(bi)liter, imperfectio, inactuosus, incarnaliter, incidentia, incognoscibiliter, incommutabiliter, incongrue, inconiunctus, inconsonus, incontinuus, indeterminatio, indiscernibilis, inexsistentialiter, inexsisto, infiguratus, ingenerabilis, inimmutabilis, innoetus, insensualis, insubstantialis, insubstantiatus, insufflatio, intellectibilis, intellectualiter, intellectuo, intellegentialis, intellegentialitas, intellegentitas, intermixtio, internundinium, intracaelestis, inuersabilis, inuersibilis, leuianimus, limitamentum, mascularis, materialiter, mutilatio, noscentia, nouissimalis, obauditor, omnicognoscens, omnicognoscentia, omniexsistens, omniexsistentia, omniintellegens, omniintellegentia, omnipotentia, omniuidens, omniuidentia, omniuiuens, omniuiuentia, optimitas, paganismus, paganus *(in the sense "pagan")*, palmalis, pertermine, pinsitor, plusquamperfectus, possibilitas, postcantatiuus, postnatiuus, potentialis, potentialiter, potentifico, praeaeternus, praecausa, praecognoscentia, praedicamentum, praeexsistentia, praeexsistentialis, praeexsisto, praeintellegentia, praenoscentia, praeprincipalis, praeprincipium, praeuidentia, praeuiuentia, praeuiuo, primiforme *(substantive, in the sense "prototype")*, primiformis, priuantia, proexsilio, propitiator, quadripotens, realis, receptibilis, reparatio, reuersim, reuersus *(4th declension)*, reuiuefacio, reuiuiscentia, risibilis, saluatio, scansio *(in the sense of metrical "scansion")*, scissio, semipodius, semisona, spiritalis *(in the sense "aspirated")*, subalternus, subauditor, subintellegentia, subsistentia, substantiatus *(participle)*, subtractio, supercino, superelatiuus, supracaelestis, syllogistice *(adverb)*, traductiuus, tripotens, uersibilis, uersidicus, uisibiliter, uiuefacio, uiuentia, unalis, unalitas, unitio, unitor, uniuoce, usitatio, uultuo.[28]

We need not suppose, of course, that Victorinus introduced all these words into the Latin language. Some of them are used by his contemporaries, and we cannot say with certainty which writer was the first to use them. We cannot even be sure of those words for which the lexicons cite Victorinus as the sole authority. For example, *realis* is quoted from him only, but Victorinus himself apparently refers to earlier unnamed authorities for the word: "alii hanc constitutionem *realem* uocarunt."[29] But after all such allowances have been made, we are left with a very large residuum of words which we certainly owe to Victorinus himself. Many of these were current coin in medieval literature, and have persisted to the present day in the languages of western Europe. Besides, to many words which had other senses before his day he gave new meanings which have remained attached to them ever since his time. Not to go outside the preceding list of words, the only meanings we attach to the words "pagan" and "scansion" are the meanings given by Victorinus to *paganus* and *scansio*. He was not the first person to use *paganus* in the sense of "pagan,"[30] of course, but he was the first, so far as we know, to raise this sense to literary status.

VI. STYLE

Of the style of Victorinus many hard things have been said. Jerome set the example. "Victorinus, an African by birth," he writes, "taught rhetoric at Rome under the Emperor Constantius. When in extreme old age he submitted to faith in Christ, he wrote books *Against Arius*, composed in dialectic style and very obscure language, which are unintelligible except to the learned. He also wrote commentaries on the Apostle."[31] The "learned" must here mean the philosophers, and Jerome, whose own great erudition was of the linguistic and textual sort, was no doubt unable to understand and appreciate Victorinus. In this, of course, he was quite different from Augustine, whose greater genius and philosophical insight perceived and valued the worth of the man who first introduced him to the thought of Plotinus and Porphyry.

   Jacques Sirmond, who at the end of the seventeenth century published some writings ascribed to Victorinus, placed two of his (alleged) works after others which were actually later in date because of what he called his "obscurity, which would have been rather unattractive on the threshold of his works. But it is chiefly in his dogmatic writings that he seems to have affected this obscurity; for in his commentaries on some of the letters of St. Paul, contained in the same codex, his style is more plain and open."[32]

   Others who mention him at various times refer to this obscurity with more or less censure, and their opinions are summed up thus by Bp. Gore:

   All these writings of Victorinus (with the exception of the commentaries which make a nearer approach to lucidity) are intensely obscure. It is a matter of astonishment that one who had Victorinus's reputation as a rhetorician should have been so wholly incapable of giving clear expression to his thoughts. His intense obscurity in treating theological subjects of themselves recondite, aggravated by the extremely corrupt condition of the text as hitherto edited, the barbarous mixture of Greek and bad Latin which he often writes, his prolixity and his repetitions, have been the causes of his being ignored more than is at all justified by his substantial merits. He has wearied the very few people who have tried to read him beyond their patience, and they have almost wholly missed his significance. Those who have read him have mostly done nothing but complain of him. "He wrote," says Jerome, "in a dialectical style some very obscure books, intelligible only to the learned" (*De Vir. Illustr.* ci). He condemns him, moreover, as a man so occupied in secular literature as to have ignored Holy Scripture (*Epist. ad Galat. Prologus*), a judgment reversed by Augustine (*Conf.* viii.2) and the evidence of his works. Petavius, besides accusing him of a heretical tendency, matched him with Heraclitus as ὁ σκοτεινός, and condemned him as "incommode balbutientem" (*De Trin.* i.v. §8). Such commentators as he has had show scant patience with him (see Migne's edition p. 1179, note 3; 1245, note 3; 1265, note 4). He is "obscurissimus," "barbarus," "ferreus." Tillemont would not trouble himself to search his works (*Mém. Eccl.*, vol. x, p. 799, l. 4). Ceillier (*Auteurs Sacrés*) commends him with an utter want of appreciation of his peculiar position. Dorner ignores him. But there is one notable exception to these severe judgments on Victorinus's style and matter and these ignorings of his significance. Thomassin, whose theological judgment is a weighty one, speaks of him as a man "inferior to none in the profundity of his insight into the inmost mysteries" of the Divine Being, and the relation of the persons of the Trinity to one another (*De Incarn. Verbi*, B. ii, cap. i, §6).[33]

A novice might well be deterred from the study of Victorinus if he paid attention to most of these judgments. But Gore's statement that "he has wearied the very few people who have tried to read him beyond their patience" is not so true today as it may have been in 1887. Patience is certainly needed to read and appreciate Victorinus, but several of his readers who have exercised this virtue have found their patience amply rewarded.

But we shall do well to review one by one the extant works which are undoubtedly his. There must surely have been some very good reason why one of the foremost rhetoricians of his day should write so obscurely as to incur these reproaches. What do we find in his writings themselves? The *Ars Grammatica* and the accompanying small treatises, both in their grammatical and metrical parts, are as plain and lucid as could be desired. There is, to be sure, a fair amount of repetition here and there, but that is only what we should expect in works which were in the first instance delivered as spoken lectures.[34]

The little work *De Definitionibus* is perhaps somewhat prolix, but certainly not in the least obscure. As for the *Explanationes in Rhetoricam Ciceronis*, if they bring down upon the author's head the editor's withering remark, "a most boring writer,"[35] it is prolixity and not obscurity which is responsible. Certainly it is a wearisome and for the most part unoriginal treatise. Victorinus may have been professionally wedded to Rhetoric, but the object of his heart's desire was Philosophy. Wherever he comes upon a philosophical reference in the course of his commentaries, he must inevitably digress. It may have been these digressions which provoked Halm's censure. At any rate, Victorinus seems to have grown weary of this treatise himself, as we may gather from the increasing rapidity with which he deals with the later part of the *De Inuentione*. (His comments on the 55 chapters of Book I occupy over 102 pages of Halm's edition; those on the 59 chapters of Book II only 47!) But the treatise is by no means obscure. In all these works his style is of the type known to the ancients as ἰσχνόν or *tenue*.

Turning to the theological works, we find that the commentaries on the Pauline epistles are specifically exempted from the general charge of obscurity. Jerome complains of them, too, it is true, but not on the ground of obscurity. Sirmond, as we have just seen, speaks of their style as *planior et apertior*, and this verdict is endorsed by Koffmane, Gore, Monceaux, Souter, and others who have written on the subject. Here, too, Victorinus is very guilty of prolixity and repetition, but his sense is for the most part quite plain. "He does not altogether escape obscurity: p. 1207, ll. 25ff. and 34ff. are good examples of the difficulty occasionally to be experienced in following him, but on the whole what want of clearness there is may be charged to the MS. tradition."[36] As a matter of fact, the passages mentioned by Professor Souter are quite in the style of the other theological works and can be paralleled from these. Their obscurity is due to causes which we are just about to deal with. They occur in the course of the exposition of the well-known Christological passage in Phil. 2:5ff., and are to be considered in the light of the two Christological treatises *De Generatione Verbi Diuini* and *Aduersus Arium*.

These two treatises, then, are alone responsible for bringing upon their author the charge of obscurity. It is these which cause Gore to say: "It is matter of astonishment that one who had Victorinus's reputation as a rhetorician should have been so wholly incapable of giving clear expression to his thoughts." The explanation, however, is not far to seek. Schanz shows us the way out of the difficulty:

People have complained of the great obscurity in his theological writings;

this obscurity is illuminated only when the Neoplatonic standpoint is taken as the basis for their study.[37]

The fact is, most of the obscure passages are almost literal translations of the language of Greek Neoplatonic writers. Victorinus's extensive borrowings from Plotinus have been recognized and noted by such authorities as M.-N. Bouillet[38] and G. Geiger[39] in the nineteenth century and E. Benz[40] and P. Henry in the twentieth. The latter, after comparing several passages in Victorinus with the *Enneads,* states his conclusions unhesitatingly as follows:

> Not only must he have read the *Enneads,* but he assimilated them to the point of reproducing their general tone, sometimes quoting extracts from them, reproducing technical formulae in the course of the argument. In a word, the mentality of his philosophico-theological writings is purely "Plotinian."[41]

Père Henry traces the influence of Plotinus not only in the syntax and style of Victorinus, but in his vocabulary as well, especially in his many compounds with *prae* and *super* and with the negative prefix *in;* the latter compounds being used when finite attributes are applied to God *via negationis,* the former when they are predicated of him *sensu eminentiore.*

The obscurity of the style of the dogmatic works is largely dispelled, then, when we read them in the light of the language of the *Enneads;* and, if there are still difficulties remaining, let us remember the exceedingly abstract and recondite nature of the thoughts which Victorinus was endeavoring to express and the fact that he was probably the first to give a systematic exposition in Latin of the Neoplatonic philosophy.

Before he himself undertook to edit the theological works of Victorinus for the Vienna *corpus* and *Sources Chrétiennes,* P. Henry had written:

> When, in obedience to the demands of present-day philology, someone thinks of re-editing the "Neoplatonic" works of Marius Victorinus (such as, for example, the *Aduersus Arium*), he will bear in mind that they have been deeply influenced not only by Plotinus's ideas, but by his style. We sometimes hear it said, as was lately said of the *Enneads,* that they are unintelligible. That is chiefly the fault of the copyists, who would have had no comprehension of what they were writing. In this case, the humble monks of the *scriptoria* might well be excused, and their corporation could invoke St. Jerome as its patron. The editor of the *Aduersus Arium* will need

much courage; he must read and re-read the *Enneads* of Plotinus, without growing weary, at the same time as the work which he is editing.[42]

How well he learned and applied this lesson is writ large on every page of his editions.[43]

Monceaux[44] suggests that familiarity with the ideas of Origen as well as of Plotinus is necessary for a proper understanding of Victorinus; this is probably an overstatement, and on a par with his statement[45] that Victorinus translated the writings of Origen.[46] There are, of course, several points of contact between Victorinus and Origen, as is only to be expected when we consider the influence of Neoplatonism on the Alexandrian school. One very obvious instance of Victorinus's indebtedness to Origen may be seen in his insistence on the eternal generation of the Divine Word, a thought first worked out by Origen and accepted from him by the Catholic Church. The treatise *De Generatione Verbi Diuini* in particular develops this idea in considerable detail. Again, Victorinus's doctrine of the Trinity, like Origen's, is frankly subordinationist. But there seems to be no *general* influence of Origen on Victorinus. Benz sums up the matter thus in the closing words of his appendix on "Viktorin und Origenes":

> Thus the theology of Victorinus does not stand in the tradition of Origen's philosophy of religion, but represents an independent Christianizing of the Neoplatonic metaphysic on Latin soil.[47]

In the extract from Gore quoted above, Victorinus's obscurity of expression is said to be aggravated, among other things, by "the barbarous mixture of Greek and bad Latin which he often writes, his prolixity and his repetitions." That there is an unusually high proportion of Greek words is true, in his pre-Christian writings as well as in his theological works. The *GVD*, in particular, as Monceaux says, "bristles" *(frissonne)* with Greek words. Sometimes the words and phrases are given in the original Greek form; sometimes they are latinized. That this does not enhance the beauty of the Latin style may be granted at once; but it does not add to the obscurity. It is clearer to retain τὸ ὄν ἢ τὸ μὴ ὄν than to attempt a Latin rendering, and τὸ εἶναι is certainly better than the circumlocution *quod est esse*, so common in the writings of Victorinus. Besides, to one acquainted with the terminology of Greek philosophy and theology the sense is immediately apparent as it would not be if native Latin equivalents were attempted throughout. "Barbarous" the mixture may indeed be, but better neat and intelligible Greek on occasion than clumsy and unintelligible Latin.

VII. VICTORINUS AND THE BIBLICAL TEXT

In addition to the almost complete texts of the three Pauline epistles on which his commentaries have survived, there are copious biblical citations in Victorinus's theological works.[48] These citations, however, make but a scanty contribution to the history of the Old Latin text of the scriptures. The reason is, quite simply, that his biblical text is "European" in character, of the kind generally in use in Italy at the time when he was writing. Naturally so: it was long after he left his native Africa for Rome that he became a Christian,[49] and only a few "African" readings are identifiable among his citations.[50]

He frequently appears to quote from memory, sometimes substituting a word or construction which he regards as better Latin, and sometimes giving an independent rendering when he is dissatisfied with the current version of a text crucial to his argument. Occasionally, as though despairing of finding any adequate Latin equivalent for a Greek word or phrase, he quotes the untranslated Greek. Frequently recurring texts tend to be quoted with a variety of wording, probably from a love of stylistic variation. He often gives a paraphrase rather than a strict translation.

A few of his quotations have more theological than textual interest. His theological concern with the adjective *consubstantialis* (ὁμοούσιος) alerts him to occurrences of the noun *substantia* (rendering either οὐσία or ὑπόστασις), even in contexts where it has originally no metaphysical significance.

For example, in Jer. 23:18, 22, Yahweh declared that the false prophets were disqualified from speaking in his name because they had not "stood in the council of Yahweh to perceive and to hear his word." Here the Hebrew word *sōḏ* ("council," "secret council") has been misleadingly rendered ὑπόστημα or ὑπόστασις in the Septuagint, and therefore by *substantia* in the Old Latin. Victorinus quotes these two verses repeatedly,[51] and links them with Tit. 2:14 (λαὸν περιούσιον): those who stand in God's *substantia*, he says, are his people *circa substantiam . . . consistens*, "standing about his 'substance.'" He finds fault with the current rendering of λαὸν περιούσιον *(populum abundantem)*: it shows, he says, that the translator did not understand the text (neither, evidently, did Victorinus). He finds a better rendering in the eucharistic prayer of oblation (in a passage based on Tit. 2:14): "munda tibi populum *circumuitalem*" (an adjective which he paraphrases *circa tuam substantiam uenientem*, "coming about thy 'substance'").[52] What precisely was understood by *circumuitalis* in this prayer by those who recited it cannot be determined: in origin it was probably a mechanical rendering of

228   *A Mind for What Matters*

περιούσιος. The Vulgate made sense of it with *populum acceptabilem;* Victorinus's Neoplatonizing treatment led him far astray from the true sense: "a people for his very own."

Another word which, like περιούσιος, seemed to contain the element οὐσία was ἐπιούσιος in the Lord's Prayer (Matt. 6:11). Victorinus knew a Latin version of the Lord's Prayer in which the petition for bread was aptly rendered: *da panem nobis hodiernum,* "give us today's bread." But the object of the petition, he thought, was the body of Christ, in whom the divine riches dwell *corporaliter.* "The Greek Gospel," he says, "has ἐπιούσιον, which is derived from the word 'substance'—that is, God's substance; the Latins could not say this either because they did not understand it or were unable to express it, and so they simply put *cotidianum* [daily], not ἐπιούσιον."[53] But how does the petition run in an adequate Latin rendering? Thus, says Victorinus: *panem nostrum consubstantialem da nobis hodie* (because Christ, for whom one actually prays in this petition, is "consubstantial" with the Father).[54] When Jerome, some twenty years later, came to translate the Gospels, he too linked ἐπιούσιος with οὐσία, but rendered the prefix accurately, not by *con-* but by *super: panem nostrum supersubstantialem da nobis hodie.*

A clue to the allegorical interpretation of the parable of the prodigal son is found by Victorinus in the statement that the prodigal wasted his "substance" (οὐσία, *substantia*) in riotous living (Luke 15:13). It is the Father's substance that is wasted, "for he who 'takes a journey' from God has neither the Spirit of God nor light nor Christ: left to himself he wastes the substance of God." [55]

The Johannine prologue, and especially its opening verses, provided Victorinus with an unrivaled wealth of texts to undergird his argument. Augustine, after quoting John 1:1-5, recalls how Simplicianus was accustomed to tell of a certain Platonist (i.e., Neoplatonist) who "used to say that these opening words of the Gospel according to John should be written in letters of gold and set up in the most prominent positions in all the churches."[56] Was this "Platonist" Victorinus?[57]

As for the second clause of John 1:1, Victorinus "almost exhausts the prepositions," wrote William Sanday, "in his attempts to translate ὁ λόγος ἦν πρὸς τὸν θεόν: 'circa Deum', 'apud Deum', 'juxta Deum', are all used in turn."[58] He prefers (like some twentieth-century translators) to retain the Greek λόγος in quoting the prologue, probably regarding all the current Latin equivalents as inadequate.

Writing to Candidus the Arian, Victorinus quotes the first two clauses of the Gospel, "In principio erat λόγος et λόγος erat circa deum," and follows them immediately with verse 18: "unigenitus filius, qui est in gremio patris." Then he asks,

How do you take or understand these words? The Romans render πρὸς τὸν θεόν as *apud deum*, as though to say "wholly within," that is, within the existence of God; and this is true. For in being, working is also present. The λόγος is in God and so is the Son in the Father. "Being" itself is the cause of action, for that in which working is present must itself first exist. . . . If therefore "being" itself is in principle the cause of working and action, action is begotten by "being." The Father is "being"; the Son therefore is "working" *(operari ergo filius)*.[59]

Only if it is decided in advance that John is teaching Neoplatonic doctrine can it be believed that this is the meaning of his words.

The statement that the Son has his being in the Father's bosom (John 1:18) is quoted several times; in one place Victorinus discusses whether *gremium* (his own preference) or *sinus* is the apter rendering of κόλπος here.

But either the one word or the other signifies that the Son is both begotten (that is, he is external to the Father) and yet also in the Father's bosom (that is, he is within the Father). That this is the essence of all the readings will be understood by the diligent and faithful inquirer.

Practically every christologically significant text in the Fourth Gospel is quoted somewhere by Victorinus, and given a Neoplatonic exposition. One of his most remarkable expositions occurs when he discusses John 20:17, where Jesus says to Mary Magdalene, "Do not touch me, for I have not yet ascended to the Father." Many readers have wondered why Mary is forbidden to touch him, whereas a week later Thomas is encouraged to do so in no merely tentative way (John 20:27). Here is Victorinus's explanation:

Before he could allow himself to be touched, Christ had to go to the Father—that is, he had to penetrate potentially and existentially into the Father's inherent essence.

This seems to mean that the human life which he had recovered from hades (as distinct from the divine life of the *logos*) had to go to the Father in order to be sanctified *(propter hanc igitur sanctificandam eundum fuit ad patrem)*.[60]

Victorinus no doubt intended to set forth the Nicene faith according to the mode of thought and language which had long since become second nature to him—in Neoplatonic terms. But in fact he was in large measure using the Nicene formularies to expound the Neoplatonic doctrine of God.[61] The one new thing that entered into his system of thought with his conversion to Christianity was the revelation that in Jesus the eternal Word became flesh.

VIII. BIBLIOGRAPHY

Altaner, B., *Patrology*, E.T. (Freiburg/Edinburgh/London, 1960), pp. 430-432.

Bardenhewer, Otto, *Geschichte der altkirchlichen Literatur*, III (Freiburg i/B, 1912), pp. 460ff.

Benz, E., *Marius Victorinus und die Entwicklung der abendländischen Metaphysik* (Stuttgart, 1932).[62]

Bömer, F., *Der lateinische Neuplatonismus und Neupythagoreismus* (Leipzig, 1936).

Busse, A., *Die neuplatonischen Ausleger der Isagoge des Porphyrius* (Berlin, 1892).

Caesar, J., *De uerborum ARSIS et THESIS apud scriptores artis metricae latinos, imprimis Marium Victorinum, significatione* (Marburg, 1885).

Citterio B., C. *Mario Vittorino* (Brescia, 1948).

Clark, Mary T., "The Neo-Platonism of Marius Victorinus the Christian," in *Neo-Platonism and Early Christian Thought*, ed. H. J. Blumenthal and R. A. Markus (London, 1981), pp. 153-159.

Erdt, W., *Marius Victorinus Afer, der erste lateinische Pauluskommentator* (Frankfurt/Bern/Cirencester, 1980).

Geiger, G., C. *Marius Victorinus Afer, ein neuplatonischer Philosoph* (Metten, 1888-89).

De Ghellinck, J., "Réminiscences de la dialectique de Marius Victorinus dans les conflits théologiques du onzième et du douzième siècle," *Revue néoscolastique de philosophie* 19 (1911), pp. 432-435.

Gore, C., "Victorinus Afer," in *Dictionary of Christian Biography*, ed. W. Smith and H. Wace, IV (London, 1887), pp. 1129-1138.

Hadot, P., *La notion de Dieu "causa sui" chez Marius Victorinus* (University of Paris thesis, 1949).

Hadot, P., *Porphyre et Victorinus*, Études Augustiniennes (Paris, 1968).

Hadot, P., *Marius Victorinus: Recherches sur sa vie et ses oeuvres*, Études Augustiniennes (Paris, 1971).

Hadot, P., "Typus Stoicisme et Monarchianisme au quatrième siècle d'après Candide l'Arien et Marius Victorinus," *Recherches de théologie ancienne et mediévale* (1951), pp. 177-187.

Hanson, R. P. C., "The Western Pro-Nicenes III, 1. Marius Victorinus," *The Search for the Christian Doctrine of God. The Arian Controversy 318-381* (Edinburgh: T. & T. Clark, 1988), pp. 531-556 (an outstanding study of the place of Victorinus in the history of the Arian controversy).

Harnack, A., *Dogmengeschichte* (Tübingen, [4]1909-10), III, pp. 33ff.; E.T. of ed. 3 (London, 1898), V, pp. 33ff. (A discussion of the relation between Victorinus and Augustine.)

Henry, Paul, S. J., "Marius Victorinus a-t-il lu les Ennéades de Plotin?" *Recherches de science religieuse* 24 (1934), pp. 432-449.

Henry, Paul, S. J., *Plotin et l'Occident: Firmicus Maternus, Marius Victorinus, Saint Augustin et Macrobe* (Louvain, 1934).

Henry, Paul, S. J., "Augustine and Plotinus," in *Journal of Theological Studies* 38 (1937), pp. 1-23.

Henry, P., "The *Adversus Arium* of Marius Victorinus," *Journal of Theological Studies* n.s. 1 (1950), pp. 42-55.

Janssen, K., *Die Entstehung der Gnadenlehre Augustins* (Rostock, 1935), pp. 28-38.

Karig, W., *Des C. Marius Victorinus Kommentare zu den paulinischen Briefen* (Marburg, 1925).

Keil, H., *Quaestionum grammaticarum partes I et II. De Marii Victorini arte grammatica. De Maximi Victorini libris de arte grammatica qui feruntur* (Halle, 1871-72).

Kiessling, A., in *Deutsche Literaturzeitung* (1881), pp. 966f., on the Neoplatonic works translated by Victorinus.

Koffmane, G., *De Mario Victorino philosopho christiano* (Breslau, 1880).[63]

De Labriolle, P., *Histoire de la Littérature Latine Chrétienne* (Paris, 1924), pp. 346ff.; E.T., *The History and Literature of Christianity from Tertullian to Boethius* (London, 1924), pp. 259ff.

De Leusse, H., "Préexistence des Âmes," *Recherches de science religieuse* 29 (1939), pp. 197-239.

Monceaux, P., *Histoire littéraire de l'Afrique chrétienne* (Paris, 1905), I, pp. 132ff.; III, pp. 373-422.

Monceaux, P., "L'Isagoge latine de Marius Victorinus," in *Philologie et Linguistique: mélanges offerts à L. Havet* (Paris, 1909), pp. 290-310.

Richter, F., *De Mario Victorino Ciceronis rhetoricorum librorum qui uocantur De Inuentione interprete* (Göttingen, 1924).

Schady, W., *De Marii Victorini libri I capite IV quod inscribitur De Orthographia* (Bonn, 1869).

Schäfer, K. T., "Marius Victorinus und die Marcionitischen Prologe zu den Paulusbriefen," *Revue Bénédictine* 80 (1970), pp. 7-16.

Schanz, M., *Geschichte der römischen Litteratur*, IV / 1 (München, 1914), pp. 149ff.

Schepss, G., "Zu Marius Victorinus De Definitionibus," *Philologus* 56 (1897), p. 382.

Schmid, R., *Marius Victorinus Rhetor und seine Beziehungen zu Augustin* (Kiel, 1895).

Schultz, G., *Quibus auctoribus Aelius Festus Aphthonius de re metrica usus sit* (Breslau, 1885).

Séjourné, P., "Victorinus Afer," in *Dictionnaire de Théologie Catholique*, XV/2 (1950), cols. 2887-2954.

Simonetti, M., *La crisi ariana* (Rome, 1965), pp. 287-298.

Souter, A., *The Earliest Latin Commentaries on the Epistles of St. Paul* (Oxford, 1927), ch. i: "Marius Victorinus" (pp. 8-38).

Stangl, Th., *Tulliana et Mario-Victoriniana* (München, 1888), including introduction to *De Definitionibus* (pp. 12-16), and "Kleine Nachträge zu K. Halms Text des Victorinischen Kommentares zu Ciceros Rhetorik" (pp. 49-60).

Teuffel, W. S., *Geschichte der römischen Litteratur*, neubearbeitet von W. Kroll und F. Skutsch, III (Leipzig, ⁶1913), pp. 231ff.; E.T., *History of Roman Literature*, authorized translation from the 5th edition by G. C. W. Warr, II (London and Cambridge, 1900), pp. 337ff.

Überweg, F., and Prächter, K., *Grundriss der Geschichte der Philosophie*, I: *Das Altertum* (Berlin, 1926), pp. 650f., 199*.

Usener, H., *Anecdoton Holderi: Festschrift zur 32ten Philologenversammlung zu Wiesbaden* (Bonn, 1877).

Vaveri, G. M., *La filosofia teologica di C. Mario Vittorino* (Palermo, 1950).

Woehrer, J., *Studien zu Marius Victorinus* (Jahresbericht des Privat-Untergymnasiums zu Wilhering, 1905).

V. ESPECIALLY FOR CHRISTIAN BRETHREN

15. *Some Reflections on the Primitive Church: In Memory of Cecil Howley (1907-1980)*

I. EARLY HOUSE-CHURCHES

If Peter or Paul could come back to earth for a week or two—say to one of the cities, such as Rome, which they knew in their day—where would they find most congenial fellowship on a Sunday morning? If this question were asked in some mixed audiences, the questioner would have to beg his hearers to answer one at a time; otherwise there would be a deafening babel of conflicting replies. Many of the replies, however, could be reduced to a common formula: With *us*, of course! But wherever they might go today, they would probably find the company and the proceedings strange, and that not only because of the changes in language and culture which the passing centuries have brought.

But if they did come back and find congenial fellowship, would they necessarily find it in one and the same company? We may assume

First published (under the title "Lessons from the Primitive Church") as a contribution to *In God's Community*, ed. D. J. Ellis and W. W. Gasque, a collection of essays presented to G. C. D. Howley (London: Pickering & Inglis, 1978), pp. 153-168. The fact that the recipient and the contributors were all associated with Christian Brethren explains the occasional references to that religious group.

that they would, but we might be wrong. There was one famous occasion, in Antioch on the Orontes, when Peter found the company kept by Paul inconveniently inclusive, and sought a more restricted fellowship—although this, we must admit, was not so much from his own choice as from a desire not to make life too awkward for his friends back home in Jerusalem.[1] One of those friends was James, the Lord's brother—and it appears, incidentally, that when they were in Jerusalem Peter and James did not belong to the same household church. If Peter belonged to the group which met in the house of Mary the mother of John Mark, he knew that James and "the brethren" (whoever they were) met somewhere else (Acts 12:17). Since the church of Jerusalem, according to Luke, was several thousand strong, it could not meet as a whole in one place; and of the household groups which it comprised, those would count themselves particularly happy which had an apostle or comparable leader in their membership. Moreover, human nature being what it is, in the first century or the twentieth, we should expect that some of these groups would attract those who preferred more cautious and conservative ways while others (like the Hellenistic groups to which Stephen and his associates had belonged before persecution drove them out) would be more liberal and adventurous.

Hypothetical questions are not very fruitful. Let us ask one of a more factual sort. Where did Peter and Paul go when they visited Rome? Not to St. Peter's or St. Paul's, of course, for in A.D. 60 there were no Christian basilicas on the Vatican hill or by the Ostian Way. Paul indeed was not in a position to "go" anywhere when first he came to Rome; he had to remain under house-arrest, and other people came to him. It would not be surprising if Paul's tenement flat became the locus for a small and variable household church during his two-year custody in Rome, over and above the many household churches already existing in the city. Some purists would discourage us from referring to the "church" of Rome in A.D. 60; the Letter to the Romans, they point out, is not addressed to a city church, as several of Paul's other letters are, and a number of separate household churches receive mention in Paul's list of greetings in Romans 16:3-16.[2] At the same time, there must have been sufficient cohesion, or at least communication, between the various groups for Paul to be confident that his letter would reach "all God's beloved in Rome, who are called to be saints" (Romans 1:7).

It was probably to one of the household churches in Rome—one with Jewish antecedents and associations—that the Letter to the Hebrews was written a few years after Paul's Letter to the Romans.[3] And a century later Justin Martyr, asked by the city prefect where he met with his disciples, gave his headquarters as "the house of Martin, by the baths of Timothy" (on the Viminal), "and," he added, "all this time (and this is my second visit to Rome) I have known no other meeting-place than his house."[4] Justin's professed ignorance of any other Christian meeting-place in Rome may simply mean that he had never been to any other; in any case, the meeting which Justin and his friends frequented could have been much more like a philosopher's school than the average household church in Rome.

Before they had church buildings of their own (as they had in several places by the end of the third century), Christians met for worship in private houses, a special room in such a house being sometimes set apart for Christian meetings. Of this we have clear evidence in some of the most ancient Christian sites in Rome—for example, in the substructure of the basilica of San Clemente. It is a moving experience for a Christian visitor to reflect that Christian worship has been carried on continuously on such sites from the days of the imperial persecutions, over a period of seventeen or even eighteen centuries.

It is almost an article of faith with Protestants that Roman Catholic worship represents a sad falling away from the practice of apostolic times. But when a Roman Catholic visits Rome, he is impressed with the sense of historical continuity. On this and that site, he feels, century by century, the holy mysteries of the faith have been celebrated from the remote beginnings of Roman Christianity, and in the same language. (He cannot be expected to know that until the end of the second century Greek was the language of the Roman church; by the middle of the third century it had been displaced by Latin.)[5] It would not be easy to persuade such a visitor that the form of Christianity which he knows, and which he believes to be attested by the most ancient Christian monuments, is a corruption of apostolic Christianity. If Peter came back to Rome, he may think, he would be quite at home in (say) Santa Pudenziana, built on the site of the house of Pudens where, according to tradition, he lived for seven years.

Well, we may say, *we* know better. But do we? Change there certainly has been during these eighteen centuries—change sometimes for the worse but sometimes for the better. But the general *pattern* of worship today in any one of these ancient churches is recognizably the same as it was by the end of the second century. Are we then bound to conclude that there were greater changes in the first two centuries of the faith than there have been since then? If so, when did these changes take place? To locate them in the "tunnel" period between A.D. 75 and 175 is easy, just because our inadequate knowledge of the details of church life in that period makes it difficult to disprove many statements that are made about what happened then. At the end of the period we are confronted by the catholic church, the catholic ministry, the catholic canon and the catholic faith in a more developed form than they had at the beginning of the period; but the roots of this fourfold development are present before we enter the tunnel.

Is such development a bad thing or a good thing?

II. DEPARTURE OR DEVELOPMENT?

When I was in my teens I read with great interest a paperback volume which came into our home, entitled *Departure*.[6] The author (G. H. Lang) indicated the main thrust of his thesis more fully in the subtitle: "A warning and an appeal addressed by one of themselves mainly to Christians known as Open Brethren." I was not unduly troubled by the current tendencies which he deplored; indeed, insofar as I knew anything about them, I may even have approved of some of them. What fascinated me chiefly was the use which he made of early church history. I realize now that he leaned too heavily on Edwin Hatch's Bampton Lectures on *The Organization of the Early Christian Churches* (1880), with his theory that the bishop was in origin the principal financial officer. But one fact emerged quite unmistakably, above all others, from Mr. Lang's comparative study: when a modern movement starts out with the deliberate intention of reproducing the life and order of the apostolic age, it will before long reproduce the features of the *post*-apostolic age, such as standardization of worship, ministry and doctrine, formalizing of interchurch relations, and so forth. These features, characteristic of what is now often called "incipient catholicism," might be regarded by some as natural or even desirable developments; what the author of *Departure* thought of them is shown by the title of his book. In fact, some of them were of the nature of development and others of the nature of departure. Development and departure are two different things and should not be confused. Development is the unfolding of what is there already, even if only implicitly; departure involves the abandonment of one principle or basis in favor of another.

More recently, Roy Coad's *History of the Brethren Movement* has enriched us in many ways with the remembrance of things past, and not least by quotations from a work nowadays known only to a few—Henry Craik's *New Testament Church Order* (1863)—which anticipated B. H. Streeter's *The Primitive Church* (1929) in pointing out that the New Testament provides adumbrations of episcopalian, presbyterian and congregational church order, alongside "what may be described as less systematic than any of the above organizations."[7] This is a matter of simple truth, but it was highly unfashionable to acknowledge such a simple truth in the middle of the nineteenth century. "It appears to me," said Craik, "that the early churches were not, in all places, similarly constituted."[8] A consideration of the constitution and government (or nongovernment) of the churches of Jerusalem, Antioch, Corinth and Rome in the apostolic church would confirm his statement.

Paul indeed seems to have attached some importance to preserving a certain measure of uniform practice throughout his churches. In writing to the volatile church of Corinth he urges it more than once to restrain its tendency to deviation and bring its practices into some kind of conformity with those of "the churches of God" (1 Cor. 11:16) or "all the churches of the saints" (1 Cor. 14:33b). While he was primarily concerned with churches of his own planting, in which he was entitled to institute his own ruling (1 Cor. 7:17), he appears to have had in mind the wisdom of maintaining in his own churches some degree of conformity with churches not of his planting, especially with the mother-church of Jerusalem and her daughter-churches. It is plain that he was always anxious to foster fellowship between his Gentile mission and the Jerusalem church, and this fellowship would have been strained even more than it was if the Gentile churches used unfettered discretion (not to speak of indiscretion) in matters of ecclesiastical order. Arnold Ehrhardt once pointed out that Paul was "one of the greatest assets for the Church at Jerusalem," despite Jerusalem's misgivings about him, because under his influence, when not by his personal action, non-Jerusalem versions of the gospel were brought into line with that which he and the Jerusalem leaders held in common.[9] Even so, diversities in primitive church order can be discerned; they would have been greater but for Paul's policy, arising out of his concern to maintain unity not only within churches but between churches.

But Henry Craik was not content with drawing attention to *diversities* of primitive church order: as Roy Coad also reminds us, he recognized a *development* of order within the New Testament. Again, in saying that in apostolic times "a more fully developed church organization and official position were introduced as occasion called for them,"[10] Craik was saying something which has only to be stated to be recognized as true. But if it is true, it rules out any idea that one uniform and unchangeable pattern is to be discerned in the apostolic writings and followed by all churches which wish to be scripturally ordered. The one uniform pattern which can indeed be discerned in the New Testament is the pattern of flexibility which facilitates instead of impeding the free movement of the Spirit as he makes provision for the churches and their members as and when the need arises.

III. SPIRIT AND STRUCTURE

"Like Jordan," wrote R. B. Rackham in expounding the Pentecostal narrative of Acts 2, "the full and plenteous flood of the Spirit 'overflows all its banks' (Josh. 3:15). At first the worn-out vessels of humanity cannot contain it; and there is a flood of strange and novel spiritual experiences. But when it has worn for itself a deep channel in the church, when the laws of the new spiritual life are learnt and understood, then some of the irregular phenomena disappear, others become normal, and what was thought to be miraculous is found to be a natural endowment of the Christian life."[11] This should be borne in mind on the recurring occasions when God does a new thing in the church, and those who are responsible to maintain decency and order are disturbed by the incursion of unfamiliar and unpredictable practices.

There was probably a time in the early days of the Brethren movement when, with the conscious abandonment of a fixed liturgy, one never knew in the course of a meeting for worship what was going to happen next. Nowadays, with the fixation in many places of another (albeit unwritten) liturgy, one often knows only too well what is going to happen next. Some of us may think that our familiar order of worship provides adequate room for the liberty of the Spirit to move in well-recognized ways. It might cause no little surprise in some places, and possibly even dismay, if (for instance) at a communion service a couple of young people contributed to the worship by singing an impromptu duet, with or without guitar accompaniment. In other places, however, their contribution might be accepted spontaneously in the spirit in which it was offered. In some places, while the liberty of the Spirit might be maintained in theory, the possibility of his exercising that liberty to speak through a woman would be ruled out in practice; in others, such an occasion would be welcomed with joy and appreciation.[12]

It is, in fact, a mistake to set the charismatic and institutional aspects of church life in opposition the one to the other: both are necessary. The floodwaters of the Spirit will drain away ineffectively without vessels or channels to contain them and convey them to the areas where they are most needed; the vessels or channels, for their part, need to be filled with the life-giving water if they are not to be empty and useless. The institutions or structures may be traditional, but they are none the worse for that if they serve a useful purpose; on the other hand, to maintain institutions or structures for their own sake when they have outlived their usefulness is traditionalism of the wrong kind.

What sort of institutions or structures, then, should be regarded as most desirable? Light and flexible ones, which can be maintained without undue cost and labor so long as they are serviceable, and be dismantled without regret when something more suited to the needs of a new day comes along. Some institutions are allowed to grow so old and venerable that the idea of scrapping them is unthinkably sacrilegious. Consider as an example the historic episcopate, which sometimes proves to be a very awkward obstacle in the path of Christian unity. At one time the historic episcopate was a safeguard against the intrusion of subversive doctrine and other dangers; does it fill this role today? If it does, good and well; but some churches which preserve it are not more obviously free from the menace of erroneous teaching and practice than are others which live happily without it.

Something to the same effect may be said about the historic formularies in which the church has traditionally confessed her faith. The ancient creeds are worthy of Christian veneration and acceptance since, as Article VIII of the Anglican Thirty-nine Articles of Religion puts it, "they may be proved by most certain warrants of holy Scripture." But the language of some of them is too technical (and technical in a fourth- and fifth-century sense) to be readily understood by many Christians who recite them today.[13] It may be reasonably answered that Christians who recite the Nicene Creed are not so much expressing their personal faith as confessing their membership in the church whose faith is set forth in these terms; but it is better when the question "Understandest thou what thou sayest?" can receive an affirmative reply. More than that: experience shows that the regular recital of the ancient creeds in a Christian community does not guarantee that it will be more immune from false doctrine than other communities in which they are rarely or never recited. To judge by fragments of confessional statements embedded in the New Testament writings, Christians of apostolic days got along with fairly simple affirmations of faith, which were yet explicit enough to exclude denials of Christ's lordship or of his incarnation. If we inherit or devise confessions of faith, let them at the same time conserve the apostolic witness and be flexible enough to accommodate whatever light the Lord may yet have to break forth from his Holy Word.

IV. UNITY IN THE APOSTOLIC CHURCH

Such unity as was maintained in first-century Christianity was not ensured by a superstructure. There were the apostles, indeed, but we should not exaggerate or idealize the extent of their authority. Paul did not care to have the authority of the Jerusalem apostles imposed by their

emissaries on his Gentile churches: after his contretemps with Peter at
Antioch he could never be sure that one of them might not yield to
pressure, as (in his judgment) Peter did, and sell the pass. He had no
thought of imposing his own authority outside the limits of his commission—we can see how careful he is in this regard when writing to the
Roman church, which was "another man's foundation"[14]—but his restraint was not always matched by others, and there were those who
questioned his apostolic status and did their best to undermine his
authority even in his own mission-field.[15]

There was, of course, a basic unity of faith and life. Paul himself
acknowledges that the outline of the gospel—Christ died, Christ was
buried, Christ was raised the third day—was common ground to himself
and the Jerusalem leaders (1 Cor. 15:3-11). And in an alien world anyone
who called Jesus Messiah or Lord or Son of God would be greeted by
Christians as one of themselves. But the extremist judaizers would have
qualified as fellow-Christians by this test, and so probably would many
of the gnosticizers. If some of the latter were so "way out" as to say "Jesus
is anathema" (1 Cor. 12:3)—meaning perhaps that the heavenly Christ
was all that mattered now, while the earthly Jesus was no longer of any
account—they would scarcely have been recognized as true believers
by the Christian majority.

The New Testament bears ample witness to the centrifugal tendencies in apostolic Christianity: we have only to think of the tensions
between Jewish and Gentile Christians, between legalists and libertari-
ans, between the rank and file who were content with the "simple
gospel" and the spiritual élite who preferred what they imagined to be
more advanced teaching. But it bears ample witness also to the centripetal forces which kept churches and Christians together, and the greatest
of these was love. Here we may think of the spontaneity with which the
young Antiochene church came to the aid of Jerusalem in time of scarcity
and of the readiness with which Paul assented to the request of the
Jerusalem leaders that he and Barnabas should go on remembering the
poor, readiness which manifested itself on the largest scale in the
Jerusalem relief fund which he organized among his Gentile churches.[16]
This example persisted in the postapostolic age. Some churches were
outstanding in charitable enterprise, especially the church in Rome. Half
a century after Paul's stay in Rome, Ignatius begins his letter to the
church there by commending it for its distinction in every noble quality,
and above all for its exercising the "presidency of love" among all the
churches—a worthy primacy indeed![17]

Later in the second century (c. A.D. 170) Dionysius, bishop of
Corinth, wrote to the Roman church and congratulated it on the way in

which it kept up its tradition of generosity to churches in need. "Your blessed bishop Soter has not only maintained this custom but enhanced it by his administration of the largesse distributed to the saints and by the encouragement given by his blessed words to the brethren who come to Rome, addressing them as an affectionate father would his children."[18]

V. PRINCIPLES OF CATHOLICITY

This letter of Dionysius illustrates another centripetal force of special interest. He refers to his own church of Corinth as being, like the Roman church, a joint foundation of the two apostles Peter and Paul.[19] Paul would certainly have disclaimed any part in the founding of the Roman church, but he might well have turned in his grave at the suggestion that the Corinthian church was founded in part by Peter. And yet Dionysius's attitude, while it outrages historical fact, reflects a sound instinct, and one which Paul himself would have approved. When, shortly after he founded it, the church of Corinth showed signs of splitting up into parties, each appropriating as its figurehead some name of renown in the Christian world of that day, Paul insisted that such a course was foolish self-impoverishment; all of them were entitled to an equal share in all the leading teachers: "whether Paul or Apollos or Cephas . . . , all are yours" (1 Cor. 3:22).

It was a mark of the catholic church of the second century (more explicitly, a mark of its catholicity) that it claimed as complete an apostolic heritage as it could. Splinter groups might restrict themselves to one strand in the Christian tradition: the Marcionites might look on Paul as the only faithful apostle and dismiss the Twelve as compromisers with Judaism, while the Ebionites might execrate Paul's name and venerate the memory of Peter and, preeminently, of James the Just. But the catholic church included in its comprehensive canon everything that could reasonably be regarded as apostolic, not (as Marcion did) the epistles of Paul only but those of other apostles and apostolic men.[20]

Whatever tensions might have existed in the apostolic age between Peter and Paul or between their respective followers, these were transcended a generation or two later. Clement of Rome, at the end of the first century, and Ignatius of Antioch, at the beginning of the second, give Peter and Paul joint honorable mention in a Roman setting.[21] More than that, the canonical Petrine literature contains a friendly reference to "our beloved brother Paul" (2 Peter 3:15), even if it is acknowledged that some of his writings are difficult to understand and liable to be seriously misconstrued.

This agreement to pay simultaneous respect to Peter and Paul, together with the other apostles, is frequently said to be a symptom of "incipient catholicism," and it would be pointless to deny this. But incipient catholicism, especially under its German designation *Früh-katholizismus*, is viewed by many theologians in the Lutheran tradition as a deplorable declension from the purity of the Pauline gospel, so much so that those New Testament books in which it appears are judged for that reason to be sub-Pauline, postapostolic and at best deuterocanonical. Other symptoms of this declension are said to be the replacement of a charismatic by an institutional ministry, the extension of the term "church" from the local congregation to cover the worldwide community of Christian people, the adoption of a codified confession of faith and the recession of the imminent hope of glory at the parousia in favor of dependence on the means of grace presently dispensed through the church and its ministry.[22]

In some measure most of these symptoms are present in the New Testament. But the last-mentioned is not to be found. The church as an institution has not yet become the guardian and dispenser of the means of grace. Even in the Pastoral Letters the church is the witness and custodian of the divine revelation, like Israel in earlier days (cf. Rom. 3:2), "the pillar and bulwark of the truth" (1 Tim. 3:15). In these letters, which contain our earliest manuals of church order, the ministry is indeed institutional but has not ceased to be charismatic. Timothy himself has been "instituted" by prophecy (1 Tim. 1:18) and the Spirit still speaks "expressly" in the church (1 Tim. 4:1), although now perhaps through apostolic writings as well as through the lips of prophets. Certainly in the Pastoral Letters the truth is well on its way to being codified (although primitive confessional fragments have been detected in the earliest New Testament documents) and "the faith" is now used not only subjectively, of the faith with which Christians believe, but objectively, of the sum of what they believe (as also in Jude 3). But these things are simply aspects of that development which Henry Craik discerned within the New Testament itself. The development did not cease when the latest New Testament document was penned, nor was there any reason why it should. If it be asked further (in the light of what has been already said) how development is to be distinguished from departure, or how it can be prevented from lapsing into departure, the answer may lie in certain criteria which the New Testament writings themselves provide.

VI. ONE BODY, ONE FAITH

Another aspect of incipient catholicism appears in the Letter to the Ephesians. "In the New Testament," says Ernst Käsemann, "it is Ephesians that most clearly marks the transition from the Pauline tradition to the perspective of the early Catholic era."[23] Repeatedly the principles of life and ministry in the local church, as we find them set out in 1 Corinthians, are universalized in Ephesians. But the universal perspective of Ephesians grows out of something already latent in 1 Corinthians. While 1 Corinthians is addressed to "the church of God that is in Corinth," it is intended also for "all those who in every place call on the name of our Lord Jesus Christ" (1 Cor. 1:1)—primarily, it may be, in the same province of Achaia, but not explicitly and probably not exclusively so. The church throughout the world is one, and its oneness depends on the fact that there is one Spirit, one Lord and one God. But the terms in which this is emphasized in Ephesians 4:4-6 are based on 1 Corinthians 12:4-6, where the collaboration of all the members for the common good in the local church is a corollary of their sharing "the same Spirit; . . . the same Lord; and . . . the same God." We might antecedently have expected Paul to think of Christians throughout his mission-field as forming a unity. "Israel after the flesh" did not exist only in local synagogues; it was an ecumenical entity. The synagogue in any place was the local manifestation of the whole congregation of Israel. So with the new Israel: what we might antecedently have expected is confirmed by the evidence in Paul's earlier letters of his deep concern for Christian unity, not only unity among his own Gentile churches but unity which bound them together with the Jerusalem church and the churches of the Jewish mission.

Again, all Christians according to Paul were baptized "into Christ," not merely into a local fellowship, and thus formed part of one spiritual whole.[24] The Christians in Corinth are reminded that they are Christ's body, and individually members thereof (1 Cor. 12:27); similarly those in Rome are told that "we" (that is, not the Roman Christians only but the Roman Christians in fellowship with other Christians), "though many, are one body in Christ, and individually members one of another" (Rom. 12:5). But to Paul's way of thinking Christ could no more be parceled out among the several congregations than he could be divided among the factions within the congregation at Corinth. Language such as he uses to the Corinthian and Roman Christians could not be locally restricted, even if the occasions of his writing to them directed its application to the conditions of local fellowship. All believers everywhere had together died with Christ and been raised with him; as participators in his risen life they could not but constitute one Christian fellowship. The explicit exposition of the universal church in Ephesians is an unfolding of the significance of Paul's phrase "in Christ" and all that goes with it. Here too we are bound to recognize authentic development within the New Testament.

VII. THE ACTS OF THE APOSTLES

But there is another New Testament document which displays the features of "incipient catholicism" more impressively still, and that is Acts. From the middle of the second century onwards it has been called "The Acts of the Apostles" not because it records the acts of all the apostles (it does not) but because it does not confine itself to one strand of apostolic tradition. Paul may be the author's hero—although in the only places where he calls Paul an apostle he makes him share the designation with Barnabas (Acts 14:4, 14)[25]—but Peter receives a fair share of attention: indeed, commentators have drawn out the parallels in this work between the "Acts of Peter" (chs. 1–12) and the "Acts of Paul" (chs. 13–28). At the Council of Jerusalem, Peter and even James come down in principle on the side of salvation through grace by faith, apart from legal works; and the letter sent to the Gentile churches by the apostles and elders of the Jerusalem church makes appreciative reference to "our beloved Barnabas and Paul" (Acts 15:25), while Barnabas and Paul, for their part, seem quite happy to accept the stipulations laid down in the letter. Acts certainly gives us the impression that trouble was always prone to break out in Jerusalem when Paul visited the city, but the tension between Paul and the leaders of the Jerusalem church, which can be discerned so pervasively beneath the surface in several of Paul's letters, has left hardly a trace in Acts. In Acts Paul and Barnabas, Peter and James, with their respective associates, appear as a happy band of brothers. On the one occasion when Paul and Barnabas have a sharp difference of opinion, it is on personal grounds, quite unlike the difference at Antioch recorded by Paul, when *even Barnabas*, the last man of whom it might have been expected, was carried away by the "play-acting" of Peter and the other Jewish Christians (Gal. 2:13).

But when Acts was written, Paul's career was at an end. That career had been marked by trials and tribulations from within the Christian community as well as from outsiders; but all this could now be recollected in tranquillity. This does not mean that an interval of a generation or two must be postulated between Paul's death and the composition of Acts. We ourselves have known highly controversial figures in church life who in old age enjoyed considerable veneration, even on the part of those who had been involved in controversy with them. At that time of day, and all the more so after their death, the general feeling was: Why recall the controversies when so much that is more edifying can be recorded? The controversy at Antioch was crucial enough when it happened, and it was still so when Paul wrote to the Galatians. A few decades later it was ancient history and, from Luke's point of view, might well remain unmentioned. It could make no contribution to the purpose for which he wrote.

VIII. THE CHURCH'S CALLING

The church is the dwelling-place of the Spirit, and "where the Spirit of the Lord is, there is freedom" (2 Cor. 3:17). Structures of ministry, government and order are of value so long as they provide vehicles for the free moving of the Spirit; when they cease to do that, they should be replaced by more suitable ones. Whatever at any time helps the church to discharge her proper functions—the worship of God, the strengthening of fellowship within her membership and the witness of outgoing and self-giving love to mankind—that is what matters. When the church thinks more of her status than of her service, she has taken a wrong path and must immediately retrace her steps. As the church's Lord was (and remains) the Man for others, the church must be the society for others, the community of the reconciled which is at the same time the instrument by which the reconciling grace of God in Christ is communicated to the world.[26] All that enables the church to be this is true development; all that hinders the church from being this is departure.

16. The Humanity of Jesus Christ

"Jesus: the man who fits no formula," is the title of one of the chapters in Eduard Schweizer's recently published book *Jesus*:[1] the same words will serve admirably as a motto for what I have to say.

If Godhead is to be revealed in the created order, it will be revealed most adequately in manhood, since man was created in the image of God. It is fitting, then, that our Lord Jesus Christ, the Divine Word who became flesh, should in his own person be both altogether God and altogether man—not something betwixt and between as so many, from Arius (and before Arius) to Jehovah's Witnesses, have supposed. The more, then, we emphasize our Lord's real humanity, the more we do justice to his true nature, for it is in that real humanity—*in* it, and not merely *through* it—that we see the Godhead shine.

I. PROLEGOMENA IN BRETHREN HISTORY

My instructions are to deal with the biblical teaching about our Lord's humanity, but to bear in mind, as I do so, the imbalances which need to be corrected in Brethren tradition. This can most easily be done if, before I survey the biblical evidence, I present some prolegomena—prolegomena which, I fear, will absorb the greater part of my time. What emerges from these prolegomena is this: a weakness on the doctrine of our Lord's

---

A paper read at the Annual General Meeting of the Christian Brethren Research Fellowship in London, October 23, 1971, and published in the *CBRF Journal*, 24 (1973), pp. 5-15, along with papers on "The Humanity of Jesus" by H. D. McDonald and on "God in Human Form" by D. J. A. Clines.

humanity, verging at times on Docetism, has been endemic in certain phases of the Brethren movement.

The reason for this is that, almost at the outset of the movement, Brethren found themselves involved in debates on the Person of Christ of a kind which, more especially among the rank and file, caused any emphasis on his *normal* manhood to be almost suspect.

The trouble, I think, really goes back to Edward Irving (1792-1834). Irving, who was a leading participant in the Albury Park conferences (1826-30) and visited Lady Powerscourt at Powerscourt Castle in September 1830, published in the latter year his work on *The Orthodox and Catholic Doctrine of our Lord's Human Nature*, in which he promulgated views which he had already ventilated in his preaching, and which led, three years later, to his conviction for heresy by the Presbytery of Annan and his expulsion from the ministry of the Church of Scotland. In his own words:

> The point at issue is simply this: whether Christ's flesh had the grace of sinlessness and incorruption from its proper nature or from the indwelling of the Holy Ghost. I say the latter. I assert, that in its proper nature it was as the flesh of His Mother, but, by virtue of the Holy Ghost's quickening and inhabiting of it, it was preserved sinless and incorruptible.[2]

In other words, since it was fallen human nature that needed to be redeemed, it was fallen human nature that Christ assumed. As Dr. H. C. Whitley paraphrases Irving's argument, "the deliverer must go into the prison-house where the captives were held, and be Himself a prisoner, so that by His own escape He might open the prison-door for His brethren."[3]

Because of Irving's popularity as a preacher, his views received wide currency, and called forth several rebuttals. The leaders of the Brethren movement probably felt themselves under a special obligation to rebut them, because Irving, like them, was intensely interested in unfulfilled prophecy and because—also, but not likewise!—he aimed at the restoration of apostolic church order.

One such rebuttal of Irving's views, entitled "Doctrine of the Church in Newman Street, considered," was contributed by B. W. Newton in 1835 to the second volume of *The Christian Witness,* and amplified by him in a second edition of the volume. (It was to Newman Street, London, that Irving and his followers moved in October 1832, five months after his deposition from the ministry of Regent Square Church.) In the course of his rebuttal of Irvingism, Newton endeavored to set forth a more biblical account of the human nature of Christ by exploring its relation to the "federal headship" of Adam. Newton stood in that

Reformed tradition which maintained the covenant theology of Johannes Cocceius and other early seventeenth-century theologians (including the Westminster Divines). According to this school of thought, God, upon creating Adam, entered into a "covenant of works" with him, a covenant which was conditional on Adam's perfect obedience. When Adam broke the covenant by eating from the forbidden tree, he incurred suffering and death not only for himself but for his descendants: since he was their "covenant head" or "federal head," his sin was imputed to them, and they reaped its fruit. Along these lines Rom. 5:12-21 was interpreted. Now, Christ was undoubtedly ("according to the flesh") a descendant of Adam, and while Newton repudiated Irving's view that Christ accordingly inherited a sinful nature, he suggested that it was because of his *federal* relationship to Adam that he inherited such side-effects of the fall as "hunger, thirst, weariness, sorrow, etc.," together with "the being possessed of a mortal body." Some years later he repudiated this view in favor of one which accounted for Christ's suffering such ills as flesh is heir to "in virtue of his having been made of a woman." He realized that the view he had previously expressed might be thought to imply the corollary that Adam's sin was imputed to Christ just as (in terms of covenant theology) it was imputed to every other member of the human family, so he not only repudiated it as an exegetical error but (so sensitive was his theological conscience) confessed it as a sin, for which he sought the Lord's pardon.[4]

In other papers Newton gave further consideration to the subject of Christ's sufferings during his life ("non-atoning" sufferings, as he reckoned them) by expounding some of the "individual laments" in the Psalter in a christological sense. It was notes of such an exposition of Psalm 6 that provided the immediate occasion for the doctrinal controversy at Plymouth in 1845-47 which split the Brethren movement.[5]

We can see, more easily than our predecessors could at that time, that much of the trouble arose from mistaken principles of Old Testament exegesis. It is an instance of the irony of history that J. N. Darby, who led the attack against Newton, ran into trouble himself twelve years later because of papers on "The Sufferings of Christ" contributed to *The Bible Treasury* in 1858 and 1859.[6] Here he distinguished, in addition to Christ's ill-treatment at the hands of men and the atoning sufferings endured vicariously on men's behalf (the "cup" which his Father gave him to drink), a third category, endured under the "governmental" dealing of God when he "entered in heart into the indignation and wrath that lay on Israel," in sympathy with the righteous remnant of the end-time. Here also the psalms of individual lament were brought into play. While Psalm 22 was (naturally) expounded in relation to Christ's atoning sufferings on the cross, Psalms 69 and 102 were related to the third category of sufferings.[7] While this thesis was not identical with Newton's, both were based on mistaken exegesis,[8] and some of Darby's most faithful followers saw little to choose between the two, since both implied that Christ endured divine wrath otherwise than vicariously and by way of atonement.

To revert to the Plymouth controversy, one of its effects was the growth of a morbid scrupulosity about the use of certain time-honored language concerning our Lord's manhood, arising from fear lest the terrible stigma of Newtonianism should be incurred. Newton, for example, had spoken of our Lord's body as "mortal," in the perfectly proper sense of its being "capable of dying." The application of the epithet to Christ in manhood had well-known orthodox precedent, as, for example, in Isaac Watts's lines:

> Arrayed in mortal flesh
> The Covenant Angel stands—

or:

> Down from the shining heights above
>   In joyful haste he sped,
> Entered the grave in mortal flesh
>   And dwelt among the dead.

But Newton's use of the word was chalked up against him as heresy. In 1850, replying to this misrepresentation, he appealed to its common use in a hymn by J. G. Deck which had been freely sung by the Brethren ever since its composition about 1837:

> Such was Thy grace that, for our sake,
>   Thou didst from heaven come down;
> Our mortal flesh and blood partake,
>   In all our misery one.

Here was a to-do, to be sure! The unfortunate hymn-writer had to wear a white sheet in public. On November 14, 1850, Deck issued a *Confession of a Verbal Error in a Hymn.* He admitted that the offending word had been "long used by godly brethren without consciousness of evil" and explained that he meant no more than "capable of death"—which no one doubted. But since Newton's use of the word had been pronounced heretical, it was thenceforth taboo among Brethren who valued their reputation for "soundness." Deck's hymn had to be altered, and was weakened in the process: the new form of the line in question—"With us of flesh and blood partake"—was but a pale reflection of the original.[9]

If the term "mortal" became taboo among Brethren, however, Newton's cousin and champion, S. P. Tregelles, reacted vigorously by making willingness to use it a test of orthodoxy: its deliberate avoidance, in his eyes, was a sign of Docetism.[10]

In October 1848 Henry Craik was severely criticized by G. V. Wigram for using language about our Lord's humanity which, while not including the taboo word, emphasized that "He was in all things made like unto His brethren, sin only excepted; that the flesh which He assumed was the flesh and blood of the children; that the physical or chemical properties of His body were the same as ours." The "necessary inference" from the critics' strictures, he said, "would be, that the Blessed One did not take our flesh, but flesh and blood essentially different from ours."[11]

Darby knew very well that there was nothing heretical in what Craik had written, and is reported to have said that, when he received Wigram's criticisms of Craik, he put them at the back of the fire. He must have seen, moreover, the docetic direction in which Wigram's arguments tended. But for purposes of ecclesiastical politics Wigram was too useful a henchman to be disowned.

One symptom of this docetic tendency appears in the description of our Lord's manhood as "heavenly humanity," found in the works of C. H. Mackintosh and others.[12] In his present exaltation he does indeed wear a heavenly humanity,[13] but if the expression is used of the manhood of the historical Jesus, the natural conclusion would be that his humanity and ours were different.

As quoted by W. B. Neatby, F. E. Raven used this expression in a context which makes its docetic intention plain. He remarked that one of his critics, Gladwell by name, appeared to be "in great ignorance of the true moral character of Christ's humanity. He did not get that character by being born of a woman, though that was the way by which He took man's form, but Manhood in Him takes its character from what He ever was divinely. 'The Word became flesh'. He does not seem to me to have any idea of a real heavenly humanity." These words, as Neatby says, are unintelligible unless they mean "that Christ was not man of the substance of His mother, but that He derived from her only the outward form of a man. It is hard to distinguish this from the doctrine that He was man in semblance only."[14]

Raven's critics charged him with Apollinarianism—the doctrine (condemned at Constantinople in A.D. 381) that in our Lord's incarnate being the Divine Logos took the place that in other men is taken by the rational mind and spirit. Whether this is the proper label to attach to him is doubtful, because of the cloudiness of his language on this subject (as on many others). But he manifestly did not believe in our Lord's *personal* humanity and would not subscribe to the affirmation of the Athanasian Creed that "God and man is one Christ." When someone, at a discussion meeting in 1895, quoted Darby's comment on Col. 1:15f. ("We say, Christ is God, Christ is man; but it is Christ who is the two"),[15] Raven replied, "Yes; but you must be careful how you take up an expression like that. In Person He is God; in condition He is Man." And again: "Unity is not a happy word as applied to the Lord. The teaching of Scripture is incarnation."[16] Raven was repeatedly urged to make his meaning plain, but on no occasion (so far as I am aware) did he make an unambiguous statement of our Lord's perfect and unimpaired manhood, although it would have been easy for him to do so, had he been so minded. On the contrary, when, in the course of the same conversations, someone referred to man as comprising body, soul and spirit, and asked if this was true of our Lord—"you do not contend against His manhood?"—Raven replied: "No; but you might be near error there. You get on dangerous ground in applying such things to the Lord. He is a divine Person in manhood."[17]

Raven's christological eccentricity provoked a healthy reaction in the group which in 1890 withdrew from association with him, the Lowe party, which united in 1926 with the Kelly party. William Kelly's followers (who had separated from the mainstream of Darbyism in 1881) were fortunate in having as their leader a master of biblical and historical theology who held intelligently to the Chalcedonian definition of our Lord's person[18] and taught his disciples accordingly. Several years ago, in conversation with the late John Weston, a well-known leader in the Lowe-Kelly party, I mentioned that Apollinarianism was the besetting heresy of evangelical Christians. He expressed interest in my opinion, but added, "Not among us." But what could happen in the Raven succession was shown in 1927, when James Boyd of Brighouse, Yorkshire, not a "Taylorite" but a "Glanton" brother, published a pamphlet on *The Incarnation of the Son* in which he said, "That the Son was the spirit of His own body I have not the slightest question. . . . The assertion that Christ has a *human* soul and spirit is in principle a denial of the incarnation of the Son."[19] These statements were made in a polemical context, and when the good man realized the furor which they created he withdrew them, but plainly he could not see what was wrong with them. It is better to remember Mr. Boyd gratefully as the author of the beautiful communion hymn, "O teach us, Lord, Thy searchless love to know,"[20] than as one who inadvertently perpetrated a doctrinal deviation which contributed to a minor ecclesiastical cleavage.[21]

The fact is that, in certain strands of Brethrenism where the issues have not been clearly faced, views subversive of our Lord's manhood find a measure of acquiescence such as would never be extended to views subversive of his deity. Have you, for example, ever come across in Brethren circles the Valentinian view that from conception to birth our Lord passed through the body of his mother "like water through a pipe," deriving no part of his humanity from her?[22] I have met it—not, of course, in a responsible teacher but in a local leader whose expression of opinion was regarded by some of his followers as doing honor to Christ. Writing in 1901, W. B. Neatby said, "A year or two ago I heard an address from a Brother of the Open Section, who actually taught that Christ did not die from crucifixion, but by a mere miraculous act. The good man was certainly not a responsible teacher, nor did I ever know a man of weight to set Holy Scripture aside with quite so much definiteness and completeness; but I have heard much that glanced in the same direction."[23] And so have I, and probably you have too. Our Lord's statement, "No one takes it [my life] from me, but I lay it down of my own accord" (John 10:18) must be taken along with other New Testament passages which state explicitly that his enemies "killed" him (e.g., Acts 2:23; 10:39; 1 Thess. 2:15, etc.). To deny the reality of his death is an ancient form of Docetism (represented in some apocryphal Gospels[24] and later in the *Qur'ān*),[25] against which John the evangelist had to polemicize as early as the first century.[26]

Or we may think of the disapproval visited even today on those who interpret our Lord's temptations realistically[27] or take at face value his words which place limits to his knowledge. I remember the criticism voiced in the 1930s by William Hoste in *The Believer's Magazine* of a statement about our Lord in C. F. Hogg's pamphlet, *The Traditions and the Deposit:* "What He did not know, He knew that He did not know."[28] Mr. Hogg's statement was based on our Lord's own unambiguous language in Mark 13:32 (= Matt. 24:36). But Mr. Hoste may well have been particularly sensitive in this regard, because the interpretation of Mark 13:32 figured in the 1923-24 controversy over Theodore Roberts' alleged unorthodoxy, in which Mr. Hoste had played a leading part.[29]

In my youth I remember the holy horror expressed by a ministering brother because someone else had, in an address, taken for granted that our Lord in his boyhood went to school. The very idea that he should have had to learn his letters from a human teacher was judged an intolerable aspersion on his perfect knowledge: "He owed *nothing* to earth," said the speaker. As I listened to him, I felt glad that Luke stated expressly that "Jesus *increased in wisdom*" as well as "in stature" (Luke 2:52), for I suspected that, if one of our own contemporaries had made such a statement on his own initiative, the speaker would have been horrified at him too. Our Lord's deity is not enhanced when men, thinking to do him honor, detract from the completeness of his manhood.

II. THE NEW TESTAMENT WITNESS

We turn now to the biblical evidence, and it will be convenient to consider the main divisions of the New Testament one by one.

The Synoptic Gospels and Acts. While the Synoptic Gospels and Acts, like all the New Testament documents, are written from a "post-Easter" perspective, yet they preserve a clear impression of the historical Jesus—Jesus as he was known to his associates and others during his Palestinian ministry. While full justice is done, especially by Mark, to his being the Son of God,[30] his real manhood is axiomatic for all three writers: it is assumed rather than asserted. The disciples realized, indeed, that he was no ordinary man: "Who then is this?" they exclaimed in amazement when he awoke and stilled the tempest (Mark 4:41)—but they knew that the one who, a few minutes earlier, had been lying asleep with his head on a cushion was a real man, whatever else might be said of him. Two of the Synoptic evangelists give some account of his birth, which was perfectly natural—it was his conception that was supernatural. The same two evangelists trace his ancestry back through many generations: Matthew back through David to Abraham (Matt. 1:1-17), Luke back through David to Adam (Luke 3:23-28). All three writers refer to his family relationships; and none leaves any doubt about the reality of his death. After his resurrection and exaltation he is described in the apostles' preaching as "a man *(anēr)* attested . . . by God with mighty works and wonders and signs which God did through him" (Acts 2:22), as the "man" *(anēr)* appointed by God to be the future judge of living and dead (Acts 17:31), and his descent from David is repeatedly emphasized (Acts 2:30f.; 13:23). If I have not adduced the designation "the Son of Man" in this connection, that is because this phrase does not primarily connote his humanity but rather his identity with a figure of Old Testament prophecy and apocalyptic who is exalted after humiliation. Even so, insofar as it comes to mean "the representative man" or

> the Proper Man
> Whom God Himself hath bidden,

it is not without its relevance here.

The Pauline Corpus. More important is the testimony of Paul, whose words about no longer knowing Christ "after the flesh" (2 Cor. 5:16) are frequently taken to mean that he had no interest in the historical Jesus,

concentrating exclusively on the now exalted Lord. What Paul is really
contrasting in these words is his own former, pre-Christian attitude with
his present attitude as a believer; his meaning is brought out well in the
NEB rendering: "With us, therefore, worldly standards have ceased to
count in our estimate of any man; even if once they counted in our
understanding of Christ, they do so now no longer." No one would
dispute, indeed, that Paul was immediately and permanently conscious
of Jesus as the exalted Lord, raised high above the universe (Phil. 2:9-11;
Eph. 1:20-23), embodying the fullness of deity (Col. 2:9), as he also
identified him with the Wisdom of God, the agent through whom all
things were brought into being and maintained in being (1 Cor. 1:24, 30;
8:6b; Col. 1:15-17). Yet for Paul he who was the eternal Wisdom and the
exalted Lord was personally continuous with the historical Jesus, true
man, "descended from David according to the flesh" (Rom. 1:3), "born
of woman, born under the law" (Gal. 4:4), who met his death upon a
cross (Gal. 3:1; Phil. 2:8, etc.). In his death the deathblow was given to
sin in the sphere of human nature where sin had usurped control, and
redemption was procured for sinners. When, in the place where he
teaches this most explicitly (Rom. 8:3), Paul says that God sent "his own
Son in the likeness of sinful flesh"—literally, "in likeness of flesh of sin"
(i.e., flesh which is dominated by sin)—he is affirming the Son's humanity while denying his sinfulness. His flesh was the same as ours, otherwise the deathblow given to sin in his death would not have broken its
power in our lives; but his flesh—his human nature—was not dominated by sin, as ours is.[31]

As "first-begotten from the dead" (Col. 1:18) Jesus is head of the
new creation, but since the new creation comprises a new humanity, not
a new order of divine beings, his own humanity persists in his risen life.

In the Pastoral Letters the one who was "manifested in the flesh"
(1 Tim. 3:16) is the "one mediator between God and men, the man Christ
Jesus" (1 Tim. 2:5), whose "good confession" before Pontius Pilate provides an example and incentive to his followers to be faithful confessors
in their turn (1 Tim. 6:13f.).

Hebrews. For the writer to the Hebrews, as for Paul, Jesus is the Son
of God "through whom also he made the worlds" (Heb. 1:2) and is
addressed in Old Testament scripture not only as "Lord" (Heb. 1:10) but
actually as "God" (Heb. 1:8f., twice); but there is no New Testament
writer who more emphatically underlines the necessity of Jesus' humanity if there was to be any gospel for mankind. "Since . . . the children
share in flesh and blood, he himself likewise partook of the same nature,
that through death" he might "deliver" them (Heb. 2:14f.). "He had to
be made like his brethren in every respect" if he was to be their effective

high priest: "it is not of angels that he takes hold; he takes hold of the descendants of Abraham"[32] (Heb. 2:16f.). Far from being an impassive visitor from another realm, playing a set part on the world stage with Olympian detachment, he sympathizes with the weaknesses of his fellow-men and knows how best to help them, for "he himself has suffered and been tempted"—tempted indeed "in every respect . . . as we are, yet without sinning" (Heb. 2:18; 4:15). There is nothing impassive, there is everything that is warmly and appealingly human in the picture of one who poured out his soul in "prayers and supplications, with loud cries and tears, to him who was able to save him from death," and "learned obedience through what he suffered" (Heb. 5:7f.), who blazed the trail of faith and persevered to the end, enduring the cross and despising the shame, putting up with sinners' hostility so that his people, profiting by his example, need not "grow weary or fainthearted" (Heb. 12:2f.).

The General Epistles. Of the General Epistles (apart from 1 John, which is considered below), the only one which contains material directly relevant to our subject is 1 Peter. In 1 Peter, as in the Pauline letters, Jesus is now the exalted one "who has gone into heaven and is at the right hand of God, with angels, authorities and powers subject to him" (1 Pet. 3:22); yet he was "put to death in the flesh" (1 Pet. 3:18), enduring unjust suffering uncomplainingly on his people's behalf, that they might learn by his example and follow his steps (1 Pet. 2:21). The writer claims to be a witness of the sufferings of Christ (1 Pet. 5:1), and there is much in his language about those sufferings which bears out this claim, even if the language be largely indebted to the fourth Isaianic Servant Song (so especially in 1 Pet. 2:22-25). Christ's sufferings and death were real: on their reality their redemptive and exemplary efficacy depends.

The Johannine Writings. The Apocalypse may be passed over briefly, since it concentrates on the exalted Christ to such a degree that it contributes but little to our purpose. Yet the exalted Christ is pictured, *inter alia,* as the Lamb that was slain (Rev. 5:6ff.), and the repeated references to the redeeming and cleansing virtue of "the blood of the Lamb" (Rev. 5:9; 7:14; 12:11) leave us in no doubt that his present exaltation is the consequence of his humiliation and death. If his followers win their victory through being faithful unto death, it is because he won his thus and has shown them the way.

But the Johannine Gospel and first two epistles are quite outstandingly germane to our theme. The evangelist who expounds so eloquently the divine character of the eternal Logos who was manifested on earth in Jesus Christ set his face uncompromisingly against docetic tendencies in the church of his day and made as sure as he could that no docetic inferences should be drawn from his exposition. (If, nevertheless, such inferences have been drawn, the fault is not his.)[33] He does not content himself with saying that the Logos assumed manhood: in the most positive terms he affirms that the Logos "became flesh" (John 1:14). This affirmation cut at the root of the dualist presupposition that the spiritual and the material orders were too incompatible to be congenially associated. The incarnate Logos, moreover, according to John, was capable of weariness, thirst and grief, and died as only men can die. John will not allow that there was anything unreal about the death of Jesus: the solemn eyewitness testimony to the effusion of blood and water which followed the piercing of his side with the soldier's lance (John 19:34f.) is adduced in order to emphasize, against much contemporary docetic speculation, that he really died.

So essential, indeed, is Jesus' true manhood to the authentic gospel that in John's first epistle the confession of this is a criterion of membership in the family of God (1 John 4:2; 5:1), while its denial is a mark of the spirit of Antichrist (1 John 4:3; cf. 2 John 7). Some Docetists might hold, as Cerinthus apparently did, that the Christ-spirit came upon the man Jesus at his baptism but left him before his passion. In the *Gospel of Peter* the cry of dereliction is reinterpreted in this sense: "My power, my power, thou hast left me!" But to all this speculation John says No: "This is he who came by water and blood, Jesus Christ, not with the water only but with the water and with the blood" (1 John 5:6). If the one who was baptized was the Son of God, as the heavenly acclamation confirmed (cf. John 1:32-34), the one who died was equally the Son of God. And the witness of the blood attests that, as the Son of God's manhood was real, so was his death.

The gospel of our salvation depends upon the genuineness of our Lord's humanity, and so does the value of his life as an example for his people to follow. The power of that example is weakened if we can say, in extenuation of our own failure, "It was different, or easier, for him." Only as he presents himself to us as perfect man can we in turn be validly encouraged to grow up, not only individually but corporately, "to the measure of the stature of the fulness of Christ" (Eph. 4:13).

"A Saviour *not quite God*," said Bishop Handley Moule, "is a bridge broken at the farther end."[34] With equal truth it must be said that a Savior—and an Exemplar—*not quite man* is a bridge broken at the nearer end. "The only Redeemer of God's elect is the Lord Jesus Christ, who, being the eternal Son of God, became man, and so was, and continueth to be, God and man in two distinct natures, and one person, for ever."[35]

17. Women in the Church: A Biblical Survey

PROLEGOMENA

The phenomenon of cultural relativity, with the adaptations it imposes, is repeatedly illustrated within the Bible itself. We see the Israelite nomads moving from the wilderness into the settled agricultural life of Canaan; we see a peasant economy giving place under the monarchy to an urbanized mercantile economy, with the attendant abuses against which the great prophets of Israel inveighed; we see the postexilic adjustment to life in a unit of a great, well-organized empire—first Persian, then Hellenistic, then Roman. Even within the limited confines of the New Testament we see the gospel transplanted from its Jewish and Palestinian matrix into the Gentile environment of the Mediterranean world. In this last respect we could pay special attention to the way in which John, while preserving the authentic gospel of Christ, brings out its abiding and universal validity in a new idiom for an audience very different from that to which it was first proclaimed.

One major concern of the scribes and Pharisees of our Lord's day was to apply to their contemporaries a code of laws originally given in quite another way of life. The sabbath law, for example, was formulated in relation to a simple pastoral or agrarian economy, in which "work"

A paper read at a seminar on "Women in the Church" organized by the Christian Brethren Research Fellowship at London Bible College, Northwood, Middlesex, on June 9, 1979, and published in *Christian Brethren Review Journal* 33 (1982), pp. 7-14.

was a clearly understood term. But what kinds of activity came within the prohibition of "work" in the more complex situation at the dawn of the Christian era? The scribes saw that detailed definition was necessary if people were to have clear guidance in this matter: in one of their schools thirty-nine categories of "work" were specified, all of which were banned on the sabbath.

That was one way to tackle the problem of cultural relativity; the way of Jesus was different. He preferred to go back to first principles: any kind of action which promoted the original purpose of the commandment fulfilled it; any kind of action which hindered that original purpose violated it. But it was for people to decide for themselves which actions promoted the original purpose and which actions hindered it: he would not lay down precise regulations.

The Gospels exhibit the contrast between the scribal way and the way of Jesus in the handling of the Old Testament. Subsequent church history, down to our own generation, exhibits the same contrast in the handling of the New Testament and the varying attempts to apply its principles to changing situations. Canon law, whether it is explicitly so called or not, exemplifies the scribal way—the tradition of the elders.

Cultural relativity is certainly to be reckoned with when the permanent message of the New Testament receives our practical attention today. The local and temporary situation in which that message was first delivered must be appreciated if we are to discern what its permanent essence really is and learn to re-apply it in the local and temporary circumstances of our own culture.

We take this for granted in the case of missionaries taking the gospel to lands of different traditions from their own. Even with our instant and worldwide intercommunication, culture shock remains a reality—a two-way reality. Let us similarly take it for granted that a sympathetic awareness of the cultures in which the Gospels and epistles first appeared will help us to understand those documents in their own setting and also to profit by them in our own setting.

I. IN CREATION

The basic teaching of the creation narratives is that when God created mankind (Adam) in his own image, he created them male and female (Gen. 1:27).[1]

In the narrative of Gen. 1 no question of priority, let alone of superiority, arises. In the narrative of Gen. 2 the female is formed after the male, to be "a help answering to him"—not, as a later interpreter put it, "he for God only, she for God in him."[2] The priority of the male in this creation narrative does not bespeak his superiority: any suggestion to this effect might be answered by the counterargument that the last-made crowns the work—but either argument is beside the point.

II. IN THE FALL

It is in the fall narrative, not in the creation narratives, that superiority of the one sex over the other is first mentioned. And here it is not an inherent superiority, but one that is exercised by force. The Creator's words to Eve, "your desire shall be for your husband, and he will rule over you" (Gen. 3:16), mean that, in our sinful human condition, the man exploits the woman's natural proclivity towards him to dominate and subjugate her. Subjugation of woman, in fact, is a symptom of man's fallen nature.[3]

If the work of Christ involves the breaking of the entail of the fall, the implication of his work for the liberation of women is plain.

III. IN THE NEW CREATION

1. *The Attitude and Teaching of Jesus*

Jesus was born into a male-dominated culture. Some of its basic presuppositions he quietly and indirectly undermined. His treatment of the divorce question, for example, not only illustrates his constant appeal to first principles; its chief practical effect was the redressing of a balance which was heavily weighted against women. His male disciples immediately realized this, as is shown by their response. "If a man cannot divorce his wife under any circumstances," they meant, "it is better not to marry" (Matt. 19:10).

Unwarranted inferences have sometimes been drawn from the fact that all twelve of the original apostles were men. But in fact our Lord's male disciples cut a sorry figure alongside his female disciples, especially in his last hours; and it was to women that he first entrusted the privilege of carrying the news of his resurrection.

He treated women in a completely natural and unselfconscious way as real persons. He imparted his teaching to the eager ears and heart of Mary of Bethany, while to the Samaritan woman (of all people) he revealed the nature of true worship. His disciples who found him thus engaged at the well were surprised to find him talking to a woman: for a religious teacher to do this was at best a waste of time and at worst a spiritual danger.

2. The Attitude and Teaching of Paul

No distinction in service or status is implied in Paul's many references
to his fellow-workers, whether male or female. Among the latter we
recall Phoebe, deacon (not deaconess!) of the church at Cenchreae (Rom.
16:1f.), who by her safe delivery of the Epistle to the Romans performed
an inestimable service to the church universal, and Euodia and Syntyche
of Philippi, who received Paul's commendation as women who "con-
tended side by side"[4] with him in the gospel together with Clement and
others (Phil. 4:3). Paul uses the designation "apostles" more comprehen-
sively than Luke does, and he may even include at least one woman
among them, if the companion of Andronicus in Rom. 16:7 is Junia, a
woman (as Chrysostom understood), and not Junias, a man.[5]

From the standpoint of Paul's upbringing he voices a revolutionary
sentiment when he declares that "in Christ Jesus . . . there is neither Jew
nor Greek, there is neither slave nor free, there is neither male nor
female" (Gal. 3:28). Already in his time the Jewish morning prayer
probably included the passage where the pious man thanks God that he
was made a Jew and not a Gentile, a free man and not a slave, a man and
not a woman. All three of these privileges are hereby wiped out: real as
they were in the Judaism of Paul's day, they are abolished in Christ. In
Judaism it was the males only who received in their bodies the visible
seal of the covenant with Abraham; it is a corollary of Paul's circumci-
sion-free gospel that any such religious privilege enjoyed by males over
females is abolished. To the present day among orthodox Jews the
quorum for a synagogue congregation is ten free men; unless ten such
males are present the service cannot begin. (We may, incidentally, be
happy that for Christian meetings we have the less stringent quorum of
"two or three," with nothing said as to whether they are men or women.)
Paul, on the other hand, expects Christian women to play a responsible
part in church meetings, and if, out of concern for public order, he asks
them to veil their heads when they pray or prophesy, the veil is the sign
of their authority to exercise their Christian liberty in this way, not the
sign of someone else's authority over them.[6]

Nothing that Paul says elsewhere on women's contribution to
church services can be understood in a sense which conflicts with these
statements of principle. This applies to the limitations apparently placed
on their public liberty in 1 Cor. 14:34 ("the women should keep silence in
the churches") and 1 Tim. 2:11 ("let a woman learn in silence with all
submissiveness"). Critical questions have indeed been raised about the
text of 1 Cor. 14:34f. (which the "Western" recension places after verse 40)[7]
or the direct authorship of the Pastoral Epistles. If it is judged that the

evidence is not sufficient to extrude 1 Cor. 14:34f. from the authentic text, the prohibition expressed in these verses refers to the asking of questions which imply a judgment on prophetic utterances (so, at least, their context suggests). The adjacent injunctions to silence in verses 28 and 30 are also limited in reference. As for the Pastoral Epistles, we have received them as canonical scripture, and that goes for 1 Tim. 2:9-15. I am disposed to agree with Chrysostom, who read the Greek New Testament in his native language, that in 1 Tim. 2:9f. we have a direction (developing the teaching of 1 Cor. 11:2-16) that women's dress and demeanor should be seemly when they engage in public prayer.[8] In verses 11 and 12 of this chapter, however, women are quite explicitly not given permission to teach or rule.[9] The relevance of the two arguments—*(a)* that Adam was formed before Eve and *(b)* that Eve was genuinely deceived whereas Adam knew what he was doing when he broke the divine commandment—is not immediately obvious; I am not too happy with the suggestion that the former is an early instance of the principle of primogeniture, in which the special rights of the firstborn are recognized.

Exegesis seeks to determine the meaning of the text in its primary setting. But when exegesis has done its work, our application of the text should avoid treating the New Testament as a book of rules. In applying the New Testament text to our own situation, we need not treat it as the scribes of our Lord's day treated the Old Testament. We should not turn what were meant as guiding lines for worshipers in one situation into laws binding for all time. (It is commonly recognized that the regulations regarding widows in 1 Tim. 5:3-16 need not be carried out literally today, although their essential principle should continue to be observed.) It is an ironical paradox when Paul, who was so concerned to free his converts from the bondage of the law, is treated as a law-giver for later generations. The freedom of the Spirit, which can be safeguarded by one set of guiding lines in a particular situation, may call for a different procedure in a new situation.

It is very naturally asked what criteria can be safely used to distinguish between those elements in the apostolic letters which are of local and temporary application and those which are of universal and permanent validity. The question is too big for a detailed discussion here. Where the writings of Paul are concerned, however, a reliable rule of thumb is suggested by his passionate emphasis on freedom—true freedom by contrast with spiritual bondage on the one hand and moral license on the other. Here it is: whatever in Paul's teaching promotes true freedom is of universal and permanent validity; whatever seems to impose restrictions on true freedom has regard to local and temporary conditions. (For example, to go to another area, restrictions on a Christian's freedom in the matter of food are conditioned by the company in which he or she is at the time; and even those restrictions are manifestations of the overriding principle of always considering the well-being of others.)

An appeal to first principles in our application of the New Testament might demand the recognition that when the Spirit, in his sovereign good pleasure, bestows varying gifts on individual believers, these gifts are intended to be exercised for the well-being of the whole church. If he manifestly withheld the gifts of teaching or leadership from Christian women, then we should accept that as evidence of his will (1 Cor. 12:11). But experience shows that he bestows these and other gifts, with "undistinguishing regard," on men and women alike—not on all women, of course, nor yet on all men. That being so, it is unsatisfactory to rest with a halfway house in this issue of women's ministry, where they are allowed to pray and prophesy, but not to teach or lead.

Let me add that an appeal to first principles in our application of the New Testament demands that nothing should be done to endanger the unity of a local church. Let those who understand the scriptures along the lines indicated in this paper have liberty to expound them thus, but let them not force the pace or try to impose their understanding of the scriptures until that understanding finds general acceptance with the church—and when it does, there will be no need to impose it.

IV. THE PRIESTHOOD OF WOMEN

The recent debates about the admission of women to the priesthood in the Church of England and similar communities arise largely from a conception of Christian priesthood which we do not share. In these debates it has been freely conceded by many that women may perform in church practically all the ministries performed by a nonconformist pastor. The one thing she may not do is to celebrate the eucharist.

The concept of priesthood implied in such a position is of a restricted order to which certain selected men are solemnly ordained. The exclusion of women from this order is defended by a variety of arguments, some of which are more unconvincing than others. Without the presence and action of such an ordained priest, it is held, a communion service is irregular, if not invalid.

Another factor which enters into this argument is the issue of headship: it is held by many that the celebrant at holy communion represents Christ as head of the church, from which some infer that, since Christ is male, so should his representative be.[10] On this let it suffice to say that, for those who believe in the real presence[11] of Christ in the holy communion, there is no need for anyone to "represent" him there. Celebrant and other communicants alike take their place on one level at his table, partakers together of his body and blood, all debtors to his grace.

Well, we may say, this question of the ordination of women to the priesthood does not affect us: we believe in the priesthood of all believers; we do not recognize a restricted order of priests. Would it be all right, then, at one of our communion services for a women to give thanks for the bread and break it, before it is distributed to the congregation? I suspect that some of our brethren would—reluctantly, it may be—concede anything to a woman rather than this. (I apologize if I am doing them an injustice; this is the impression I sometimes get.) But why? The thanksgiving and the preliminary breaking of the bread at the table are priestly acts only insofar as the person who performs them does so as representative of the other communicants who are there exercising their common priesthood. Why should not a Christian woman who shares our common priesthood perform such a representative act on behalf of her fellow-worshippers as well as a Christian man? This is not a rhetorical question; I should like to be given a scriptural answer.[12]

At some of our women's conferences, I am told, while every other part of the program is run very competently by women, it is thought desirable for one or two token men to be imported to conduct the communion service.[13] This is not the fault of the conveners; they know very well, however, that some of their sisters would be discouraged from attending if their spiritual directors thought that the communion service would be conducted by women.

J. N. Darby was no feminist, but he had a strong vein of common sense. He thought it a little out of place for a woman even to start a hymn, "but I do not object," he added, "if she does it modestly." But when he was asked if Christian women might take the Lord's Supper together in the absence of men, he said, "If three women were on a desert island, I do not see why they should not break bread together, if they did it privately."[14] Herein he showed his common sense. Of course, they could scarcely do it otherwise than privately, if they were alone on a desert island; and there are other desert islands than those which are entirely surrounded by water.

V. BRETHREN TRADITIONS AND PRACTICES

The mention of J. N. Darby may suggest that the Brethren movement—unlike (say) the Society of Friends—has tended to be male-dominated from its inception. I do not forget that elect lady, Theodosia, Viscountess Powerscourt, but even she "knew her place."

Two factors have perpetuated such an attitude: one, the continuing high-church tradition in our movement; the other, the scribalism (not to say legalism) of our application of scripture.

There have indeed been outstanding exceptions. The Brethren assembly on the Hohenstaufenstrasse, Berlin, was founded by Toni von Blücher (a female descendant of Wellington's comrade-in-arms at Waterloo) and some like-minded women. When in due course a man joined their fellowship, he was (unlike themselves) so utterly ungifted that his presence made no difference to their procedure. And I know of one Brethren meeting in the northeast of Scotland—at Rhynie, Aberdeenshire—which in the fourth quarter of the nineteenth century obstinately persisted in allowing liberty of ministry to women as well as men.[15] In my boyhood I met a very old lady, Mrs. Lundin-Brown, who used to spend the summer in our part of the world. Her Christian activity went back well before the revival of 1859, and she enjoyed the fellowship of the Brethren despite her assiduity in the public preaching of the gospel. By the time I knew her she was nearing her century and could no longer continue her preaching, but would not be restrained from taking part audibly in prayer-meetings in the most traditionalist Brethren assemblies in the north of Scotland. An old lady of indomitable will can get away with anything!

Such an exercise of liberty was atypical for that age in most denominations. But nineteenth-century attitudes tend to persist in quarters where they are not clearly distinguished from first-century principles.

CONCLUSION

What was said at the beginning of this paper about relativity in earlier days applies to our own times also. We too are culturally conditioned; only we do not notice it. The women's liberation movement has conditioned not only our practices but our very vocabulary. But, in such an important matter as we are now considering, it would be a pity if we were influenced by contemporary world-movements in thought and practice rather than by the guidance of the Spirit, as he speaks his liberating word to men and women today through the ministry of our Lord and his servant Paul. That ministry, that liberating word, is enshrined for us in the pages of scripture: to use scripture aright is to hear what the Spirit is saying through it to the churches of the twentieth century as well as what he said to those of the first.

VI. ENVOI

18. The Bible and the Faith

When I was invited to address you on "The Bible and the Faith," it was primarily the sense of honor done me that made me accept the invitation with alacrity. In addition, I realized that my own mind required clarification on this subject, and I hoped that the preparation of this address would help clarify it. At the same time I had no illusions about my fitness to speak to you on this aspect of biblical study. I am by predilection and practice a biblical critic and exegete. It is my business to study and teach such things as the textual evidence for the books of the Bible, their structure, date and authorship, and especially what their authors meant by them and what their first readers might have been expected to understand. I feel at home when I am examining the biblical documents in their historical setting.

I know very well, of course, that for all the importance of these studies, they are far from exhausting the significance of the Bible. As a Christian, I recognize that in the biblical writings the Spirit speaks to the churches of the twentieth century as surely as he spoke to those of the first, and that, as we read them or hear them read, we shall not be disappointed if we listen for his voice. But this is an area in which I can claim no professional expertise. In this auditorium there are theologians much more competent to deal with it than I am. If you will permit me, Moderator, I might refer to your own very helpful book *The Bible Says,*[1] which I read with appreciation when it first appeared fourteen years ago

---

An address delivered at Eastbourne on March 23, 1976, to the Annual Congress of the Free Church Federal Council, under the Moderatorship of the Rev. Dr. John Huxtable, and published in *Free Church Chronicle* 31.4 (Winter 1976), pp. 8-16.

and have reread more recently while preparing for the present occasion. But, having accepted the invitation to address you, I can at least share with you my thinking on this important topic.

I. THE LIVING ORACLES

After this preamble, let me begin to tackle my theme by quoting two distinguished English churchmen of the sixteenth and seventeenth centuries—Richard Hooker and John Robinson.

The judicious Hooker was not, of course, a *free* churchman, but much that he said merits serious attention for all that. Writing about the source of authority in the church in the fifth book of his *Laws of Ecclesiastical Polity*, he says:

> What Scripture doth plainly deliver, to that the first place both of credit and obedience is due; the next whereunto, is whatsoever any man can necessarily conclude, by force of Reason; after these, the voice of the Church succeedeth.[2]

John Robinson—who should perhaps be described nowadays, to avoid confusion, as John Robinson the elder—was indubitably a free churchman. I should like to quote some of his immortal words addressed to the Pilgrim Fathers at Leiden before their departure for the new world, but no one who undertakes to quote them can have any assurance that he is quoting them *verbatim*, for they have come down to us as they were summarized from memory in later years by one of his hearers, Edward Winslow. (This is a situation with which we are not unfamiliar in biblical criticism.) But here they are, as reproduced by W. H. Burgess in *John Robinson: Pastor of the Pilgrim Fathers* (London, 1920), pp. 239f.:

> He charged us, before God and his blessed angels, to follow him no farther than he followed Christ; and if God should reveal anything to us by any other instrument of his, to be as ready to receive it, as ever we were to receive any truth by his Ministry. For he was very confident that the Lord had more truth and light yet to break forth out of his holy Word.

He went on to bewail the failure of the churches of the Reformation to venture a step beyond the point to which their respective leaders—Luther and Calvin particularly—had brought them. He reminded them of that part of their church covenant whereby "we promise and covenant with God and one with another to receive whatsoever light or truth shall be made known to us from his written Word." He exhorted them to

"examine and compare and weigh" with the relevant scriptures anything that was proffered to them as Christian truth.

> "For," saith he, "it is not possible the Christian World should come so lately
> out of such thick antichristian darkness; and that full perfection of knowl-
> edge should break forth at once."[3]

To return to Hooker: when he gives reason the second place after
the authority of Scripture, he does well. If the authority of Scripture is to
be invoked and applied, Scripture must be interpreted reasonably. Reason by itself is an insufficient guide, but reason must not be decried:
where reason is expelled through the door, fanaticism comes in by the
window, and the church has suffered great harm through the irrational
use of Scripture. "I will pray with the spirit," says Paul, "and I will pray
with the understanding also"; and if the point had been put to him he
might well have added: "I will read Scripture with the spirit and I will
read it with the understanding also." For this, indeed, Old Testament
precedent could have been cited: when the book of the law was read
publicly in Jerusalem in Ezra's day, the readers "gave the sense, so that
the people understood the reading" (Neh. 8:8).

The Westminster Divines (whose heirs some of us are) professed a
different churchmanship from Hooker's, but on this they are in agreement with him. While the authority of Scripture is paramount in all
matters relating to saving faith, "there are some circumstances," they say,
"concerning the worship of God, and government of the Church, common to human actions and societies, which are to be ordered by the light
of nature and Christian prudence, according to the general rules of the
word, which are always to be observed."[4] They do not here speak
expressly of "the force of Reason," as Hooker does, but their appeal to
"the light of nature and Christian prudence" is to much the same effect.

As for "the voice of the Church," to which Hooker gives the third
place after Scripture and reason, this includes what is commonly called
tradition. On this point, Moderator, I take leave to commend the reading
and digesting of what you have written in the foreword to our Congress
handbook. You point out that, when the church as a whole, or a local and
particular church, feels the need to issue a ruling on some new and
unprecedented situation, it is prone to frame that ruling as far as possible
in accordance with the principles discernible in earlier rulings. It is not
my purpose here to deal in any detail with the problem of Scripture and
tradition, but one thing is plain: when appeal is made to the authority of
Scripture, even to the authority of *sola Scriptura* (that is, Scripture apart
from tradition), what is often meant is Scripture as traditionally interpreted—Scripture as understood in *our* tradition. I have known a new

independent congregation to be founded on the avowed basis of eschewing all tradition and relying on the guidance of Scripture alone. But what the founders meant by "Scripture alone" was "Scripture as we have learned to look at it." Very well, so long as all of them had learned to look at Scripture the same way; but when they were joined by others who had been brought up to look at Scripture differently, their basis was severely tested and became subject to predictable strains and stresses.

When we are concerned (as we are here) with Scripture in the church, Scripture considered as the standard of the church's faith, the tradition in terms of which Scripture is interpreted is inevitably ecclesiastical tradition. The possession of a common Bible is not enough if the common Bible is read through incompatible pairs of spectacles. In the second-century *Dialogue* between Justin Martyr and Trypho the Jew the fact that both parties shared a common Bible (a common Old Testament, as we should say), apart from occasional textual variants, did not help them to reach a common judgment, because they read their common Bible with irreconcilable presuppositions—Justin in the light of Christian tradition and Trypho in the light of Jewish tradition. On several individual questions of Old Testament exegesis, indeed, a modern Christian interpreter will concede that Trypho was nearer the truth than Justin; yet he will agree with Justin's main emphasis—that Christ is the fulfiller of the Old Testament revelation—while differing from him on many details of this fulfillment.

If later, at the time of the Reformation, the Reformers broke loose from medieval tradition and interpreted Scripture as accurately as they could in accordance with the grammatical and historical methods which the new learning had taught them to apply to ancient texts in general, yet in a generation or two their fresh insights had become a new tradition, as influential for the Protestant understanding of Scripture as the old tradition, revised at Trent, was for the understanding of Scripture on the Roman side of the fence. Anything which threatened to impair the authority of the new tradition was discouraged. In the first generation the editors of the Geneva Bible might cheerfully draw attention in their marginal notes to variant readings in the manuscripts, but a century later John Owen deprecated Brian Walton's collection of such variants in the apparatus to his *Biblia Sacra Polyglotta*. "We went from Rome," said Owen darkly, "under the conduct of the *purity* of the originals. I wish none have a mind to return thither under the pretence of their *corruption*."[5]

It is here that John Robinson comes in with his breath of fresh air. Scripture must not be treated as a legal document but as a living oracle. The Vincentian canon *quod ubique, quod semper, quod ab omnibus* is not to be jettisoned, but alongside it we must say *quod nusquam, quod nunquam, quod a nullo*—which is as much as to say, "What no eye has seen, nor ear heard, nor the heart of man conceived. . . ." The Lord may say something to this generation or the next from his word which no previous generation has heard him say. True, it will not conflict with what he has said to previous generations, for the Holy Ghost, as John Knox told Queen Mary, "is never contrarious to himself";[6] but faith may expect new insights for a new age.

An earlier Free Churchman than John Robinson—Henry Barrow, whose free churchmanship brought him to the gallows under the first Elizabeth in 1593—described "a true planted and rightly established church of Christ" as "a brotherhood, a communion of saints, each one of them standing in and for their Christian liberty to practice whatsoever God has commanded and revealed unto them in his holy Word."[7] But such a church, or fellowship of churches, will be prepared to accept and obey whatsoever God may yet command and reveal unto them in his holy Word, by way of that further truth and light which John Robinson expected to break forth from it.

II. WITNESS TO CHRIST

For the Christian, the nature of biblical authority is expressed with unsurpassed clarity in a passage in the Fourth Gospel where Jesus says of the Hebrew scriptures, "it is they that bear witness to me" (John 5:39). We take it for granted that the New Testament writings bear witness to Jesus; here it is affirmed—in harmony, indeed, with the consentient testimony of the New Testament—that the *Old* Testament writings bear witness to him also, although manifestly in a different way. It could be, in fact, that herein lies the essential principle of canonicity: it is their witness to Christ that brings the heterogeneous biblical documents together and gives them their unity for the life and faith of the church.

In the book to which I have already referred, Moderator, you quoted a passage from J. K. Mozley to the effect that, when the Bible is called the *record* of revelation, the word "record" is used in a deeper sense than when one speaks, for example, of a gramophone record: it includes interpretation as well as reproduction.[8] The Bible both attests and interprets the divine revelation; preeminently, it serves as witness and interpreter to that revelation as it finds its climax in Christ. In the Fourth Gospel the same Jesus who affirms that Scripture bears witness to himself makes a similar affirmation of the role of the Holy Spirit: "he will bear witness to me, . . . he will take what is mine and declare it to you" (John 15:26; 16:14f.). It is distinctively in Scripture that the Spirit bears this interpretative witness; any other form of witness he bears can be recognized as *his* witness by its consistency with his witness in Scripture.

It was their insight into this teaching that led Calvin and other Reformers to lay such stress on the inward witness of the Spirit as a corroboration of his witness in Scripture. The Westminster Confession of Faith, for example, declares that, beside and above all the other considerations which move us to "an high and reverend esteem of the holy scripture, . . . our full persuasion and assurance of the infallible truth, and divine authority thereof, is from the inward work of the Holy Spirit, bearing witness by and with the word in our hearts." The Confession envisages this ministry of witness as exercised in the hearts of individual believers, in which it acknowledges "the inward illumination of the Spirit of God to be necessary for the saving understanding of such things as are revealed in the word"; at the same time it indicates that it is exercised also in a wider setting.

> The supreme Judge by which all controversies of religion are to be determined, and all decrees of councils, opinions of ancient writers, doctrines of men, and private spirits, are to be examined and in whose sentence we are to rest, can be no other but the Holy Spirit speaking in the scripture.[9]

Certainly, if "the Holy Spirit speaking in the scripture" is to provide guidance in defining the faith, it is the church that must hear his voice. One man's faith is—one man's faith. But one Christian's faith cannot be simply one Christian's faith. When, several years ago, Professor J. V. Langmead-Casserley chose the title *No Faith of My Own* for one of his books (1950), he meant that, while his faith *was* his own, it was not exclusively his own: it was the faith of the church universal of which he was a member.

The earliest statements of this faith are preserved in the New Testament writings. If we belong to the church of the apostles, if the faith we profess is in a historical sense *Christian* faith, it must be organically related to the New Testament witness. This is a different matter from supporting each article of faith by the citation of proof-texts. The edition of the Westminster Confession which I consulted in quoting from it above is equipped with a copious apparatus of proof-text references. An examination of these in their biblical contexts shows that some of them are only remotely relevant to the statements of doctrine to which they are appended. In our use of Scripture we pay careful attention to the context—the speaker, the occasion, the persons addressed and so forth. We bear in mind the distinctive vocabularies and idioms of the various authors. We consider the particular stage in the progress of revelation to which any passage belongs; otherwise we may imitate the inconsequence of those friends who quote the pessimistic observation of Ecclesiastes, "the dead know nothing," as though it said the last word about the state of the faithful departed.[10]

The church's use of the Bible is richer and more diversified than the academic exegete's use of the Bible. The church has been using the Bible for a long time and has developed a corporate understanding of it that is not confined to any single generation—whether the apostles' generation or ours. Since the church is the family of God, the Bible is in a special sense our *family* Bible. Professor John Knox, in his *Limits of Unbelief* (1970), has compared the church's confession to a family's memory: whatever an individual member of the family may experience in the way of doubt or forgetfulness, the corporate memory of the community continues unimpaired. Thus the living community preserves the memory not only of Jesus' existence but of his character, and this, says Professor Knox, is as trustworthy evidence as his own personal memory of his parents is of *their* existence and character.[11] Some of you may feel that it would be good if this argument could be sustained, but may wonder if a communal memory stretching back over so many generations can have the same probative force as a memory going back for one generation only. Paul Tillich criticized the argument because it denies to the historian the jurisdiction which is properly his. Rudolf Bultmann agreed that Tillich's criticism was valid "except in the moment of faith"—but in this qualification Professor Knox discerns the primary fault in Professor Bultmann's position, because its phrasing implies the faith of an individual, not of a community, and even so only a single instance of that individual's experience. Professor Knox himself would replace "the moment of faith" by "the life of the church."[12]

The relevance of the New Testament writings to Professor Knox's argument is that they are the earliest surviving expression of the church's corporate memory.

III. THE VOICE OF THE SPIRIT

In this earliest surviving expression of the church's corporate memory, then, what are the dominant features—the features which should be dominant in a biblically based confession of our faith today? In answering this question I find much help in a work by a great contemporary English Free Churchman.

When Dr. Norman Snaith delivered his Fernley-Hartley Lecture in 1944, on *The Distinctive Ideas of the Old Testament*, he found that the distinctive ideas were those aspects of the prophetic message which were taken up and brought to perfection in the New Testament, not least in Paul's teaching about justification by faith, while "the true development from the Pauline theology is to be found in Luther and John Wesley."[13] Some people might regard it as a surprising coincidence that the finest flowering of the biblical revelation should be seen in that tradition of which Dr. Snaith himself was for long so worthy and devoted an exponent. I believe that he established his case, especially if the Bible is viewed as a basis for Christian doctrine. If Christian doctrine is our concern, its basis is most likely to be found in that which (in Luther's phrase) "urges Christ" on the reader and hearer.

Dr. Snaith was no undiscriminating student of Scripture. As he saw it, this revelation of God's pardoning grace in the Hebrew Bible is bound in a hard, iron binding of "separation," which is done away with in Christ. Perhaps it was providential that the revelation should be protected in this way until the fulfillment came and the middle wall of partition could be demolished.

That the fulfillment came with the ministry of Jesus is, as we have seen, the testimony of the New Testament and of subsequent Christian tradition: it finds expression in the words of Jesus himself, established by the strictest criteria of multiple attestation. But when we examine the gospel records closely we can discern which particular strands of Old Testament religion Jesus claimed to fulfill, and it is then difficult to disagree with Dr. Snaith's thesis that Jesus stood in the tradition of the great prophets of Israel and crowned it with his own life and teaching, death and exaltation. The use of the *Old* Testament for the establishment of Christian doctrine will be, then, as it was in the apostolic age, the use of the Old Testament as interpreted and fulfilled by Christ. (That this use does not always coincide with the historico-critical exegesis of the Old Testament is something for which Dr. Snaith himself might be cited as a witness.) And when we examine the central teaching of the great New Testament theologians—Paul, the fourth Evangelist, the writer to the Hebrews—we find that the same mainstream flows through their writings: the message of the prophets embodied and brought to perfection in Jesus.

This onward-moving stream of evangelical interpretation—God forbid that the adjective "evangelical" should be used in a party sense!—makes an essential contribution to what Professor Knox calls the church's family memory. The church's family memory includes also the corporate understanding of Scripture which has grown up over the centuries. To quote now a scholar from another Christian tradition than Professor Knox and Dr. Snaith, Father Y.M.-J. Congar describes this corporate understanding as a *thésaurisation* or constant accrual of meditation on the text of

Scripture from one generation to another, "the living continuity of faith quickening the people of God."[14] We may think of the special significance which Psalm 46, paraphrased as *Ein' feste Burg*, has acquired in the Lutheran tradition, or of the special place occupied in English folk-memory by Isaac Watts's version of Psalm 90: "O God, our help in ages past." But such interpretation and application of Scripture, even if it accrues at compound interest, cannot get more out of the text than what is there already—implicitly, at least. When, in William Cowper's words,

> The Spirit breathes upon the word
> And brings the truth to sight—

this truth must in some valid sense be antecedently present in the word.

The living tradition, the continuity of Christian existence and witness, is indispensable. Without it, the interpretation of Scripture would lose its context. Suppose the church had been wiped out in the last imperial persecution about the beginning of the fourth century and all her scriptures had been lost, to be rediscovered in our day like the Dead Sea Scrolls, what would their effect be? Would their witness prove even so to be God's power for salvation, as we know it to be in our experience, or would the scriptures, like the scrolls, be little more than an archaeological curiosity and a subject for historical debate? It is a question worth pondering.

On the other hand, the living tradition without the constant corrective of Scripture, without the possibility of "reformation according to the Word of God," might have developed in such a way as to be distorted beyond recognition, if it had not slowly faded and died.

The interaction between the living tradition and the text of Scripture is interestingly discussed in the Vatican II *Constitution on Divine Revelation*, not least in Chapter VI, "Sacred Scripture in the Life of the Church" (section 24):

> Sacred theology rests on the written word of God, together with sacred tradition, as its primary and perpetual foundation. By scrutinizing in the light of faith all truth stored up in the mystery of Christ, theology is most powerfully strengthened and constantly rejuvenated by that word. For the sacred scriptures contain the word of God and, since they are inspired, really *are* the word of God; and so the study of the sacred page is, as it were, the soul of sacred theology.[15]

A higher critic, analyzing this quotation, might be pardoned for concluding that the passage was composed by a biblicist, and that the phrase "together with sacred tradition" was inserted in the first sentence by a redactor, for the reassurance of more conservative Catholics.

IV. THE WORD OF AUTHORITY TODAY

But let us come home to current trends in western Protestantism. In an article in the *Journal of Ecumenical Studies* for Spring 1971, on "The Influence of Ecumenical Developments on New Testament Teaching," Dr. Paul S. Minear commented on a disquieting feature of Christian concern today: "on virtually every controverted issue," he says, "appeals are made to Christ as Lord of the Church, but almost never does such an appeal involve a sustained reasoned study of his teachings or example. There are, of course, many kinds of docetism, but the kind most widely current today is the partisan claim that Christ is a protagonist for some contemporary messianism without any initial effort to define his own historical message and mission by reference to the Gospel sources."[16]

You may think that Dr. Minear's complaint is exaggerated, or you may suspect that it is more applicable to his American environment than it is to ours. But we must all be aware of one aspect of the tendency to which he draws attention—that relating to the use of violence as a means of liberation. The issue is not whether the use of violence to such an end is right or wrong, but whether or not it can be supported by the teaching and example of Jesus. As a practitioner of Gospel criticism I am bound to say that it cannot be so supported: quite the contrary. The proper course, then, for Christians who counsel the use of violence is to say: "We recognize that our Lord repudiated the use of violence; *nevertheless*, we believe that in this situation it is the proper course to adopt." There is nothing unfamiliar about this argument; many Christians adopted it during World War II. What is not permissible is to obfuscate the Gospel evidence and pretend that it is other than it really is.

More generally; whereas the Faith and Order Commission in its early days acknowledged the primacy of the biblical basis for the churches' belief and practice—an acknowledgment reflected in the addition of the words "according to the scriptures" to the definition of the World Council of Churches at the New Delhi Assembly of 1961—a failure of nerve in this regard is registered in the Louvain Faith and Order Report of 1971: because "in the ecumenical movement a certain perplexity has arisen over the Bible" and its application to specific problems, "the tendency has been more and more to abandon the appeal to biblical grounds altogether."[17] The effect of this tendency has been particularly evident in one realm where Christians might have been expected to be of the same mind—the church's mandate to evangelize the world.

The application of biblical principles to the complicated issues of the world today is no easy matter, but what norm is to regulate our thinking and action as Christian churches or councils of churches if the normative function of Scripture receives at best our lip-service? Let us not be put off by the argument that the witness of the Bible in general, or of the New Testament in particular, is so ambiguous or diverse. Amid all the admitted diversity there is, as I have maintained, an essential unity of witness to Christ. Jesus Christ is Lord; in him God's pardoning grace has come near to the world of mankind. In him God's loving purpose was conceived before the universe came into being; in him that purpose was realized when, in the fullness of time, he accomplished his redeeming and reconciling work; in him the same purpose will be consummated. He who is our righteousness and our peace is also our hope; and the New Testament knows no other Christ.

Christianity ceases to be Christianity if it does not remain founded on the person, the teaching and the saving work of this Christ, crucified Savior and risen Lord; and to his person, teaching and saving work the New Testament writings constitute our unique source of testimony. To sit loose to Scripture is thus to sit loose to the Christ to whom it bears witness, and to sit loose to him is to relax our Christian faith and life.

Of the New Testament writings as a whole in the church today we may say, as Hans Lietzmann said more especially of the four Gospels in the early church, that "the reference to their apostolic authority, which can only appear to us as a reminder of sound historical bases, had the deeper meaning that this particular tradition of Jesus—and this alone— had been established and guaranteed by the Holy Spirit working authoritatively in the Church."[18] History has preserved no alternative to "this particular tradition."[19] Whatever distinct strands of varying traditions may be recognized within "this particular tradition," it is its unity that has been most evident to the corporate consciousness of the church.

In these writings we have the foundation documents, the title deeds, the charter of our faith. (If the precise relation of the charter to the faith has to be determined, perhaps after all you will decide to treat the critic and exegete as a consultant.) But this is far from imprisoning the free Spirit within a closed collection of books. Repeatedly, new liberating movements of this Spirit have been launched by a rediscovery of the living power which resides in these writings. They are not the prison-house but the power-house of the Spirit. The New Testament, in Adolf Deissmann's words, "is not one of the paralysing and enslaving forces of the past, but is full of eternal and present strength to make strong and to make free."[20]

End Notes

NOTES TO CHAPTER 1

1. See L. J. Macfarlane, *William Elphinstone and the Kingdom of Scotland 1431-1514* (Aberdeen, 1985), pp. 324-326; G. P. Edwards, "Aberdeen and its Classical Tradition," *Aberdeen University Review* No. 176 (Autumn 1986), pp. 410-426. Even before King's College received its charter in 1505, Hector Boece had probably been teaching Latin and conducting university examinations in Aberdeen since 1497. When this address was delivered, I could not have foreseen, nor would I have believed it possible, that in November 1987 the authorities of Aberdeen University would so repudiate their noble heritage as to decree the axing of the Department of Classics—a sacrifice on the altar of cost-effectiveness.

2. F. Lyall, "Roman Law in the Writings of Paul—The Slave and the Freedman," *NTS* 17 (1970-71), pp. 73-79, later reprinted in his *Slaves, Citizens, Sons: Legal Metaphors in the Epistles* (Grand Rapids, 1984), pp. 27-46.

3. A. Souter, *The Earliest Latin Commentaries on the Epistles of St. Paul* (Oxford, 1927), p. 139.

4. *Ibid.*, p. 6.

5. *Ibid.*, p. 3.

6. W. M. Ramsay, *The Bearing of Recent Discovery on the Trustworthiness of the New Testament* (London, 1915), p. 16.

7. *Ibid.*, p. 30.

8. *The Church in the Roman Empire* (London, ⁴1896), p. xiii.

9. Cf. *The Bearing of Recent Discovery* . . . , pp. 386f., also 193; *Pictures of the Apostolic Church* (London, 1910), pp. 180f.

10. Prepared for publication by his former pupil J.G.C. Anderson, who also contributed the entry under Ramsay's name to the *Dictionary of National Biography 1931-40* (London, 1949), pp. 727f. For judicious appraisals of Ramsay's achievement see W. F. Howard, *The Romance of New Testament Scholarship* (London, 1949), pp. 138-155; W. W. Gasque, *Sir William M. Ramsay: Archaeologist and New Testament Scholar* (Grand Rapids, 1966).

11. Cf. I. H. Marshall, "Palestinian and Hellenistic Christianity: Some Critical Comments," *NTS* 19 (1972-73), pp. 271-287.

12. Cf. R. H. Gundry, "The Language Milieu of First-Century Palestine," *JBL* 83 (1964), pp. 404-408; J. N. Sevenster, *Do You Know Greek?* (Leiden, 1968).

13. J. B. Skemp, *The Greeks and the Gospel* (London, 1964), pp. 3-24.

14. Herodotus, *Hist.* 7.143 *et passim*.

15. Thucydides, *Hist.* 1.89-93, 135-38.

16. He will, for example, apply himself to such a detail as the sorting out of the conflicting evidence of Strabo (*Geog.* 10.1.2) and Dio Chrysostom (*Orat.* 7.2) on the precise location of the "Hollows of Euboea" which figure in Herodotus' narrative of events leading up to the encounter at Salamis (*Hist.* 8.13f.); cf. G. C. Richards, "The Hollows of Euboea," *Classical Review* 44 (1930), pp. 61f.

17. Aeschylus, *Persae* 249-432.

18. D. E. Nineham, "Eye-witness Testimony and the Gospel Tradition," *JTS* n.s. 11 (1960), pp. 253-264, especially 260.

19. Among older writers, T. Mommsen, *Römisches Staatsrecht* (Leipzig, 1876-77) and *Römisches Strafrecht* (Leipzig, 1899), and L. Mitteis, *Reichsrecht und Volksrecht* (Leipzig, 1891), provide useful background information in this area; more recent works of similar relevance are A. H. M. Jones, *Studies in Roman Government and Law* (Oxford, 1960), A. N. Sherwin-White, *Roman Society and Roman Law in the New Testament* (Oxford, 1963), and D. Nörr, *Imperium und Polis in der hohen Prinzipatszeit* (Munich, 1966).

20. Some unfashionable reflections on the common estimate of Thucydides as a "scientific" historian are offered by M. I. Finley, *Ancient History: Evidence and Models* (London, 1985).

21. *Hist.* 1.22.4 (κτῆμα ἐς αἰεί).

22. F. M. Cornford, *Thucydides Mythistoricus* (London, 1907), p. viii.

23. *Ibid.*, p. x.

24. *Ibid.*, pp. ixf.

25. The Melian episode (5.84-116) is immediately followed by the Athenian plan to invade and conquer Sicily (6.1ff.).

26. *Hist.* 2.2.1.

27. F. F. Bruce, *The Acts of the Apostles* (London, 1951), revised edition (Grand Rapids, 1990).

28. Lord Hewart, "Presidential Address," *Proceedings of the Classical Association* 24 (1927), p. 21.

29. *Handcommentar zum Neuen Testament*, I/2 (Freiburg i/B, 1889), p. 421; cf. J. Smith, *The Voyage and Shipwreck of St. Paul* (London, ⁴1880); H. Balmer, *Die Romfahrt des Apostels Paulus und die Seefahrtskunde im römischen Kaiseralter* (Bern, 1905); W. Stammler, *Apostelgeschichte 27 in nautischer Beleuchtung* (Berlin, 1931).

30. Thucydides, *Hist.* 1.22.1 (see p. 166 and p. 311, n.1).

31. Polybius, *History* 2.56.10-12; cf. Dionysius of Halicarnassus, *De Thucydide* 34.

32. On the speeches in Acts in general see M. Wilcox, "A Foreword to the Study of the Speeches in Acts," *Christianity, Judaism and Other Greco-Roman Cults* (Studies for Morton Smith at Sixty), ed. J. Neusner, I, *New Testament* (Leiden, 1975), pp. 206-225.

33. Aeschylus, *Eumenides* 647f. (words spoken by Apollo at the institution of the Areopagus Court by Athene):

ἀνδρὸς δ' ἐπειδὰν αἷμ' ἀνασπάσῃ κόνις
ἅπαξ θανόντος οὔτις ἔστ' ἀνάστασις.

34. *The Beginnings of Christianity,* ed. F. J. F. Jackson and K. Lake, I/5 (London, 1933), p. 406.

35. E. Meyer, *Ursprung und Anfänge des Christentums,* III (Stuttgart/Berlin, 1923), p. 105.

36. *Ibid.,* p. 92.

37. Thus P. Vielhauer criticized E. Meyer because he "approaches Acts with the presuppositions of a historian of antiquity and treats it with the greatest confidence," and so "misunderstands the nature of its accounts and the way in which they are connected" ("On the 'Paulinism' of Acts" [1950-51], E.T. in *Studies in Luke-Acts,* ed. L. E. Keck and J. L. Martyn [Nashville/New York, 1966], p. 50, n. 37). For later approaches to Acts from the perspective of ancient historiography see E. Plümacher, *Lukas als hellenistischer Schriftsteller: Studien zur Apostelgeschichte,* SUNT 9 (Göttingen, 1972); C. J. Hemer, *The Book of Acts in the Setting of Hellenistic History,* WUNT (Tübingen, 1989).

38. Wilamowitz could not be included among "the classicists" referred to by Cadbury; he thought that the religious sentiment of the *Areopagitica* lay closer to the religious sentiment of his day (even among theologians) than Paul himself did.

39. U. von Wilamowitz-Moellendorff, *Die griechische Literatur des Altertums = Die Kultur der Gegenwart,* ed. P. Hinneberg, I/8 (Berlin/Leipzig, ³1912), p. 232.

40. Cf. 2 Cor. 11:22.

41. Cf. H. Chadwick, "St Paul and Philo of Alexandria," *BJRL* 48 (1965-66), pp. 286-307.

42. Cf. Acts 22:3, taking ἀνατεθραμμένος with ἐν τῇ πόλει ταύτῃ. See also W. C. van Unnik, *Tarsus or Jerusalem: The City of Paul's Youth,* E.T. (London, 1962).

43. E. A. Judge, "St. Paul and Classical Society," *Jahrbuch für Antike und Christentum* 15 (1972), p. 21.

44. Cf. also N. Hugedé, *Saint Paul et la culture grecque* (Geneva, 1966).

45. Cf. A. H. M. Jones, *The Greek City from Alexander to Justinian* (Oxford, 1940), and *Cities of the Eastern Roman Provinces* (Oxford, ²1971); L. Robert, *Villes d'Asie Mineure* (Paris, ²1962).

46. A study of one particular group of cities in a defined area is presented by B. Levick, *Roman Colonies in Southern Asia Minor* (Oxford, 1967).

47. See now J. E. Stambaugh and D. L. Balch, *The New Testament in its Social Environment* (Philadelphia, 1986); W. A. Meeks, *The Moral World of the First Christians* (Philadelphia, 1986).

48. Cf. L. Bieler, *Theios Anēr: Das Bild des "göttlichen Menschen" in Spätantike und Frühchristentum* (Darmstadt, 1967); C. R. Holladay, *Theios Anēr in Hellenistic Judaism,* SBLDS 40 (Missoula, MT, 1977).

49. A phrase borrowed from the title of A. R. Johnson, *The Vitality of the Individual in the Thought of Ancient Israel* (Cardiff, 1949).

50. J. B. Skemp, *The Greeks and the Gospel,* p. 82.

51. Virgil, *Aeneid* 2.49 (see p. 95 and p. 297, n. 60).

52. John 12:32.

53. For a detailed and lively survey of the interaction between classical and New Testament studies see F. W. Danker, *A Century of Greco-Roman Philology: Featuring the American Philological Association and the Society of Biblical Literature,* SBL Centennial Publications (Atlanta, 1988).

NOTES TO CHAPTER 2

1. Cf. *Apion* 1.134-141.

2. Megasthenes, Diocles, Philostratus; cf. *Apion* 1.144.

3. Insofar as Josephus's narrative can be compared with the two ancient Greek versions of Daniel, it has closer affinities with the LXX than with the Theodotionic text. Thus Josephus agrees with Dan. 1:12 LXX in translating *zērō'îm* by ὄσπρια (*Ant.* 10.190), as against the Theodotionic σπέρματα, and with Dan. 4:13 (16) LXX in the rendering ἐπτὰ ἔτη (*Ant.* 10.216f.) where Theodotion adheres to the Aramaic wording with ἐπτὰ καιροί. He is closer to Dan. 8:5 LXX (ἀπὸ δυσμῶν) with his ἀπὸ τῆς δύσεως (*Ant.* 10.209; cf. εἰς τὴν δύσιν, § 270) than to Theodotion's ἀπὸ λιβός. But no great significance attaches to these coincidences; in other places Josephus's wording agrees with Theodotion's against LXX, e.g., in the transcription of the writing on the wall at Belshazzar's feast.

4. Herodotus, *Hist.* 1.185-187.

5. Xenophon, *Cyrop.* 1.5.2, etc.

6. At Ecbatana (mod. Hamadan) is the reputed tomb of Esther and Mordecai, but this appears to be later than Josephus's time.

7. Perhaps a variant reading of the 1290 days of Dan. 12:11, or a conflation in memory of these 1290 days with the 1260 days implied in Dan. 7:25; 9:27. Cf. p. 285, n. 27.

8. The last clause, "how Jerusalem would be captured by them and the city laid waste," is not found in the MSS. of Josephus but is included in Chrysostom's excerpt in *Adv. Iudaeos* 5.8. It certainly corresponds to Josephus's belief.

9. V. Tcherikover, *Hellenistic Civilization and the Jews* (Philadelphia, 1959), p. 420. He discusses the significance of this tale preserved by Josephus and the similar one preserved in *Megillath Ta'anith* (*op. cit.*, pp. 42-48).

10. By W. E. Vine (London, *c.* 1925). Cf. P. O. Ruoff, *W. E. Vine: His Life and Ministry* (London, 1951), p. 78.

11. That the second year of Darius I is meant seems plain from the mention of Haggai, whose prophetic ministry belongs to that year (Hag. 1:1; 2:1, 10), as Josephus recognizes (*Ant.* 11.96, 106); although elsewhere Josephus distinguishes between the first foundation of the Second Temple in the second year of Cyrus and its resumption in the second year of Darius (*Apion* 1.154; *Ant.* 11.78). (According to the manuscript tradition of Josephus he calls Artaxerxes I Cyrus in *Ant.* 11.184, but here Gutschmid's emendation of 'Ασύηρον for Κῦρον should perhaps be accepted.) In *Ant.* 20.234 Josephus reckons 414 years from the edict of Cyrus to the accession of Antiochus V (164 B.C.)—an error of 40 years.

12. In *BJ* 1.70 Aristobulus's accession is dated 471 years and 3 months after the return from exile; the later calculation in *Ant.* 13.301 is probably a correction of this figure. If the figure given in *BJ* 1.70 was based on the reckoning of the seventy heptads from the edict of Cyrus, the seventieth heptad would end in 85 B.C., so that Jannaeus's vengeance on the leaders of the revolt against him would fall "in the midst of the week." For a later reckoning (that of Hippolytus?) by which the seventy heptads terminated with Alexander Jannaeus, see Eusebius, *Dem. Ev.* 8.2.

13. This is equivalent to 62 heptads (cf. Dan. 9:25b, 26)—by a mere coincidence.

14. M. Anstey, *The Romance of Bible Chronology* (London, 1913), vol. 1, pp. 275ff., on the basis of an *a priori* interpretation of the seventy heptads, reduces the interval

between Cyrus and Alexander by over 80 years, dating Cyrus's decree for the rebuilding of the temple in 453 B.C. By a similar reckoning P. Mauro, *The Chronology of the Bible* (Boston, Mass., 1922), pp. 99ff., dates Cyrus's decree in 457 B.C.

15. So also in TB *Arakhin* 12*b* the Second Temple is said to have stood for 420 years.

16. In *Ant.* 12.413f. the people give the high-priesthood to Judas after the death of Alcimus; in *Ant.* 12.434 Judas "had held the high-priesthood for three years when he died."

17. A. Ehrhardt, *The Apostolic Succession* (London, 1953), p. 50. I am greatly indebted to this section of Ehrhardt's book. Cf. also G. R. Driver, "Sacred Numbers and Round Figures," in *Promise and Fulfilment,* ed. F. F. Bruce (Edinburgh, 1963), pp. 62-90.

18. Usually interpreted of the murder of Onias III in 171 B.C.

19. In Ezek. 41:21 LXX "the holy place and the sanctuary were open four-square," i.e., "on four sides" (τετράγωνα, Heb. *rᵉḇûʿāh*); but there is no question of the destruction of *Ezekiel's* temple, any more than of the city foursquare of Rev. 21:16 (ἡ πόλις τετράγωνος κεῖται—the only NT occurrence of the adjective). (According to Josephus, *Ant.* 8.96, the court of Solomon's temple corresponding to the Court of the Israelites in Herod's temple was built "in the form of a quadrangle," ἐν τετραγώνου σχήματι.)

20. Heb. *rᵉḥōḇ wᵉḥārûṣ;* that *ḥārûṣ* means "water-channel" or "conduit" is now confirmed by the appearance of the word in 3 Q 15, col. 5.8; cf. J. M. Allegro, *The Treasure of the Copper Scroll* (New York, 1960), pp. 41, 148.

21. The Greek equivalents are LXX πλάτος and Theod. πλατεῖα ("broadway"); neither suggests τετράγωνος.

22. Dr. M. Wallenstein and Dr. M. Gertner have kindly supplied me with valuable evidence on this point.

23. Thackeray compares *Or. Sib.* 4.115-129, a passage which is probably too late (*c.* A.D. 80) to have served as a source for *BJ;* if it is not entirely a *vaticinium ex eventu* it may have a common source with Josephus.

24. Reading ἀρνῶν for ἀνδρῶν of the MSS.

25. Cf. 1Q p Hab., col. 6.2-5, for the practice of the Kittiʾim of sacrificing to their standards.

26. Cf. *BJ* 2.169-174; *Ant.* 18.55-59.

27. The intervals indicated in Dan. 7:25 (with 9:27); 12:11 and 12:12 respectively for the suspension of the daily burnt-offering and establishment of the abomination of desolation. Cf. p. 284, n. 7 above.

28. The Slavonic version adds: "Some understood that this meant Herod; others, the crucified miracle-worker Jesus; others again, Vespasian." Compare the astrological assurances given to Nero that, if he were compelled to leave Rome, he would find another throne in the east, some even specifying Jerusalem (Suetonius, *Nero* 40).

29. KJV/AV, followed by ASV (1901), departs from the Masoretic punctuation, which is followed by RV and RSV.

30. Cf. 1Q M, col. 11.6; CD 7.19-21; 4 Q *Testimonia* 9-13.

31. In TB *Yoma* 39*b* he prophesies the destruction of the temple on the basis of Zech. 11:1.

32. 1Q p Hab., col. 7.1-4.

33. Cf. Luke 20:18*b*.

NOTES TO CHAPTER 3

1. See P. R. Davies, *Qumrān* (Grand Rapids, 1983); *Behind the Essenes: History and Ideology in the Dead Sea Scrolls* (Atlanta, 1987).

2. Heb. *môrēh ṣedeq*, derived perhaps from Hosea 10:12 or Joel 2:23 (AV/KJV margin, "he hath given you a teacher of righteousness"); on the sense of the title at Qumran see J. Weingreen, *From Bible to Mishna* (Manchester, 1976), pp. 100-114.

3. See my *Second Thoughts on the Dead Sea Scrolls* (Exeter, [3]1966). There is no better or more up-to-date introduction to the subject than G. Vermes, *The Dead Sea Scrolls: Qumran in Perspective* (London, [2]1982). See also E. Schürer, *History of the Jewish People in the Age of Jesus Christ*, new edition, III/1 (Edinburgh, 1986), pp. 380-469, and (for a provisional reconstruction of the history which refuses to go beyond the available evidence) P. R. Callaway, *The History of the Qumran Community: An Investigation*, Journal for the Study of the Pseudepigrapha Suppl. 3 (Sheffield, 1988).

4. In the conventional abbreviations for Qumran manuscripts 1Q denotes Cave 1 at Qumran, 2Q Cave 2 at Qumran, and so forth.

5. This Psalms scroll includes the Hebrew text of Ps. 151 (previously known in Greek from the Septuagint), and of three apocryphal psalms previously known in the Syriac version, with two or three other poetical compositions; see J. A. Sanders (ed.), *The Psalms Scroll of Qumran Cave 11, DJD* 4 (Oxford, 1965).

6. See p. 41.

7. Cf. H. M. Orlinsky, "Qumran and the Present State of Old Testament Studies: The Septuagint Text," *JBL* 78 (1959), pp. 26-33. The most significant Greek Old Testament find in the Dead Sea region has been made not at Qumran but in the Ḥever (Ḥabra) ravine, which was occupied at the time of the second Jewish revolt (A.D. 132-135). This find is a fragmentary copy of a Greek version of the Twelve Prophets, whose text is in agreement with that used by Justin and has been tentatively identified with Origen's *Quinta;* cf. now E. Tov and R. A. Kraft (eds.), *The Seiyâl Collection, I: The Greek Minor Prophets Scroll from Naḥal Ḥever, DJD* 8 (1990).

8. TB *Sanhedrin* 115a.

9. *Ten Years of Discovery in the Wilderness of Judaea,* E.T., SBT 26 (London, 1959), p. 31.

10. *NTS* 3 (1956-57), p. 313 (in the final paragraph of an article, "The Recovery of the Language of Jesus," pp. 305-313). See also G. Vermes, *The Dead Sea Scrolls in English* (Sheffield, [3]1988), p. 252: "It is a mixture of Targum, Midrash, re-written Bible and autobiography."

11. The best translation of the principal Qumran documents, apart from biblical texts and versions, is G. Vermes, *The Dead Sea Scrolls in English* (Sheffield, [3]1988).

12. See P. R. Davies, *The Damascus Covenant,* JSOT Suppl 25 (Sheffield, 1983).

13. See Y. Yadin, *The Scroll of the War of the Sons of Light against the Sons of Darkness,* E.T. (Oxford, 1962).

14. First edited by Y. Yadin, *The Temple Scroll,* 3 vols. (Jerusalem, 1983). For a useful introduction, translation and commentary see J. Maier, *The Temple Scroll,* JSOT Suppl 34 (Sheffield, 1985).

15. It has indeed been held that "the record of the prophet's work closes with the triumphant strains of the thirty-third chapter" (W. R. Smith, *The Prophets of Israel* [Edinburgh, 1882], p. 354), the oracles from Isa. 34 onwards being the work of later

prophets; but it would be precarious to relate this critical judgment to the scribal space between chapters 33 and 34 of 1Q Isaᵃ.

16. *The Servant of the Lord* (London, 1911).

17. *Das Buch Jesaia übersetzt und erklärt*, HKAT (Göttingen, ⁴1922).

18. Cf. A. Dupont-Sommer, *The Dead Sea Scrolls*, E.T. (Oxford, 1952), p. 96.

19. Cf. P. W. Skehan, "The Qumran Manuscripts and Textual Criticism," VTSuppl 4 (Leiden, 1957), pp. 148-160; H. M. Orlinsky, "The Textual Criticism of the Old Testament," in *The Bible and the Ancient Near East: Essays in Honor of W. F. Albright*, ed. G. E. Wright (London, 1961), pp. 113-132.

20. Caution must be exercised in distinguishing these lines of transmission and relating the Qumran biblical texts to one or another. There are features of affinity between the "Egyptian" and "Palestinian" lines which mark them off from the "Babylonian" line. Some of the Qumran biblical texts are of "mixed" type, and some may belong to another line of transmission than the three mentioned here. The situation is not much less fluid in 1989 than it was when this address was delivered thirty years ago.

21. Cf. P. W. Skehan, "Qumran and the Present State of Old Testament Textual Studies: The Masoretic Text," *JBL* 78 (1959), pp. 21-25.

22. These fragmentary exceptions are portions of Hebrew Scripture, of the sixth century A.D. and later, found towards the end of last century in the genizah of the ancient synagogue in Old Cairo.

23. *The Cairo Geniza* (Oxford, 1947), p. 148.

24. Cf. F. G. Kenyon, *Our Bible and the Ancient Manuscripts* (London, 1939), p. 48.

25. See F. M. Cross, *The Ancient Library of Qumran and Modern Biblical Studies* (Garden City, N.Y., ²1961; Grand Rapids, MI, ³1980); S. Talmon, "The Old Testament Text," in *Cambridge History of the Bible*, I, ed. P. R. Ackroyd and C. F. Evans (Cambridge, 1970), pp. 159-199; F. M. Cross and S. Talmon (ed.), *Qumran and the History of the Biblical Text* (Cambridge, 1975).

26. Cf. M. Burrows, *The Dead Sea Scrolls* (New York, 1955), pp. 304-311.

26a. New RSV (1990): "Out of his anguish he shall see light."

27. Cf. J. Ziegler, "Die Vorlage der Isaias-Septuaginta (LXX) und die erste Isaias-Rolle von Qumran (1Q Isᵃ)," *JBL* 78 (1959), 34-59.

28. So RSV on the basis of the Greek version; 4Q Dt�q was not known when the RSV was made. MT agrees with Exod. 1:5 MT: if the number of the "children of Israel" who went down into Egypt was 70, their number corresponds to that of the nations of the earth, as listed in Gen. 10:2-32. But if the "children of Israel" were 75 in all, then the statement in Deut. 32:8 MT is inappropriate, whereas no conflict arises with the reading "sons (angels) of God" (4Q Dt�q and LXX). See G. Vermes, *The Dead Sea Scrolls: Qumran in Perspective*, pp. 204f.

29. Skehan, "Qumran and the Present State of Old Testament Studies: The Masoretic Text," p. 22.

30. Ibid., p. 24.

31. First published by J. M. Allegro, "Messianic References in Qumran Litera-ture," *JBL* 75 (1956), pp. 174-187 (especially 182-187). At an early stage in the study of the scrolls J. M. Allegro earned the gratitude of scholars for his prompt publication of several texts well in advance of their official publication in *DJD*.

32. *Ten Years of Discovery . . .* , pp. 25f.

33. For example, Hab. 1:17 MT reads "Is he then to keep on emptying his net?" (RSV), but for *ḥermô* ("his net") the text used in the Qumran *pesher* on Habakkuk reads *ḥrbw* ("his sword," to be vocalized *ḥarbô*), and this reading underlies NEB "Are they then to unsheathe the sword every day?"

34. No trace has been found of the "Parables of Enoch," which include the much canvassed "Son of Man" passages (1 Enoch 37–71). This, says Milik, "can scarcely be the work of chance" (*Ten Years of Discovery . . .* , p. 33), concluding that the "Parables" belong to a later period than that of the Qumran literature. This conclusion is probably justified, although later, in his edition of the Enoch fragments from Qumran, *The Books of Enoch* (Oxford, 1976), he has argued for an improbably late date for the "Parables."

35. Dupont-Sommer concludes that the Qumran community acknowledged a more comprehensive Old Testament canon than the rabbis, and finds it significant that the early Christians did the same (*The Essene Writings from Qumran*, E.T. [Oxford, 1961], pp. 297f.).

36. Cf. TB *Megillah* 7a; *Sanhedrin* 110b.

37. It is omitted from the list of OT books published by Melito of Sardis (*c.* A.D. 170); and it is reckoned as deuterocanonical, along with Wisdom, Ecclesiasticus, Judith and Tobit, by Athanasius (A.D. 367).

38. F. M. Cross, discussing the "proto-Masoretic tradition" of the Qumran manuscripts of Daniel, concludes "that the extraordinarily free treatment of Daniel at Qumran in at least four different copies strongly suggests its noncanonical status" ("Qumran Cave 1," *JBL* 75 [1956], p. 123). D. Barthélemy (in *Discoveries in the Judaean Desert*, I [1955], pp. 150f.) adds the following considerations against the canonical recognition of Daniel at Qumran: (a) all the biblical manuscripts from Cave 1 whose format can be determined have columns whose height is twice their breadth, whereas 1Q Dan^a has columns of roughly equal length and breadth; (b) in Cave 6 a papyrus copy of Daniel was found, whereas no other papyrus fragment from Cave 4 or Cave 6 contains a canonical book in its original language. None of these arguments strikes one as being particularly strong. In any case, since Barthélemy wrote this, a papyrus copy of Kings (an undoubtedly canonical work) has been identified from Cave 4. And now that the full text of 4Q *Florilegium* (4Q 174) has been shown to contain a quotation of Dan. 12:10 and 11:32, said to be "written in the book of Daniel the prophet" (cf. Matt. 24:15), all doubt about the canonical status of Daniel at Qumran is at an end (*DJD* 5 [Oxford, 1968], pp. 53-57). See now E. Ulrich, "Daniel Manuscripts from Qumran," *BASOR* 268 (1987), pp. 17-37; 274 (1989), pp. 3-26.

39. Cf. further additions in Josephus, *Ant.* 10.260f., 264f.

40. C. H. H. Wright, *An Introduction to the Old Testament* (London, 1891), pp. 193f.

41. Milik (*Ten Years of Discovery . . .* , p. 37) expresses the opinion that this account, in an oral or written form, seems to have been the source of Dan. 4: Nabonidus, of course, was the father of Belshazzar, and it is the father of Belshazzar (albeit named Nebuchadnezzar) to whom the seven years of madness are ascribed in Dan. 5:20f. Cf. D. N. Freedman, "The Prayer of Nabonidus," *BASOR* 145 (February 1957), pp. 31f.

42. Among several points of interest in this cycle is the occurrence of the name *blkrws*, i.e. Balakros, the full form of which Balas (Alexander Balas) is a hypocoristic (*balakros* is an adjective meaning "bald," the Macedonian equivalent of the general Greek *phalakros*). Fragments of other proper names survive in the same context, where it is said that ". . . *rhws*, son of . . . *ws*, [reigned . .] years"—possibly "Demetrius, son of Demetrius" (1 Macc. 10:67).

43. I have dealt with this subject more fully in *Biblical Exegesis in the Qumran Texts* (London, 1960).

44. The revelation, that is to say, is given in two stages: first the "mystery" *(rāz)* is communicated to the prophet, but it remains a mystery until the "interpretation" *(pesher)* is communicated to the Teacher, and through him to his followers. Members of the community therefore praise God in the *Hôḏāyôt* that he has made known to them his wonderful mysteries (cf. Mark 4:11f.; 1 Peter 1:10-12). We may compare how, in the book of Daniel, part of a divine revelation is conveyed as a "mystery," as in Nebuchadnezzar's dreams or the writing on the wall at Belshazzar's feast; not until the other part of the revelation is conveyed as "interpretation" to Daniel, and declared by him, is the revelation completed and understood.

45. Cf. "The Dead Sea Habakkuk Scroll," *Annual of the Leeds University Oriental Society* 1 (1958-59), pp. 5-14.

46. Further details of this war are given in the *Rule of War* (1QM).

47. Cf. the implication of the "forty years" in Heb. 3:9ff.

48. Cf. 4Q *Florilegium*, where a comment on Ps. 2:1f. refers to "the chosen ones of Israel in the last days, that is, the time of trial which is coming." On the interpretation of 4Q *Florilegium* see G. J. Brooke, *Exegesis at Qumran: 4Q Florilegium in its Jewish Context*, JSOT Suppl 29 (Sheffield, 1985).

49. The Teacher is expressly called "the priest" in col. 2, line 15, of this same *pesher*; cf. 1Q p Hab., col. 2, lines 8f.: "the priest into whose [heart] God has put [wisdo]m, to interpret all the words of his servants the prophets."

50. As in 1 Macc. 1:1; 8:5.

51. As in Dan. 11:30.

52. J. T. Milik, who supplements some lacunae in 4Q *Testimonia* here with the help of 4Q *Psalms of Joshua* (thus far unpublished), renders the beginning of this sentence "And he stood forth and [made his sons] rulers" (*Ten Years of Discovery . . .*, p. 61).

53. In 1Q p Hab. the town built with blood of Hab. 2:12 is perhaps interpreted figuratively; cf. the builders of the wall in CD 4:19.

54. *The Ancient Library of Qumran and Modern Biblical Studies* (³1980), p. 149. For Simon's death, cf. 1 Macc. 16:11ff.; for the subsequent invasion of Antiochus VII, cf. Josephus, *Ant.* 13.236-248.

55. *Ten Years of Discovery . . .*, pp. 63f.

56. Cf. C. Roth, *The Historical Background of the Dead Sea Scrolls* (Oxford, 1958), p. 37: "This could well be a reference to Vespasian's capture of Jericho in 68, though there is no need to insist on this point." (In a footnote Roth suggests that the execrated builder of Jericho might be Herod.)

57. J. L. Teicher considered that in this passage from 4Q *Testimonia* "Joshua" is to be understood typologically as Jesus, and that the son of Belial is the future Antichrist, who is to rebuild Jerusalem as his capital ("Dead Sea Fragment of an Apocryphal Gospel," *Times Literary Supplement*, 21 March 1958).

58. The aposiopesis could be avoided if one were to translate "because of one hung up alive . . . ," for then the Scripture pronounces the doom of the person responsible for the outrage in the words of Nah. 2:13: "because of one hung up alive on a tree the Scripture says, 'Behold, I am against you, says the LORD of hosts. . . .'" See G. Vermes, *The Dead Sea Scrolls in English*, p. 280.

59. In 11QT 64.6-13, however, regulations are formulated for hanging a man

"on a tree, that he may die," as well as for hanging the corpse of an executed criminal "on a tree," and both forms of hanging are related to Deut. 21:22f. There is no evidence, even so, that the regulation for hanging a person alive was ever put into effect by Israelite authorities in the period under consideration.

60. Other historical names—*šlmṣywn* (Salampsio, i.e. Queen Salome Alexandra), *hwrqnws* (Hyrcanus) and *'mlyws* (Aemilius, i.e. Aemilius Scaurus, Roman governor of Syria, 65-62 B.C.)—appear in a fragmentary sectarian calendar from Cave 4 (Milik, *Ten Years of Discovery . . .* , p. 73); cf. also p. 288, n.42 above.

NOTES TO CHAPTER 4

1. See p. 38.

2. A. Dupont-Sommer, *The Dead Sea Scrolls*, E.T. (Oxford, 1950), p. 99.

3. E.g., by J. L. Teicher, who in a series of papers in the *Journal of Jewish Studies* from Vol. 2 (1951) to Vol. 5 (1954) argued that the members of the Qumran community were Jewish Christians (Ebionites) and that the Wicked Priest was Paul. More recently an Australian scholar has suggested that the Wicked Priest was a designation given to Jesus himself by some partisans of John the Baptist (B. E. Thiering, *The Gospels and Qumran* [Sydney, 1981], pp. 192f.; cf. *The Qumran Origins of the Christian Church* [Sydney, 1983], pp. 185f., 193).

4. Now in its third edition (1988), published by the JSOT Press, Sheffield. See also E. F. Sutcliffe, *The Monks of Qumran* (London, 1960), pp. 129-223; A. Dupont-Sommer, *The Essene Writings from Qumran*, E.T. (Oxford, 1961); T. H. Gaster, *The Dead Sea Scriptures* (Garden City, N.Y., [3]1976).

5. Many documents from Cave 4 and some from Cave 11 still await publication.

6. I call him the "effective founder" because the godly remnant out of which the community developed wandered aimlessly for twenty years before he was raised up (CD 1.8-12). But it does not appear that he had any predecessor who could be called absolutely the "founder" of the community, although A. R. C. Leaney envisages a "founder" who was followed twenty years later by the Teacher of Righteousness, "who was not the founder but a re-founder" (*The Rule of Qumran and its Meaning*, NTL [London, 1966], p. 115). Similarly E. F. Sutcliffe describes the Teacher as "the second founder and organizer of the sect" (*The Monks of Qumran*, p. 97).

7. 2 Maccabees 4:34.

8. Josephus, *BJ* 2.433-448.

9. *The Zadokite Fragments and the Dead Sea Scrolls* (Oxford, 1952), pp. 67-71; cf. also A. Michel, *Le Maître de Justice* (Avignon, 1954), pp. 293-298; M. Black, *The Scrolls and Christian Origins* (London, 1961), p. 20.

10. Cf. also H. E. Del Medico, *The Riddle of the Scrolls*, E.T. (London, 1958), pp. 140-145; C. Roth, *The Historical Background of the Dead Sea Scrolls* (Oxford, 1958), pp. 6ff.

11. *The Judaean Scrolls* (Oxford, 1965), p. 6.

12. For this identification cf. G. Vermès, *Les manuscrits du désert de Juda* (1953), pp. 90ff.; J. T. Milik, *Ten Years of Discovery in the Wilderness of Judaea* (1959), pp. 65-72; P. Winter, "The Wicked Priest," *Hibbert Journal* 58 (1959-60), 53ff.; E. F. Sutcliffe, *The Monks of Qumran*, pp. 42-49; G. Jeremias, *Der Lehrer der Gerechtigkeit*, SUNT 2 (Göttingen, 1963), pp. 36-78. F. M. Cross prefers to identify the Wicked Priest with Jonathan's brother Simon (143-135 B.C.), who succeeded him as ruler and high priest (*The Ancient*

Library of Qumran, pp. 136-156). J. M. Allegro's identification of him with Alexander Jannaeus (103-76 B.C.), Simon's grandson (*The Dead Sea Scrolls: A Reappraisal* [Harmondsworth, ²1964], pp. 107-109), is not so well founded as his identification of Jannaeus with the "raging young lion" of the Qumran commentary on Nahum ("Further Light on the History of the Qumran Sect," *JBL* 75 [1956], pp. 89-95); see pp. 47f. Jannaeus's son Hyrcanus II is preferred by A. Dupont-Sommer (*The Dead Sea Scrolls*, pp. 37-41; *The Essene Writings from Qumran*, pp. 351- 357). Any Hasmonaean high priest would have been *ex officio* a "wicked priest" in Qumran eyes. A pre-Hasmonaean identification is Menelaus, preferred by H. H. Rowley (*The Zadokite Fragments*, pp. 67- 70); a post-Hasmonaean one is Eleazar ben Hananiah, captain of the temple in A.D. 66, preferred by G. R. Driver (*The Judaean Scrolls*, pp. 267-281).

13. Josephus, *Ant.* 13.171 (along with the Pharisees and Sadducees).

14. Hippolytus (*Ref. Omn. Haer.* 9.21) can speak of Zealots and *sicarii* as a variety of Essenes.

15. See p. 289, n. 49.

16. 1QS 8.1. For this interpretation, cf. E. F. Sutcliffe, *The Monks of Qumran*, p. 97; A. R. C. Leaney, *The Rule of Qumran and its Meaning*, pp. 210-213. The parallel with the twelve apostles of the New Testament is imperfect; the apostles were a group of twelve *including* an inner circle of three, and they were all laymen.

17. 1QS 6.3ff.

18. Not only in the primitive Jerusalem church but in the earlier days of the apostles' itinerant association with Jesus, when Judas Iscariot had charge of the common purse (John 12:6; 13:29).

19. CD 1.11f.

20. Cf. O. Betz, *Offenbarung und Schriftforschung in der Qumransekte*, WUNT 6 (Tübingen, 1960).

21. Cf. C. H. Dodd, *According to the Scriptures* (London, 1952), pp. 109f.

22. CD 20.1, 14.

23. Cf. CD 6.10f., "until there stands up one who will teach righteousness in the end of days."

24. If he is the "expounder of the law" who is to stand up with the Davidic Messiah in the end-time, according to the document provisionally called 4Q *Florilegium* 1.11 (J. M. Allegro, "Fragments of a Qumran Scroll of Eschatological *Midrāšîm*," *JBL* 77 [1958], pp. 350-354; cf. G. J. Brooke, *Exegesis at Qumran*, JSOT Suppl 29 [Sheffield, 1985]; G. Vermes, *The Dead Sea Scrolls in English* [Sheffield, ³1988], pp. 293f.).

25. Cf. A. S. van der Woude, *Die messianischen Vorstellungen der Gemeinde von Qumran* (Assen, 1957).

26. CD 20.1; 12.23f.

27. 1QSa 2.11ff.

28. 4Q *Testimonia;* 1QS 9.11.

29. Luke 4:18; Acts 10:38.

30. Acts 3:22f.; 7:37.

31. Rom. 1:3, etc.

32. Heb. 5:6, etc.

33. In fact, the Qumran conception of the character and function of the Davidic Messiah must be included among those which Jesus decisively and repeatedly repudiated (cf., e.g., John 6:15).

34. There is a historical foundation for the application of Ps. 110:4 to Christ in

the Epistle to the Hebrews, in that the acclamation as a perpetual priest of Melchizedek's order is addressed to the Davidic king of Ps. 110:1, although the writer to the Hebrews may not have been greatly interested in such a foundation.

35. See M. Casey, *Son of Man* (London, 1979).

36. See T. W. Manson, *The Servant-Messiah* (Cambridge, 1953), pp. 72-74 (I am bound to concur with his judgment). For a contrary view see M. D. Hooker, *Jesus and the Servant* (London, 1959).

37. 1QS 8.6, 10; 1QSa 1.3.

38. 1Qp Hab. 5.3-6.

39. Heb. *dôrᵉšê (ha)hălāqôt* (1QH 2.15, 32; 4Qp Nahum 1.7; cf. CD 1.18; there may be an allusion to Isa. 30:10, "speak to us smooth things").

40. Cf. CD 4.19f.

41. Luke 14:5; cf. Matt. 12:11, where a sheep is mentioned instead of an ox or an ass.

42. CD 11.13f.

43. Mark 2:17.

44. The term "covenantal nomism," in which E. P. Sanders sums up Jewish existence in the New Testament period (*Paul and Palestinian Judaism* [London, 1977], pp. 75, 236 *et passim*), would be as applicable to the Qumran community as to (say) the Pharisees, but for the community the covenant was more narrowly defined and the requirements of nomism more strictly interpreted and applied.

45. See H. Braun, *Qumran und das Neue Testament*, 2 vols. (Tübingen, 1966).

46. *The Setting of the Sermon on the Mount* (Cambridge, 1964), pp. 235-315.

47. Gk. ἄνθρωποι εὐδοκίας. Cf. the phrase *bᵉnê rāṣôn*, lit. "sons of (God's) good pleasure" (1QH 4.32f.; 11.9).

48. Cf. W. F. Albright, "Recent Discoveries in Palestine and the Gospel of St. John," in *The Background of the New Testament and its Eschatology*, ed. W. D. Davies and D. Daube (Cambridge, 1964), pp. 153- 171; G. Baumbach, *Qumran und das Johannes-Evangelium* (Berlin, 1957); J. H. Charlesworth (ed.), *John and Qumran* (London, 1972).

49. The light–darkness antithesis appears also in the Pauline corpus; cf. Eph. 5:7-14.

50. Cf. J. Thomas, *Le mouvement baptiste en Palestine et Syrie* (Gembloux, 1935).

51. Cf. A. S. Geyser, "The Youth of John the Baptist," *NovT* I (1956), 70-75; J. A. T. Robinson, "The Baptism of John and the Qumran Community" (1957), in *Twelve New Testament Studies*, SBT 34 (London, 1962), pp. 11-27; W. H. Brownlee, "John the Baptist in the New Light of Ancient Scrolls," in *The Scrolls and the New Testament*, ed. K. Stendahl (1958), pp. 33-53; J. Pryke, "John the Baptist and the Qumran Community," *Revue de Qumran* 4 (1963-64), 483-496.

52. It is noteworthy that the language of Isa. 40:3, used in the New Testament as a *testimonium* for John the Baptist (Mark 1:3; Matt. 3:3; Luke 3:4-6; John 1:23), is quoted in 1QS 8.14 with reference to the Qumran community's withdrawal to the wilderness.

53. 1QS 6.24f.

54. Cf. O. Cullmann, "The Significance of the Qumran Texts for Research into the Beginnings of Christianity," in *The Scrolls and the New Testament*, ed. K. Stendahl, pp. 18-32, esp. p. 29; E. P. Blair, *Jesus in the Gospel of Matthew* (New York, 1960), pp. 142ff., and the summary of such views in W. D. Davies, *The Setting of the Sermon on the Mount*, p. 254.

55. Cf. K. Bornhäuser, *Empfänger und Verfasser des Briefes an die Hebräer* (1932); C. Spicq, *L'Épitre aux Hébreux* (1952), I, pp. 226-231. See p. 61, and n. 68 below.

56. There is thus far no means of certainty on this question.

57. Gal. 1:17; Acts 9:10.

58. E.g., CD 1.13; 2.6; 1QS 9.17f., 19, 21; 10.21; 11.11. Cf. E. Repo, *Der "Weg" als Selbstbezeichnung des Urchristentums* (Helsinki, 1964).

59. Especially in the "Hymn of the Initiants" at the end of 1QS (e.g., 10.12f.; 11.3-15); cf. 1QH 4.30-38. See pp. 67, 70.

60. Close resemblances to Qumran thought and language have been recognized also in 2 Cor. 6:14–7:1; cf. J. A. Fitzmyer, "Qumrân and the interpolated Paragraph in 2 Cor. 6:14–7:1" (1961), in *Essays on the Semitic Background of the New Testament* (London, 1971), pp. 205-217; J. Gnilka, "2 Cor. 6:14–7:1 in the Light of the Qumran Texts and the Testaments of the Twelve Patriarchs" (1962), in J. Murphy-O'Connor (ed.), *Paul and Qumran* (London, 1968), pp. 48-68.

61. H. Chadwick, "All Things to all Men," *NTS* 1 (1954-55), pp. 261-275, especially p. 272.

62. J. B. Lightfoot, *Saint Paul's Epistles to the Colossians and to Philemon* (London, [2]1879), pp. 73-113, 349-419.

63. Cf. K. G. Kuhn, "The Epistle to the Ephesians in the Light of the Qumran Texts," E.T. in *Paul and Qumran*, ed. J. Murphy- O'Connor (London, 1968), pp. 115-131. (All the contributions to that volume of essays are of high value.)

64. The Melchizedek fragment from Qumran Cave 11 (11Q Melch) is most interesting in its own right, but its conception of Melchizedek has little enough in common with that of the writer to the Hebrews. In it Melchizedek is promoted to be head of the heavenly court, judging the spirits of Belial's lot and fulfilling a ministry of liberation for the people of his own lot, the children of light. The *editio princeps* is A. S. van der Woude, "Melchisedek als himmlische Erlösergestalt in den neugefundenen eschatologischen Midraschim aus Qumran Höhle XI," *OTS* 14 (1965), pp. 354-373; cf. also M. de Jonge and A. S. van der Woude, "11Q Melchizedek and the New Testament," *NTS* 12 (1965-66), pp. 301-326.

65. *RB* 62 (1965), p. 37 (in article "L'arrière-fond judaïque du quatrième Évangile et la Communauté du l'Alliance," pp. 5-44.

66. "The Dead Sea Scrolls and the Epistle to the Hebrews," *Scripta Hierosolymitana* 4 (1958), pp. 36-55.

67. *Hebräer-Essener-Christen* (Leiden, 1959).

68. "L'Épître aux Hébreux: Apollos, Jean-Baptiste, les Hellénistes et Qumrân," *Revue de Qumran* 1 (1958-59), pp. 365-390 (see p. 59, and n. 55 above).

69. *Hebrews, James, I and II Peter* (1962), pp. 13-16. For a critique of all such views see J. Coppens, *Les affinités qumrâniennes de l'Épître aux Hébreux* (Bruges / Paris, 1962).

70. Cf. the pre-baptismal bath for the removal of impurity on the Thursday preceding Easter Day (*The Apostolic Tradition of St. Hippolytus*, ed. G. Dix [London, [2]1968], p. 31). See also S. Giet, "Un courant judéo-chrétien à Rome au milieu du IIe siècle?" and G. Kretschmar, "Die Bedeutung der Liturgiegeschichte für die Frage nach der Kontinuität des Judenchristentums in nachapostolischer Zeit," in M. Simon *et al.*, *Aspects du judéo-christianisme* (Paris, 1965), pp. 95-111, 113-136. See p. 295, n. 12.

71. The "forty years" of Ps. 95:10 seem to be applied in Heb. 3:7ff. to the forty years following the death of Jesus, in a manner comparable to the conception of a

probationary period of forty years in Qumran literature; cf. CD 20.14f.; 1QM 2.6-16; 4Qp Ps 37, 2.8-11. See pp. 44f. above.

72. This is probably the place to mention the skillful but unsuccessful attempt by R. H. Eisenman to identify the Teacher of Righteousness with James the Lord's brother: *James the Just in the Habakkuk Pescher* (Leiden, 1986).

73. K. G. Kuhn, *The Scrolls and the New Testament*, ed. K. Stendahl, p. 268, n. 34 (in notes to article "New Light on Temptation, Sin, and Flesh in the New Testament," pp. 94-113).

74. Jude 14f., 9. See p. 300, n. 11.

75. Caves 1, 2, 4, 5 and 11; those from Caves 1, 2 and 5 (1Q32, 2Q24, 5Q15) have been published in *DJD* 1 (1955), pp. 134f.; 3 (1962), Texte, pp. 84-89; 184-193.

76. 1QH 3.9f.

77. Cf. O. Cullmann, "Die neuentdeckten Qumran-Texte und das Juden-christentum der Pseudoklementinen," in *Neutestamentliche Studien für R. Bultmann*, BZNW 21 (1954), pp. 35-51.

78. J. B. Lightfoot, *Saint Paul's Epistles to the Colossians and to Philemon*, pp. 82-98; cf. F. J. A. Hort, *Judaistic Christianity* (London, 1894), pp. 201f.

79. Many years ago R. Bultmann remarked towards the end of his influential article "Die Bedeutung der neuerschlossenen mandäischen und manichäischen Quellen für das Verständnis des Johannesevangeliums" (*ZNW* 24 [1925], pp. 100-146) that further knowledge about the Essenes might provide the missing link between Johannine Christianity and the Mandaeans. The whole question is highly problematical and demands much critical scrutiny, but cf. R. Macuch, "Alter und Heimat des Mandäismus nach neuerchlossenen Quellen," *TLZ* 82 (1957), cols. 401-408; K. Rudolph, "War der Verfasser der Oden Salomos ein Qumran- Christ?," *Revue de Qumran* 4 (1963-4), 523-555.

80. John 1:28ff.; 10:40; 11:54.

81. On back of "Signet Key Book" edition of A. P. Davies, *The Meaning of the Dead Sea Scrolls* (New York, 1956).

82. 2 Cor. 13:8.

NOTES TO CHAPTER 5

1. *Biblical Exegesis in the Qumran Texts* (London, 1960), p. 82.

2. Compare τὸν δικαιοῦντα τὸν ἀσεβῆ (Rom. 4:5) with οὐ δικαιώσεις τὸν ἀσεβῆ (Exod. 23:7, LXX).

3. E. F. Sutcliffe, "Hatred at Qumran," *Revue de Qumran* 2 (1960), pp. 345-356. But see the observations on his argument in W. D. Davies, *The Setting of the Sermon on the Mount* (Cambridge, 1964), pp. 242-251.

NOTES TO CHAPTER 6

1. K. P. Donfried (ed.), *The Romans Debate* (Minneapolis, 1977).

2. *BJRL* 31 (1948), 224-40, reprinted in T. W. Manson, *Studies in the Gospels and Epistles*, ed. M. Black (Manchester, 1962), pp. 225-41.

3. Cf. C. E. B. Cranfield, *The Epistle to the Romans*, I-II, ICC (Edinburgh, 1972-79);

E. Käsemann, *Commentary on Romans*, E.T. (London, 1980); H. Schlier, *Der Römerbrief*, HTK (Freiburg, 1977); U. Wilckens, *Der Brief an die Römer*, EKK (Neukirchen-Vluyn, 1978-82). [See now A. J. M. Wedderburn, *The Reasons for Romans* (Edinburgh, 1989).]

4. H. Y. Gamble, Jr., *The Textual History of the Letter to the Romans*, SD 42 (Grand Rapids, 1977).

5. C. H. Dodd, *The Epistle of Paul to the Romans*, MNTC (London, 1932), pp. xvii-xxiv, 236-40.

6. Spain was annexed and organized as two Roman provinces (Hispania Citerior and Hispania Ulterior) in 197 B.C., soon after the Second Punic War. Sicily was the first Roman province, annexed in 241 B.C., at the end of the First Punic War; Sardinia and Corsica were annexed shortly afterwards (238 B.C.), and were administered as one province from 231 B.C. to the beginning of the fourth century A.D.

7. Romans 15:20.

8. Cf. 1 Corinthians 3:10-15; 2 Corinthians 10:12-16.

9. Romans 1:13-15.

10. Romans 1:8; 15:14.

11. Ambrosiaster, *Ad Romanos* (ed. H. J. Vogels), CSEL 81.1 (Vindobonae, 1966), p. 6.

12. This appears from nonliterary (as well as literary) evidence, such as the indebtedness of early Christian catacombs to the Jewish catacombs of Rome (like that on Monteverde). As for literary evidence, the surviving influence of Jewish lustral practice in the Christian worship of Rome has been traced in Hippolytus, *Apostolic Tradition* 20.5, where a purificatory bath on Maundy Thursday is prescribed for those preparing to be baptized on Easter Day; cf. R. J. Zwi Werblowsky, "On the Baptismal Rite according to St. Hippolytus," *Studia Patristica* 4 = *TU* 54 (Berlin, 1957), pp. 93-105.

13. Acts 6:9.

14. Suetonius, *Divus Claudius* 25.4.

15. Chrestus was as common a slave-name as its near-synonym Onesimus. For the incidence of Chrestus in Rome cf. *CIL* VI.668, 880, 975, 1929, 3555, 7460, 7846, 11707, 14058, 14433, 14805, 20770, 21531, 22837, 26157, 28324, 28659, 37672, 38735. While Suetonius has the spelling *Chresto* here, he has *Christiani* in *Nero* 16.2. But in Tacitus, *Ann.* 15.44.3 the MS Mediceus 68.2 had originally (it appears) *Chrestianos*, which was corrected to *Christianos* by a later hand. Tacitus himself, however, may have spelled the word *Christianos*, since he links it closely with Christus ("auctor nominis eius"). In the NT the first hand in Vaticanus consistently shows the spelling Χρηστιανός. The apologists exploit the confusion between the two forms: "We are accused of being χριστιανοί but it is unjust that one should be hated for being χρηστός" (Justin, *Apol.* 1.4.5).

16. Cf. R. Eisler, *The Messiah Jesus and John the Baptist* (London, 1931), p. 581. E. A. Judge and G. S. R. Thomas, "The Origin of the Church at Rome: A New Solution," *Reformed Theological Review* 25 (1966), p. 87, refer to Simon as "the most suggestive example" of the type of agitator in question. Simon's presence in Rome in the time of Claudius is mentioned by Justin (*Apol.* 1.26.2). The identification of Chrestus with James the Just has been proposed by B. E. Thiering, *The Gospels and Qumran* (Sydney, 1981), p. 271.

17. That he was indeed there at that time is argued by R. Graves and J. Podro, *Jesus in Rome* (London, 1957).

18. Tacitus, *Ann.* 15.44.4. See p. 297, n. 39.

19. Orosius (writing A.D. 417-18) quotes Suetonius on the expulsion and says that Josephus dates the incident in A.D. 49 (*Hist.* 7.6.15f.). But there is no reference to the incident in the extant writings of Josephus. See pp. 138-140.

20. The question arises of the relation of the expulsion recorded by Suetonius to an action of Claudius dated by Dio Cassius (*Hist.* 60.6) to the first year of his principate: "When the Jews [*sc.* of Rome] had again multiplied to a point where their numbers made it difficult to expel them from the city without a riot, he did not banish them outright but forbade them to meet in accordance with their ancestral way of life." If this ban on meetings was later lifted, then perhaps Claudius, "annoyed that his relaxation . . . had led to a repetition of disorder, reacted more severely than before, this time with an expulsion" (E. M. Smallwood, *The Jews under Roman Rule* [Leiden, 1976], pp. 215f.).

21. On the date of Gallio's entry on his proconsulship see p. 140.

22. Cf. A. Harnack, "Probabilia über die Adresse und den Verfasser des Hebräerbriefs," *ZNW* 1 (1900), 16-41.

23. This is a reasonable inference from Romans 1:13; 11:13.

24. See J. B. Lightfoot, *Saint Paul's Epistle to the Philippians* (London, 1868), pp. 171-178.

25. Cf. C. H. Dodd, *The Epistle of Paul to the Romans*, p. xxii; F. F. Bruce, *Paul: Apostle of the Free Spirit* (Exeter, 1977), pp. 386f.; *The Letter of Paul to the Romans*, TNTC (Leicester/Grand Rapids, ²1985), pp. 259f.

26. E.g., the expulsion under Tiberius in A.D. 19 (Josephus, *Ant.* 18.65, 81-84; Tacitus, *Ann.* 2.85; Suetonius, *Tiberius* 36), ascribed by Philo (*Leg.* 159f.) to the malignity of Sejanus.

27. T. W. Manson, "St. Paul's Letter to the Romans," pp. 226-29 (*Studies*, pp. 227-30; *The Romans Debate*, ed. K. P. Donfried, pp. 3-6); see, however, H. Gamble, *The Textual History*, pp. 29-33, 100-124.

28. Cf. A. Harnack, *The Mission and Expansion of Christianity*, E.T. (London, 1908), I, pp. 74f.; H. J. Cadbury, *The Book of Acts in History* (New York, 1955), pp. 60f.; G. Bornkamm, *Paul*, E.T. (London, 1971), pp. 51-54; E. A. Judge and G. S. R. Thomas, "The Origin of the Church at Rome," p. 90.

29. The date A.D. 57 is indicated by reckoning forward (from Gallio) and backward (from Festus). By Pentecost of the year in which Romans was written Paul had arrived in Judaea; not long after his arrival he was detained in custody in Caesarea, and remained there for two years, until Festus became procurator (Acts 24:27). There is numismatic evidence for dating the accession of Festus in A.D. 59 (cf. F. W. Madden, *History of Jewish Coinage* [London, 1864], p. 153; A. Reifenberg, *Ancient Jewish Coins* [Jerusalem, ²1947], p. 27; see also E. Schürer, *The History of the Jewish People in the Age of Jesus Christ*, I [Edinburgh, 1973], p. 465, n. 42). See pp. 143-145.

30. See pp. 98-113.

31. See B. M. Metzger, *A Textual Commentary on the Greek New Testament* (London/New York, 1971), pp. 539-41; H. Gamble, *The Textual History*, pp. 121-24, 129-32.

32. Where he refers to slanderous charges (βλασφημούμεθα) that his preaching amounts to saying, "Let us do evil, that good may come."

33. Acts 6:9f.; see p. 82.

34. Romans 10:1.

35. Romans 9:1-3.

36. Cf. Acts 22:17-21, on which see O. Betz, "Die Vision des Paulus im Tempel

von Jerusalem," in *Verborum Veritas: Festschrift für G. Stählin,* ed. O. Böcher and K. Haacker (Wuppertal, 1970), pp. 113-123.

37. Gk. ἀπόδοτε in both places.

38. See pp. 109-111.

39. Cf. the only mention of the trial of Jesus by a pagan author: "Christus Tiberio imperitante per procuratorem Pontium Pilatum supplicio adfectus erat" (Tacitus, *Ann.* 15.44.4).

40. Notably Gallio, who refused to take up a complaint against him at Corinth (Acts 18:12-16).

41. See p. 112.

42. Acts 15:28f. Cf. C. K. Barrett, "Things Offered to Idols," *NTS* 11 (1964-65), pp. 138-153, reprinted in *Essays on Paul* (London, 1982), pp. 40-59.

43. Cf. Juvenal, *Sat.* 14.96-106.

44. The varieties need not be demarcated so distinctly as in P. S. Minear, *The Obedience of Faith,* SBT 2.19 (London, 1971), pp. 8-35, where five different outlooks are identified.

45. Cf. 1 Corinthians 8:13; 10:33; Romans 14:14.

46. 1 Corinthians 9:19-23.

47. Chrysostom goes farther: "he mentions Spain in order to show his eagerness and warmth towards them [the Roman Christians]" (*Homilies on Romans* 30 [on 15:28]).

48. Cf. W. P. Bowers, "Jewish Communities in Spain in the Time of Paul the Apostle," *JTS* n.s. 26 (1975), pp. 395-402, for evidence that Jewish settlement in Spain was later than Paul's time.

49. Cf. 1 Corinthians 16:1-4; 2 Corinthians 8:1–9:15.

50. See p. 144.

51. Galatians 2:2-10.

52. See p. 148.

53. See F. F. Bruce, "Paul and Jerusalem" (New Zealand Tyndale Lecture, 1966), *Tyndale Bulletin* 19 (1968), pp. 3-25.

54. A. A. T. Ehrhardt, *The Framework of the New Testament Stories* (Manchester, 1964), p. 94.

55. H. Chadwick, "The Circle and the Ellipse: Rival Concepts of Authority in the Early Church" (1959), *History and Thought of the Early Church* (London, 1982), pp. 3-17, especially p. 6.

56. On this see J. Munck, *Paul and the Salvation of Mankind,* E.T. (London, 1959), *passim.*

57. See p. 87 above, and p. 296, n. 36.

58. Cf. 1 Clement 5:7 (τὸ τέρμα τῆς δύσεως).

59. For the argument that the "full number of the Gentiles" (Romans 11:25) will not "come in" until Paul "has brought Christian representatives from Spain to Jerusalem as part of his collection enterprise" see R. D. Aus, "Paul's Travel Plans to Spain and the 'Full Number of the Gentiles' of Rom. xi.25," *NovT* 21 (1979), pp. 232-62.

60. Virgil, *Aeneid* 2.49, where Laocoon voices his distrust of the Trojan horse: "I fear the Greeks even when they bring gifts." See p. 15.

61. J. D. G. Dunn thinks it most likely that "the Jerusalem church refused to accept the collection" (*Unity and Diversity in the New Testament* [London, 1977], p. 257). (For my part, I think it more likely that they did accept it.) See pp. 171f.

62. Amplifying the suggestion of E. Fuchs that the "secret address" of the letter is Jerusalem (*Hermeneutik* [Bad Canstatt, 1963], p. 191), J. Jervell argues that "the essential and primary content of Romans (1:18–11:36) is a reflection upon its major content, the 'collection speech,' or more precisely, the defense which Paul plans to give before the church in Jerusalem" ("The Letter to Jerusalem" [1972], in *The Romans Debate*, ed. K. P. Donfried, p. 64).

63. So Y. M. Park, "The Effect of Contemporary Conditions in the Jerusalem Church on the Writing of the Epistle to the Romans" (unpublished Ph.D. thesis, University of Edinburgh, 1979).

64. Gk. πορεύομαι.

65. Vegetius, *De re militari* 4.39. Even a journey by land could not have begun much earlier.

66. It would not have made much difference to the timing if Phoebe went to Rome by the Via Egnatia rather than all the way by sea. The promptest journey from Rome to Judaea took nearly five weeks; for example, news of the death of Tiberius on 16 March A.D. 37 (Tacitus, *Ann.* 6.50) reached Jerusalem on the eve of Passover (Josephus, *Ant.* 18.122-24), which in that year coincided with the full moon of 17 or 18 April. Cf. A. M. Ramsay, "The Speed of the Roman Imperial Post," *JRS* 15 (1925), pp. 60-74.

67. "The Circle and the Ellipse," p. 9.

68. And later, no doubt, during his two years' residence among them. This much may be said with confidence, even if we do not go so far as to say with Henry Chadwick that, "if there is one man who more than any other man may be regarded as founder of the papacy, that man is surely St. Paul" ("The Circle and the Ellipse," p. 17).

NOTES TO CHAPTER 7

1. Mainly on the ground that Tertullian, in his running commentary on Marcion's Pauline edition (*Against Marcion* 5.14.11-14), makes no reference to Romans 13:1-7. But there was probably no reason why he should refer to it.

2. There are good bibliographical notes in C. E. B. Cranfield, *The Epistle to the Romans*, ICC, II (Edinburgh, 1979), pp. 651-657.

3. J. Kallas, "Romans XIII.1-7: An Interpolation," *NTS* 11 (1964-65), pp. 365-374.

4. Cf. the dictum of Rabbi Ḥanina, deputy high priest (Paul's contemporary): "Pray for the peace of the empire, since but for the fear of it men would swallow one another alive" (*Pirqê Abôth* 3.2). The "Pharisaic principle of retribution" is in fact Deuteronomic.

5. Gk. τοὺς ἐξουθημένους ἐν τῇ ἐκκλησίᾳ.

6. See H. Gamble, *The Textual History of the Letter to the Romans*, SD 42 (Grand Rapids, 1977). Cf. p. 80 above.

7. A targumic paraphrase of Deut. 32:35 (cf. Heb. 10:30).

8. W. Munro, *Authority in Paul and Peter*, SNTSM 45 (Cambridge, 1983), p. 3.

9. *Ibid.*, pp. 56-67.

10. *Ibid.*, p. viii. In the correspondence columns of the *British Weekly* for 9 September 1983, a letter-writer remarked, as if it were something which hardly needed stating, that Paul would not have said that "the powers that be are ordained

of God" had Nero been emperor at the time—but of course Nero *was* emperor. (Admittedly we know facts about Nero which Paul could not have known in A.D. 57.)

11. This is the reading of one manuscript from Qumran, which exhibits the Hebrew text presumably followed in LXX ἀγγέλων θεοῦ. MT reads "sons (children) of Israel." See pp. 38f., and p. 287, n. 28.

12. Psalm 82:7.

13. For the view that they are angels see M. Noth, "The Holy Ones of the Most High," E.T. in *The Laws of the Pentateuch and Other Studies* (Edinburgh, 1966), pp. 215-228; L. Dequeker, "'The Saints of the Most High' in Qumran and Daniel," *Oudtestamentische Studiën* 18 (1973), pp. 108-187; for a conclusive statement of the view that they are faithful Jews see M. Casey, *Son of Man* (London, 1979), pp. 7-70.

14. O. Cullmann, *Christ and Time*, E.T. (London, 1951), pp. 191-210; cf. *The State in the New Testament*, E.T. (London, 1957), pp. 50-70 (on p. 64 of the latter work Cullmann finds that "Romans 13:1ff., I Cor. 6:1ff., and I Cor. 2:8, taken together, furnish a uniform picture, which coincides astonishingly with Jesus' conception of the State").

15. *Christ and Time*, p. 194.

16. *Ibid.*, p. 195 (Cullmann's italics).

17. Irenaeus, *Against Heresies* 5.24.1.

18. *Christ and Time*, p. 196.

19. K. Barth, *Church and State*, E.T. (London, 1939); *Church Dogmatics*, E.T., II/2 (Edinburgh, 1957), pp. 721-724. See also C. D. Morrison, *The Powers That Be*, SBT 29 (London, 1960), which includes a useful account of the state of the question up to the time when it was written.

20. In Winsome Munro's eyes, the relevant passages in the Pastorals and 1 Peter belong themselves to the later "pastoral stratum."

21. These rulers, then, are not the same as the "angels, authorities and powers" which, according to 1 Peter 3:22, have been subjected to the risen and exalted Christ.

22. 1 Clement 60:2–61:2.

23. *Martyrdom of Polycarp* 10.3.

24. See pp. 183f.; also my *New Testament History* (London, [2]1971), pp. 290-294; *1 & 2 Thessalonians*, WBC 45 (Waco, 1982), pp. 159-188.

25. Tertullian, *On the Resurrection of the Flesh* 24.

26. Chrysostom, *Homilies on 2 Thessalonians* 4.

27. Gk. ἀπόδοτε, the same word as is used in Romans 13:7. See pp. 87f.

28. The adherents of the "fourth philosophy," followers of Judas the Galilaean, maintained that it was contrary to divine law for the people of God in the land which he gave them to acknowledge the sovereignty of a pagan ruler.

29. C. E. B. Cranfield, *The Epistle to the Romans*, II, p. 653.

30. Acts 17:5-7. See F. F. Bruce, *Paul, Apostle of the Free Spirit/of the Heart Set Free* (Exeter/Grand Rapids, 1977), pp. 224-227.

31. See F. F. Bruce, "Christianity under Claudius," *BJRL* 44 (1961-62), pp. 310-21.

32. See J. Friedrich, W. Pöhlmann, P. Stuhlmacher, "Zur historischen Situation und Intention von Röm 13, 1-7," *ZTK* 73 (1976), pp. 131-166.

33. E. Käsemann, *New Testament Questions of Today*, E.T. (London, 1969), p. 215.

34. 1 Peter 3:13-18 (cf. 2:12).

35. J. Kallas, "Romans XIII.1-7: An Interpolation," pp. 370f.

36. Cf. S. S. Smalley, "The Delay of the Parousia," *JBL* 83 (1964), pp. 41-64.

37. Acts 18:12-17.

38. Cf. C. E. B. Cranfield, "The Christian's Political Responsibility according to the New Testament," *SJT* 15 (1962), pp. 176-192.

NOTES TO CHAPTER 8

1. *BJRL* 56 (1973-74), pp. 317-35 (especially p. 325), substantially reproduced in *Paul: Apostle of the Free Spirit* (Exeter, 1977) = *Paul: Apostle of the Heart Set Free* (Grand Rapids, 1977), pp. 95-112 (especially p. 101).

2. Cf. *Paul, Apostle . . .* , pp. 70, 190.

3. Cf. Mark 12:35-37.

4. Perhaps the compound verb ὑπερύψωσεν echoes ὑψωθήσεται ("shall be exalted"), used of the Servant of Yahweh in Isa. 52:13. Cf. Eph. 1:20-22.

5. Whether the passage Phil. 2:6-11 is Pauline or pre-Pauline, Paul makes it his own. See E. Lohmeyer, *Kyrios Jesus* (Heidelberg, 1928, ²1961); E. Käsemann, "A Critical Analysis of Philippians 2, 5-11" (1950), E.T. in *JTC* 5 (1968), pp. 45-88; D. Georgi, "Der vorpaulinische Hymnus Phil. 2, 6-11," in *Zeit und Geschichte: Dankesgabe an R. Bultmann,* ed. E. Dinkler (Tübingen, 1964), pp. 263-293; R. P. Martin, *Carmen Christi* (Cambridge, 1967); I. H. Marshall, "The Christ-Hymn in Philippians 2:5-11," *Tyndale Bulletin* 19 (1968), pp. 104-127; C. F. D. Moule, "Further Reflexions on Philippians 2:5-11," in *Apostolic History and the Gospel,* ed. W. W. Gasque and R. P. Martin (Exeter, 1970), pp. 264-276; M. D. Hooker, "Philippians 2:6-11," in *Jesus und Paulus: Festschrift für W. G. Kümmel,* ed. E. E. Ellis and E. Grässer (Göttingen, 1975), pp. 151-164; O. Hofius, *Der Christushymnus Philipper 2, 6-11* (Tübingen, 1976); J. D. G. Dunn, *Christology in the Making* (London, 1980), pp. 114-121.

6. Cf. A. R. Johnson, *Sacral Kingship in Ancient Israel* (Cardiff, 1955), pp. 120-122; H. Ringgren, *The Messiah in the Old Testament,* SBT 18 (London, 1956), pp. 13-16.

7. Quoted by Paul in Rom. 14:11 with the appended comment: "So each of us shall give account of himself to God" (i.e., before his judgment seat).

8. Another example is 1 Pet. 3:15, where Isa. 8:13, "Yahweh of hosts (LXX κύριον αὐτόν), him you shall sanctify," is adapted in the form: "sanctify Christ as Lord in your hearts."

9. See *Paul, Apostle . . .* , pp. 116-119.

10. Cf. H. Lietzmann, *Mass and Lord's Supper,* E.T. (Leiden, 1979), p. 193; C. F. D. Moule, "A Reconsideration of the Context of *Maranatha,*" *NTS* 6 (1959-60), pp. 307-310, reprinted in his *Essays in New Testament Interpretation* (Cambridge, 1982), pp. 222-226.

11. Cf. M. Black, "The Christological Use of the Old Testament in the New Testament," *New Testament Studies* 18 (1971-72), p. 10; "The Maranatha Invocation," in *Christ and Spirit in the New Testament: Studies in Honour of C. F. D. Moule,* ed. B. Lindars and S. S. Smalley (Cambridge, 1973), pp. 189-196; and see especially *The Books of Enoch: Aramaic Fragments of Qumran Cave 4,* ed. J. T. Milik (Oxford, 1976), pp. 171, 175. The form *maryā* corresponds to ὁ κύριος in (Greek) 1 Enoch 1:9 (cf. Jude 14).

12. Cf. 2 Cor. 13:4a.

13. There is a close connection between his being "designated Son of God in power" and the coming of the kingdom of God "in power" in Mark 9:1. During Jesus' earthly ministry the kingdom of God was subject to limitations (cf. Luke 12:50).

14. Like the oracle of Ps. 110:1, this one also probably had its original life-setting in the enthronement of a Davidic king. The clause "You are my Son" is part of the utterance of the heavenly voice to Jesus at his baptism in Mark 1:11 (cf. John 1:34, "I have seen and have borne witness that this is the Son of God"); in the Western text of the parallel in Luke 3:22 the heavenly voice repeats the full wording: "You are my Son; today I have begotten you."

15. Cf. A. D. Nock, "'Son of God' in Pauline and Hellenistic Thought" (1961), in his *Essays on Religion and the Ancient World*, ed. Z. Stewart, II (Oxford, 1972), pp. 928-939; M. Hengel, *The Son of God: The Origin of Christology and the History of Jewish-Hellenistic Religion*, E.T. (London, 1976).

16. Cf. the Q-logion Matt. 11:27 // Luke 10:22; but Jesus' use of *Abba* is evidence enough. See p. 130 and p. 303, n. 60.

17. Gal. 4:9. See further on these "elemental forces" F. F. Bruce, *Galatians*, NIGTC (Exeter/Grand Rapids, 1982), pp. 193f., 202-205; *Colossians-Philemon-Ephesians*, NICNT (Grand Rapids, 1984), pp. 99f., 124f.

18. Compare the challenge of the Servant of Yahweh in Isa. 50:8f.

19. Cf. the abortive attempt to prosecute Joshua the high priest in the heavenly court in Zech. 3:1-5.

20. This intercession is obscured in LXX, but the Targum of Jonathan introduces the theme elsewhere in the fourth Servant Song, e.g., at Isa. 53:4, 11 ("for their trespasses he will make entreaty"), 12 ("he will make entreaty for many trespasses").

21. Cf. E. G. Rupp, "The Finished Work of Christ in Word and Sacrament," in *The Finality of Christ*, ed. D. Kilpatrick (Nashville/New York, 1966), pp. 175-192.

22. As the coming "shoot from the stump of Jesse" is endowed with the Spirit in Isa. 11:2, so is the Servant of Yahweh in Isa. 53:1.

23. Joel 2:28-32, quoted in the context of the first Christian Pentecost in Acts 2:17-21. Part of the peroration of the prophecy ("every one who calls upon the name of the Lord will be saved") is quoted by Paul as a gospel *testimonium* in Romans 10:13.

24. Acts 2:22-33; John 7:39.

25. Mark 1:8; Matt. 3:11 // Luke 3:16; John 1:33.

26. 1 Cor. 12:12-26.

27. Cf. Eph. 2:20-22; also 1 Pet. 2:4f.

28. Cf. 1QS 8.5f., where the community is the holy place and its inner council the holy of holies. See B. Gärtner, *The Temple and the Community in Qumran and the New Testament*, SNTSM 1 (Cambridge, 1965).

29. Cf. J. D. G. Dunn, "2 Corinthians iii.17—'the Lord is the Spirit'," *JTS* n.s. 21 (1970), pp. 309-320; C. F. D. Moule, "2 Cor. 3:18b, *Kathaper apo kuriou pneumatos*," in *Neues Testament und Geschichte: Oscar Cullmann zum 70. Geburtstag*, ed. H. Baltensweiler and B. Reicke (Zürich/Tübingen, 1972), pp. 231-237, reprinted in *Essays in New Testament Interpretation*, pp. 227-234.

30. Cf. Paul's use of παρρησία in 2 Cor. 3:12; see W. C. van Unnik, "With Unveiled Face," *NovT* 6 (1963), pp. 153-169.

31. See *Paul, Apostle . . .* , pp. 188-202.

32. G. Smeaton, *The Doctrine of the Holy Spirit* (Edinburgh, 1882), p. 57.

33. E. Käsemann, *Religion in Geschichte und Gegenwart*[3], II (Tübingen, 1958), col. 1274 (*s.v.* "Geist").

34. C. H. Pinnock, "The Concept of Spirit in the Epistles of Paul" (unpublished Ph.D. thesis, University of Manchester, 1963), p. 105.

35. Cf. H. J. Holtzmann, *Lehrbuch der neutestamentlichen Theologie,* II (Tübingen, ²1911), p. 88: "eine gewisse Entpersönlichung desselben Christusbegriffes."

36. Cf. 2 Cor. 13:14; also the "unity of the Spirit" in Eph. 4:3.

37. Cf. Col. 1:8, "your love in the Spirit." This is the only reference to the Spirit in Colossians. The role of the Spirit in other Pauline letters is in Colossians filled by the risen Christ. Thus, if in other letters the indwelling Spirit is believers' hope of glory (Rom. 8:11, 14-16, 23; 2 Cor. 5:5; Eph. 1:13f.), in Col. 1:27 it is the indwelling Christ ("Christ in you, the hope of glory"). If in Colossians the present ministry of Christ is emphasized rather than that of the Spirit, the reason may be that the former emphasis was judged to be more helpful to its readers in their current situation.

38. Actually it is the "offering" of the Gentile Christians, presented to God by Paul in pursuance of his "priestly service" (ἱερουργία) in the gospel, that is "sanctified by the Holy Spirit," but since they are the offering, it is they who are so sanctified.

39. Cf. Eph. 4:4-6, "one Spirit, . . . one Lord, . . . one God and Father of all." On such triadic patterns in the New Testament see C. F. D. Moule, "The New Testament and the Doctrine of the Trinity," *Expository Times* 88 (1976-77), pp. 16-20.

40. This quotation is introduced by Paul with the words "as it is written," implying that it comes from holy writ, but the source cannot be identified. The words resemble Isa. 64:4, but are not directly derived from it. Origen (on Matt. 27:9; cf. Jerome on Isa. 64:4 and Ambrosiaster on 1 Cor. 2:9) says they appear in the *Secrets (Apocalypse) of Elijah;* in *Acts of Peter* 39 and *Gospel of Thomas* 17 they are ascribed to Jesus. See also E. von Nordheim, "Das Zitat des Paulus in 1 Kor 2,9 und seine Beziehung zum koptischen Testament Jakobs," *ZNW* 65 (1974), pp. 112-20 (this Coptic work is a christianized version of a Jewish testament from which, it is suggested, Paul may have quoted), with reply by H. F. D. Sparks, "1 Kor 2,9 a quotation from the Coptic Testament of Jacob?" *ZNW* 67 (1976), pp. 269-276.

41. It was through their ignorance of this hidden wisdom that the "rulers (ἄρχοντες) of this age" were so misguided as to seal their own doom by "crucifying the Lord of glory" (1 Cor. 2:8); cf. p. 104.

42. 1QH 12.11-12.

43. 1 Cor. 12:8-10, 28; 14:1-6.

44. "The spirits of prophets are subject to prophets" (1 Cor. 14:32).

45. For the parallel invocation of God as *Abba* see p. 130 and p. 303, n. 60.

46. CD 2.12.

47. CD 1.11f.; 1QpHab. 7.1-8; cf. 1 Pet. 1:10-12. See pp. 43, 53.

48. For the foundation of Paul's appreciation of Christ as the image of God see Seyoon Kim, *The Origin of Paul's Gospel,* WUNT 2.4 (Tübingen, ²1984), pp. 193-268.

49. 2 Cor. 3:18 (see p. 122); cf. Gal. 4:19.

50. 1 Cor. 15:49.

51. Paul says this of the ἀνήρ, the male, although in Gen. 1:26f. it is said of ἄνθρωπος, mankind. But he read Gen. 1:26-30 in the light of Gen. 2:18-23, and concluded that it was first in the form of the male that mankind was created to bear the image of God: "male and female he created them" being taken to mean "first male and later female."

52. Wisdom 7:26, where wisdom is also described as "a reflection (ἀπαύγασμα, cf. Heb. 1:3, where the Son is the ἀπαύγασμα of God's glory) of eternal light, a spotless mirror of the working of God" (with ἔσοπτρον, "mirror," cf. κατοπτριζόμενοι, "beholding," "reflecting," in 2 Cor. 3:18 and δι' ἐσόπτρου, "in a mirror," in 1 Cor. 13:12).

53. Cf. Rev. 3:14, where Christ speaks as "the Amen, . . . the beginning of God's creation"—an echo of Prov. 8:22, 30 where Wisdom speaks as "the beginning of his way," his *'āmôn* ("master workman") at the creation.

54. The wording echoes that of Isa. 52:13–53:12, but in another Greek rendering than that of the Septuagint (where the servant is παῖς, not δοῦλος as here): ἐκένωσεν ἑαυτὸν . . . εἰς θάνατον reflects "he poured out his soul to death" (Isa. 53:12).

55. Cf. Rabbi Aqiba in *Pirqê Abôth* 3.19.

56. Cf. Rabbi Eleazar in TB *Pesaḥim* 68b.

57. See my *Paul, Apostle . . .* , pp. 190-193.

58. Heb. *rûaḥ haqqōdeš*.

59. Cf. Rom. 5:2; Col. 1:27.

60. Cf. Mark 14:36. See J. Jeremias, *The Central Message of the New Testament* (London, 1965), pp. 9-30; *Abba* (Göttingen, 1966), pp. 15-67; also G. Vermes, *Jesus and the World of Judaism* (London, 1983), pp. 39-43; J. Barr, " 'Abba, Father' and the Familiarity of Jesus' Speech," *Theology* 91 (1988), pp. 173-179.

61. John uses τέκνα, not υἱοί, of the children of God, reserving υἱός for the Son of God *par excellence;* Paul uses both words interchangeably.

62. In this context "seal" and "guarantee" are practically interchangeable. Gk. ἀρραβών is derived from a Phoenician mercantile term, which appears in Hebrew as *'ērābôn*, and even if it is nothing more than a coincidence, it is worth recalling that on the first occasion where *'ērābôn* appears in the Hebrew Bible, in the sense of "guarantee" or "pledge" for the payment of a debt, the debtor's "seal" (Heb. *ḥōtām*) was an important part of the pledge (Gen. 38:18, 25).

63. Cf. G. W. H. Lampe, *The Seal of the Spirit* (London, 1951).

64. E.g., RSV, NEB; cf. GNB ("the Holy Spirit he had promised"), New American Bible ("the Holy Spirit who had been promised").

65. Cf. Acts 1:4; 2:33.

66. A. Schweitzer, *The Mysticism of Paul the Apostle*, E.T. (London, 1931), p. 165.

NOTES TO CHAPTER 9

1. In Arnold Ehrhardt's opinion "much animosity, so it seems, had also died with them" (*The Acts of the Apostles* [Manchester, 1969], p. 50).

2. A. N. Sherwin-White, *Roman Society and Roman Law in the New Testament* (Oxford, 1963), p. 189.

3. See pp. 144f., 167.

4. C. J. Cadoux, "The Chronological Division of Acts," *JTS* 19 (1918), pp. 333-341; "A Tentative Synthetic Chronology of the Apostolic Age," *JBL* 56 (1937), pp. 177-191.

5. Acts 2:47b; 6:7; 9:31; 12:24; 16:5; 19:20; 28:31. C. H. Turner calls them "rubrics of progress" ("Chronology of the New Testament," *Hastings' Dictionary of the Bible,* I [Edinburgh, 1898], p. 424).

6. Cf. E. Haenchen, *The Acts of the Apostles*, E.T. (Oxford, 1971), p. 60, n. 1.

7. *Hastings' Dictionary of the Bible,* I, p. 415.

8. Cf. E. Schürer, *History of the Jewish People in the Age of Jesus Christ,* II (Edinburgh, 1979), pp. 129f.

9. Cf. E. Schwartz, "Die Aeren von Gerasa und Eleutheropolis," *Nachrichten der kgl. Gesellschaft der Wissenschaften zu Göttingen* (1906), pp. 367f.; E. Meyer, *Ursprung*

und Anfänge des Christentums, III (Stuttgart/Berlin, 1923), p. 346; E. A. Knauf, "Zum Ethnarchen des Aretas 2 Kor 11,32," *ZNW* 74 (1983), pp. 145-147.

10. Josephus, *BJ* 2.181-183; *Ant.* 18.237.

11. Josephus, *Ant.* 18.252; 19.274f.

12. Josephus, *BJ* 2.214; *Ant.* 19.351.

13. Josephus, *Ant.* 19.236-296.

14. News of Tiberius's death, which took place on 16 March, A.D. 37 (Tacitus, *Annals* 6.50.7), was delivered to Vitellius, legate of Syria, in Jerusalem on the fourth day after Passover (Josephus, *Ant.* 18.124), which in that year coincided with the full moon of 17/18 April. Such official news would travel by the fastest means. (In A.D. 41 Passover fell on 6/7 April.)

15. Josephus, *Ant.* 19.343. The institution of these games in 9 B.C. is recorded in *BJ* 1.415; *Ant.* 16.136-144. When Josephus says they were celebrated quinquennially (κατὰ πενταετηρίδα), he uses inclusive reckoning. The date of Caesarea's *dies natalis* (5 March) is known from Eusebius, *Martyrs of Palestine* 11.30.

16. But if, as is possible, the games celebrated Claudius's birthday, which fell on 1 August (Suetonius, *Claudius* 2.1), the Passover of Acts 12:4 could have been that of A.D. 44. (In that year Passover fell on 3/4 April.)

17. Suetonius, *Claudius* 18.2.

18. In Rome, at the beginning of his principate (Dio Cassius, *Hist.* 60.11), and again between his ninth and eleventh years (Tacitus, *Annals* 12.43; Orosius, *Hist.* 7.6.17); in Greece, in his eighth or ninth year (Eusebius, *Chronicle,* anno Abr. 2065); in Egypt, in his fifth year (P. Mich. 123, 127). See K. S. Gapp, "The Universal Famine under Claudius," *HTR* 28 (1925), pp. 258-265.

19. Josephus, *Ant.* 20.101, where the manuscripts read ἐπὶ τούτοις ("under these," i.e., the two procurators mentioned above) but the Epitome reads ἐπὶ τούτου ("under him," i.e., Alexander).

20. Josephus, *Ant.* 20.51-53.

21. J. Jeremias, "Sabbathjahr und neutestamentliche Chronologie," *Abba* (Göttingen, 1966), pp. 233-238.

22. *CIL* VI.31545.

23. *IGRR* III.935, corrected reading in J. L. Myres, *Handbook of the Cesnola Collection of Antiquities from Cyprus* (New York, 1914), 1903 (pp. 319, 548); but see T. B. Mitford, "Roman Cyprus," *ANRW* 2.7.2 (Berlin, 1980), p. 1300, n. 54, p. 1330, n. 195.

24. *IGRR* III.930.

25. See T. B. Mitford, "Notes on Some Published Inscriptions from Roman Cyprus," *Annual of the British School at Athens* 42 (1947), pp. 201-206.

26. D. G. Hogarth, *Devia Cypria* (London, 1889), p. 114. See also K. Lake, "The Chronology of Acts," *Beginnings of Christianity,* I.5 (London, 1933), especially pp. 455-459; B. Van Elderen, "Some Archaeological Observations on Paul's First Missionary Journey," in *Apostolic History and the Gospel,* ed. W. W. Gasque and R. P. Martin (Exeter, 1970), pp. 151-156.

27. Josephus, *Ant.* 18.65-80 (the Isis scandal), 81-85 (the Jewish scandal).

28. Dio Cassius, *Hist.* 60.6.6.

29. Suetonius, *Claudius* 25.4. See pp. 82f.

30. F. F. Bruce, "Christianity under Claudius," *BJRL* 44 (1961-62), pp. 315-318.

31. So G. Lüdemann, *Paul, Apostle to the Gentiles: Studies in Chronology,* E.T. (London, 1984), pp. 164-171.

32. So A. Suhl, *Paulus und seine Briefe: Ein Beitrag zur paulinischen Chronologie* (Gütersloh, 1975), p. 326; R. O. Hoerber, "The Decree of Claudius in Acts 18:2," *Concordia Theological Monthly* 31 (1960), pp. 690-694.

33. So, convincingly *(me iudice)*, E. M. Smallwood, *The Jews under Roman Rule* (Leiden, 1976), pp. 210-216. See p. 296, n. 20.

34. See A. Momigliano, *Claudius: The Emperor and his Achievement* (Cambridge, ^{2}1961), p. 30.

35. Orosius's words are: "anno eiusdem [*sc.* Claudii] nono expulsos per Claudium urbe Iudaeos Iosephus refert" (*Hist.* 7.6.15).

36. E.g., H. J. Leon, *The Jews of Ancient Rome* (Philadelphia, 1960), p. 25.

37. *SIG* II^3, 801; for the text see also A. Deissmann, *Paul: A Study in Social and Religious History*, E.T. (London, ^{2}1926), pp. 261-284; E. M. Smallwood, *Documents Illustrating the Principates of Gaius, Claudius and Nero* (Cambridge, 1967), p. 376 (p. 105).

38. From *CIL* III.476, VI.1256, with Frontinus, *De aquis urbis Romae* 1.13, it appears that by 1 August he had been acclaimed *imperator* for the 27th time.

39. See A. Plassart, "L'inscription de Delphes mentionnant le Proconsul Gallion," *Revue des Études Grecques* 80 (1967), pp. 372-378; also A. Brassac, "Une inscription de Delphes et la chronologie de Saint Paul," *RB* 10 (1913), pp. 36-53, 207-217; J. H. Oliver, "The Epistle of Claudius which mentions the Proconsul Junius Gallio," *Hesperia* 40 (1971), pp. 239f.; B. Schwank, "Der sogenannte Brief an Gallio und die Datierung des 1. Thess.," *Biblische Zeitschrift* 15 (1971), pp. 265f.; K. Haacker, "Die Gallio-Episode und die paulinische Chronologie," *ibid.* 16 (1972), pp. 252-255; C. J. Hemer, "Observations on Pauline Chronology," in *Pauline Studies*, ed. D. A. Hagner and M. J. Harris (Exeter, 1980), pp. 6-9.

40. Dio Cassius, *Hist.* 60.17.3.

41. Cf. Seneca, *Epistulae Morales* 104.1.

42. Josephus, *Ant.* 19.354.

43. *Ibid.*, 19.362.

44. Josephus, *BJ* 2.223, 247; 3.56f.; *Ant.* 20.104, 138, 159.

45. Josephus, *Ant.* 20.138f.

46. *Ibid.*, 20.141-143.

47. *Ibid.*, 20.200f.

48. *Ibid.*, 20.137f.

49. "Claudius sent out Felix . . . as procurator of Judaea, Samaria, Galilee and Peraea" (Josephus, *BJ* 2.247)—a form of words compatible with his having exercised authority in one of those regions already.

50. Tacitus, *Annals* 12.54.7.

51. *Ibid.*, 12.54.3.

52. M. Aberbach, "The Conflicting Accounts of Josephus and Tacitus concerning Cumanus' and Felix' Terms of Office," *JQR* 40 (1949-50), pp. 1-14, suggests that Cumanus had been procurator of Judaea and Samaria, while Felix was in charge of Galilee (but this is the opposite of what Tacitus says).

53. See L. H. Feldman, *Josephus* (Loeb Classical Library), IX (Cambridge, Mass./London, 1965), pp. 461-463, n. *e;* E. M. Smallwood, *The Jews under Roman Rule*, p. 266, n. 32; E. Schürer, *History of the Jewish People in the Age of Jesus Christ*, I (Edinburgh, 1973), p. 459, n. 15.

54. Josephus, *Ant.* 20.103f.

55. Tacitus, *Annals* 12.54.1.

56. *Ibid.*, 12.54.7.

57. E. M. Smallwood, *The Jews under Roman Rule*, p. 269, n. 40. See F. W. Madden, *History of Jewish Coinage* (London, 1864), p. 153; A. Reifenberg, *Ancient Jewish Coins* (Jerusalem, 1947), p. 27; cf. H. J. Cadbury, *The Book of Acts in History* (New York, 1955), p. 10.

58. Josephus, *Ant.* 20.182.

59. *Ibid.*, 20.162.

60. Tacitus, *Annals* 13.14.1.

61. *Ibid.*, 13.14.2.

62. *Ibid.*, 14.65.1.

63. Eusebius, *Chron.*, anno Abr. 2072.

64. Josephus, *BJ* 2.252.

65. See C. Erbes, "Die Todestage der Apostel Paulus und Petrus," *TU* N.F. 4.1 (Leipzig, 1899), esp. pp. 16-36.

66. See G. Ogg, *The Chronology of the Life of Paul* (London, 1968), pp. 140-145, and R. Jewett, *Dating Paul's Life* (London, 1979), pp. 48-50, for discussions of the correlation of the Jewish and Julian calendars at this season from A.D. 52 to 60.

67. W. M. Ramsay, "A Fixed Date in the Life of St. Paul," *Expositor* 5.3 (1896), pp. 336-345; *St. Paul the Traveller and the Roman Citizen*, pp. xiv-xx, 289f.; *Pauline and Other Studies* (London, 1906), pp. 345-353. The same conclusion was reached by D. Plooij, *De Chronologie van het Leven van Paulus* (Leiden, 1918), pp. 83-85.

68. Vegetius, *De re militari* 4.39.

69. Tacitus, *Annals* 15.38-44.

70. J. A. T. Robinson, *Redating the New Testament* (London, 1976), pp. 143-146, following G. Edmundson, *The Church in Rome in the First Century* (London, 1913), pp. 141-143.

71. F. F. Bruce, "Galatian Problems: 1. Autobiographical Data," *BJRL* 51 (1968-69), pp. 292-309; "Is the Paul of Acts the Real Paul?" *BJRL* 58 (1975-76), pp. 282-303, especially pp. 285-293.

72. J. Knox, "'Fourteen Years Later': A Note on the Pauline Chronology," *Journal of Religion* 16 (1936), pp. 341-349; "The Pauline Chronology," *JBL* 58 (1939), pp. 15-29; *Chapters in a Life of Paul* (New York, 1950 / London, 1954); also D. W. Riddle, *Paul, Man of Conflict* (Nashville, 1940); P. S. Minear, "The Jerusalem Fund and Pauline Chronology," *Anglical Theological Review* 25 (1943), pp. 389-396; C. H. Buck, Jr., "The Collection for the Saints," *HTR* 43 (1950), pp. 1-29; "The Date of Galatians," *JBL* 70 (1951), pp. 113-122; J. C. Hurd, Jr., *The Origin of 1 Corinthians* (London, 1965); "Pauline Chronology and Pauline Theology," in *Christian History and Interpretation: Studies Presented to John Knox*, ed. W. R. Farmer, C. F. D. Moule, R. R. Niebuhr (Cambridge, 1967), pp. 225-248; G. Lüdemann, *Paulus der Heidenapostel, 1. Studien zur Chronologie* (Göttingen, 1980). Lüdemann's argument is more detailed and thoroughgoing than any of its predecessors; the English translation of this volume (see n. 31 above) is appropriately commended in an introduction by John Knox.

73. Cf. J. Knox, *Chapters*, pp. 54-58; G. Lüdemann, *Paul*, pp. 77-78.

74. It is disputed whether the "fourteen years" of Gal. 2:1 are reckoned from the same point of departure as Paul's earlier Jerusalem visit "after three years" (Gal. 1:18) or from that earlier visit itself.

75. J. Knox, "'Fourteen Years Later,'" p. 345. That Macedonia may have been Paul's earliest mission-field was argued by M. J. Suggs ("Concerning the Date of

Paul's Macedonian Ministry," *NovT* 4 [1960], pp. 60-68) on the basis of Phil. 4:15f. (cf. Phil. 1:15; 2 Thess. 2:13). But ἐν ἀρχῇ τοῦ εὐαγγελίου (Phil. 4:15) probably means "when you first heard the gospel" rather than "when I first preached the gospel."

76. J. Knox, *Chapters*, pp. 68-70; G. Lüdemann, *Paul*, pp. 147-157. The visit of Acts 18:22 had already been equated with that of Gal. 2:1 by E. Barnikol, *Die drei Jerusalemreisen des Paulus: Die echte Konkordanz der Paulusbriefe mit der Wir-Quelle der Apostelgeschichte*, FEUNTK 2 (Kiel, 1929). The same equation is maintained by J. van Bruggen, *"Na veertien Jaren"* (Kampen, 1973), pp. 40-43, 223-225; but he does not regard the visit of Acts 18:22 as a duplicate of any other visit in Acts. The widespread identification of the visits of Acts 11:30 and 15:4 prompts a question about the historical status of Barnabas and Paul's missionary journey in Cyprus and Asia Minor, recorded in Acts 13–14. C. H. Buck derives the record of this journey from a source which begins at Acts 13:1 and (after the interruption of 15:1-33) continues further from 15:35 to 18:23; the journey took place indeed, but before the famine, not after it ("The Collection for the Saints," pp. 18f.). H. Conzelmann takes the whole journey to be Luke's construction, "a 'model journey,' furnishing the pattern for subsequent missionary activity" (*Acts of the Apostles*, E.T., Hermeneia [Philadelphia, 1987], p. 98).

77. G. Lüdemann, *Paul*, pp. 172, 262f.; cf. J. Knox, *Chapters*, p. 85. This dating would go well with the Eusebian date for Felix's deposition (A.D. 55).

78. G. Lüdemann, *Paul*, pp. 158-173. He dates Paul's first visit to Corinth in A.D. 41, the year (he argues) of Claudius's expulsion edict. N. Hyldahl, *Die paulinische Chronologie*, Acta Theologica Danica 19 (Leiden, 1986), adheres in general to the newer chronology of Knox and others, but he commands greater confidence than Lüdemann when, for example, without any forcing of the evidence, he dates Paul's first visit to Corinth between A.D. 49 and 51, so that it overlaps Gallio's brief proconsulship (pp. 121-124).

79. The present tense of "remember" (μνημονεύωμεν) may have continuous force: "it is a temptation to translate here, 'they wanted us to continue to remember the poor' " and to take the aorist ἐσπούδασα as having inceptive force, "which very thing I began to busy myself with" (C. H. Buck, "The Collection for the Saints," p. 12, n. 15). On the continuous force of μνημονεύωμεν see also E. D. Burton, *The Epistle to the Galatians* (Edinburgh, 1921), p. 99. C. W. Emmet takes the aorist ἐσπούδασα as having pluperfect force, which "fits in well with the fact that Paul had actually just brought alms to Jerusalem" ("The Case for the Tradition," *Beginnings of Christianity*, ed. F. J. Foakes Jackson and K. Lake, I.2 [London, 1922], p. 279); so also D. R. Hall, "St. Paul and Famine Relief: A Study in Galatians 2:10," *Expository Times* 82 (1970-71), pp. 309-311.

80. The delivery of the gift in Jerusalem would be the "seal" on this phase of his ministry (Rom. 15:28).

81. C. H. Buck, "The Collection for the Saints," p. 26.

82. The instructions to the Galatian Christians to set aside a proportion of their income week by week were given before similar instructions were given to the Corinthians.

83. G. B. Caird, "Chronology of the NT," *Interpreter's Dictionary of the Bible*, I (New York/Nashville, 1962), p. 606.

84. "Galatian Problems: 4. The Date of the Epistle," *BJRL* 54 (1971-72), pp. 250-267; cf. *The Epistle to the Galatians*, NIGTC (Exeter/Grand Rapids, 1982), pp. 43-56.

NOTES TO CHAPTER 10

1. Gk. ἐν ' Ἀντιοχείᾳ κατὰ τὴν οὖσαν ἐκκλησίαν. This attributive use of the present participle of the verb "to be" with ἐκκλησία is practically equivalent to our expression "the local church" (cf. Acts 11:22).

2. The churches of Antioch (Acts 11:26; 14:27; 15:3), South Galatia (Acts 14:23; 16:5), Syria and Cilicia (Acts 15:41), Ephesus (Acts 20:17, 28).

3. M. Hengel, *Between Jesus and Paul*, E.T. (London, 1983), p. 110.

4. On these and other postulated sources see A. Harnack, *The Acts of the Apostles*, E.T. (London, 1909), pp. 162-202; J. Dupont, *The Sources of Acts*, E.T. (London, 1964), pp. 17-72.

5. Cf. S. G. F. Brandon, *The Fall of Jerusalem and the Christian Church* (London, 1951), pp. 27f., 46f.

6. By Hegesippus, quoted in Eusebius, *Hist. Eccl.* 2.23.4.

7. See p. 136.

8. There is a contrast between 5,000 *men* (ἄνδρες) in Acts 4:4 and 3,000 *persons* (ψυχαί) in Acts 2:41. Harnack (*Acts*, p. 183) discerns two narratives of the same events.

9. See p. 310, n. 53 for the view that these μυριάδες are all the Jews of Jerusalem and not only the members of the church.

10. J. Jeremias, *Jerusalem in the Time of Jesus*, E.T. (London, 1969), pp. 83f.; cf. "Die Einwohnerzahl Jerusalems zur Zeit Jesu," in his *Abba* (Göttingen, 1966), pp. 335-341.

11. Acts 6:1.

12. Cf. C. F. D. Moule, "Once More, Who were the Hellenists?" *Expository Times* 70 (1958-59), pp. 100-102; M. Hengel, *Between Jesus and Paul*, pp. 1-29.

13. On the "synagogue of the Hebrews" in Corinth see *CIJ* 718; B. Powell, "Greek Inscriptions from Corinth," *American Journal of Archaeology*, series 2, 7 (1903), pp. 60f., No. 40; on that in Rome see *CIJ* 291, 317, 510, 535 (also pp. lxxvif.); H. J. Leon, *The Jews of Ancient Rome* (Philadelphia, 1960), pp. 147-149.

14. *CIJ* 1404. See R. Weill, *Comptes rendus de l'Académie des Inscriptions*, 29 mai 1914, pp. 333f.; "La cité de David . . . Campagne 1913-14," *Revue des études juives* 69 (1919), annexe, pl. XXVa; 71 (1920), pp. 30-34; A. Deissmann, *Light from the Ancient East*, E.T. (London, ²1927), pp. 439-441. Deissmann considered the identity of the "Theodotus" synagogue with that of Acts 6:9 to be "not impossible, but . . . not probable" (p. 441).

15. This is indicated not only by the subject-matter but also by the transitional formula ἐν δὲ ταῖς ἡμέραις ταύταις.

16. For example, we know from Paul of his difference with Barnabas over a serious point of principle (Gal. 2:13), but when they part company in Acts, it is over a personal issue (Acts 15:36-39).

17. See I. H. Marshall, "Palestinian and Hellenistic Christianity," *NTS* 19 (1972-73), pp. 271-287; M. Hengel, *Judaism and Hellenism*, E.T. (London, 1974), *passim;* R. Kuntzmann and J. Schlosser (ed.), *Études sur le judaïsme hellénistique* (Paris, 1984).

18. See W. L. Knox, *Some Hellenistic Elements in Primitive Christianity* (London, 1944), pp. 30-33, commenting on TB *Soṭah* 49b.

19. Philippians 3:5; cf. 2 Corinthians 11:22.

20. See C. F. D. Moule, "Once More . . . ," p. 102 (cf. n. 12 above); M. Hengel (*Between Jesus and Paul*, p. 11) agrees.

21. Acts 4:36.

22. Acts 6:5.

23. As they are called by W. M. Ramsay, *St. Paul the Traveller and the Roman Citizen* (London, [14]1920), p. 375.

24. Acts 3:1, 11; 5:12-21.

25. Acts 7:44-50.

26. This indeed is part of the testimony of the "false witnesses" at Jesus' trial, but the expression is no doubt his own, and entered into the Christian vocabulary.

27. See pp. 163f. below.

28. The tradition is attested in the Western text of Acts 11:28 ("when we were gathered together") and in the so-called anti-Marcionite prologue to Luke's Gospel.

29. Mark 14:57-59, a passage not reproduced in Luke's trial narrative.

30. Acts 7:58; 22:20; cf. Leviticus 24:14; Deuteronomy 13:9; 17:7.

31. Acts 8:1. Luke sometimes uses "all" in a hyperbolic way.

32. See p. 310, n. 53 below.

33. That it is the same visit is scarcely to be doubted, although some have denied this; cf. P. Parker, "Once More, Acts and Galatians," *JBL* 86 (1967), pp. 175-182.

34. O. Linton, "The Third Aspect: A Neglected Point of View," *Studia Theologica* 3 (1949), pp. 79-95.

35. Luke normally restricts the term "apostles" to the Twelve; for an exception (Acts 14:4, 14) see n. 40 below.

36. Acts 10:17-48.

37. Acts 11:1-18.

38. Acts 12:1-23.

39. James appears to have retained this esteem until his death in A.D. 62; his judicial murder at the instance of the high priest Ananus II outraged public opinion (Josephus, *Ant.* 20.200).

40. But when he and Paul are called ἀπόστολοι in Acts 14:4, 14 (see n. 35 above), Luke refers to them as emissaries of the church of Antioch (Acts 13:2f.).

41. Acts 10:1-4.

42. Acts 15:1, 5.

43. Acts 15:19f., 28f.

44. Martin Hengel sees in the decree evidence of "an astounding magnanimity" on the part of the Jerusalem leaders, for "this bold step necessarily meant defamation for them and persecution by the Jewish majority in Palestine" (*Victory over Violence*, E.T. [London, 1975], p. 87).

45. Cf. T. W. Manson, *Studies in the Gospels and Epistles* (Manchester, 1962), p. 186 (reprinted from "The Problem of the Epistle to the Galatians," *BJRL* 24 [1940], p. 77).

46. Acts 16:4. For an argument against the authenticity of this verse see A. S. Geyser, "Paul, the Apostolic Decree and the Liberals in Corinth," in *Studia Paulina in honorem J. de Zwaan*, ed. J. N. Sevenster and W. C. van Unnik (Haarlem, 1953), pp. 124-138.

47. It is argued, however, that Paul paid no visit to Jerusalem between that recorded in Galatians 2:1-10 and his last visit, to deliver the proceeds of the collection (the visit projected in Romans 15:25); cf. J. Knox, *Chapters in a Life of Paul* (London, 1954), pp. 51-60, 85. See p. 147.

48. H. J. Cadbury thought that the Jerusalem church was understood here by most commentators under the influence of the Western text of the preceding verse (*Beginnings of Christianity*, I.4 [London, 1933], pp. 230f.). J. Knox (*Chapters*, pp. 68-70)

argues that the visit of Acts 18:22 is identical with that of Galatians 2:1-10; cf. G. Lüdemann, *Paul, Apostle to the Gentiles: Studies in Chronology*, E.T. (London, 1984), p. 149, for "the thesis that Acts 11:27ff.; 15:1ff.; and 18:22 are a tripling of Paul's second visit to Jerusalem and that Acts 18:22 represents its original historical location." See p. 147.

49. As in Acts 11:22; 13:1 (see p. 308, n. 2).

50. "It seems likely that Luke had some knowledge of the offering as a motive for the final journey. . . . Luke had good sources, or a good source, for his journey (J. Knox, *Chapters*, p. 71).

51. See pp. 170-172.

52. Acts 21:20a ("when they heard it, they glorified God").

53. J. Munck, "without any authority in the manuscript[s]," as he acknowledged, proposed to delete the words "of those who have believed" (τῶν πεπιστευκότων) from Acts 21:20b, reading in consequence: "how many myriads there are in Judaea; they are all zealots for the law"—the reference being to Jews in general, not Jewish Christians in particular (*Paul and the Salvation of Mankind*, E.T. [London, 1959], pp. 240f.; cf. his *The Acts of the Apostles*, Anchor Bible [Garden City, N.Y., 1967], p. 209). The same deletion was proposed, on different grounds, by F. C. Baur (*Paul: His Life and Works*, E.T., I [London, ²1876], pp. 201-204).

54. To pay the expenses of Nazirites who were discharging their vows was a charitable act: Herod Agrippa I contributed to his reputation for piety by paying the expenses of many Nazirites (Josephus, *Ant.* 19.294).

55. Cf. 1 Corinthians 9:20. According to Acts 18:18, Paul had undertaken a Nazirite vow on his own behalf some years before (the construction is ambiguous, but the reference is more probably to Paul than to Aquila).

56. Acts 21:27-29. The leader of these Asian Jews may have been "Alexander the coppersmith," who did Paul "great harm" (2 Timothy 4:14), if he is to be identified with Alexander, a Jew of Ephesus mentioned in Acts 19:33.

57. The "gates" (θύραι) were those leading from the inner courts (the sacred area proper) down into the outer court (cf. Mishnah, *Middoth* 1:4, 5).

58. T. D. Bernard, *The Progress of Doctrine in the New Testament* (London, ⁵1900), p. 121.

59. See p. 155 above.

60. See p. 309, n. 26. When James, Cephas and John are said to have been reputed as "pillars" in the Jerusalem church (Galatians 2:9), this probably means that they were reckoned to be pillars in the new temple, not made with hands (see C. K. Barrett, "Paul and the 'Pillar' Apostles," in *Studia Paulina in honorem J. de Zwaan*, ed. J. N. Sevenster and W. C. van Unnik, pp. 1-19).

61. Cited by Eusebius, *Hist. Eccl.* 2.23.6. Cf. A. Ehrhardt, *The Apostolic Succession* (London, 1953), pp. 64f.

62. So A. J. Mattill, "The Purpose of Acts: Schneckenburger Reconsidered," in *Apostolic History and the Gospel*, ed. W. W. Gasque and R. P. Martin (Exeter/Grand Rapids, 1970), pp. 115f. J. D. G. Dunn suggests that, if James and his colleagues did not refuse to accept the collection, they postponed acceptance of it until Paul, by adopting their proposed course of action, "had proved his good Jewish faith" (*Unity and Diversity in the New Testament* [London, 1977], p. 257). See p. 312, n. 13.

63. H. Chadwick, "The Circle and the Ellipse," Oxford inaugural lecture, 1959, reprinted in his *History and Thought of the Early Church* (London, 1982), pp. 3-17.

64. See pp. 79-97.

65. J. A. Bengel, *Gnomon Novi Testamenti* ([1742] London, 1862), p. 489: "Victoria Verbi Dei. Paulus Romae, apex evangelii, Actorum finis. . . . Hierosolymis coepit; Romae desinit."

66. Cf. Isaiah 2:3, "Out of Zion shall go forth the law, and the word of the Lord from Jerusalem," with a discussion of its relevance to the apostolic church in B. Gerhardsson, *Memory and Manuscript* (Lund, 1961), pp. 273-280.

67. Other aspects of the subject of this lecture were dealt with by G. W. H. Lampe in his Ethel M. Wood lecture *St. Luke and the Church of Jerusalem* (London, 1969).

NOTES TO CHAPTER 11

1. Thuc., *Hist.* 1.22.1. See A. W. Gomme, "The Speeches in Thucydides," in *Essays in Greek History and Literature* (Oxford, 1957), pp. 156-189; T. F. Glasson, "The Speeches in Acts and Thucydides," *Expository Times* 76 (1964-65), p. 165; P. A. Stadter (ed.), *The Speeches in Thucydides* (Chapel Hill, N.C., 1973); M. I. Finley, *Ancient History: Evidence and Models* (London, 1985), pp. 13-15; G. H. R. Horsley, "Speeches and Dialogue in Acts," *New Testament Studies* 32 (1986), pp. 609-614.

2. See also F. Veltman, "The Defense Speeches of Paul in Acts," in *Perspectives in Luke-Acts*, ed. C. H. Talbert (Edinburgh, 1978), pp. 243-256.

3. See pp. 91f., 146-148.

4. See H. Chadwick, "The Circle and the Ellipse," in *History and Thought of the Early Church* (London, 1982), p. 16.

5. It is evident from a comparison with Paul's letters that these fellow-travelers were carrying their respective churches' contributions to the Jerusalem relief fund.

6. See W. C. van Unnik, *Tarsus or Jerusalem: The City of Paul's Youth*, E.T. (London, 1962).

7. Exceptionally, the Romans allowed the Jewish authorities in Judaea to retain the right of capital jurisdiction in this sphere, especially with regard to Gentile trespass into the inner courts of the temple (cf. Josephus, *BJ* 5.194; 6.124f.).

8. Cf. Josephus, *Ant.* 18.17.

9. See n. 5 above (on Acts 20:4).

10. See K. Berger, "Almosen für Israel: Zum historischen Kontext der paulinischen Kollekte," *New Testament Studies* 23 (1976-77), pp. 180-204.

11. These so-called God-fearers have been the subject of much literary debate in recent years; see L. H. Feldman, "Jewish 'Sympathizers' in Classical Literature and Inscriptions," *Transactions of the American Philological Association* 81 (1956), pp. 200-208, and "The Omnipresence of the God-fearers," *Biblical Archaeology Review* 12.5 (Sept.-Oct. 1986), pp. 58-69; A. T. Kraabel, "The Diaspora Synagogue: Archaeological and Epigraphic Evidence since Sukenik," in *Aufstieg und Niedergang der römischen Welt*, 2/19 (Berlin, 1979), pp. 477-510, and "The Disappearance of the 'God-fearers,'" *Numen* 28 (1981), pp. 113-126; M. Wilcox, "The 'God-fearers' in Acts—A Reconsideration," *Journal for the Study of the New Testament* 13 (1981), pp. 102-122; T. M. Finn, "The God-fearers Reconsidered," *Catholic Biblical Quarterly* 47 (1985), pp. 75-84; J. Reynolds and R. F. Tannenbaum, "Jews and God-fearers at Aphrodisias," *Proceedings of the Cambridge Philological Society*, Supp. Vol. 12 (Cambridge, 1987).

12. See J. D. G. Dunn, *Unity and Diversity in the New Testament* (London, 1977), pp. 256f. Cf. p. 95 and p. 297, n. 61; p. 164 and p. 310, n. 62.

13. It has even been suggested that members of the Jerusalem church drew Paul into an ambush "by luring him into the Temple" and that Luke suspected as much; see A. J. Mattill, "The Purpose of Acts: Schneckenberger Reconsidered," in *Apostolic History and the Gospel,* ed. W. W. Gasque and R. P. Martin (Exeter, 1970), pp. 115f.

14. On the theory that the famine-relief visit to Jerusalem of Acts 11:28-30 is an antedating of Paul's present visit see p. 137.

15. Compare the serious charges brought against him and his friends at an earlier date, in Thessalonica (Acts 17:5-7). See p. 110.

16. An echo of Isa. 42:6 (cf. Luke 2:33; Acts 13:47).

17. Cf. the prologue to Luke's twofold work (Luke 1:1-4); see L. C. A. Alexander, "Luke's Preface in the Context of Greek Preface-Writing," *Novum Testamentum* 28 (1986), pp. 48-74.

18. Josephus, *Vita* 14.

19. So M. von Aberle, "Exegetische Studien: 2. Über den Zweck der Apostel-geschichte," *Theologische Quartalschrift* 37 (1855), pp. 173-236; D. Plooij, "The Work of St. Luke: A Historical Apology for Pauline Preaching before the Roman Court," *Expositor* series 8, 8 (1914), pp. 511-523, and "Again: The Work of St. Luke," *ibid.,* 13 (1917), pp. 108-124; J. I. Still, *St. Paul on Trial* (London, 1923); G. S. Duncan, *St. Paul's Ephesian Ministry* (London, 1929), pp. 97f.

20. Cf. Acts 16:19-21; 19:23-28.

21. P. W. Walaskay, *"And so we came to Rome,"* SNTSM 49 (Cambridge, 1983).

22. Tert., *Ad Nationes* 1.7.

NOTES TO CHAPTER 12

1. For the majority reading "every spirit which does not confess Jesus" some versions (notably the Latin) and patristic witnesses read "every spirit which disunites (Gk. *lyei*) Jesus"—i.e., disunites the earthly Jesus and the heavenly Christ (an error against which John in this letter guards his readers).

2. Literally "who will not acknowledge Jesus Christ coming in flesh," which in some contexts might imply a denial of his future coming but in this context more probably implies a denial of his incarnation.

3. Polycarp, *Ep.* 7.1.

4. Irenaeus, *Against Heresies* 3.3.4.

5. Not, as RSV has it, "you know what is restraining him now"; the order of the Greek words demands that "now" be taken along with "you know," in a resumptive rather than a temporal sense: "as it is, you know" (they knew because they had been told; we have not been told, so we have to guess).

6. A fuller exegesis and discussion of this passage is given in F. F. Bruce, *1 and 2 Thessalonians,* WBC (Waco, TX, 1982), pp. 159-178.

7. NEB rightly: "when you see the 'abomination of desolation' usurping a place which is not his."

8. Philo, *Legation to Gaius* 203-346; Josephus, *Ant.* 18.261-301.

9. It is probable that Heb. *ba'al šāmayim* (corresponding to Aram. *ba'al šāmēn*), was referred to by Jews at this time by the derogatory pun *šiqqûṣ šômēm,* "the

abomination that lays waste" (*ba'al*, the unspeakable name of a pagan divinity, being replaced by *šiqqûṣ*, "abomination"), rendered literally into Greek as *bdelygma erēmōseōs* (cf. E. Nestle, "Der Greuel der Verwüstung," *ZAW* 4 [1884], p. 248).

10. Josephus, *BJ* 6.316 (see p. 27).

11. C. C. Lattey, *The Book of Daniel*, WVSS (Dublin, 1948).

12. The forecast of the decline and fall of Antiochus (Dan. 11:40-45) follows Isaiah's foretelling of the downfall of the Assyrian invader (Isa. 14:24-27; 31:8f.) and Ezekiel's description of the end of Gog (Ezek. 39:1-8).

13. J. Calvin, *Commentaries on Daniel*, E.T., II (Edinburgh, 1853), pp. 338-367.

14. P. Mauro, *The Seventy Weeks and the Great Tribulation* (Boston, Mass., 1923), pp. 139-167. The work by Farquharson was *Daniel's Last Vision and Prophecy* (Aberdeen, 1838).

15. Before its publication in book form, Mauro's work appeared as a series of papers in his periodical *The Last Hour*.

16. E. J. Young, *The Prophecy of Daniel* (Grand Rapids, 1949). Compare the gap which some interpreters posit between the sixty-ninth and seventieth "weeks" of Dan. 9:24-27 (an interpretation which Young dismisses, although his own theory of a gap between vv. 35 and 36 of Daniel 11 is open to the same objections).

17. Leviathan's heads (Ps. 74:14) are given as seven in the Ugaritic texts (where he is "the accursed one of seven heads") and in *Od. Sol.* 22:5 ("the dragon with seven heads").

18. The expectation of the returning Nero took two forms: for the first twenty years after his death the belief persisted that he was not dead but had gone into hiding, and would come back at the head of a Parthian army and resume his sovereignty; after 88 this gave way to the expectation that he would return to life and rule once more.

19. Even pagan writers regarded Domitian as a second Nero, but "Domitian cannot be identified with Nero redivivus. . . . It is not an actual Roman emperor, but a supernatural monster from the abyss that is to play the part of the Nero redivivus, and that in the immediate future" (R. H. Charles, *The Revelation of St. John*, ICC, I [Edinburgh, 1920], pp. lxxvif.).

20. The spelling *nrwn qsr* (which in the Hebrew / Aramaic alphabet yields 666) is found in an Aramaic document from Wadi Murabba'at (Mur 18.1), dated in Nero's reign.

21. E. Stauffer, *Christ and the Caesars*, E.T. (London, 1955), p. 179. But it is not clear that the series of Domitian's abbreviated titles, yielding (in Greek) a total of 666, actually appears on any one coin.

22. *Ascension of Isaiah* 4:1-4.

23. *Didachē* 16.3-8.

24. This cannot be identified as a precise quotation from the extant Enoch literature.

25. Dan. 7:19f.

26. *Epistle of Barnabas* 4:3-6.

27. *Or. Sib.* 5.222-224; cf. 4 Ezra 12:23-25 (?).

28. *Hist. Eccl.* 6.7.

29. Justin, *Dialogue* 32 (a "time" being interpreted as a century).

30. *Dialogue* 110.

31. Irenaeus, *Against Heresies* 5.30.3 (see p. 204, and p. 315, n. 16).

32. *Against Heresies* 5.30.2.

33. Tertullian's understanding of "temple of God" in 2 Thess. 2:4 (quoted in *Against Marcion* 5.16, *On the Resurrection of the Flesh* 24 and *On the Soul* 57) is indicated by his comment on Isa. 2:3, where the "house of the Lord" is "the catholic temple of God, in which God is worshipped" (*Against Marcion* 3.21.3).

34. Hippolytus, *On Christ and Antichrist* 14, 15.

35. Hippolytus, *On Christ and Antichrist* 56.

36. Hippolytus, *On Christ and Antichrist* 52.

37. Hippolytus, *On Christ and Antichrist,* 54-58.

38. See pp. 198-212.

39. J. R. Harris, *Testimonies,* I (Cambridge, 1916), p. 118.

40. Charles, *Studies in the Apocalypse* (Edinburgh, 1913), pp. 10f.

41. CSEL 49, p. 100, line 5–6; 102, line 10. That Nero, who succeeded Claudius in A.D. 54, was not yet emperor when 2 Thessalonians was written (*c.* A.D. 50) would not have occurred to Victorinus.

42. CSEL 49, p. 114, lines 7-15.

43. *Against Heresies* 5.30.3.

44. CSEL 49, p. 120, line 8–p. 122, line 1.

45. This is his paraphrase of the LXX version: "between the seas and the mountain. . . ."

46. Augustine, *City of God* 20.19.

47. Chapter 25, para. 6. On 11 October 1988, as Pope John Paul II began to address the European Parliament in Strasbourg, the member for one of the United Kingdom constituencies rose to denounce him as Antichrist and was escorted from the chamber.

48. H. Grotius, *Annotationes in Novum Testamentum,* I (Amsterdam, 1641), II (Paris, 1646).

49. Compare G. Salmon's mock-serious comment: "There are three rules by the help of which I believe an ingenious man could find the required sum in any given name. First, if the proper name by itself will not yield it, add a title; secondly, if the sum cannot be found in Greek, try Hebrew, or even Latin; thirdly, do not be too particular about the spelling" (*Historical Introduction to the Study of the Books of the New Testament* [London, 1889], p. 233).

50. See, for example, D. Brady, *The Contribution of British Writers between 1560 and 1830 to the Interpretation of Revelation 13.16-18,* BGBE 27 (Tübingen, 1983).

51. See V. Solovyev, "Short Narrative about the Antichrist," E.T. in *War and Christianity,* ed. S. Graham (London, 1915), pp. 144-188.

52. G. Salmon, *Historical Introduction,* p. 253. The consonants are *mr slmwn,* to be vocalized *mar šalmôn.*

NOTES TO CHAPTER 13

1. R. H. Charles, *Commentary on the Revelation,* ICC (Edinburgh, 1920), I, p. clxxxiv.

2. R. H. Charles, *Studies in the Apocalypse* (Edinburgh, 1913), pp. 10f.

3. *De Viris Illustribus* 74. The Victorinus to whom Jerome refers elsewhere (*Ep.* 84.7; *Against Rufinus* 3.14) as a translator of Origen has usually been taken to be

Victorinus Afer, but E. Benz has shown good reason to believe that the reference is to Victorinus of Pettau (*Marius Victorinus und die Entwicklung der abendländischen Willensmetaphysik* [Stuttgart, 1932], pp. 23-29). As for the work *Against All Heresies* mentioned by Jerome, this has been identified by some scholars with the *Collection of Thirty-Two Heresies* appended in the manuscript tradition to Tertullian's *De Praescriptione Haereticorum*. There is no firm ground for J. Woehrer's suggestion (*Studien zu Marius Victorinus*, Jahrbuch des Privatgymnasiums Wilhering, 1905; *Eine kleine Schrift, die vielleicht dem hl. Märtyrerbischof Viktorin von Pettau angehört*, Jb. d. Pg. Wilhering, 1927, 3/8) that Victorinus of Pettau was the author of the two treatises *De Verbis Scripturae*, "*Factum est uespere et mane dies unus*" (*PL* 8.1009-1014) and *De Physicis* (*PL* 8.1295-1310). The latter at any rate is not his: its Latinity is quite different from that of the martyr-bishop of Pettau, and it exhibits an African biblical text, whereas Victorinus of Pettau seems to make his own translation from the Greek (and Marius Victorinus shows a European text). Woehrer also hazarded the guess (*Victorini ep. Petavionensis (?) ad Iustinum Manichaeum*, Jb. d. Pg. Wilhering, 1928, 3/7) that Victorinus of Pettau was the author of the *Liber ad Iustinum Manichaeum* (*PL* 8.999-1010).

4. J. Haussleiter (ed.), *Victorini episcopi Petauionensis opera*, CSEL 49 (Vienna, 1916), pp. 167-194.

5. H. A. Wilson, *Dictionary of Christian Biography*, ed. W. Smith and H. Wace, IV (London, 1887), pp. 1128f. (*s.v.* "Victorinus of Pettau").

6. Jerome's letter to Anatolius appears as a prologue to his edition of Victorinus's commentary.

7. It is of this recension that an English translation is given in ANF VII, pp. 344-360 (following a translation of *De fabrica mundi* on pp. 341-343).

8. See p. 217, and p. 317, n. 15.

9. All the contents of these MSS, except this commentary on the Apocalypse, were published for the first time by Mai in his *Scriptorum Veterum Nova Collectio e Vaticanis codicibus edita*, III/2 (Rome, 1828).

10. "Difficillima quaedam loca breuiter tractauit" (*Institutiones* 9).

11. As though the seals confirm the divinely decreed judgment, the trumpets proclaim it, and the bowls give effect to it.

12. Dan. 7:8.

13. Dan. 11:37.

14. Not Isaiah but Ezekiel (31:4). The king of Assyria, or the Assyrian, of Isa. 8:7; 10:5-34; 31:8 and of Ezek. 31:3ff. was identified with Antichrist by patristic interpreters, as was also the Assyrian of Mic. 5:5f. (see p. 192).

15. *Against Heresies* 5.30.3.

16. *Teitan* is mentioned with some favor by Irenaeus (*ibid.*). But the only reason for preferring the itacistic spelling Τειτάν to the normal Τιτάν is that the letters of the former, but not of the latter, yield a total of 666.

17. Genseric the Vandal (A.D. 429-477). See p. 195.

18. Perhaps Anthemius, Roman consul A.D. 455, Western emperor A.D. 467-472.

19. The rule of faith in the British church in the first half of the fifth century was an adaptation of Victorinus's rule of faith; see R. P. C. Hanson, "The Rule of Faith of Victorinus and of Patrick," *Studies in Christian Antiquity* (Edinburgh, 1988), pp. 319-331.

20. Cf. Irenaeus, *Against Heresies* 1.23.

21. 1 Thess. 4:15-17.

22. 1 Cor. 15:52.

23. Cf. Rom. 10:15, quoting Isa. 52:7.

24. Cf. Muratorian Canon, lines 56-59; Cyprian, *Exhortation for Martyrdom* 11.

25. *Against Heresies* 3.11.8.

26. See T. Zahn, *Introduction to the New Testament*, E.T., III (Edinburgh, 1909), pp. 405f.

27. Cf. John 5:22, 27.

28. A fairly free Latin rendering of LXX. "Nebroth" is Nimrod: in the Hebrew text "the land of Nimrod" stands in synonymous parallelism with "the land of Assyria."

29. See p. 187.

30. John 2:21.

31. Matt. 24:15.

32. The beast has the same color *(roseus)* as the dragon of Rev. 12:3 and, like the dragon, has seven heads and ten horns.

33. Irenaeus, *Against Heresies* 5.33.1.

34. *Ibid.*, 5.33.3, 4.

35. Cf. J. R. Harris, *Testimonies*, I (Cambridge, 1916), p. 118 (see pp. 192f.); M. J. Hommes, *Het Testimonialboek* (Amsterdam, 1935), pp. 225-230.

36. Nepos's chiliasm called forth a reply from Dionysius, bishop of Alexandria, *c.* A.D. 250 (cited by Eusebius, *Hist. Eccl.* 7.24.1-5).

37. A. Souter, *The Earliest Latin Commentaries on the Epistles of St. Paul* (Oxford, 1927), p. 7.

38. 2 Tim. 3:12.

39. F. Bacon, *Advancement of Learning,* II (*Ecclesiastical History* 2.2: "History of Prophecy") in *Works*, ed. B. Montagu, II (London, 1825), p. 117.

NOTES TO CHAPTER 14

1. "Victorinus orator sui temporis ferme doctissimus" (*In Porphyrium a Victorino translatum* 1.1). As late as the twelfth century Theodoric of Chartres in his *Heptateuchon* mentions Cicero, Quintilian and Marius Victorinus as favorite models in rhetoric.

2. "Ille doctissimus senex et omnium liberalium doctrinarum peritissimus quique philosophorum tam multa legerat et diiudicauerat, doctor tot nobilium senatorum, qui etiam ob insigne praeclari magisterii, quod ciues huius mundi eximium putant, statuam Romano foro meruerat et acceperat" (*Conf.* 8.2.3).

3. "Nonne aspicimus, quanto auro et argento et ueste suffarcinatus exierit de Aegypto Cyprianus doctor suauissimus et martyr beatissimus? Quanto Lactantius? Quanto Victorinus, Optatus, Hilarius, ut de uiuis taceam?" (*De doctr. chr.* 2.40.61).

4. *Prologue to Commentary on Galatians.*

5. Augustine, *Conf.* 8.2.4.

6. See p. 222.

7. "Victorinus rhetor et Donatus grammaticus praeceptor meus Romae insignes habentur; e quibus Victorinus etiam statuam in foro Traiani meruit" (Jerome, *Chron. ad ann. Abr.* 2370).

8. "*Et nunc* Valens et Ursacius . . . destructi sunt . . . *et nunc* Valens et Ursacius reliquiae Arii" (*Aduersus Arium* 1.28.1061c). [The final indicator in references to Victorinus's theological works is to the relevant column in Migne's *PL* 8.] Valens and Ursacius, two Pannonian bishops, were Arian leaders. This passage must have been written between their excommunication by the Council of Ariminum and the prompt reversal of the Council's judgment at the instance of Constantius.

9. "Imperatoris Iuliani temporibus lege data prohibiti sunt christiani docere litteraturam et oratoriam, quam legem ille amplexus loquacem scholam deserere maluit quam uerbum tuum, quo linguas infantium facis disertas" (Augustine, *Conf.* 8.5.10). This last clause is a quotation from Wisdom 10:21b.

10. The Council of Nicaea is referred to by Victorinus in *Aduersus Arium* 1.28.1061b: "forty years ago, when the faith was confirmed in the city of Nicaea by three hundred and more bishops" (*ante XL annos, cum in Nicaea ciuitate fides confirmata per CCC et plures episcopos*—Migne, following earlier editions, reads wrongly and, indeed, impossibly, *ante undecim annos*. See the introduction to the works of Victorinus in Migne's *Patrologia Latina* 8.998. It is easy to see how XI could be read by mistake for XL). But we cannot date *Aduersus Arium* so late as 365. The reference to the excommunication of Valens and Ursacius as a contemporary event (*Ar.* 1.28.1061c) practically fixes 359 as the date of the first book at least. Besides, Constantius was still emperor, as may be seen from *Ar.* 2.9.1096a, where Victorinus, referring to the part played by the word ὁμοούσιος at the Council of Nicaea, adds: "and it was approved by the emperor, the father of our emperor" (*probatum autem ab imperatore imperatoris nostri patre*), i.e., by Constantine, the father of Constantius. This reference, quite apart from the mention of Valens and Ursacius, makes it certain that *Aduersus Arium* was composed not later than 361, the year of Constantius's death. So we must apparently understand "forty" as a round number, meaning simply that Victorinus was writing in the fourth decade after the famous Council.

11. The five φωναί being *genus, species, differentia, proprium, accidens.*

12. See also J. C. von Orelli (ed.), *Cicero*, V/1 (Turin, 1833), pp. 2-174.

13. The edition in "Sources chrétiennes" includes a French translation by P. Hadot; cf. *Christlicher Platonismus: Die theologischen Schriften des Marius Victorinus,* übersetzt von P. Hadot und U. Brenke, eingeleitet und erläutert von P. Hadot (Zurich: Artemis, 1967).

14. Galland's edition of *GVD* is a mixture of two traditions, represented respectively by the printed texts *(a)* of J. Herold, *Orthoxographa* (Basel, 1555) and J. Ziegler, *Expositio in Genesim et Exodum* (Lyons, 1585), and *(b)* of J. Mabillon, *Analecta* IV (Paris, 1723). The latter is more trustworthy.

15. The codices used by Mai are Ottobonian 3288a and 3288b (the latter being a copy of the former), and Vatican 3546 (a copy of one or the other of the two Ottobonian manuscripts). J. Haussleiter dated Ottobonian 3288a in the 15th century, A. Souter in the 14th century. See p. 201, and p. 315, n. 9.

16. See A. Souter, *The Earliest Latin Commentaries on the Epistles of St. Paul* (Oxford, 1927), pp. 8-38; W. Erdt, *Marius Victorinus Afer: der erste lateinische Pauluskommentator* (Frankfurt/Bern/Cirencester, 1980).

17. C. Gore (*Dictionary of Christian Biography,* IV, p. 1130) says that the *Liber ad Iustinum Manichaeum* "may with reasonable certainty be ascribed to Victorinus"; similarly F. Bömer (*Der lateinische Neuplatonismus,* pp. 126f.) regards it as his. But Dom G. Morin attributed it to Pacian of Barcelona (d. 392) on the ground of similari-

ties of language (*Revue Bénédictine* 30 [1913], pp. 286ff.), and J. Woehrer to Victorinus of Pettau (see p. 315, n. 3 above).

18. See P. Monceaux, *Histoire littéraire de l'Afrique chrétienne,* III (Paris, 1905), pp. 391ff.; E. Benz, *Marius Victorinus und die Entwicklung der abendländischen Willens-metaphysik* (Stuttgart, 1931), pp. 15-38.

19. P. Henry, *Plotin et l'Occident* (Louvain, 1934), pp. 60-62, 94f., 104, 136, 209, 222f., 231, 234.

20. F. Bömer, *Der lateinische Neuplatonismus und Neupythagoreismus* (Leipzig, 1936), pp. 80ff.

21. P. Monceaux, *Histoire littéraire de l'Afrique chrétienne,* III, pp. 373-422; M. Schanz, *Geschichte der römischen Litteratur,* IV/1 (Munich, 1914), pp. 149-161 (§§ 828-831).

22. H. Keil (ed.), *Grammatici Latini,* VI (Leipzig, 1874), p. xvii.

23. Schanz, *Geschichte,* IV/1, § 829. Schanz goes on to speak of the importance of the metrical work attributed to Aphthonius: "The significance of Aphthonius's work for the history of metre is not to be underestimated."

24. Monceaux, *Histoire littéraire,* III, p. 389.

25. W. S. Teuffel, *History of Roman Literature,* E.T., II (London/Cambridge, 1900), pp. 337f.

26. Although Victorinus's dogmatic works are chiefly concerned with Christology, and his doctrine of the Holy Spirit is markedly inadequate, it is important to note that, as Gore points out, he "is the first theologian to speak of the Spirit as the principle of unity in the Godhead, the bond or 'copula' of the eternal Trinity, completing the perfect circle of the Divine Being, the return of God upon Himself" (*Dictionary of Christian Biography,* IV, p. 1134).

27. Victorinus uses many words of Greek origin, especially technical terms of grammar and meter, but only those which give evidence of having been naturalized in Latin are included here. For other word lists see CSEL 48, pp. 354ff. (asterisked words); A. Souter, *The Earliest Latin Commentaries on the Epistles of St. Paul* (Oxford, 1927), pp. 31-38; E. Benz, *Marius Victorinus,* pp. 432-436.

28. In 1927 A. Souter wrote: "Victorinus's latinity deserves a monograph after the fashion in which Tertullian, Cyprian, Hilary, Jerome, and others have already been studied" (*The Earliest Latin Commentaries on the Epistles of St. Paul,* p. 30). Under his direction I endeavored to supply this need with a monograph, *The Latinity of Gaius Marius Victorinus Afer,* written during my tenure of the Croom Robertson Fellowship of the University of Aberdeen, 1933-36. It is now housed in the Manuscripts and Archives Section of Aberdeen University Library. Professor Souter acknowledges its value in *A Glossary of Later Latin to 600 A.D.* (Oxford: Clarendon Press, 1949), p. xx.

29. *Rhet.* 1.8, p. 180, line 20.

30. See L. R. Palmer, *An Introduction to Modern Linguistics* (London, 1936), p. 156.

31. "Victorinus, natione Afer, Romae sub Constantio principe rhetoricam docuit et in extrema senectute Christi se tradens fidei scripsit *Aduersus Arium* libros more dialectico ualde obscuros, qui nisi ab eruditis non intelleguntur, et commentarios in Apostolum" (*De Viris Illustribus* 101). Although Augustine (*Conf.* 8.2.3) calls him a *senex* at the time of his conversion, Jerome's *in extrema senectute* is an exaggeration.

32. J. Sirmond (ed.), *Opera Varia,* I (Paris, 1696/Venice, 1728), between cols. 344

and 345: "obscuritas, quae primo in limine fuisset ingratior. Ceterum, obscuritatem hanc Victorinus in dogmaticis praecipue libris sectatus uidetur. In commentariis enim aliquot epistolarum S. Pauli, quos idem codex continebat, stylus planior et apertior." The codex to which he refers, from the monastery of Herenthals in Belgium, no longer exists; unfortunately Sirmond did not publish its text of the Pauline commentaries. See Souter, *Earliest Latin Commentaries*, pp. 9f.

33. *Dictionary of Christian Biography*, ed. W. Smith and H. Wace, IV (London, 1887), pp. 1130f. (*s.v.* "Victorinus Afer").

34. Keil (*GL* VI, p. xxvi) remarks on the custom at that time for grammarians to repeat their work, writing first in a style intended for the education of the young, and then in a manner suitable for learned readers. There is some evidence of such a twofold purpose in Victorinus's grammatical work.

35. C. Halm (ed.), *Rhetores Latini Minores* (Leipzig, 1863), p. viii: "scriptor taedii plenus."

36. A. Souter, *Earliest Latin Commentaries*, p. 28.

37. M. Schanz, *Geschichte*, IV/1, p. 150.

38. M.-N. Bouillet, *Les Ennéades de Plotin* (Paris, 1857-61), II, pp. 554ff.

39. G. Geiger, *C. Marius Victorinus Afer, ein neuplatonischer Philosoph* (Metten, 1888-89), I, pp. 17ff.

40. E. Benz, *Marius Victorinus, passim.*

41. P. Henry, *Plotin et l'Occident*, p. 60.

42. *Ibid.*, p. 241.

43. See p. 216.

44. P. Monceaux, *Histoire littéraire*, III, p. 416.

45. *Ibid.*, p. 397.

46. E. Benz (*Marius Victorinus*, pp. 23-29) shows conclusively that the Victorinus mentioned by Jerome (*Ep.* 84.7 and *Adu. Rufin.* 3.14) as a translator of Origen was not our author but the martyr-bishop of Pettau (died *c.* 304).

47. E. Benz, *Marius Victorinus*, pp. 422-429. As regards another alleged influence of Origen, A. Souter says, "The question whether Victorinus used Origen for his commentary on Ephesians is to be answered in the negative, as no certain case of borrowing can be produced" (*Earliest Latin Commentaries*, pp. 26f.).

48. See F. F. Bruce, "The Gospel Text of Marius Victorinus," in *Text and Interpretation*, ed. E. Best and R. McL. Wilson (Cambridge, 1979), pp. 69-78.

49. It is initially disconcerting for one who knows him as Victorinus Afer to find him cited as "Victorinus-Rome" in the United Bible Societies *Greek New Testament* (New York/London, etc., ³1975).

50. The thoroughly "African" character of Bible citations in *De Physicis* is a conclusive argument against its attribution to Marius Victorinus.

51. *Ar.* 1.30.1063b-c; 1.59.1085b; 2.3.1091c-d; 2.5.1093a; 2.12.1097d; 4.4.1115c; *HR* 2.1138c.

52. *Ar.* 1.30.1063b; 2.8.1094c.

53. *Ar.* 2.8.1094c.

54. Cf. *Ar.* 1.30.1063b, where *hodiernum* is quoted as an Old Latin rendering of ἐπιούσιον.

55. *Ar.* 2.6.1093b; cf. *Ar.* 1.59.1085c.

56. *De ciu. dei* 10.29.

57. It was from Simplicianus that Augustine learned the story of Victorinus's

conversion (*Conf.* 8.2.4). Augustine tells how, shortly before his own conversion, he found in the Latin translation of some Neoplatonic writings much that agreed with the Johannine prologue, but nothing corresponding to the statement that "the Word became flesh and dwelt among us" (*Conf.* 7.13, 14).

58. *Old-Latin Biblical Texts* II (Oxford, 1886), p. lxxxv. We find also *ad deum* (*Ar.* 2.1.1088d) and *cum deo* (*Phil.* 2.9.1209d).

59. *GVD* 20.1030c-1031a.

60. *Ar.* 3.15.1110b-c.

61. Cf. H. Lietzmann, *From Constantine to Julian*, E.T. (London, ²1953), pp. 253f.

62. See also reviews of Benz by A. E. Taylor in *Classical Review* 47 (1933), p. 86; by W. Theiler in *Gnomon* 10 (1934), pp. 493-499; by H. Leisegang in *Philologische Wochenschrift* 54 (1934), 1195f.

63. Koffmane provides a list of MSS of Victorinus (pp. 9f.).

NOTES TO CHAPTER 15

1. Gal. 2:11-14.

2. The Roman destination of these greetings is here assumed, for reasons set out elsewhere; cf. F. F. Bruce, *The Epistle to the Romans*, TNTC (Leicester/Grand Rapids, ²1985), pp. 253-257.

3. F. F. Bruce, *The Epistle to the Hebrews*, NICNT (Grand Rapids, ²1990), pp. 3ff.

4. *Acts of Justin* 3.

5. Victor, bishop of Rome towards the end of the second century, is said to have been the first pope to write in Latin (Jerome, *On Illustrious Men* 34).

6. G. H. Lang, *Departure* (London, 1925).

7. H. Craik, *New Testament Church Order* (Bristol, 1863), pp. 3f., quoted by F. R. Coad, *A History of the Brethren Movement* (Exeter, 1968), p. 255. Henry Craik (1805-66), St. Andrews graduate and Hebrew scholar, was joint-pastor with George Müller at Bethesda Chapel, Bristol.

8. *Ibid.*

9. A. A. T. Ehrhardt, "Construction and Purpose of Acts," *The Framework of the New Testament Stories* (Manchester, 1964), p. 94.

10. Craik, *New Testament Church Order*, pp. 24f., quoted by Coad, *History*, p. 256.

11. R. B. Rackham, *The Acts of the Apostles*, WC (London, 1901), pp. 15f.

12. See pp. 264-266.

13. No question is raised here about the validity of what was expressed in the language they used; see some helpful explanations in R. P. C. Hanson, *The Attractiveness of God* (London, 1973), pp. 71-137.

14. Rom. 15:20.

15. Cf. 2 Cor. 10:1–11:15.

16. Acts 11:27-30; Gal. 2:10; 1 Cor. 16:1-4; 2 Cor. 8:1–9:15; Rom. 15:25-31.

17. Ignatius, *To the Romans*, preface.

18. Dionysius of Corinth, quoted by Eusebius, *Hist. Eccl.* 4.23.9-11.

19. Quoted by Eusebius, *Hist Eccl.* 2.25.8

20. Cf. F. F. Bruce, *The Canon of Scripture* (Glasgow, 1988), pp. 150-154, 261f.

21. Clement, *To the Corinthians* 5:4-7; Ignatius, *To the Romans* 4:5.

22. Cf. the opposing viewpoints of Ernst Käsemann, "The Canon of the New

Testament and the Unity of the Church," E.T. in *Essays on New Testament Themes*, SBT 41 (London, 1964), pp. 95-107, and Hans Küng, *The Living Church*, E.T. (London, 1963), pp. 233-293.

23. E. Käsemann, "Ephesians and Acts," in *Studies in Luke-Acts*, ed. L. E. Keck and J. L. Martyn (New York, 1966), p. 288.

24. 1 Cor. 12:13.

25. Outside Acts 14 Luke restricts the designation "apostle(s)" to the Twelve. See p. 305, n. 40.

26. Cf. Col. 1:21f.; Eph. 1:9f.; 2:14-17; 3:9-11.

NOTES TO CHAPTER 16

1. E. Schweizer, *Jesus*, E.T. (London, 1971), p. 13.

2. E. Irving, *Doctrine of the Incarnation Opened* (1830), Preface, in his *Collected Writings*, V (London, 1865), p. 4.

3. H. C. Whitley, *Blinded Eagle* (London, 1955), p. 90.

4. Newton's *Statement and Acknowledgment respecting Certain Doctrinal Errors* (Plymouth, 1847) is conveniently reproduced as Appendix B in F. R. Coad, *A History of the Brethren Movement* (Exeter, ²1976), pp. 296-300. It is surprising that W. B. Neatby was unable to procure a copy of "this important tract," as he justly calls it in *A History of the Plymouth Brethren* (London, 1901), p. 344. It contains salient quotations from Newton's *Christian Witness* article of 1835.

5. Cf. Neatby, *History*, pp. 130-155.

6. Reproduced in a revised edition in J. N. Darby, *Collected Writings* (London, 1867-1900), VII, pp. 212-361.

7. *Collected Writings*, VII, pp. 240, 273n., 306; cf. the exposition of Psalm 102 in Darby's *Synopsis of the Books of the Bible*, II (London, n.d.), pp. 212f.

8. For another example of this mistaken principle of exegesis—mistaken, for all the noble precedent it could claim—cf. S. P. Tregelles's difficulty in interpreting Ps. 119:67, 176 as words of Christ, according to his own account in *Three Letters to the Author of "A Retrospect of Events that have taken place amongst the Brethren"* (London, 1849, ²1894), pp. 53-57.

9. Cf. S. P. Tregelles, *Five Letters to the Editor of "The Record" on Recent Denials of our Lord's Vicarious Life* (London, ²1864), pp. 29f. The amended line stands as quoted in *Hymns for the Little Flock* (3rd edition, 1903), No. 327, *Hymns for Christian Worship*, No. 328, and *Hymns of Light and Love*, No. 70. The wiser path was perhaps followed in *The Believers' Hymn Book*, No. 128, which omits the controversial stanza. One might have thought that objection would have been taken to the word "confessed" in the couplet

> "Our sins, our guilt, in love divine,
>   Confessed and borne by Thee"—

but evidently not. (Perhaps Ps. 69:5 was held to justify it.)

10. "The orthodox word 'mortal' has become a kind of keynote. Let it be observed, that no one professing to be a *teacher* can be accepted as sound in connection with our Lord's spotless and vicarious life of obedience, who does not, without hesitation or equivocation, avow his acceptance of this term, as used habitually by

sound Christians. He who *rejects* it, cannot *really* hold the incarnation of our Lord, that He took the same flesh and blood as His brethren: he must hold some part at least of the false doctrine of the 'heavenly humanity'" (*Five Letters*, p. 30). This was carrying the war into the opposing camp with a vengeance!

11. Cf. Heb. 2:14ff.; 4:15. In the issue of *Pastoral Letters* which Wigram attacked, Craik allegorized the "shittim" (acacia) wood, of which the ark of the covenant was made, in terms of our Lord's humanity, linking it with the words of Isa. 53:2, "a root out of a dry ground." See Neatby's account of the matter (*History*, pp. 165-172).

12. See C. H. Mackintosh, *Notes on the Book of Leviticus* (London, [2]1961), pp. 28-66 (the exposition of the meal offering of Lev. 2:1ff. in terms of our Lord's humanity), especially pp. 35-38. Some unguarded expressions in the first edition (1860), which I have not seen, were removed or modified in the second edition. So unprejudiced a critic as Horatius Bonar, in the *Quarterly Journal of Prophecy* (which he edited), charged him with Valentinianism! But this was absurd for, in spite of the imprecision of his devotional style, Mackintosh on p. 37 made it plain that our Lord had "a real human body—real 'flesh and blood.'" Darby, while finding Mackintosh's occasional expression "objectionable" (and rightly so), wrote trenchantly in his defense (*Collected Writings*, X, pp. 49-66).

13. The "heavenly man" or "man of heaven," whose image believers are to wear (1 Cor. 15:49), is Christ in his resurrection life. This is the reference also of 1 Cor. 15:47, "the second man is (the Lord) from heaven," which Mackintosh (*Notes on Leviticus*, p. 35) seems to apply to our Lord's earthly existence.

14. Neatby, *History*, p. 317.

15. Darby, *Synopsis*, V, p. 16. On our Lord's personal humanity Darby expressed himself wisely: "the simple faith that Jesus was God and man in one person can be easily accepted as plain and vital truth, but the moment you *deny* personality in the man Christ Jesus you run into a thousand difficulties and errors. What is really denied is Christ's individuality as a man" (*Collected Writings*, XXXIX, p. 322). (See J. Murray, "The Person of Christ," *Collected Writings*, 2. *Systematic Theology* [Edinburgh, 1977], pp. 137-139.)

16. *Notes of Addresses and Readings at Quemerford* (London, 1895), pp. 132f.

17. *Ibid.*, p. 135. N. F. Noel (*The History of the Brethren* [Denver, 1936], p. 511) quotes Raven as saying, "Where the unity of the Person is got from, I know not. It seems to me perfect nonsense."

18. This definition, so called from the Council of Chalcedon (A.D. 451), where it was adopted, uses the term "person" in a rather different sense from that in which it is now commonly used. The modern concept of personhood is much richer than anything denoted by *prosōpon* and its derivatives in the fifth century.

19. J. Boyd, *The Incarnation of the Son* (Philadelphia, 1927), pp. 14f. In an open letter dated March 28, 1927, he said the pamphlet should have ended with p. 13, and took the "opportunity of withdrawing the passage referred to as extraneous to the main question."

20. *Hymns for the Little Flock* ([3]1903), No. 350.

21. The "West Philadelphia Cleavage" (Noel, *History*, pp. 407-430).

22. Cf. the summary and scriptural refutation of the Valentinian doctrine in Irenaeus, *Against Heresies* 1.7.2; 3.16. The doctrine is sometimes called Melchiorite, after the Anabaptist Melchior Hoffmann (d. 1542).

23. Neatby, *History*, p. 170.

24. Compare what is said on p. 258 about the *Gospel of Peter*. Basilides is said to have taught that Simon of Cyrene was crucified in Jesus' place, while Jesus stood by wearing Simon's form (Irenaeus, *Against Heresies* 1.24.4).

25. Sura 4:156 ("they did not kill him, neither did they crucify him; he was made a semblance to them"). By an unhappy accident, Muhammad apparently derived his knowledge of the gospel story from a docetic source.

26. John 19:34f.

27. As witness some reactions to G. F. Hawthorne's note on Heb. 4:15 in *A New Testament Commentary*, ed. G. C. D. Howley (London, 1969), p. 547.

28. *The Traditions and the Deposit* (London, n.d.), p. 4. The edition which evoked Mr. Hoste's critical review was published by Pickering and Inglis; it was a reprint of a pamphlet originally issued by so orthodox a body as the Bible League. It is to this earlier issue (I think) that reference is made by T. Roberts in *The Word became Flesh* (London, 1924), p. 6, where he points out that Mr. Hogg used "our Lord's assertion that He did not know the time of His Second Advent as proof of His infallibility where He claims to know."

29. See *The Doctrine of Christ* (London, 1924), a document signed by thirteen brethren; criticizing T. Roberts' teaching on biblical inerrancy and on the person of Christ. Controversy on the latter issue was sparked off by a letter to *The Christian* early in 1923 in which Mr. Roberts wrote, with reference to Mark 13:32, of "our Lord's plainly stated ignorance of the date of His second advent." That Mr. Hogg did not agree with the thirteen signatories to *The Doctrine of Christ* (one of whom was Mr. Hoste) is evident from an open letter of his, dated July 17, 1924, in which he reported that at an interview "what Mr. Roberts put before us seemed to me an explicit acknowledgment of the true, essential and unchangeable Deity of Christ."

30. Cf. Mark 1:1. That Jesus is the Son of God is twice proclaimed from heaven (Mark 1:11; 9:7), but is for the most part concealed on earth until it is affirmed in Jesus' reply to the high priest (Mark 14:62) and acknowledged at the climax of the passion narrative by the centurion (Mark 15:39).

31. As for another instance of "likeness" in reference to our Lord's incarnation (Phil. 2:7), the phrase "having been born in human likeness" may (like the following phrase, "having been found in human form") be a paraphrase of "one like a son of man" (i.e., like a human being) in Dan. 7:13.

32. The RSV rendering "it is not with angels that he is concerned but with the descendants of Abraham" is too weak; the verb is that found in the phrase "I took them by the hand" in Heb. 8:9.

33. Our Lord's words in John 4:32, "I have food to eat of which you do not know" (namely, the doing of the Father's will and accomplishment of his work), do not imply that he was immune from bodily hunger.

34. H. C. G. Moule, in prefatory note to Sir Robert Anderson, *The Lord from Heaven* (London, 1910), p. vi.

35. Westminster Shorter Catechism (1647), answer to Question 21.

NOTES TO CHAPTER 17

1. Cf. P. K. Jewett, *Man as Male and Female* (Grand Rapids, 1975).

2. J. Milton, *Paradise Lost* IV. 299.

3. Cf. H. L. Ellison, *The Message of the Old Testament* (Exeter, 1969), p. 20.

4. The verb is *synathleō*, used already in the last clause of Phil. 1:27.

5. Chrysostom, *Homilies on Romans* 31. No certain occurrence of the name Junias is attested.

6. On the "veil" in general, Paul seems to say in 1 Cor. 11:2-16, nature intends a woman's head to be covered, for she has been given a natural head-covering—her hair. Convention ought to follow nature's example: as nature covers a woman's head with hair, so convention ought to cover it with a veil. If it is unseemly for a woman to be deprived of her natural head-covering (i.e., to be shorn or shaved), so it is unseemly for her to be deprived of her conventional head-covering (i.e., to be unveiled), especially in such public exercises as praying or prophesying. This argument, which has affinities to some aspects of Stoic thought, makes the whole passage cohere: it would not have seemed so strange in the Mediterranean world of the first century as it may seem in the Western world today.

7. The case for regarding 1 Cor. 14:34f. as an addition to Paul's original text is defended by G. D. Fee, *The First Epistle to the Corinthians*, NICNT (Grand Rapids, 1987), pp. 699-708.

8. Chrysostom, *Homilies on I Timothy* 8.

9. There is a striking contrast between the Paul of the Pastoral Epistles and the Paul of the later *Acts of Paul* (c. 160). In the Pastorals women are forbidden to teach or rule but encouraged to marry (1 Tim. 5:14); in the *Acts of Paul* they (and specifically Thecla) are encouraged to exercise a public ministry but discouraged from marrying.

10. Another aspect of headship—that indicated in 1 Cor. 11:3, "the head of the woman is man" (NIV) or "the head of a woman is her husband" (RSV)—belongs to the order of the old creation, and is irrelevant in the context of Christian worship. The primary sense of the word "head" in 1 Cor. 11:3 (cf. Eph. 5:23) is "source," i.e., "source of life," understood here in the light of 1 Cor. 11:12, "woman was made from man" (according to the creation narrative of Gen. 2:21-23). See S. Bedale, "The Meaning of κεφαλή in the Pauline Epistles," *JTS* n.s. 5 (1954), pp. 211-215; G. D. Fee, *First Corinthians*, NICNT, pp. 491-505.

11. "Real presence" as in the closing couplet of Charles Wesley's hymn "Victim divine":

> To every faithful soul appear,
> And show Thy real presence here.

12. Let it not be pretended that such an act involves an exercise of authority over men in the sense of 1 Tim. 2:12.

13. This was so when this paper was read in 1979; happily, I learn that the situation has changed since then.

14. "Notes of a Reading on 1 Corinthians" (on 1 Cor. 14:34), *Collected Writings*, XXVI, p. 429. In the next sentence he says, "A man and his wife being alone, I see no objection to their breaking bread, if they themselves feel free and are disposed"—but that is not quite germane to the text under discussion.

15. According to Dr. John A. Anderson, later missionary in China, who was associated with the Rhynie meeting in the 1870s and 1880s, "notwithstanding the urgent request of leading brethren in both Scotland and England, the Rhynie meeting refused to prohibit women from taking part. The consequence was that we were

ostracised, although all visitors from other Assemblies freely stated that the power of the Holy Spirit was realized more in Rhynie than in other meetings" (*Autobiography of John A. Anderson, M.D.* [Aberdeen, [2]1950], pp. 21f.).

NOTES TO CHAPTER 18

1. J. Huxtable, *The Bible Says* (London: SCM Press, 1962).

2. R. Hooker, *Laws of Ecclesiastical Polity*, V (London, 1597), 8.2. See now B. Drewery and R. J. Bauckham (ed.), *Scripture, Tradition and Reason: A Study in the Criteria of Christian Doctrine. Essays in Honour of R. P. C. Hanson* (Edinburgh, 1988).

3. W. H. Burgess, *John Robinson: Pastor of the Pilgrim Fathers* (London, 1920), pp. 239f.

4. Westminster Confession of Faith 1.6.

5. J. Owen, *Considerations on the Prolegomena and Appendix to the late Polyglotta* (1659), in *Works*, ed. W. H. Goold, XVI (London, 1853), p. 370.

6. J. Knox, *History of the Reformation in Scotland*, ed. W. C. Dickinson, II (London, 1949), p. 18.

7. H. Barrow, *A True Discourse of the Visible Congregation of the Saints* (Amsterdam, 1589).

8. *The Bible Says*, pp. 118f., quoting J. K. Mozley, "The Bible," in *The Christian Faith*, ed. W. R. Matthews (London, 1936), pp. 51f.

9. Westminster Confession of Faith 1.5, 6, 10.

10. Eccles. 9:5.

11. J. Knox, *Limits of Unbelief* (London, 1970), pp. 39f., 70-79.

12. For these comments by Tillich and Bultmann (made orally to Dr. Knox) see *Limits of Unbelief*, pp. 70-73.

13. N. H. Snaith, *The Distinctive Ideas of the Old Testament* (London, 1944), p. 186. (Snaith died in 1982.)

14. Y. M.-J. Congar, *Tradition and Traditions*, E.T. (London, 1966), pp. 3f.

15. See *The Documents of Vatican II*, ed. W. M. Abbott and J. Gallagher (London, 1967), p. 127.

16. P. S. Minear, "The Influence of Ecumenical Developments on New Testament Teaching," *Journal of Ecumenical Studies* 8 (1971), p. 287.

17. "The Authority of the Bible," *Faith and Order Louvain 1971*, Faith and Order Paper 59 (Geneva, 1971), p. 9.

18. H. Lietzmann, *The Founding of the Church Universal*, E.T. (London, 1950), p. 97.

19. I pass over such temporary "alternatives" as second-century Gnosticism, which was too much bound up with a passing world-outlook to survive.

20. A. Deissmann, *Light from the Ancient East*, E.T. (London, 1927), p. 409.